SHAKESPEARE STUDIES

Historical and Comparative in Method

ELMER EDGAR STOLL

Comedien: C'est comme cela que je sens le rôle.

Sarcey: Eh! malheureux! il ne s'agit pas
de le sentir mais de le comprendre.

Quarante ans [1900], *iii,* II

FREDERICK UNGAR PUBLISHING CO.
NEW YORK

Republished 1960

Based on second edition 1942
with additional corrections

PR
2976
S76
1960

Printed in the United States of America

Library of Congress Catalog Card No. 59-10885

PREFACE

THIS is not quite the book that I have for years had it in mind to write as I penned my articles and monographs on Shakespeare and the Elizabethan drama. I had hoped, with these as a nucleus, to develop a rounded and reasoned whole. But as time went on and material accumulated, with no end yet in sight, I came to the conclusion that if ever I was to write a book at all it must be, as indeed this one is, a collection of studies or essays, and no more.

With those who may have troubled to read some of these as they were first published, it is only fair that I should be more explicit. I have here included two new studies (chapters iii and iv) and six which have already appeared in print, though these last have been entirely recast—much altered and even more enlarged. I have, however (though sometimes quoting from them), made no attempt to incorporate matter from articles such as my *Anachronism in Shakespeare Criticism, Recent Hamlet Criticism,* and *Drama Old and New,* or from my monographs on *Hamlet* and *Othello.* In particular I have avoided reproducing purely technical discussions, on the one hand, such as my article on *Hamlet, Marston, and the Malcontent Type,* and rather popular ones, on the other, such as my introductions to *Titus Andronicus* and *Henry V.* In short, I have here put together those of my writings which are least easily accessible, or are of most general interest, or seem, because of the fresh material in my hands, most worth revision. To each of the chapters not entirely new I have appended the date of its first appearance.

My indebtedness to previous writers I have endeavoured adequately to indicate. This, as they themselves would admit, is not always so simple as it seems. Sometimes one's own thought becomes inextricably bound up with that of another writer, and one is fearful of making an acknowledgment which may not be welcome. Sometimes, too, this process has taken place almost subconsciously; and one is in the sad state of not quite knowing what one has borrowed. One's only consolation or compensation in the predicament is the perception of the fact that a like process has taken place in the minds of others—though then one is in the further quandary whether to bow and make acknowledgments as, in a new and poignant sense, *on prend son bien où on le trouve*. But oftener it is the case that two students, following a like historical method, light upon the same thought or arrive at the same conclusion independently. In all these various conjunctures I have striven to be more than just.

Through so long a period of investigation I have incurred still further obligations, for services rendered not merely to the world at large but to me personally; but these obligations are more than can be appropriately recorded here. Like everyone who has read in the British Museum I think, at such a time, not only of the vast treasures gathered there but of the courteous and intelligent assistance given in making these available. That, however, is a less personal and particular service than another—the frank criticism of scholars upon the various articles or monographs as they have appeared. It is no light task to read a disquisition encumbered with references, and then pen the writer something more than a perfunctory—a polite, yet honest—note. And there is still another service so particular and intimate that without it there would have been no articles or monographs—and no book as a result—that of the editors who read and printed them. Among these I wish to thank by name those who have now kindly given me permission to use copyrighted material: the Editors of the *Contemporary Review*, the *Modern Language Review*, and the *North American Review;* and the publishers Messrs Ginn and Company and Messrs Henry Holt and Company.

CONTENTS

CHAPTER I

The academic, somewhat apologetic attitude of Shakespeare's first editors, which he may complaisantly have shared. (1) His neglect of his own writings, whether printed or unprinted. (2) His indifference like that of his literary contemporaries to his work and to him. (3 and 4) His failure to assert himself or his opinions even in his plays, or reveal his love-story in the Sonnets. (5 and 6) His personality elusive and sunk in his creations, as Keats says the greatest poet's should be. (7) Improbable that he refers to. himself in the *Tempest*. He is thinking not of his end but of the great conclusion. (8) Regardless of fame, though he presents the aspiration for it in his characters. (9) Regardless of fame and the rules, but intent on his subject and in perfect sympathy with his audience. (10) Hence his imperfections and supreme perfections. (11 and 12) The vitality of his work owing to his freedom but above all to his creative, uncritical, and unconscious genius.

CHAPTER II

The fallacy that literature is the image of the contemporary life. (1) Fainting or swooning, ancient and modern; women wooing the men. (2) Maidens as pages, and the spirit of romance. (3) The seventeenth-century comedy of manners as a veracious picture of Restoration corruption or of ethical enfranchisement. (4) The failure of the critics to enter into the spirit of the Restoration humour and morals. (5) The philosophy of conduct in Etherege or Congreve not that of the age but that of comedy, in Saturnalian rebellion. The striking contrast between seventeenth-century English and French drama betrays differences in taste not in morality of the age. (6) Class distinctions not faithfully reflected in

CHAPTER III

CHAPTER IV

CONTENTS

CHAPTER V

CHAPTER VI

CHAPTER VII

CHAPTER VIII

SHAKESPEARE STUDIES

CHAPTER I

ON THE ANNIVERSARY OF THE FOLIO

THREE hundred years ago, seven years after the death of
the writer, appeared 'Mr. William Shakespeare's Comedies, Histories, and Tragedies,' or what is commonly known
as the First Folio. The editors, John Heminge and Henry
Condell, Shakespeare's fellow actors and shareholders in
the Globe, were remembered along with another more
famous fellow actor, Richard Burbage, in his will. They
had lived almost their whole lives in the parish of St Mary
the Virgin, Aldermanbury; and—the days of 'Merry England' (though numbered) having not yet come to an end—
they were, at different times, wardens of the church, not a
stone's throw from which, in Silver Street, lived Shakespeare
himself. In the churchyard, now a little oasis (in oldest
and dingiest London) of grass and stooping plane-trees,
alongside a placid white stone structure of Sir Christopher
Wren's—streaked with the soot and dust and rains of centuries, though it replaces their church, levelled in the Great
Fire—stands a monument to the men, lying there, who
rescued more than half of Shakespeare's plays for us from
oblivion, from that or other fires. There are carved the
touching words: 'We have but collected them and done an
office to the dead . . . without ambition either of self-
profit or fame; only to keepe the memory of so worthy
a Friend and Fellow alive, as was our Shakespeare.' Shakespeare and his Thespian church-wardens had worked together, acted together, in a manner lived together, the
least of which experiences is notoriously a trial and test of

affection, often the death of it; and yet he thought of them
—and left them mourning rings that they might afterwards
think of him—before the end.   And they thought of him
indeed.

For theirs was an act of friendship far more than of
fealty and homage. 'They pleased the living,' as the verses
recently discovered by Sir Israel Gollancz record; but it
was because 'they loved the dead.' 'These trifles' they call
the plays in their dedication of the volume to Pembroke
and Montgomery, using the conventional language—*haec
novimus esse nihil*—which would be appropriate only in the
modest mouth of the poet; though by their felicitous words
in the address 'To the Great Variety of Readers' they
show that, if unaware of his genius, they were not insensible
to his charm:—'who, as he was a happie imitator of Nature,
was a most gentle expresser of it.' Even Shakespeare's fellow actors at such moments bowed, with the rings upon their
fingers, before the rigours of the academic standard.   Perhaps Shakespeare, as we shall see, bowed too.

I.

Twenty plays thus found a refuge in print, among them
*As You Like It, Twelfth Night, Julius Cæsar, Macbeth,
Coriolanus,* and *Antony and Cleopatra.*   *Othello* had, for
the first time, been printed only the year before.   Twenty-
one plays, therefore, more than half his output and the
more precious part of it, Shakespeare had unnaturally left
to the mercy of fortune, the treachery of chance.   In 1611,
or thereabouts, he retired from the stage to Stratford.   He
did not, like Lope and Calderón (who, nevertheless, printed
a number of theirs) go on writing to the end; he was not,
like Molière, hindered from carrying out his intention to
publish a complete edition of his works, 'in their final perfection,' by the absorbing duties of an actor and manager;
nor was he stopped by sudden death.   'The latter part of
his life,' says Rowe, who was also a popular playwright,

'was spent, as all men of good sense will wish theirs may
be, in ease, retirement, and the conversation of his friends.'
His work was done, he thought. He collected his rents
instead of his writings, mingled with his neighbours instead
of the poets, founded an estate in strict entail at Stratford
instead of his fame for ever through all the world, and, in
due time, made deliberate but simple preparations for his
exit. Though he dictated his will in January, he did not
die until April, and in the interval he revised it; but in all
the long and particular document he mentions no books, his
own or anyone else's, and no manuscripts; and in no way
recalls the fact that he was a poet or dramatist, or remembers any poet or dramatist—among so many. He remembers eight of his friends in Stratford and three of his 'fellows,' as we have seen, in London; but not Ben Jonson,
Drayton, Fletcher, Dekker, Webster, Heywood, or any of
the others of that galaxy of luminaries, more truly (one
would think) congenial, with whom he must have held converse, high or low, at the Mermaid Tavern; and he is concerned who should have his sword, his broad silver-gilt bowl,
and who only the second-best bed, but unconcerned, it would
seem, for all that the Globe had recently burned to the
ground, what should become of the unprinted manuscript of
Othello or *Macbeth.*

Except in two instances, those of *Venus and Adonis* and
the *Rape of Lucrece,* he seems not to have sought publication or thought of it. All the other publications were by
pirates, or, apparently, by the Company to steal a march
upon the pirates. The plays, to be sure, were sold to the
Company outright, and, like companies nowadays, the
King's Men preferred not to publish them so long as they
could be kept on the stage. But it was so that Jonson, Chapman, and Webster sold their plays; and yet, though not like
Shakespeare shareholders in the purchasing company, they
attended, in many instances, to the matter of publication
themselves. Shakespeare did not even do what was done

by many Elizabethans, and by Molière, Calderón, and Lope de Vega—endeavour to forestall the pirates, or print the correct text to replace the one already pirated to its damage. In several instances, indeed, better editions appeared after the unauthorized; but if authorized, they were not authentic; and these bungled and garbled texts Shakespeare must certainly have seen. He would then have read, even in the better quarto, 'according to the true and perfect coppie' as the title-page has it, such lines as the last of these from Hamlet's speech to his mother in the closet scene:—

> That to the vse of actions faire and good
> He likewise giues a frock or liuery
> That aptly is put on to refraine night.

Even if he was not concerned for the twenty-one plays still unprinted, how could he have rested through the idle days and quiet nights the long five years at Stratford, thinking of this and similar errors descending to posterity, to plague the reader and for ever employ the commentator —to plague then the reader anew—in the printed sixteen? 'Oh, what a wounded name, things standing thus unknown, shall live behind me!' But that, in things literary, were a thought for Bacon, Jonson, Milton—conscience is for the conscious.

And the sonnets received no tenderer care. His stage plays Shakespeare held in slight regard as the contemporary Lope de Vega held his. They were admired, but, in the poet's time, very seldom admired in print. Such things were 'trifles,' as Heminge and Condell called them, or, to apply another Elizabethan phrase, 'staled by the stage, clapper-clawed with the palmes of the vulger.' Critics, scholars, and many of the aristocrats despised them, partly because they were not according to Aristotle, but partly because they served for the delectation of the rabble; and the classically-minded Chapman, Jonson, and Webster came out, with the products of their pens, in prefaces, half complaining, half boasting of their failure on the stage. Most of the little praise which Shakespeare received in print during his lifetime was for his poems and sonnets; in his sonnets (though echoing the very words of the Petrarchans and the ancients) he seems to expect immortality for his poetry; and, again like Lope de Vega, he may well have thought that his poetry alone was careful and academic enough to be literature, and afforded his only claim or title. Yet for years he permitted his sonnets to circulate in manuscript; and when they were printed, it was without his knowledge or consent. It seems, indeed, to have been the aristocratic and genteel thing not to print, in order to be above all suspicion of literary gain; and these considerations Shakespeare, who was founding a family and estate, applying for a coat of arms and taking to himself the style of 'gentleman,' may have permitted to weigh with him in regard to both sonnets and plays. And it may have been the correct thing not to print sonnets because of their extremely amorous character.[1] As an actor he had no social status, and his indifference to publication, which he shared with most Elizabethan and Spanish playwrights, may, then, have had its origin not only in the requirements of his business, but also in his social aspirations and his rooted regard for decorum. Yet genius, if of itself aware, has higher aspirations, which considerations of profit,[2] social status, and decorum, or of literary custom, cannot daunt; and here was no fixed

[1] J. Q. Adams, *Life of Shakespeare* (Boston, 1923), 164-5. I much doubt if this principle was widely accepted; the evidence produced seems to me to indicate rather the aristocratic and genteel prejudice mentioned above. Amorous as they were, the sonnets circulated in manuscript freely; and against amorousness the Elizabethans, like other poets, had small scruple.

[2] Professor Adams (*ibid.* p. 524) thinks Shakespeare's failure to collect and publish his dramatic works is by such considerations 'fully explained.' It is—if Shakespeare did not realize their literary value, an admission which Mr Adams apparently would not make. The editors or the publishers of the Folio probably had to pay the Companies for the rights in 1623, as the publishers of the Beaumont and Fletcher folio declare that they had to do in 1647 (Adams, p. 536); and why did Shakespeare not attend to the matter himself?

custom in the way. Spenser had printed—Chapman, Jonson, and Webster had printed—four of them poems and three of them plays; and all but Webster had far higher pretensions to learning, gentility, and literary eminence, and, so far as one knows, won in their own day fuller recognition for them. As for the sonnets, Daniel, Constable, Barnes, Fletcher, and Drayton printed theirs in the very years in which Shakespeare is supposed to have been writing his. And, since the Company printed some of the plays, why did not Shakespeare see to it that they printed them well, and (even though he had to reimburse them for it) printed them all, if rightly he valued either his life-work or the good opinion of readers in his own time or in times to come?

2.

He did not rightly value his work—he accepted the opinion of his contemporaries. Jonson's high praise came after Shakespeare's death, prefixed to the Folio—an epitaph on the monument, a garland upon his grave. In his own day, nobody of real importance, save Webster,[3] who (though he deprecates that interpretation) clearly ranks him, in his preface to the *White Devil,* lower than Chapman, Jonson, Beaumont, and Fletcher, took public notice of his merits as a playwright at all; and like Meres in 1598 (though Meres also singles him out as the best both in tragedy and comedy, and for that alone is famous), and Camden in 1603, Webster puts him in the same class with such as Dekker, Marston, Heywood, Daniel, and Hugh Holland, as well as others now unknown. Although more than twenty years in London, Shakespeare seems there to have made no stir. With his kindly nature and supreme gifts of expression he should have been the social light of the city; but though the common people knew and delighted in his plays, and though

---

[3] See footnote 6 below. To the names of Webster and Drayton should be added that of Beaumont, if the lines signed *F.B.,* and first published in 1921, be really his.

some few writers alluded familiarly to Falstaff or Hamlet, to Benedick and Beatrice, they seem generally (like present-day play-goers and novel-readers for that matter) not to have known the author's name or cared to know it. Bacon was of a larger calibre; with him style would have counted and the author have been of some concern. In his report concerning the insurrection of Essex in 1601, he tells of 'a Play of deposing of King Richard II,' which the conspirators 'procured to bee played before them'; but neither there nor elsewhere, although in the *Advancement of Learning* he wrote some of the noblest words ever penned on the subject of poetry, and in the second book of the *De Augmentis* an acute paragraph on the nature of drama, does he betray any knowledge of the author of the writings which some day were to be thought, by some people, too good to have been written by any one but himself. Here is no nodding—or tipping the wink, either—of Jove to Jove in the guise of a player-playwright. Two ships—tall five-masters —passing in the night! Did Bacon read the book, go to the play, or trouble to inquire after the author? Or, as Attorney-general finding no treason against the Queen, did he, as greatest of poets in prose, find, instead, treason in plenty against the Muse and Aristotle? Idle questioning, vain surmise, and there is irony enough in the incident without it.

And what of those who, though they knew not him, must have known his name and face? Francis Beaumont, who died in 1616, wrote in his later days a celebrated verse epistle to Jonson upon the Mermaid, recalling the words heard there, so nimble and so full of subtle flame, but does not remember Shakespeare's; Robert Herrick, in still later verses to Jonson on 'the lyric feasts made at the Sun, the Dog, the Triple Tunne,' does not either; and one wonders whether Fuller's celebrated account of 'the wit-combats betwixt him and Ben Jonson, like a Spanish great Gallion and an English Man of War,' in which Shakespeare carries off the honours by his lighter sailing and the quickness of his wit and invention, were not a tradition ill-founded, arising out of the poet's posthumous fame. Fuller, born in 1608, could not himself have witnessed them; Herrick, born in Cheapside, where stood the Mermaid, in 1591, easily could. Beaumont and Herrick do not there mention other poets either—to do so might have been not so palatable to the rather grudging Ben; but how, then, does it come about that neither of them, nor any one else, writes verses about the Mermaid to Shakespeare if he it was who bore the palm away? To the victor is the praise, and why recall to Ben the scene of his discomfiture? The very few who speak of Shakespeare personally cherish the memory of his gentle and courteous nature—he was, then, approachable enough —but no one hails him either lord of poets or king of men. He was not a great actor,—according to tradition, he played minor parts, such as that of Adam in *As You Like It* and the Ghost in *Hamlet,*—and (if we dared to say so) he seems not to have been a dominating or magnetic personality, though a master of the written, not of the spoken word. For if his conversation was as interesting as Jonson's, why, since it was so much gentler and more agreeable, did no poets allude to it, no London or Stratford Drummond take the trouble to jot it down? All the anecdotes and nearly all the personalia concerning Shakespeare appeared late, myths born of his reputation.

It may have been simply that he was too modest and unassuming, that he did not assert himself, did not in society boldly enough disclose the world of imagination wherein he lived and moved and had his being, or claim and take his intellectual throne. It was Jonson who took it, and sat squarely and solidly on it a score of years. It was Jonson who was the chief figure, not only at the Mermaid, but at the Dog, the Sun, and the Tun; and who, his convivial commandments graven on the marble mantel-piece before him, presided in regal state in the Apollo room at the Devil. It was Jonson, Chapman, Webster, Beaumont and Fletcher, not Shakespeare in his lifetime or afterwards, whom the poets looked up to and addressed. It was Jonson who knew the King, the Lord Chancellor Bacon, Sir Walter Raleigh, Camden and Selden, and almost all the poets, scholars, and men of rank and renown; and who founded schools (an expression in America now misleading) not only of comedy but of lyric verse. And yet, though one of the learned, as Shakespeare was not, Jonson was of neither university, and had been, like him, an actor, as well as a common writer for the theatres; and if Shakespeare was provincial and rustic, what was Jonson but the stepson of a brick-layer, if not a brick-layer himself, and branded on the thumb? The better dramatist, the finer poet, the infinitely sweeter nature—did Greek and Latin and other learning then outweigh all these? We have seen such things in society as well as in poetry, and know what a pitiful showing of themselves they make; and surely some other gift at the beginning must have been added unto him to turn the scale in favour of rare old Ben.

And it was Jonson, even, who bestowed on Shakespeare posthumously all authoritative title to the name of genius in that age; his is the only famous name among the writers of commendatory verses in the Folio; while Webster, in the same year, though as yet no object of piety, comes before the public, in his *Duchess of Malfi,* as the recipient of such verses from the pens of Middleton, Rowley, and Ford. All three of them we here miss, as well as Webster himself, Fletcher, Massinger, Shirley, and others of the double score of those who wrote verses for Jonson's plays, whether for his folio in 1616 or simply as a tribute at large to his personality and genius. 'No writer in his day published his poems without laudatory lines from his friends; Shakespeare never gave or requested any' [4]—or received any, we may add, even at his death. [5] Why did Beaumont and Fletcher, who had more in common with Shakespeare than with

[4] J. J. Jusserand, British Academy Lecture, p. 234.
[5] Save from Basse, in 1622, six years after.

Jonson, write only in the latter's praise—Beaumont, who was more indebted to Shakespeare than anyone, doing it again and again? And why did Herrick, who lived after Jonson had set his seal on Shakespeare's fame, write (also again and again) in praise of Jonson's comedies, his poetry and his wit, and 'upon Master Fletcher's incomparable playes,' and say never a word of one who composed plays and poems so incomparably better than either? Was it only because of the romantic irregularity of Shakespeare's style? There is nothing of that in his songs. It is somewhat, no doubt, because, like others, he shared Jonson's opinion, imparted to Drummond of Hawthornden, that 'Shakespeare wanted arte'; somewhat that Shakespeare had no theory of art or program; but somewhat also that he had not, whether through immediate contact with Shakespeare or through tradition, fallen under the spell of a personality such as your party leader like Jonson must of necessity have. He knew Jonson—Shakespeare no one knew.

Jonson himself, in the lines prefixed to the Folio, 'To the memory of my beloved, the Author, Mr William Shakespeare, and what he hath left us,' writes, though finely and nobly, as one who rises to the occasion; he indulges here and there in the humanist's hyperbole, and, as was then (and is even now) expected when recommending the book of a friend, particularly one issued posthumously, sets out to pen a panegyric. In his *Conversations* with Drummond, he mentions Shakespeare but twice, then only as a writer, and both times disparagingly; and while, in his *Discoveries,* he declares that he 'loved the man and do honour his memory on this side idolatry as much as any,' he is there defending himself against the charge of having made a malevolent speech. Idolatry there has been, but Ben does not crook the knee. 'He was, indeed, honest [honourable] and of an open and free nature; had an excellent fancy, brave notions, and gentle expressions, wherein he flowed with that facility that sometime it was necessary he should be stopped.' Now and then, he complains, Shakespeare makes himself ridiculous. 'But he redeemed his vices with his virtues. There was ever more in him to be praised than to be pardoned.' It was not too much to say.

A quiet and a minor part, therefore, Shakespeare seems to have played in life, as on the stage, though that was no less than justice from a jealous heaven to one who boldly played every part in the ample theatre of his imagination. He created a 'boon companion' or 'good-fellow' like Falstaff, lord of misrule, the life of the tavern, but, however it was in Eastcheap, he seems at the Mermaid (if indeed he was much there) not to have been given the delight of being such; he was king of poets at a time when the poets were kings, but he seems not to have been given the delight of knowing it or of receiving homage. He had friends, but not followers or worshippers; he founded no school and gathered about him no coterie; and he was at home among the players and the people, not the poets. He slipped through life in London without getting much noticed by the great world around him; and, about 1611, he was permitted to retire for good and all to Stratford, and bury himself in the country. No one noticed it. No one lamented it (or his death either) in elegiac strains. Beaumont and Fletcher took his place at the Globe, if they had not taken it already. And Stratford thereupon, not London, became the centre and hub of England and of Europe; but neither Stratford, London, nor Shakespeare himself was aware.[6]

[6] Both Sir Sidney Lee and Professor Adams in their *Lives* insist that Shakespeare enjoyed a great literary reputation during his life-time. But in such a matter authority counts for little, and evidence for nearly all. His plays were very popular, as I have recognized; his name was valuable enough on title-pages to be put there by some fraudulent publishers without warrant; but stage-plays were not considered literature, and no really literary person in his life-time praises Shakespeare save Webster and Drayton, the latter not exuberantly, either, and but for Lucrece. Spenser may have referred to him as Aëtion, but that is exceedingly dubious. And certainly the evidence is insufficient for Mr Adams' statement (pp. 237-8) that by 1599 he had 'won frank recognition as England's chief man of letters'— which, as Mr Adams acknowledges, a playwright was not supposed to be.

3.

Even in his writings, where he sits enthroned and enshrined above all the world, Shakespeare does not assert himself as do his contemporaries in drama—Marlowe, Marston, Chapman, Jonson, Beaumont and Fletcher, and Webster—any more than at the Mermaid or the Sun. As every one knows, we cannot easily make out his character, his likes or dislikes, his convictions or principles. He is too fair, too tolerant, too indulgent: the creator is lost in the multitude of his creations, and, a god in his own world, he is invisible. No partisan, or satirist, no reformer or propagandist—he stays his hand, lets things be. He has no word of abuse, or of sympathy either, for the Puritans, for the hungrily invading Scotch or the turbulent and truculent

Instead, as Creizenach notices (q.v., *Geschichte des Dramas,* iv, 191-211 for a juster estimate), Shakespeare's existence is ignored even by the greatest thinkers of the time who are much inclined to the poets—by Bacon, William Harvey, Gilbert, Hobbes, and Burton; though the last-named does once allude to *Venus and Adonis* as by 'an elegant poet of ours,' and mentions Benedick, Beatrice, and Romeo. This is after Shakespeare's death, however; after that, and particularly, after the publication of the Folio, with Jonson's encomium, he came into greater literary credit.—On the point of going to press I have consulted a book which I have inexcusably neglected, Professor Schücking's *Shakespeare im Urtheil seiner Zeit* (1908); but it gives me pleasure to see that my conclusions are by him fully justified. Professor Schücking interprets Jonson and Fuller much as I have done, and recognizes the unimportance of Meres' testimony, the only high praise recorded in Shakespeare's life-time which clearly concerns his plays rather than his poems. Meres has no reputation as a writer and in his discussion and praise of other playwrights shows little discrimination or taste. Evidently, as Professor Schücking says, he reflects popular rather than literary opinion. And the case of Drummond of Hawthornden is much in point. He was not only a writer of merit but was widely read both in continental and contemporary English literature and drama, and yet, though from his records it appears that he had read *Romeo and Juliet, Love's Labour's Lost,* and *Midsummer Night's Dream,* he seems not to have been sufficiently interested to go farther. The testimony in the *Return from Parnassus*—'Why, here's our fellow Shakespeare puts them all downe, I and Ben Jonson too,' and similar passages—is, as Professor Schücking shows, not to be taken seriously, written as it is by a scholar and put in the mouth of a gross clown. This indifference the critic attributes not only to the classical prejudice of littérateurs but to their dislike for Shakespeare's propensity to borrow instead of inventing his plots (pp. 94-6).

Irish; no gibes at tobacco-taking, tooth-picking, or the other highly fashionable affectations of the time. And he betrays no bias in affairs of church or state. He has, directly or indirectly, nothing to say of the Spanish or the Catholics, of the sale of honours or monopolies, or of the struggles then beginning between throne and people; has no opinions with regard to Ireland, no curiosity with regard to America, no interest even in that most fundamental of questions (a great nineteenth-century poet, even, vowed that he himself neither knew nor cared) whether the sun rose and set or the earth instead turned round. Theories and questions, creeds, problems, parties, these were not for him. Not new ideas but familiar ones interested him and served his popular dramatic purpose—pagan, Catholic, or royalist notions, for instance, not those of the newer faith. Like most of the great poets and artists he is no seer or prophet, no philosopher.[7] Even what may seem to be his aversions are not personal, but wholly traditional and inherited:—his aversion to Jews if he had any; his disgust for the sweaty, ill-smelling mob, frequently given expression, which belonged to many of the writers of his time; his patriotic contempt for the French. He was prejudiced only as England was prejudiced, or the ruling classes of England. His is the most real, solid, and variously coloured world in all drama; but he himself is out of it. And London is out of it, and, as Professor Tucker Brooke has noticed, all the noisy momentous matters of the hour. He is the supreme spectator, even a dreamer, as—to live—a spectator must well-nigh be. 'This world is too big to be all a dream'—too little if it were none. In that boisterous day he was the one prominent playwright to stand aloof—from everything he stood aloof, though not afar—from the free fight called the 'war of the theatres,' in which Jonson beat Marston and took his pistol from him, and roughest of all, wrote his Poetaster on him. Only once, for a moment, does Shake-

[7] See below, chapter iii, and *passim*.

speare grow personal (for the remarks upon the little eyases, rivals to his company, in *Hamlet,* have to do with a Company affair), when, remembering his poaching days, perhaps, he gives Justice Shallow a 'dozen white luces on his old coat,' in allusion (with the boyish prank of a pun on his enemy's name intended) to the coat of arms of Sir Thomas Lucy, who had prosecuted him. The old legend may, then, be true, we are delighted to discover; the spectator was sometimes an actor; like Prince Hal, he too for once in his days was a madcap, a minion of the moon.

4.

He was no doubt a lover. But in the sonnets, where he might safely have unlocked his heart, as people once fondly thought that he did, and as poets did in some measure before him, and in far greater measure after him, he did nothing of the sort, to the unending disappointment of all us inveterate prowlers and eavesdroppers to-day. Sonnets they are, not love-letters. Of many it is not possible to say even whether they are addressed to a woman or a man; indeed, that any of them was addressed to a man was for eighty years in the eighteenth century forgotten; and that two of them, the 110th and the 111th, contain a complaint against the poet's lot as an actor, is even now only conjecture. The critics cannot agree, no one knows. Though so concrete and specific in his plays, Shakespeare here embraces conventional and traditional language as his medium, or, where there is none to fit, deliberately betakes him to vagueness and draws the veil. Some scholars think the sonnets only a poetical exercise; some think they were written (as in rustic communities still) in behalf of another; in any case, whatever of his own experience is there he does not definitely disclose. He lets others, even delicate maidens, in his romantic dramas, tell their love, as if they were treading, not our earthly turf, but the amaranth or asphodel; yet for himself, though furnished with the immemorial warrant and license of lyric poetry to do likewise, he shyly puts off the poet, and keeps his heart with all an Englishman's diligence.

5.

He was no doubt a friend, a husband and father, a citizen of London and Stratford, and really walked their streets. But where in his verse do we find him or them? Not only do no poets write to him or of him, as Spenser, Jonson, Beaumont, Chapman, Drayton, and the rest freely did together, but he himself writes neither to them nor of them, neither these nor others. Two lines (in passing) to Marlowe, the dead Shepherd, in *As You Like It,* form the only exception. In the sonnet the Elizabethans kept pretty closely to tradition and convention; but in couplets and stanzas, in elegy, eulogy, epigram, or verse-letter, they often poured out their hearts to friends and fellow poets, living or dead, with a delightful intimacy and frankness. Jonson lost a son, and lamented him without pastoral or elegiac formality or circumstance. Shakespeare lost his son, but in verse said not a word, in public dropt not a tear. Jonson paid tribute to Edward Alleyn and Salathiel Pavy, the actors. Shakespeare, who had had so many more occasions to be grateful for their services, left all his actors, alive or dead, unsung, though in celebrating their triumphs he would have commemorated his own. All the poets praised Elizabeth alive, mourned her dead, and hailed the advent of her successor [8]—all but Shakespeare. And friends and enemies, male and female, whether of high or of low degree, and places and occasions, also, without number, these poets freely apostrophized, sometimes for profit, indeed, though generally for sheer pleasure in the song. But he who had more poetry in him than all these others together kept to the vague or riddling sonnet, and his few and doubtful other

[8] It has been thought by some that the 107th sonnet refers to Elizabeth's death and the advent of James, but this is not definite or certain.

poems are as impersonal as *Venus and Adonis* and *Lucrece*. Not a word has he for Marlowe, Greene, or Lyly, whose mantle had descended upon him, for Burbage or Lowin, Heminge or Condell, who filled the rôles he made for them, for any friend who talked with him or drank with him in London or Stratford, in youth or age, or even for the town or tavern itself. Jonson, Beaumont, Herrick and the rest celebrated such company, such places; and Drayton wrote his lines to Henry Reynolds about the long delicious winter evenings, when they

> Haue past the howres contentedly with chat,
> Now talk of this, and then discours'd of that,
> Spoke our owne verses 'twixt our selves, if not
> Other men's lines, which we by chance had got
> Or some Stage pieces famous long before . . .

It was with Drayton and Jonson, as in after-times the story runs, that Shakespeare had a merry meeting which was the death of him, but of any whatsoever in which he played a part we find nothing in his or others' verse. And Drayton wrote verses to the town of Coventry, near which (in Shakespeare's own county) he was born and where his lady lived, and Jonson wrote on the fire which burned up his books and papers; but Shakespeare wrote nothing to Stratford where he was cradled, or to the woman there whom he wedded, or to London where he triumphed, or to Oxford, where he tarried pleasantly at the Crown Inn as he journeyed to and fro, or on the fire that burnt the Globe and not improbably some of his manuscripts with it.

How did he thus contain himself, having 'poetry enough in him for anything'—for everything? Mere songs, such as Burns wrote so abundantly, but not more easily, would, one would think, have, all his life through, come flowing from his pen. Possibly they did; and careless of them as of his plays he took no pains to preserve them. But of his poems, as we have seen, he did take care, as not of his plays; with his sonnets he tooks pains in the penning if he did not

see them safe into print; and another explanation there must
be. Shakespeare seems to have been a dramatist by nature,
to use Mr Woodberry's words in another connection, as
well as by profession. Conventionality, reticence, imperson-
ality it appeared to be in the man, but it was absorption
in the poet. He it was—not Webster, who said the words,
and thus belied them—that 'rested silent in his own work.'
The songs seem all to have been written for the occasion in
the play, and not to have been the utterance of a personal
or private joy or woe. And if it be a personal and private
joy or woe in the sonnets, Shakespeare has artfully or
instinctively taken every precaution, and availed himself of
every convention, to make us think the contrary or keep
from us both fact and cause. With greater store of passion
and resources of expression within him than had ever any
who touched the sonnet before him or after, he, so conventional, is the last sonneteer of note before Milton, who
dropped convention almost altogether. Within it that
doughty personality would not be confined.

Indeed, it goes so far with him that in that time—the
Renaissance—and in that country—England—in which
more than anywhere else personality or character was esteemed, the man who prized it most seems to have been then,
and is to us now, hardly a character at all. Where is he but
in his style? [9] What is he but the spirit behind the radiant
and passionate, racy and humorous, poignant and terrible
drama? Why, a name, and some half dozen legal signa-
tures. By indirection and cunning inference something of
the man behind the mask has, with various degrees of certi-
tude, been detected by Bagehot, Sir Leslie Stephen, and Professors Bradley and Manly, and in some measure intui-
tively by us all, as virtuous and kindly, not religious yet not
irreverent, not cynical yet not fond of the rabble, and scorn-

[9] Ce langage, il sait le mesurer selon chaque personnage, mais pas si
bien que ce ne soit Shakespeare qui parle, qui rie, qui pleure, qui chante,
qui gambade ou gémisse selon son humeur Shakespearienne.—Gourmont,
Promenades, iv, 312.

ful of affectation, painted cheeks, and false hair. He is, to
be sure, not quite so impartial as he has been thought. Many
of the questions we raise he does not answer; but which is
the villain, which the hero—often who is wise, who foolish
—he leaves us in little doubt.[10]   Still, directly and definitely
we know nothing or next to nothing. In his work we find a
personality—diffused, all-embracing, well-nigh invisible—
not a person. Spenser, for all his allegory, seems nearer to
us. Chaucer, in the dim Middle Age, cursing his scrivener
and complaining to his empty purse, has more the voice and
semblance of a man. And if the same personality is to be
found in the sonnets, there is the gentleness, sweetness, and
affectionateness that some few of his contemporaries com-
mended in him, but also (apparently) an abjectness and
timorousness of spirit in the presence of his high-born faithless friend and in the face of society's disapproval of his
profession as a player,—not an imposing nature, but one not
out of keeping with the flexibility and impressionableness of
a dramatist, on the one hand, and with this particular dramatist's conventionality and obscurity in private life, on the
other. A very different person he must have been from the
exquisite and esthetic Flaubert, but still the objective facts
of his life and work would seem not unlike those of Flaubert's as seen by Gourmont. His work too is commonly
called impersonal; Gourmont insists that it is the most profoundly personal known—just as there is more personality
in the lectures of Claude Bernard on Experimental Physiol-
ogy than in *La Confession d'un enfant du siècle*. But there
we have all of him! 'Flaubert incorporait toute sa sensibilité
à ses œuvres—hors de ses livres, où il se transvasait goutte
à goutte, jusqu'à la lie, Flaubert est fort peu intéressant;
il n'est plus que lie.'[11]   The personality of most poets and
artists, indeed, proves prodigiously disappointing. What

[10] See, below, the discussions of Shylock and the Criminals, especially
section 2 in the latter.

[11] Gourmont, *Problème du style*, p. 107. Cf. pp. 50, 51, what he has to say
of Racine and Rousseau.

they aspired to be but are not may comfort them, not us, as we meet them or read their lives or correspondence.

The poet nowadays taken by some excellent critics to be in spirit nearest akin to Shakespeare is Keats. And however it be with the quality and calibre of his genius he has indeed much of Shakespeare's freedom and detachment of imagination and his character as a man. He too sees his vision to the point of self-forgetfulness, and he also has Shakespeare's disinclination to insist or argue, to teach or exhort. A character—what do we generally mean by it but a bundle of principles or predilections, prejudices or prepossessions, self-consciousness or self-assertion? Of this there is little in either of these poets, so different in their accomplishment. But the younger poet, being also a critic, was (in the better sense of the word) self-conscious enough to realize this quality in the elder poet and even in himself. Mr Murry in his recent book, *Keats and Shakespeare,* has quoted passages from the young man's letters which indicate it clearly:

. . . and at once it struck me what quality went to form a man of achievement, especially in literature, and which Shakespeare possessed so enormously—I mean *Negative Capability,* that is, when a man is capable of being in uncertainties, mysteries, doubts, without any irritable reaching after fact and reason. Coleridge, for instance, would let go by a fine isolated verisimilitude caught from the Penetralium of mystery, from being incapable of remaining content with half knowledge.

—To his Brothers, Dec. 22, 1817.

The only means of strengthening one's intellect is to make up one's mind about nothing—to let the mind be a thoroughfare for all thoughts, not a select party.

—To George Keats, Sept. 17, 1819.

As to the poetic character itself (I mean that sort, of which, if I am anything, I am a member; that sort distinguished from the Wordsworthian, or egotistical Sublime; which is a thing *per se,* and stands alone), it is not itself—it has no self—it is everything and nothing—it has no character—it enjoys light and shade; it lives in gusto, be it foul or fair, high or low, rich or poor, mean or elevated. It has as much delight in conceiving an Iago as an Imogen. What shocks the virtuous philosopher delights the chameleon poet. It does no harm from its relish of the dark side of things, any more than from its taste for the bright one, because they both end in speculation. A poet is the most unpoetical of anything in existence, because he has no Identity—he is continually in for (sic) and filling some other body. . . . When I am in a room with people, if I ever am free from speculating on creations of my own brain, then, not myself goes home to myself, but the identity of everyone in the room begins to press upon me, so that I am in a very little time annihilated—not only among men; it would be the same in a nursery of Children.

—To Woodhouse, Oct. 27, 1818.

There is the difference—between Shakespeare and Keats and, say, Burns and Browning on the one hand, and Jonson, Milton, Wordsworth, and Tennyson on the other.

6.

Even at those points where he must needs come out into the open, as in his two dedications to Southampton and in his will, Shakespeare intentionally or unintentionally wears a mask. He is by nature an actor too. What could be more conventional than either will or dedications? And though penned by the scrivener, the will, drawn up, as we have seen, not at the last moment, and later even reconsidered, might not only in the style but at least in the mere dispositions of it have permitted a great personality or individuality to appear. But here is none like that of Francis Bacon nine years later; or even that, the year before, of Edmund Heywood, uncle of Thomas the playwright—nothing familiar, intimate, or particular, no sign of tenderness or devotion in word or phrase for any person mentioned or not mentioned, or even the conventional and traditional signs of it, such as 'my beloved daughter' or 'my well-beloved wife.' The religious exordium is formal and perfunctory, and the bequests and arrangements are all purely business-like and humdrum—the strict entail, ten pounds for the poor of Stratford, sword, bowl, bed, and mourning rings. Not a second thought would you give it if it were not William Shakespeare's will. Heywood speaks tenderly of his wife whom he leaves behind him and arranges anxiously for her welfare;[12] and Bacon bears in mind, not only (as well he might) his name and memory, not only the disposition of his books and his own writings and the founding of lecture-ships at the two universities, but also (as of Shakespeare we should have expected rather than of him) the sweet individuality of the legatees he was taking leave of—'my loving wife,' 'my ancient good friend,' 'my very good friend,'—and, having no children of his own, does not forget those of others—'and to her son Charles, some little jewel, to the value of thirty pounds'—or leave unremembered or ungratified his servants. Surely with greatness of any sort this farewell to the world of the man of Stratford is difficult to reconcile, but most of all with greatness conscious and regardful of itself; yet less with the man who neither printed his dramas nor corrected them when printed, neither claimed nor denied the authorship of any, wrote no verses to the poets and received none, and retired when he had a competence, bought the best house in his native town, got him a coat of arms, went to law again and again to recover petty debts, and was buried in the chancel of the church.

Yet, since he was not conscious, it was not really a farewell. It was mere business, and like Shakespeare's other business we know of, as the part he took in the matter of the enclosing of the Stratford commons, nothing else. But if in such affairs he was dryer, more impersonal, and more

---

[12] Professor Adams (p. 466) quotes from this will to 'help us to understand Shakespeare's possible arrangements with respect to his wife.' Such indeed he may have made, but the known facts are these: (1) that in the first draft Shakespeare does not mention his wife at all ('leaving her to her right only,' as Bacon does in the postscript to his will); (2) that he later authorized the interlineation, 'Item, I gyve unto my wief my second best bed with the furniture.' Feeling then himself that the light thus shed upon the matter was uncertain, if not unfavourable, Mr Adams turns round and calls Heywood 'loquacious and sentimental, more communicative about his private affairs than the reticent Shakespeare.'

unregardful of ultimate appearances than other men, it is
not likely that in his art, which in so far as it was an actor's
he laments, and in so far as it was a dramatist's he forgets,
he would have gone a great length in the opposite direction.
And if he made no gesture of farewell in his will, he is not
likely to have made one where it was least to be expected or
comprehended—in a play.

7.

Nothing is more improbable than that a man like this
should in his dramas refer to himself, and in the last of all,
the *Tempest,* go so far out of his way as to speak of his own
'potent art,' now to be laid aside, of breaking *his* staff and
burying *his* book, while Prospero is bidding farewell to the
elves. Some excellent critics think Prospero is the poet;
but Creizenach [13] is right when he says that Shakespeare
and the other Elizabethans did not choose materials which
should give them occasion for personal confessions in the
style of Goethe; and in the sonnets, we have seen, he even
avoided such. Tennyson and Browning and Goethe thus
remembered their ends in lyrics, and might possibly have
made such a gesture of adieu in a drama; though even they
would hardly have dared to say that they had bedimmed
the noontide sun or called forth the mutinous winds, or that
graves at their command had waked their sleepers, oped,
and let 'em forth.[14] And to refer to no one else in his
plays as Shakespeare does, and thus to himself, would
be monstrous. Far more in keeping with what we know
of him would it be that in one play he should mention
another, or himself as author of both, as do Jonson,
Shirley, Molière, and modern authors sometimes, but Shakespeare not at all. Milton, no doubt, not more a poet than a

[13] *Geschichte des Dramas,* iv, 174-5.
[14] Exactly these details and the reference to his 'potent art' are seized
upon by the critics as referring to the poet himself. But see below p. 78f.
For an apt criticism of the allegorizing of Ariel and the other characters,
mentioned below, see Schücking, *Character Problems,* pp. 258-9.

prophet, had himself, blind too among the Philistines, at the back of his mind in his *Samson*.   But in stage plays, in Shakespeare's time or even ours, it is another matter; and the notion that Shakespeare, of all men, should think or say of himself the like of the above is owing to our irresistible desire to lay hands on the man's protean personality somewhere, at whatever cost.   Or is it rather that unesthetic biographical bent which in criticism, as I show in the next chapter, generally abounds, and (at less cost to the dramatist's sense of humour) turns Ibsen's *Master-Builder*—the churches, the homes for human beings, and the castles in the air—into an allegory of Ibsen's artistic development?   So Ariel has been turned into the imagination, Caliban into the vulgar public, Miranda into the drama. In the case of either poet it troubles both poetry and biography, but in Shakespeare's more.   Such meanings, though more plainly indicated, there are in Goethe, alas! and in Ibsen there may be.

Probably he never spoke or even thought of himself (though in these all-knowing days every magazine writer or college girl is free to do it) as having an art (save the mere poet's art) at all.   And how much better so—that in this last play he should not be thinking of himself but should be (as he was) simply mindful of the end, not his end merely but the great conclusion.   There is indeed an autumnal mood pervading the play,—a mellow light upon the scene and a melancholy overtone to the happiness.   The thought in the hero's mind is not only of death but of ultimate universal dissolution, and of death as a sleep, and of life as a dream. The thought is not pursued by the poet—it steals upon him and whispers in his ear.   A tendency to reverie has grown upon him, and with it a change in the character of his imagery. In his heyday, abstractions and the elements of nature took on for him, as for other Elizabethans, a clearly outlined human form:—

> Full many a glorious morning have I seen
> Flatter the mountain tops with sovran eye.

And jocund day stands tiptoe on the misty mountain-top.

How still the evening is
As hushed on purpose to grace harmony.

Heaven doth stop the nose at it, and the Moon winks.

There is a cliff whose high and bending head
Looks fearfully in the confined deep.

And this plastic power he never quite lost. Yet now the outlines tend to become vast, vague, and wavering, as they will
to one whose eyes are resting on the horizon, whose thoughts
brood upon the beginning and the end, over

the dark backward and abysm of time.

And whereas nature then took on the semblance of man,
man's life, in its changes, now often takes on the semblance
of cloud, wind, or water, most fleeting and mutable of
things :—

Sometimes we see a cloud that's dragonish;
A vapour sometime like a bear or lion,
A tower'd citadel, a pendent rock,
A forked mountain, or blue promontory
With trees upon't, that nod unto the world,
And mock our eyes with air. Thou hast seen these signs;
They are black vesper's pageants.
Eros.　　　　　　　　　　　　Ay, my Lord.
Antony. That which is now a horse, even with a thought
The rack dislimns, and makes it indistinct,
As water is in water.
Eros.　　　　　　　It does, my lord.
Ant. My good knave Eros, now thy captain is
Even such a body.

The cloud-capped towers, the gorgeous palaces,
The solemn temples, the great globe itself,
Yea, all which it inherit shall dissolve
And, like this insubstantial pageant faded,
Leave not a rack behind. We are such stuff
As dreams are made on, etc.

Age has told on him, thoughts of the end importune him, but still he is not writing of himself. If he were, he would not be himself,—so disengaged and noble, like the ancient poets.

8.

As in his will there are no literary men, so there are none in either his plays or his poems, and himself Shakespeare scarcely accounts one of them. Yet most of his finer characters—Henry and Hotspur, Brutus and Antony, Hamlet and Othello—live and die, like those of the ancients, mindful of fame and glory. He had heard the sound thereof. For himself possibly he was above it, and anticipating the bleak idealism of our day, thought, with Fichte, thirst for fame a contemptible vanity, or with Tennyson, 'merely the pleasure of hearing oneself talked of up and down the street.' But to such sentiments he never gives utterance, and when he touches on the subject it is in the spirit of the first words of his earliest comedy:—

> Let fame that all hunt after in their lives
> Live registered upon our brazen tombs. . . .

It is remarkable that Shakespeare never treats the subject ironically, in modern style, the fruits of ambition crumbling at a touch to ashes. He is neither disappointed nor cynical. Honour is 'a word'—is but 'air'—only for one man in his theatre, who is fat and old, who had already preferred the inconvenience of flight to the terrors of combat, and who likes not the grinning honour that Sir Walter hath.[15]

It is all well enough for Ruskin to make Shakespeare too lofty, or for Sir Leslie Stephen to make him too ironical and indifferent. There is, in his precise and meticulous will and all his orderly business-like life in London and Stratford, evidence to the contrary. 'Literary glory, though one may talk of it in sonnets, is a trifle'; but what are 'land and

[15] See the chapter on Falstaff, section 23.

beeves,' houses and furniture, a coat of arms and the title of
gentleman? And surely fame for ever, if you know you
have duly earned and won it, is a better thing than founding
a family in Stratford and leaving an estate in strict entail.
It may be better even for the heirs. But Shakespeare sought
that form of self-perpetuation which he most craved, or
had a right, he thought, to expect. In *Ratseis Ghost* (1605)
a player is by Ratsey the highwayman given advice (which
he takes) to 'buy thee some place or lordship in the country, that growing weary of playing, thy money may bring
thee to dignity and reputation.' And in the *Return from
Parnassus* (c. 1601) it is said of actors that, profiting by
the poor poets who write for them,

> They purchase land and now esquires are made.

So did Heminge and Condell, Burbage, Phillips, and
Alleyn, and for that matter, ambitious Englishmen generally in Shakespeare's day, as in this. What but an
actor, manager, and playwright—but a successful man
from Warwickshire—was he? London had not thought
him more, nor did he think of appealing from it to
posterity or all-judging Jove. Like his fellow playwrights, he did not publish his plays; like his fellow
players he saved money, bought land, and got him a
little title; like his fellow Englishmen, he retired to the
country—went home again—when his work was over; and
when the time came he wrote his will like a player and solid
country gentleman, nothing more. As with the simplest of
men (and certainly the happiest) instinct in him chimed
with his country's custom; and he followed it save when he
had reason to choose another course. He did as others
did, who, both as a man and as the supreme dramatist,
thought and felt like others—even as regards himself. A
sweet irony is in the thought that the few who see themselves somewhat as others see them, are, like the many who
do not, mistaken.

9.

And he wrote accordingly;—still as an actor, a manager, and a maker of stage-plays, which were not literature. Hence his indifference to what he had written—his happy indifference, in a way, while he wrote, having only himself and pit and gallery to please. No one has regarded readers less, for he expected none; he had no critics to fear and face but those in gallery and pit, who can be wooed to forget to be critical; and he wrote only for immediate effect, with otherwise unlimited liberty of utterance. So according to Monsieur Donnay wrote even Molière,[16] though he printed his plays. Shakespeare was writing only playbooks for his company, like Lope de Vega, not, like Corneille and Racine, immortal verse; his art satisfied him and his company only as it swayed audiences at the Globe; and since he thought only of swaying them and not of himself or his fame, he wrote often faultily, yet he has swayed the world. Shylock or Falstaff or the Ghosts he made only for himself and the Elizabethan audience, not one Shylock or Falstaff or Ghost for them, and another, lurking in the lines, for enlightened you and me.[17] To us, for all our learning and fine feelings, he, like Cervantes, gave no thought; the treatises on Shakespeare (as on Cervantes) the seer and philosopher, doctor, lawyer, naturalist, or geographer (*teneatis risum*), are vain; and as has been said of the Spaniard, 'his learning is naught, his reasonings are futile. . . . He is immortal [and universal] only by reason of his creative power, his imaginative resource, his wealth of invention, . . . his inimitable humour, his boundless sympathy.'[18]

He was free (and therefore was his audience spellbound), free of the trammels of self-consciousness and of those dread requirements of art which cow and confine the spirit.

[16] *Molière*, p. 357.
[17] See below, chapter vi, section 23.
[18] Fitzmaurice Kelly, *Spanish Literature*, pp. 229-30.

Hence the virtues of his writing, and hence its defects. It is, in the best of circumstances, notoriously a difficult thing to write a play, to hold an audience of all sorts and descriptions fast and breathless in their seats, pack a significant story into the compass of three hours—not much more, not much less—and meet all the exacting and capricious demands of stage, company, and occasion; but it is immeasurably a more difficult thing to write a play which also conforms to the rules or requirements of literature. These last, Shakespeare, we have seen, could ignore, not only the arbitrary precepts of academic criticism, the canons of Aristotle and the Renaissance critics, the unities, the trappings of chorus and prologue, and the principles of *decorum*—if Shakespeare knew them, he, like Lope, deliberately though apologetically, disobeyed them,—but those rules (if such there be) which hold good and are in force for ever. Writing rapidly and impetuously, careless and thoughtless of the cool and carping reader in his closet, he disregarded minor matters of consistency and plausibility, whilst he framed his great stage-stories, as no other great writer, even for the theatres, has done. In the twentieth line of the first scene of *Othello*, Cassio has a wife, though not long after it is clear enough that he not only has none but had never had any. He has one in the original story; and, unlike the dramatist, who, on being asked about his play, said it was finished—he had only to write the verses—Shakespeare here was already writing the verses before he had finished the play. So, Lady Macbeth, in the first act of the tragedy, seems, as she spurs her husband on, to have had a child:—

> I have given suck, and know
> How tender 'tis to love the babe that milks me;

but Goethe is certainly right in thinking that she is made to say this only to lend emphasis to the desperate speech which ensues. Why in *King Lear* should the Fool vanish with the tempest, nevermore to be thought of or mentioned by Lear or by Cordelia? Do Timon, Lady Macbeth, and Ophelia kill themselves? And there is 'young Hamlet,' can he really be fat and over thirty? Why does Richard II stop the combat between Bolingbroke and Mowbray? Is Mowbray guilty? Why does Cleopatra flee from battle and Antony? Why do Banquo and Desdemona's Emilia hold their tongues, and the Courts at Forres and Elsinore take so little notice of the remarkable deportment of royalty at functions? And why does Polixenes save his own skin and leave Hermione in the lurch? There is no answer, nor in this world will there be any. These are a few of the oversights or omissions, inconsistencies or improbabilities, in the text, not to be laid at the door of the printer, out of a multitude. Something like a dozen of the sort have been pointed out by Dr Bradley and others in *King Lear* alone.

Such are the fruits of freedom—defects due to rapid and careless workmanship (for, as several critics have observed, Shakespeare was little troubled by the literary conscience), and to a concern for immediate effect which at times becomes no more than a concern for the momentary. And as for the quibbles and rant—'his comick wit, as Dryden puts it, 'degenerating into clenches, his serious swelling into bombast,'—though his audience delighted in rant and revelled in puns and clenches, it is a delight which he must not have entirely disdained himself. Not for long can a man delight others who is not himself delighted. When we see how frequently he falls into bad taste it seems less improbable that he should not have known that he was one of the greatest of poets. That he was, like many poets, not a sure critic of his own or others' work appears from Hamlet's warm words of praise for the turgid and bombastic lines about Pyrrhus and Hecuba which the Player at his request repeats for him; but it appears more clearly from the prodigal manner in which he heaps imperfections upon perfections in almost every play.

10.

Yet there are no perfections like the perfections of Shakespeare. They, too, are spontaneous—the wildings of poetry—and that but enhances their charm. 'Les choses exquises, quand elles sont naïves, sont doublement exquises;' —for they are doubly, more exquisitely, human. This is oftener acknowledged in respect of the product of art than of the process; but the purest poetry is what it has from of old been thought to be—a song, a flight, a play or sport, without taint of self-consciousness or professionalism; and sad though it be that the greatest of us all had not the joy of knowing he was so great, we have no reason to be sad. To eat of the fruit of that knowledge means exile from the garden, or at least from the Muses' mount. He was earning his living, and that in the case of some of the greatest artists, strange to say, like the moral purpose in such as Dante, Milton, or Dickens, is not only a necessary incentive but a safeguard. For all that play of their imagination in excess of what is expected or appreciated by the public or required for the task, is their gift to mankind, their precious but spontaneous tribute to creation, which comes or goes unnoticed. Shakespeare and Molière earned their bread with their pens—but the immortal spirit within them was disengaged and free, untroubled and unspoiled by the attentions of the public or the wooings of the author himself. Luckily their work was not wholly dissociated from that of their companies; and having no reputation to live painfully up to, they were not tempted to strain their voices, keep beating their wings after they no longer rose from the earth, or go on making phrases and jests after virtue and savour, mirth and cleverness, had forsaken their thoughts.

Not that Shakespeare was a child of nature or impulse merely, and ignored art. That no great dramatist can be or do, not even a great lyric poet. Profuse strains of unpremeditated art are poured forth only by those who have in

some measure previously meditated their art and mastered
it. Sport is labour—eager and joyful labour—at the first.
And Shakespeare was conscious enough of his immediate
and practical aims and (less clearly) of his methods, though
unconscious of his eminence, and little learned in the methods or qualities of others. His art was more direct and
spontaneous than that of most dramatists, in that he had
learned it, not out of books, in the schools, or from the
ancients, but on the stage and in the audience, studying and
imitating only his contemporaries, receiving and consum-
mating a vital tradition. This art he knew, and (though
he had read examples of the classical) knew no other. He
had not so much studied it as breathed its atmosphere—it
was his element, and he became its tutelary spirit. Manners
you learn not from your dancing-master or etiquette-book
but in society; and a foreign language, not out of grammars
and dictionaries but in the country itself. So, without a
grammar, he had possessed himself of the language of the
stage, of the means of communication established by a current convention, or understanding between author and audience—the style, high or low, the verse, the stage-devices,
the loose but mobile structure of the story, the bold but
artful minglings of the emotions (tragic and comic)
together, the changes of scene,—all that in a generation the
audience had taught their authors and the authors had
taught their audience; and now nothing else under heaven
mattered, not rules of the drama, or canons of taste, or any
other question, but only how he, an author, could move the
audience anew. If any one, he could do it; not posing for
posterity, he had his eye fixed on no alien consideration such
as the example or precept of antiquity or the laurels to
crown his brow, but 'on the object,' solely on the characters
he was calling upon the stage and on the audience to assem-
ble before it; and into this business he threw his whole soul.

He had, then, a technique, but a technique of which he was
as little aware, and to which he was as little attached, as

any great artist that ever lived. The books which reduce it for us to a system or formula serve but to reveal the lack of system or formula. And, as Professor Alden has observed, he seems not to have studied and delighted in technique for its own sake as masters of it generally do, and to have varied it not for the sake of variety or ingenuity either, but only to secure greater and finer effects and fit it to the subject more adequately. The *Tempest* approaches to the unities more closely than any of his plays save that which in his youth he adapted from Plautus, simply because, as some one has noticed, the subject lent itself to them, not because they were imposed upon it.

II.

Such, I suppose, are the ideal conditions for the making of art—the supremely gifted genius, master of his medium and immediate heir to an artistic tradition, throwing himself into the undertaking prodigally and exuberantly, ignorant or regardless of esthetic rules or principles, guided and guarded only by the healthy instincts and customs of his race, his temperament, and his day. It is the difference between Homer and Milton, Æschylus and Seneca, Burns and Gray, the painters of the Renaissance and the painters of the schools. If in practical affairs the better part of a man's intelligence is 'his capacity to take account of the intelligence of others,' it is in a special way true in the artistic. Closet drama is not drama; no one paints, or writes either, as Browning's Andrea thinks he does, for himself alone. The drama's laws the drama's patrons give; but at these rare and happy conjunctures patrons and poet, in perfect understanding and accord, give the laws together. He speaks—and their hearts echo back to him—a living idiom. And in thus speaking for himself and to them only, Shakespeare, without knowing it, spoke to the ages to come. It is only so, perhaps, that the poet can full surely do that— forgetful and neglectful of ages to come or ages gone, careless of aught else than the work (with its attendant delight) of creation and communication. Afterwards come the critics, with their ancient models and antiquated standards; but they have reached and assisted only the lesser spirits; to the supreme artist they, in the end, come only to register and confirm his fame. The rules and principles are always retrospective, out-of-date as soon as formulated; great art when it appears is something new and strange. The manuals of play-writing are many—the courses in play-writing and story-writing are now many, but never are they for those who write. Regularity and symmetry, flawlessness of structure and finish, are to be found in the new only if it be still and cold; great art, of course, is impulsive, and as a result inevitably a little wayward—to give life it must be alive.

This the art of Shakespeare is, this it does. *Ex vivo vivum*. Like Browning's, the touch of his hand, at least with the pen in it, is like an electric shock; and as with Browning and Dickens both, even the inanimate things it touches start and quiver—whether it be jocund day standing tiptoe on the misty mountain top, or Mrs Todgers' dingy skylight looking distrustfully down her staircase. Like no one before or after him he teems with tropes and metaphors,—his thoughts come to the light of day metamorphosed into images, and no doubt that is the ultimate and perfected state of thought; his verse palpitates, his words have wings. But it is to the human beings he fashions that he gives life most abundantly—here, if anywhere, are the forms more real than living man. Victor Hugo writes of him more like a half-mad prophet than like a critic, but often only as a poet can write of a poet. 'As for the real, we insist, Shakespeare overflows with it, everywhere there is the living flesh; he has emotion, instinct, the true cry (*le cri vrai, l'accent juste*), all the human multitude with its clamour.' That sounds dangerously like the dark sayings about Shakespeare's characters as real persons, bits of life, not art. But Hugo is not confounding fiction with biography; long before him, though less deftly and vividly, ample Dryden and meagre Pope paid like tribute to Shakespeare's supreme life-giving power; and more and more the world does this to-day. The logic or even the psychology may be at fault, the motivation may be summary or inadequate, and character and conduct may now and then be difficult to reconcile; but at his best Shakespeare lends the persons on the stage—and lends it to them for ever—each a particular and individual voice. Whatever they do, whatever they say, by the way they say it we know them, and that is to love them. It is Cordelia, weeping, and no other, who says to Lear when he thinks, or fain would think, this lady to be his child Cordelia, 'And so I am, I am.' It is Rosalind, smiling, and no other, who says to Orlando as she plays the part of the person she really is, 'Come woo me, woo me, for now I am in a holiday humour and like enough to consent. What would you say to me now an I were your very, very Rosalind?' It is Falstaff—when comes such another?— laughing, and rolling the jest on his tongue, who says of his conscripts to the jeering Prince, 'Tush, man, mortal men, mortal men.' And who is it but Cleopatra, deep in the love of love, feeding herself with most delicious poison, that bids Antony, 'If it be love indeed, tell me how much'; and in his absence, as she pines and writhes, cries to Charmian, 'Ha, ha! Give me to drink mandragora,' or 'Give me some music, music, moody food of us that trade in love?' The words are theirs only, and these are none other than the words they spoke—one man, one woman, not a type or man the species. And like a thousand such in Shakespeare they are not literary, not bookishly beautiful (having indeed not been destined for books), not 'appointed to be read' in the study or university by generations yet unborn (and therefore by them now read and pondered) but the 'real thing,' as we call it, the true and troubled accents of the human voice. They come broken with laughter or palpitating with happi-

ness, tingling with pain or heavy-laden with desire, melting
with languor or choked with tears.   This, for all the conventions involved in it, is quick and passionate speech, not,
as in Racine, the rhetoric or eloquence of passion; a voice out
of a throbbing human throat, not the less intimate note of
flute or trumpet; the cry of the soul as alone we can ever
know it, fluttering in its tight tenement of clay, not aloft and
on the wing; and it is such as, now long after, the greatest
of the French, Russian, and English novelists have been
endeavouring to conjure forth again.   It is indeed the *cri
vrai,* the right accent and native idiom of the heart—a language we do not speak, or write, or often hear, but happily
still understand.   But the art whereby Shakespeare attained
to the deep reality of this utterance is not so much that of
the adage—which conceals itself—as an art which has out-
stripped and outdone itself, so engrossed in its purpose and
delight that for the moment it has forgotten all other art
in the world and makes it to be forgotten.

12.

The main thing, of course, is that it was Shakespeare.
He might have been given his full meed of praise in his
lifetime, and might have been made so fully aware of his eminence as to publish all his plays correctly before his
death.   Still he would not really have known himself, still
his plays would not have been 'correct.'   He was not
elegant or exquisite—when he tried to be he wrote badly,
like Burns.   He wrote, not like Congreve, without fault or
blemish, but, like Molière, hastily, far better plays.   'He
wanted arte'—was unselfconscious—not merely because he
was unrecognized and unaware, but because he was intent,
engaged, and inexhaustible.   Not critical, he was—oh, word
abused!—creative; and when he recognized a defect or
crudity in play or passage, his way, I presume, was not to
rewrite it but—almost before he knew—to write another.
In rewriting it he could not but write another, such was the

teeming abundance of his brain. There is in his work a vast
development but, one might say, no improvement or meas-
urable approach to perfection. He took to himself new
virtues, but put from him few faults or defects. 'He
redeemed his vices with his virtues,' as Jonson says—did not
amend them. He soared to greater heights, and if he
escaped pitfalls it was only while his inspirations lasted, and
because he was now stronger of wing. Not passion's slave,
he was nevertheless a prey to the poetic mood or impulse;
as with Scott, a demon seated himself on the feather of his
pen. From first play to last play, no one ever changed in
style and metre so much; but it was almost as an organism
changes, out of itself and in response to its environment,
not as a result of criticism. And in the construction of his
latest plays there are curious lapses into methods to be
found in the earliest.

Between the impulsive and the deliberate artist nowhere
is the difference clearer than in their conclusions—the last
act, last scene, last lines of play or poem all-important to
the effect—and there Shakespeare's power often flags. His
virtues are positive, opulent, redundant, not negative or
corrective, frugal or austere. Taste, as Mr Middleton
Murry says, will not carry you far; 'mieux vaut l'exubér-
ance,' said Flaubert, 'que le goût'; chastity, it is but a 'bar-
ren, beggarly virtue.' Though more complex and compact,
more varied, powerful, and subtle, his art in his later days is
nowise purer or chaster; it is even less logical and orderly;
it is more intricate, tortuous, and obscure. It is also less
consistent; his greatest characters, like Hamlet, Falstaff,
and Cleopatra, grow upon him, change as Don Quixote
changes in Cervantes' hands, and the creature, like Pyg-
malion's statue, captivates and takes possession of its
creator.[19] Here, if ever, the art is the man; of the man
we are ever reminded for all that he loses and forgets himself; and, the man being greater, the art is better, simply

[19] That is, of course, metaphorically. See below, chapter ii, section 14.

because the vast and mighty things are better than the puny. It grew—branched and soared, twined and tangled, with neither pruning nor training—as a work of nature grows. *King Lear* or *Antony and Cleopatra* is less balanced and harmonious than the *Merchant of Venice,* though either outweighs the last. In none of the plays is there much of the fine logical unity of Racine, which is achieved by the critical and selective action of the mind, and still less of it is there in the later ones. But there is another unity which is richer and more precious, that of an all-pervading, all-assimilating life. Metaphor, not simile, is his spontaneous and continual mode of expression, the perfect union of thought and form, of the spirit of thought (so to speak) and its body. And whereas the comic and the tragic in drama had been kept separate, or else been harshly and unhappily brought together, in Shakespeare's greatest work, as nowhere in the world, humour blends with sentiment and fancy, with pathos, with the tragic and terrible itself, not only in the same work but even in the same situation and moment. Here is art too, but not so much the art which rejects as that which embraces:—more matter is involved than is needed, but with every natural light upon it; more emotions than a single one, as the current of consciousness flows and eddies.

And hardly could it have been otherwise. Though greater, Shakespeare is, like Browning, Balzac, Scott, and Dickens, too preoccupied with life to study perfection in art, or strictly meditate the Muse. Yet to him she was not thankless—her supreme favour, like that of other ladies, is for him who does not too strictly woo her—and the human figures, the thoughts and images, words and rhythms, came only too thick and fast. He was no Flaubert or Pater, to chase the phrase till nightfall; out of his infinite riches he had not for long to pick and choose. He wrote easily, impetuously, for money, to be sure, but also because he liked it—because, once started, he could not easily stop—

because, once stopped, he could, in the same mood and temper, hardly get started again. In twenty years he wrote thirty-seven plays, more in the same time, despite his duties as actor and man of affairs, than any other Englishman. And yet he was not one of those to whom, either literally or metaphorically, art and life are one and the same; and he retired to Stratford. There he might have penned a dozen more, had there been an occasion. There he might have worked on, fashioning new plays or correcting the old, and like Plato have died writing,—were it not that he could talk and listen, dream and idle, and, till it sank, hold both hands before the fire of life. It and not art was his refuge and shrine. His facility when he did take pen in hand was the one trait fully appreciated in his day. 'His mind and his hand went together,' say Heminge and Condell; 'and what he thought, he uttered with that easinesse that we have scarce received from him a blot in his papers.' Swiftly he wrote down what the spirit spoke. 'He never blotted a line,' echoes Jonson with a grunt, writing not for the Folio but for himself, in his *Discoveries;* 'would he had blotted a thousand!' But the world (both then and now) does not join him and the other judges of his time, who loved what they called 'art' rather than what they called 'nature,' in their wish. If Shakespeare had been the man to do that, nature—life—would then have yielded to art; he would have known himself, which is no doubt the sum of wisdom, but, whether for him or for us, there would have been less to know. The master of them that know—*di color che sanno*—was not a poet.

1923

CHAPTER II

LITERATURE AND LIFE

The temptation is sometimes considerable to reconstruct in imagination past societies from the works of art they have left. How dangerous this fascinating game can be is shown by one who was an adept, by Addington Symonds in his essay on Perugia, where he works out the paradoxical situation that Perugino's frail sentimentalities were produced at the time when the streets of the town were bloody with civil war. If, as some people suppose, the arts were always an expression of contemporary life, then the paintings of Perugino would be a phenomenon almost inexplicable. But we know that great art may well be an expression of something quite alien to the society from which it came.—*The Times,* March 24, 1922.

The 'cave man,' it is said, is now hero in popular fiction. The 'best-sellers' no longer present a hero who bows as a true knight before the will of his lady, but one with hair on his chest, as the current vernacular would have it, who, little thinking of the needs of the state, carries her off like a Sabine, and strikes her if she turn on him and bite. These books I do not know. But I think that Mrs Gerould,[1] who does, must be right in holding the opinion that this new hero is not copied from life, and that the change in literature does not reflect a change taking place around us. It is not the war, it is not the rise of a fierce type of woman and of the man to match her, it is not to any degree a change in either our character or our manners. Literature reflects the taste of the time rather than the time itself, and often the two are widely different. We like what we are not, or we are not what we think we are. Literature is, of course, not life, neither history nor material for history, but a scroll whereon are traced and charactered the unfettered thoughts of writer and reader,—a life within a life, fancy somewhat

[1] In an article in *Harper's Magazine,* October, 1922.

at odds with fact.   But by critics and historians this is often
forgotten—'to pass from the art of a time to the time itself,'
says Wilde, 'is the great mistake that all historians commit.'

I.

Take the simple matter of swooning or fainting, recently
considered by Mr Chesterton.   At first it looks like evidence to the contrary, for there is little or none of it in
present-day practice or in our novels either.   But that is
only because the fashion had been worn to tatters, and the
taste for it had palled.   Ladies and maidens for centuries
had freely swooned or fainted both in poetry and in prose,
and in life, no doubt, as well.   They swoon in the Victorian
novel; in Scott; in eighteenth-century novel, tragedy, and
comedy; in seventeenth-century comedy and tragedy; in
Shakespeare and Spenser; in the romances, whether in prose
or in verse, English or foreign.   Was woman, through all
this effusion of emotion and unlimited liberty of deliquium,
frailer or more affected then?   It cannot be, though nowadays rather than yield to this particular frailty she will dig
her nails into her palms or bite her lips to the quick.   For
in modern literature the *motif* first appears in the heroic
epics of the dark ages, the *Song of Roland,* for instance,
when life was at its roughest and boldest; and the fainting
here is not so much by the women as by the men.   Roland
and Charlemagne's other peers weep and faint, not from loss
of blood only, but from grief and passion, and so do their
Saracen foes.   In the later Arthurian epics the knights of
the Round Table weep and swoon at times for pure sorrow.
The mighty and terrible Rustum, not only in Arnold's poem
but in the ancient chronicle, swoons on recognizing Sohrab;
and the poet of the *Inferno,* in his story, falls, on hearing the
tale of Francesca's love, as a dead body falls.   But in life
it was the ladies.

For the taste of the people is always romantic. It delights
in high colours and in strong situations, in deeds, gestures,

and outcries, with sober reality or 'the modesty of nature' ill content. Charlemagne, the great king, weeps on receiving bad news and tears his beard. Roland, the paladin, in the saddle, swoons at the sight of the dying Olivier. And in the old ballads of the fifteenth and sixteenth centuries youths in love take to 'care-bed,' or when they hear of their true-love in distress, throw the cup (ever in hand) into the fire, kick over the table, and go down the stairs a half dozen at a step. Or if the occasion call for passion merely, the buttons fly off their coats, and their hearts they burst in three. Yet these are the heroes of the poetry of the people —of phlegmatic Danes and Englishmen. The Franks under Charlemagne, I daresay, never swooned save when they were bled white. The stout knights of Philip Augustus or Richard the Lionhearted, I daresay, never swooned at all like King Arthur or Sir Gawain in the story. All this knightly and uneffeminate swooning must have happened in story or poem alone, in the land of dreams. People liked to read of it, not because it was true, but because it wasn't, though thinking, under the spell of the moment—the blessed spell of romance—that true it must have been. What made them believe in it was the high cause and occasion, the poet's art—that and their inner inclination.

The men's swooning or taking to care-bed is like Shakespeare's women wooing the men or following them up in hose and doublet. Out of the strong cometh forth sweetness, out of the sweet cometh forth strength—the man turns woman, and the woman man—when love constrains them. There is something in that, no doubt, but the way of romance in general—love at first sight is another instance— is ever the way of wonders and miracles. And this Mr Shaw for the moment forgets:

In Shakespeare's plays the woman always takes the initiative. In his problem plays and his popular plays alike the love interest is the interest of seeing the woman hunt the man down. She may do it by blandishment, like Rosalind, or by stratagem, like Mariana;

but in every case the relation between the woman and the man is the same: she is the pursuer and contriver, he the pursued and disposed of.

'The Shakespearean law,' he adds, 'is the law of life'; and for once Mr Shaw gives Shakespeare's philosophy a pat of approval. But not of a law or of fact was Shakespeare thinking—not so women act now or acted then, but so men fancy that they would have them act. A man, he was writing for men, the women in the audience being few and masked. It is in the interests of romance that the men should be pursued by the women, for thus—as a little feminist once said to me—the men are flattered. What is romance if not flattery? and the women spectators are flattered too: they see now what can be done. In a fiction, moreover, or in sport, as in some children's games, both sexes are for the moment delighted to change places.

> Teach me to flirt a fan
> As a Spanish lady can,

cried Browning's lover; and Shakespeare's Cleopatra, playing a like game with Antony, 'put my tires and mantles on him, whilst I wore his sword Philippan.' In this real world, to be sure, and when in earnest, and with a purpose, the change is not so pretty or pleasant. By an ordinary woman no man, however backward, cares to be pursued and disposed of, nor do the women themselves, mindful of the rules, approve it; but, in one's day-dreams, to be pursued by a beautiful woman—in charming fashion, timorously, in elegantly becoming hose and doublet—or to be oneself that woman—is another thing. And your day-dreams you must needs find in drama, as in the novel, not the reality which, as you turn to either, you are for the moment thinking to escape. In a way, to be sure, ladies then pursued gentlemen even as they do now,—according to the rules, without seeming to do it. But Shakespeare was writing romance.

2.

A nice woman in man's clothing is not realism either. Here the argument from history rather than that from present life has been employed, although it fits no better. Women did not then resort to men's clothing much more than they do to-day, just as they did not all fall in love at sight, though they do in Shakespeare. The spirit of romance, again, works these quick changes, external and internal,—but also the desire for lively and striking situations in a story; and to that end before his day young women had been freely represented in male garb both on the stage—English, Spanish, and Italian—and in the Italian and Spanish novels from which he took his plots. There they accompany or follow up their lovers as pages; just as the women in the medieval romances and in Ariosto and Spenser disguise themselves in armour, overthrow famous warriors with their good right arms, and traverse continents as they seek their mates. In all things, that is, dress and deportment alike, they are the ladies of romance. And they are but the more romantic for being a little irregular in their conduct: the irregularity is the outward sign and measure of their love. Generally it is apparent that this disguise is of the nature of an adventure; in one sixteenth-century Italian comedy,[2] at least, it is made clear that in life only the loose girls take to it; and so for a girl to take to it for true love makes her the more interesting. The good are interesting only if they are not unlike the bad: the romantic way is to make them seem a little bad though they be not; the realistic, to make them a little bad indeed. Shakespeare's heroines are like the girl in Spanish comedy who drops a glove or trips in the street (things strictly forbidden in the code of etiquette) to have occasion to speak to the youth, standing by, who shall come to her assistance. Braving the

[2] *Gl' Ingannati*, I, iii.

rebuke of the duenna, she flutters free of the proprieties out into the liberties of romance. The impropriety endears her to the cavaliers in the audience, who would have been of a different mind had she been off the stage and of their own flesh and blood.

The old doctrine, of course, runs counter, even from the days of Cicero. The popular dramatist or novelist likes to think that he does but hold 'the mirror up to nature'; his public like to think that his dream, which is for the moment theirs, is the 'image of truth.' Nothing is so rare as realism —nothing in itself so hateful or by name so dear. Artist and public alike would think that they are dealing boldly and directly with life, while they veil it or evade it. Both are like the lady of Shalott, though their mirror reflects a mirror and the image upon it is a shadow's shadow. And the critic and the historian, for other reasons, like to think this still more. Both give a large place in their pages to the pictures of the times provided in novel and drama, finding such even in Elizabethan drama, which is romantic through and through. But the scene there being often foreign—Italian—the historians find a less dubious foothold in the Comedy of Manners after the Restoration, the comedy of Etherege, Wycherley, Congreve, Vanbrugh, and Farquhar. There the scene is in England, London, the City or the West End; and they think themselves at home.

3.

Here again and again has been found a vivid picture of the time, and it has been reproduced by no mean pens. Macaulay long ago traced it for us as he saw it; and Mr John Palmer, not long ago, as he saw it himself. Macaulay makes of it a picture of Restoration vice and wickedness; Mr Palmer, 'a veracious picture of a particular golden moment in the history of actual English manners and morals.' [3] With the same premise, how dif-

[3] *Comedy of Manners,* (1913).

ferent a conclusion, and I cannot but think the premise false.

It seemed false to Lamb, though in this direction he goes too far:

They [these comedies of manners] are a world of themselves almost as much as fairyland. . . . They [the characters] seem engaged in their proper element. They break through no laws, or conscientious restraints. They know of none. They have got out of Christendom into the land—what shall I call it?—of cuckoldry— the Utopia of gallantry, where pleasure is duty, and the manners perfect freedom. It is altogether a speculative scene of things, which has no reference whatever to the world that is. . . . When we are among them, we are amongst a chaotic people. We are not to judge them by our usages. No reverend institutions are insulted by their proceedings,—for they have none among them. No peace of families is violated,—for no family ties exist among them. No purity of the marriage bed is stained,—for none is supposed to have a being. . . .

'In fact,' says Mr Palmer, 'as Lamb might have concluded, but did not think fit to conclude, here was a perfect reflection of the genius of early Restoration society.' But from Lamb's premises there could have been no such conclusion. 'For Etherege and his friends,' Mr Palmer says again, 'pleasure was a wise young man. They based their conduct upon inclination, and squared religion and morality with the life of the twenty-four hours. There was never in English history a time when the conscience of society was more at ease; when precept and practice were so clearly connected.' But Lamb insists that this comedy does not corrupt us just because it is so far removed from life, and because the people presented are a chaotic people—a people without ties or law or order—and that is not a society at all. Were what Mr Palmer says true, London after 1660 must have been more chaotic than was ever Munich under the Communists, or Petrograd or Moscow under Lenin and Trotsky—'which is impossible,' as at such a juncture we

learned in geometry to say.⁴ Wives—our title in them, dear
as that in our lands and tenements, cannot so lightly be
taken from us.

As for the three, Lamb says that the Comedy of Manners
is beautiful and delightful because it is unreal—morality is
not in question; Macaulay (whom we cannot undertake to
quote) says that it is tedious and corrupting because it is
altogether too real—sound morality is made contemptible;
Mr Palmer says that it is not only beautiful but also highly
moral, for it reflects and represents the morality of the age.
Lamb and Macaulay are utterly opposed; Mr Palmer
agrees a little with both but adds a great deal, contrary in
spirit, of his own. But why they differ so widely it is easy
to discover. Lamb is here, as usual, the dreamy, subtilizing
Elia, and Macaulay, the early Victorian; Mr Palmer, the
very enlightened cosmopolitan critic of to-day, who knows
all contemporary literature, and French realism, and French
criticism.   Accordingly, each sees one thing and not
another. Lamb remembers that these are comedies and
works of art, but forgets their necessary ultimate relation
to morality and life; Macaulay remembers morality, but
forgets that these are comedies and works of art; and Mr
Palmer remembers life, remembers that these are works of
art, but almost forgets that they are comedies. Mr Palmer
belongs to that great school of contemporary dramatic
critics, and dramatists, too, such as Mr A. B. Walkley and
Mr Shaw, who are enamoured of French frankness and sincerity in realism and the criticism of life. Their *bête noire*
is English prudery, sentiment, and romance. They seek

⁴ Mr Archer (*The Old Drama and the New*, Boston, 1923, pp. 173, 176,
especially) criticizes Mr Palmer much as here and below I am attempting
to do. At p. 176 he says: 'Had the theatre fairly represented its age,
the British nation could never have emerged from such a morass of levity,
cynicism, corruption, and disease.' I do not agree with Mr Archer,
however, in contemning the Comedy of Manners because it is not representative. The present essay, in sum and substance, was read before the
London branch of the Modern Humanities Research Association in December,
1921.

reality to the point of brutality. They aspire to see things in a 'dry' light; and Flaubert and Balzac, and such as Becque and Brieux, are their seers and prophets. And when Mr Palmer turns to the Restoration Comedy of Manners, he seems in Etherege, Wycherley, and Congreve to find his idol again, this dry unromantic veracity in the portrayal of life such as he would have to-day prevail. He even says that 'the comic dramatist's attitude towards Mr Pinchwife, one of Wycherley's characters, is precisely the attitude urged to-day with every symptom of moral fervour and righteousness by an energetic group of contemporary authors.' He does not realize that these are not relentless studies of reality such as appear at the Renaissance or the Vieux Colombier, but comedies, written before *drame* or social drama was invented. He does not realize that if our contemporary authors are earnest and morally fervid their attitude cannot be at all like that of the Restoration comic dramatists—which is comic. It is the spirit of the presentation which makes the difference, as in art it always is. Here are not the words of truth and soberness—this is not the world as it is, was, or, D.V., ever shall be, but the 'land of cuckoldry,' of comic topsy-turvydom.

So even the very philosophy of conduct must needs be altered, and the young gallants of Etherege and Wycherley openly invert and pervert the maxims of the received morality.[5] Here is the vein of Etherege and Congreve, as we

[5] Mr Archer's book, cited above, p. 173: 'a sort of perverted would-be morality.' Mr Allardyce Nicoll, in his excellent book on *Restoration Drama* (1923), pp. 186-88, takes a somewhat similar attitude to the question, though he inclines to conceive of the Comedy of Manners as the expression of the life of the upper classes and allows insufficiently, as it seems to me, for the distortion of the comic mirror. And though he clearly presents the fact that 'Save for the first year or two of the Restoration two theatres, and for over twelve years one theatre, supplied the wants of the play-going public' (p. 5), and that there were no theatres in the provinces, he explains the fantastic and unreal heroism of Restoration tragedy as owing to the debilitated, unheroic age; and following M. Charlanne, contrasts this tragedy with that of Corneille and Racine. There is, then, only one inference, that of the corresponding superiority of the French people, which I consider below, section 5, last paragraph, but which Mr Nicoll does not face.

find it in the *Man of Mode*. 'Constancy at my years,' cries
young Dorimant so gaily, ''tis not a virtue in season. You
might as well expect the Fruit the Autumn ripens in the
Spring.' This, though far from the worst, is typical; and
it is surely not, as Mr Palmer would have it, precisely the
morality which Etherege and Congreve followed in their
serious pilgrimage. It is manifestly startling, and partly
because it is startling is it witty and comic. 'Monstrous
principle,' cries Loveit in reply, and morality looms up in
the background, not utterly forgotten.

Vainlove. Could you be content to go to heaven?
Bellmour. Hum, not immediately, in my conscience not heartily.
    I'd do a little more good in my generation first to deserve it.
                      —*Old Bachelor,* III, ii.

Old Jeremy Collier, in 1698, saw here the *double entente,* no
doubt, though he was more concerned for the blasphemy;
but Mr Palmer drolly takes this for 'the conscientious belief
of a believer who did not believe in very much.' To me it
is no more than reckless ribald jesting, nothing conscientious in any sense. And though all this topsy-turvyism of
morality arose indeed out of these men's loose lives, it is
not the complete expression of them. It is not naïve and
simple, like the knightly morals of the Troubadours and the
conversations of Launcelot and Guinevere, Tristram and
Iseult. For these men are cynics, are drolls and wits.

4.

The trouble, as we have suggested, is that Mr Palmer, in
his modern preconceptions and his eagerness for a veracious
picture of life, has, fine and clever as he is, failed to enter
into the spirit of seventeenth-century humour, which at bottom, however, is but the humour of to-day; and Sparkish,
in Wycherley's *Country Wife,* is, though Mr Palmer does
not see it, meant to be as ridiculous as Pinchwife. Unlike
Pinchwife, his foil, he is ridiculous because he is not knowing enough to be jealous. A husband or a lover is sup-

posed, when occasion arises, to have spunk enough to be a
little jealous, even now, in life or on the stage. Though
much is taken much abides, and we are still human.

Sparkish. That's a good one! I hate a man for loving you!
If he did love you, 'tis but what he can't help; and 'tis your fault,
not his, if he admires you. I hate a man for being of my opinion!
I'll ne'er do't, by the world.

Alithea. Is it for your honour, or mine, to suffer a man to make
love to me, who am to marry you to-morrow?

Spark. Is it for your honour, or mine, to have me jealous? That
he makes love to you, is a sign you are handsome; and that I am not
jealous, is a sign you are virtuous. That, I think, is for your honour.

This is not the 'new morality' before its time; but the
vapourings of one who, according to the clever characters,
can no more think the men laugh at him than that the
women jilt him, who 'cannot drink'—so little is he of a man
—and 'tries to pass for a wit.' Any cause he espoused he
would discredit. And it is as likely that the dramatist would
have us here enter sympathetically into Sparkish's opinions
of sex matters as that Shakespeare would have us enter into
Shylock's opinions of race prejudice, or Jack Cade's of
social and fiscal matters, or Falstaff's of military glory,
though in substance they happen to approximate to the spirit
of Fraternity and Equality, and the communism and pacifism, of to-day. 'The study of literature is mainly a study in
emphasis,' says Professor Tupper; and even in life the tone
and accent of an utterance count in the way of an opinion
often for more than the substance, the spirit for more than
the letter—and indeed may enter into it with the diminutive
all-importance of a negative. The words on Fitzgerald's
tomb—'It is he that hath made us and not we ourselves'—
are taken literally from one of the Psalms, but are here
meant to convey something totally different, over the dust
of the modern Omar. The words are the Psalmist's, not the
sense.

Yet this Mr Palmer in all seriousness takes for the doctrine of sex equality in the days of the Restoration,[6] and wears a sad brow as he ponders Wycherley's irony and raillery. It is true that were it not for the situation and for the plight which befalls him—were it not for his foolish character and the context, both of which cast a glaringly ludicrous light upon him and his opinions too—Sparkish might here be thought to be expressing the ideas of, say, Mr Shaw, who thinks the graceful thing for a man in the position Othello thinks he is in, is to make haste and get out of the way himself. If poison is to be taken, he is to take it; if choking is to be done, he is not the one to do it. But that is 'advanced' thinking, not native to our common human nature, our manly but ignoble blood; that is the new chivalry, the 'new freedom,' as it were. How many in the seventeenth century could have taken it seriously—in a comedy—when put forth by one so evidently little better than a fool? We to-day do not jest about cuckolds, the very word having no longer a place in the drawing-room vocabulary, but in the seventeenth and earlier centuries— in drama or in life, in court or cottage—men freely did. Thirteen years earlier, in 1660, before an audience reputed to be not only more advanced in thinking but more refined in feeling, Sganarelle, in the *Cocu imaginaire*,[7] had expressed a philosophy of sex-morality almost equally enlightened, with the same ridiculous effect. Molière, behind him, banters quite as Wycherley jeers. The time simply had not come for taking cuckolds seriously, for 'taking their point of view,' as we say, which in the case not only of them but other hapless people, is nowadays the chief spiritual business of us all, to the baffling and stifling of the comic spirit. Where men once laughed we pause and consider, and soon we shall be less human than humane.

[6] Mr Palmer here seems to be ridden by a theory. Meredith (whom he has read) says that 'a state of marked social inequality of the sexes' is inimical to comedy. Now the seventeenth-century Comedy of Manners is unquestionably (*pace* Mr Archer!) fine and clever comedy, *ergo!*—

[7] See his long droll soliloquizing, scene 17; and below, p. 460.

One might as well look for a perfect picture of Elizabethan life in Elizabethan comedy, or of medieval life in the medieval French farces and *fabliaux*—one might as well find sex equality there. There, as here, the cuckold and the wittol, the jealous husband and the too complaisant one, are, like the miser, the standing comic types. It is in the same spirit that Wycherley and Congreve treat them, only more airily. If extreme suspicion and extreme confidence on the part of lover or husband are made ridiculous here at the Restoration, such they have always been; and if they argue a new morality in the time, they argue a new morality in every period of the comic drama and literature of which we are aware, Greek, Latin, or Medieval. But the comedy is the same. The reason that the sympathy has always been on the side of the lover betraying the husband, particularly the jealous or suspicious husband, is exactly the same reason that sympathy has always been with the young spendthrift eluding the money-lender, or with the servant or son deceiving the old master—from the days of Plautus and before. There is no great fun—very little of a lark— in siding with authority and backing up old father antic the law. Paying one's debts on the comic stage? There such humdrum, work-a-day duties cannot presume to show their face. Jeremy Bentham, that apostle of the gospel of cash payment as sole nexus betwixt man and man, sadly shaking his head, once said, 'I question whether among all the instances in which a borrower and a lender of money may have been brought together upon the stage, from the days of Thespis to the present, there ever was one in which the former was not recommended to favour in some shape or other, either to admiration, or to love, or to pity, or to all three; and the other, the man of thrift, consigned to infamy.' So it has always been on the stage in this era of property and cash payment, nor is it likely to be otherwise till the age of communism be fully come. Then first out of his infamy will the man of thrift emerge; then first will his virtue take on that rare and romantic quality which the stage requires. But the misers of Wycherley and Congreve, meantime, are all in one boat with the foolish and luckless husbands—wittol or cuckold. These are ridiculous,—the latter, because, like the miser, he guards his treasure as churlishly as a dog does a bone; the former, because he does not think of guarding it at all. Now Pinchwife, in the play above considered, is the one; Sparkish, though not actually married, is the other. And both were more ridiculous then than now, mainly because then a sense of property-rights in this particular sort of treasure was not weaker but stronger.

5.

And so with the Etherege and Congreve philosophy of conduct or 'code.' It is comical because it is gay; but also, as Lamb would forget, because it is so bold, bad, and different—because so wittily but also so startlingly phrased. It is not the philosophy or code of the period. For it is of the very essence of comedy that it should not express the code of the period, but that Saturnalian spirit of rebellion against the code, in those who nevertheless acknowledge it, which in all ages takes the form of wit and laughter. Comedy is ever in league with nature, against the virtues. Comedy is under the rule of the Lord of Misrule—a Feast of Fools. Indeed, this is not even wholly the philosophy of Etherege, Wycherley, and Congreve themselves. And when they stop writing comedy and betake them to satire, when Wycherley quits the *Country Wife,* which Mr Palmer admires, and turns to the *Plain Dealer,* which he (for good reason) disparages, the difference is disclosed. When serious, Wycherley is severe, and, though not edifying, moral enough. There was then a golden moment, according to Mr Palmer, of enfranchisement and innocence, 'when precept and practice were clearly connected,' and the precept was Rabelais's *fais ce que vouldras.* But England was Puritan before the Restoration, and after it; and the time when precept and practice were connected was not in the supposed golden moment but after and before. Even in that moment there was no change of faith, principle, or precept, but of practice alone. All Jeremy Collier, in his *Short View of the Immorality and Profaneness of the English Stage* (1698), had to do, was appeal to the old faith—their faith still—and Congreve and Vanbrugh were routed, and the stage purged.[8] Believing as England did, as she believed before the Restoration, during it, and ever after, her conscience could not possibly have been so much at ease as now when the stage (in a sense) was clean again. Pepys and the pages of history show that the excesses were only those of reaction, and that men had not taken up a new point of view but were adjusting themselves more humanly to the old. A moment—of glittering license—had intervened.

What, then, of Restoration life do we get from the Comedy of Manners? Literature utterly divorced from life, dreamy and fantastic as Lamb (on the other hand) seems to make it, would not touch us, or at least would not tickle us as all right comedy must. We get, not a faithful presentation of the men of the Restoration, but a specimen of the entertainment they delighted in, not a reflection of their life and morality and social conditions, but of their dramatic taste as they dealt with these; and, however highly coloured, it is a reflection of a reflection— however loud, an echo's echo. Life is only these dramatic writers' point of departure and return; it is not life that they are presenting, though life is ever in the background as they write. There are, indeed, continual reverberations from it, the looser, noisier part of it—Vauxhall, Spring

[8] To put it roughly, that is to say. As historians recognize, Collier was not the only one to protest, and the stage was not immediately cleansed. Cf. Archer, *op. cit.*, p. 204. Indeed, by present-day standards, the stage was hardly cleansed for a generation or two, and for the matter of that it is always in arrears. But morality was now recognized on the stage and paid homage, not flouted; though it was for long a thin and ostensible allegiance, perfunctory and insincere. Cf. Nicoll (*op. cit.*) pp. 252-53.

Garden, St James's Park, Westminster, the Royal Exchange; and the language, the customs and manners, all the local colour, as we call it, are real and vivid enough. Yet the customs and manners are those of a very restricted class. The indecency, at least, in idea though not in wording far in excess of anything in Elizabethan comedy, has been supposed to be representative of the licentious and indecent Restoration. There is something in that. But the theatre at this time was no longer popular and national as it was in Elizabeth's time. The playhouses had been closed by the Puritans and were opened again under Charles; yet Puritanism was not dead, and by the vast body of the middle classes they were not frequented. In the reign of James I there were nearly twenty theatres going at one time in London; in the reign of Charles II and James II, when the population had greatly increased, not more than two or three. The stage, therefore, reflected the taste of a much smaller proportion of the population. Since the drama's laws the drama's patrons give, and those patrons were no longer so respectable an element, the drama tended to be more and more immodest and immoral. Then, when Collier blew his blast, and the walls and ramparts of iniquity toppled, the respectable ones came again, or at least those who came were no longer ashamed. For we have Colley Cibber's testimony that ladies had come to first nights only when masked, but changed in this regard after Collier's onslaught. This shows, if anything, that the immorality in the drama was not the reflection of the morality of the time, but only of the immorality, and that of the faster set. The colours of the picture were taken from nature, but not the proportions and the perspective, the light and shade.

As we quit this subject, we cannot avoid facing a contrast—that between the drama of the Restoration and the contemporary drama in France. In comedy: on the one hand, the license of Wycherley and Vanbrugh, the gross-

ness of Dryden, and the corrupt imaginings of Aphra
Behn; on the other, the almost unspotted pages of Corneille, Molière, and Regnard. In tragedy: on the one
hand, the violence and unbridled passion of Dryden,
Lee, and Otway; on the other, the dignity and self-control
of Corneille and Racine. In French classic tragedy characters are guided and ruled by the reason, heroes and
heroines are not the mere victims of passion and impulse,
often they resist passion and impulse, sometimes they put
them down. And that cannot be said of Restoration
tragedy; it cannot be said of Elizabethan tragedy, either,
though it is infinitely nobler, or even of the heroes and
heroines of Shakespeare himself. Corneille's and Racine's
heroes bow the knee to duty and often arise and follow it
—in Shakespeare only Hamlet and Brutus can be said to
do this; and if the women follow duty, it is oftenest the
duty which is identical with the dictates of their hearts.
Are we then to draw conclusions touching the life of the
English in the seventeenth century and the life of the
French? How startling and untenable the conclusions,
though Taine and others of his school arrive at them. If
for the moment we accepted them, we should have immediately to reject them again on looking at the French tragedy
and comedy before Corneille, that is before the triumph
of the classical standard of taste. And it is just as likely
that the calm and poise of all French literature since then
but reflects these qualities of the French people, in contrast with the passion and violence in English literature
reflected from the English people, sober and sedate as the
English people have always been thought to be. To this
day, men and women on the French stage are shy of
kissing one another—how French! On the English, they
kiss passionately and freely—how English! And certainly
the age of Elizabeth and the Stuarts was not barbarous as
Taine and even some English critics call it, though so the
drama may in some ways seem. What we have is only

the reflection of what the French on the one hand and the
English on the other delighted in at the theatre. The one
people took all their virtues—like their families—there
with them; the other for a time left theirs comfortably at
home.

6.

Another case in point is the earlier one of Jonson's
comedy of 'humours'. The sudden overwhelming popular-
ity after 1600 of this comedy of class types and distinctions is supposed by Professor Tucker Brooke to reflect a
change in Elizabethan society, a new definiteness and fixity
in social distinctions which contrasts with the social democ-
racy in Shakespeare, 'the motley society of the *Henry IV*
plays and the *Merchant of Venice,* the frank independence
of the gardener in *Richard II,* the grave-digger in Hamlet,
and the sergeant in Macbeth, and the freedom everywhere
accorded to the clown.' Another golden moment! So
protean then, this society so stiff and unchanging ever
after! Shakespeare began writing about 1590, and did
the society, which he reflected, so change without his detecting it by 1600, although Ben Jonson detected it, who was
but nine years younger than he? That would be as if the
cave-man were to appear as lover, not only in fiction but
in the flesh, in the matter of a year or so. Only taste, or
the art which ministers to it or creates it, turns about so
suddenly. Really, the strongly marked class life appears
in reaction against the highly romantic figures which went
before; and its appearance is promoted by the principles
announced—or rather proclaimed—in the celebrated Prologue to Every Man in his Humour (1598),[9] by the example of Greek and Latin comedy, by the precept of Aristotle and Horace, by the Renaissance doctrine and practice
of 'decorum,' and by the growing taste for the 'character'
of Theophrastus. Classicism—realism—habitually fol-

[9] The prologue, to be sure, is probably later.

lows romanticism as a necessary reaction: even with the
Greeks the New Comedy had to follow the Old.

The free and easy ways of the earlier Elizabethan comedy, on the other hand, are due wholly to the liberty of
romantic art. Surely nothing can be inferred concerning
Elizabethan society from the fact that on the stage clowns
elbow kings and have a say in their counsels,—'all-licensed
fools,' they are openly recognized to be exceptions—or
that 'decorum' is not kept, the proprieties or distinctions
not observed, in ordinary social intercourse. What is that
but the sort of thing we notice in early art in general? If
the comparative dearth of social distinctions and formali-
ties in Shakespeare's histories and comedies indicate a
dearth of them in the real life of his day, then the greater
dearth of such distinctions in the plays of his primitive
predecessors must indicate a corresponding condition in
the real life of only thirty years before. And the ballads,
in which king or noble mingles freely with cottagers, does
his own work or rather the work of his servants, and fine
ladies make beds for their sons, or, without exciting suspicion, fry eels or snakes (though in a pan of gold) to
feed their faithless lovers, must indicate a total absence
of such distinctions in the preceding century. But George
Whetstone ought to have known, and in his Dedication to
Promos and Cassandra (1578) he attributes this mingling
and mixing up of the classes on the stage merely to the
disregard of propriety and an effort to produce comic
effect. 'Manye tymes (to make mirthe) they make a
Clowne companion with a Kinge; in theyr graue Counsels
they allow the advise of fooles; yea, they vse one order of
speach for all persons.' So says Sir Philip Sidney (1581):
'But besides these grosse absurdities, how all theyr Playes
be neither right Tragedies, nor right Comedies; mingling
Kings and Clownes, not because the matter. so carrieth it,
but thrust in Clownes by head and shoulders to play a part
in maiesticall matters, with neither decencie nor discre-

tion!' And likewise the author of the *Pilgrimage to Parnassus* (1598-99): 'Why, what an ass art thou! dost thou not knowe a playe cannot be without a clowne! Clownes have bene thrust into playes by head and shoulders ever since Kempe could make a scurvey face.' Actual society, it seems, was different, and, in comparison at least, was decorous and orderly enough. Where otherwise would have been the 'mirthe'? [10]

A perfect parallel to this comic freedom is to be found in early seventeenth-century Spanish drama, indeed a better instance of it, for in Spanish life, of course, etiquette and the proprieties must have been much more rigidly observed than in England at this time or before. The *gracioso* jests with kings and noblemen as freely as do Touchstone and Panurge, and goes into battle or council of war as unplausibly and improperly as Panurge and Falstaff. Why, in the name of propriety or common sense, should the crackbrained clown and swineherd Pelayo in Lope's *El mayor Alcalde el Rey,* accompany Sancho on the serious mission of reclaiming Elvira, Sancho's betrothed, out of the hands of Don Tello, through the mediation of the King? 'To make mirthe,' again, can be the only conclusion; to furnish the stage with a contrast.

What, moreover, is the impertinence of Elizabethan or Spanish clowns and servants to that of the valet Scapin beating his master's father, or of the free-spoken maids in almost every comedy of Molière? There is Toinette, for instance, in *Le Malade imaginaire,* who intrudes into the matrimonial affairs of the family, and jeers at her master's infirmity. In the *Légataire* of Regnard, the maid Lisette takes even greater liberties, making light of Géronte's being in love as he is, with one foot in the grave. Though he gets angry enough, he cannot curb her. It is utterly

---

[10] See the discussion of Falstaff and the *miles gloriosus,* below, chapter viii, section 8.—In one or more of the above passages clown may mean 'country-fellow', rather than 'comic figure,' but that is immaterial.

improbable that such situations should be representative, as they have been seriously said to be, of the domestic liberty of Parisian bourgeois life. If they be representative of domestic liberty anywhere, it is not in seventeenth-century France but somewhat nearer home and the present. In reality this is only the chance for a piquant situation— the master fuming against his maid; and it is like the situation of the husband fuming against his wife in farce late or early. Why is it that in this farce and *fabliau* literature, as in Boccaccio, it is nearly always the women who cheat and abuse the men? Because it conduces to comedy that the weaker should get the better of the stronger—the underling, of the one above him—and that Hercules, having had a club, should be brought down to the distaff. There can be comedy in a man's getting the better of a woman only when (as in the farces and *fabliaux*, indeed, is sometimes the case) it is plain that she herself is the stronger and ordinarily holds her husband in mental or bodily fear. From the farces and *fabliaux*, therefore, we could not, if we were so minded, infer the liberty of women in medieval times. Nor could we, in the Renaissance, from Tirso de Molina, the great Spanish dramatist. His plays have been by many Spanish scholars and critics thought to be faithful pictures of the age, though in them the women, wilful and intriguing, passionate and unscrupulous, rule and control the men—as they have done, stoutly and truly says the writer in the *Enciclopedia Hispano-Americana,* at no time. Neither could we, in ancient times, from Plautus. In the *Casina* his wife and his slaves, both male and female, thwart, mock, insult, even abuse the master. Chalinus, his slave, beats him; both he and the bailiff Olympio browbeat him; and Pardilisca, the maid, is impudent to him and insolent. His wife plays a trick on him and thereupon takes him—and he not her—to task. Can this be Rome, in the days of Cato? But so in play after play of Plautus and Terence the master of the house is by son

or servant bamboozled and abused, for naught but the
delight of an audience who know that he has power of life
and death in his hands. In ancient Rome or seventeenth-
century Paris or London the beating and abuse was for the
servant. The real picture of life we get in comedy incidentally, allusively. 'I know my lady will strike him," says
Maria as she describes Malvolio's behaviour. Martine, in
the *Femmes savantes,* complains of the beatings she has had
from Chrysalis' wife, and Arsinoë, in the *Misanthrope,* is
charged with beating her servants and not paying them.
But it is funnier on the stage to turn things round.

7.

And what of fathers nowadays? Samuel Butler, in *The
Way of all Flesh,* takes Richardson and Fielding, Smollett
and Jane Austen, for evidence when he says that 'at the
beginning of the nineteenth century, the relations between
parents and children were still far from satisfactory'; and
the drama no doubt for evidence when he makes out such
relations in Elizabethan times to have been 'on the whole
more kindly.' The relapse in the seventeenth and eighteenth centuries he lays at the door of the Old Testament
and Puritanism. No doubt the stormy father, like his wil-
lowy daughter, has of late disappeared from both the
printed page and life itself. If in fact he storms still, he
goes unheeded. But on the printed page his raging, like
her fainting (as we have seen), was a motive long outworn. He must needs step down and out, after the false
steward, the cruel stepmother, the ridiculous duenna. In
the eighteenth and the early nineteenth century, moreover,
and even so late as in Thackeray, Meredith, and Mr
Hardy, the clash between father and daughter was part
and parcel of that more violent action, and that more obvious, but more expeditious, means of effecting a complication which novelists nowadays avoid. The father rages
at the discovery, the lover retires, the daughter sinks down

in a swoon, and there we have a story started. Now that there was less of this in Elizabethan times is owing to the fact that the serious drama then, unlike the novel since, being patrician and public in character (not bourgeois and domestic), and dealing with affairs of state as well as with those of the heart, the menacing element in it, or villainy, needed not arise in the family or the house. But when occasion comes, the fathers in Shakespeare, as Juliet's and Hero's (to take two who have not the privilege and license of a king), can be as violent and tyrannical as any. Squire Western, in his paternal affection and abuse, is but Capulet over again. 'My fingers itch,' cries Capulet; 'these hands shall tear her,' cries Leonato; and in that fine old Jacobean mansion, Aston Hall, near Birmingham, is still shown the upper chamber where, in those days, Sir Thomas Holt shut up his daughter who would not marry to suit him, till she died.

8.

In the eighteenth and nineteenth centuries, especially in the novel, we no doubt find a greater measure of fidelity to the life of the times; although any one conversant with the narrative, as well as the drama—in prose or in verse— of the preceding centuries, can see at once how risky it is here to deduce anything at all definite and exact as regards the life of the period in which the particular book was penned. Or one needs but to fall back upon one's common sense, nowadays a bit upset by the historical spirit. In a recent interesting article Mr E. T. Raymond,[11] intent upon the contrast between the humour of the Victorians and that which happily now prevails, sees in it often also a picture of the two periods—not merely of their humour and ours, of our taste and theirs. He thinks that then there really were Winkles and Pickwicks, who would undertake to drive horses without knowing how, but that now (quite

[11] *London Mercury*, August, 1924.

apart from the fact that there is no horse-driving) there
are none. 'All moderns,' says he, 'are saturated with the
expert spirit.' (And yet he complains of the Victorians'
complacence and sense of superiority impairing their sense
of humour!) If what he says be true, Winkle and Pickwick were then hardly funny. And if now Winkle and
Pickwick here seem to us a little silly, and to the best judges
of those days—to Thackeray, for instance—seemed no
more than comic, surely the change is not so much in what
Englishmen do and are as in what they are willing to laugh
at. It is only an instance of Dickens's unbridled extravagance in the tradition of Fielding and Smollett, Hogarth
and Cruikshank. Taste has changed—whether the number of fools to the thousand inhabitants has changed too,
there is no right way to tell. Fiction-reading is not the way,
at any rate.

Fielding and Smollett, those brave fantasts and rich
humorists, bear the proud title of realists; and in comparison with the novelists (and still more with the dramatists) of the time preceding, they on the whole deserve it.
But not conspicuously at the critical moments, in the *scènes
à faire*. How unrestrained is the conduct at least of the
heroes! When they hear bad news or are smitten with
passion, prodigiously vigorous and stalwart young men, like
Tom Jones and Peregrine Pickle, though quite out of their
nonage, weep and rave, tear their hair or strike their heads
against the wall, beat their breasts and toss away their
pocket-books, totter as they walk or like the ladies sink
down in a swoon. Even in the Renaissance drama, for all
its emphasis, there is more of physical restraint and decorum, and (though from this novel the Victorian Epoch is
not a century off) more of British soberness and phlegm.
The young men are as frantic and extravagant as the
fathers who have charming daughters to force into matrimony are brutal and violent, though these last, to be sure
—Sophia Western or Emilia Gauntlet—are far less dif-

ferent than Cleopatra from 'our dear Queen.' But even their modesty and propriety is perhaps less a reflection of eighteenth-century life than a pastoral or romantic convention; and how the picture of life is, in their concern for contrasts, further troubled through the novelists' ignoring of the facts and results of heredity and environment! Could such a barbarous being as Squire Western have had such a daughter as Sophia, loving her, and loved and reverenced in return? In society the sexes cannot be so different and alien: with such fathers about, Sophia, Clarissa, Amelia, Emilia, and their like, would have been wretched enough even had they not had to suffer from their tyranny.

And what a picture these novelists give of human existence when in lighter vein! Man vies with fortune, and fortune with man, in caprice and mischief, and it is hard to tell which outdoes the other. In *Joseph Andrews* it is fortune, it is man in *Peregrine Pickle*. In this and many other eighteenth-century novels, the hero and his associates, it seems, live only to play boisterous and outrageous pranks upon their friends and to get more than even with their enemies. Life as depicted in the seventeenth-century Comedy of Manners is, we found, too lawless and chaotic to have been possible; here it is still more so; not only wives but almost everything else is in continual jeopardy. Even physically one could not have endured it. 'Such a bustle of coarse life,' says a writer in the *Quarterly Review* quoted by Sir Walter Raleigh, 'such swearing and rioting and squalor, and, above all, such incessant thumping and fighting and breaking each others' heads and kicking each others' shins could never have taken place in any conceivable community or under any system of police, unless the human skeleton had been of much harder construction that it is at present.' And yet as a fact we know that life in England in the eighteenth century was safe and peaceable, in greater measure, at least, than it had ever been before. Fielding and Smollett, again, are a reflection of eighteenth-century taste, as is also Hogarth.

One may think himself on safer ground as he draws conclusions from the changes he notices, from decade to decade, in the course of eighteenth-century poetry:

> I shall compare two decades. The first extends from 1730 to 1740; and the second from 1740 to 1750. The first of these, that of the 'Thirties, was critical, satirical, given largely to condemnation of the existing social customs and life. The second of these, the 'Forties, was gloomy, anti-social, disgusted with people, and quite content with country churches and tottering tombstones where one might regret through many a solemn hour the sadness of life and its unhappiness. The limits of the periods are not exact . . . yet the correspondence is close enough for the general purpose.[12]

Here are the abrupt changes again, and I wonder whether any one has ever suggested that at the beginning of the various Romantic periods there was in life, as in art, an outburst of banditry—in the day of *Tamburlaine* or of *Rob Roy,* of the *Räuber* and *Götz von Berlichingen,* of *Hernani* and Jean Valjean. But even without much knowledge of the eighteenth century one ought, I think, to conclude from the above account itself that this change took place in the minds of a few poets, and (as they slowly got a hearing) of a few readers, and is not at all fairly to be considered 'a reflection of the temper of the mind of the nation.' If in the satire of the Thirties the society of the Thirties was reflected faithfully, we may rest assured that that society went on for more than a decade pretty much as it was, and did not abundantly share in the poets' contemplative gloom of the Forties. A long time it takes to leaven so great a lump. But that the poets should fairly of one accord write graveyard poetry in 1740, and that even the same poets should, within a year or so, write first the one way and then the other, is comprehensible enough. The changes in literature and art to-day are as swift, from

[12] Elbridge Colby, *Mod. Lang. Notes,* 1923, p. 475.

out of the minds of a few writers or artists. And within a year or so Shakespeare wrote, on the one hand, the *Midsummer Night's Dream* and, on the other, *Titus Andronicus* and *Richard III,* Elizabethan society remaining unchanged.

Instead of a mirror, indeed, which reflects the age, literature is as likely to be a picture which the age slowly (though only in slight measure) learns to resemble; and in the eighteenth and nineteenth centuries, in which records are more abundant, we have for this some evidence. No doubt the taste of ordinary people, in the Thirties and Forties changed little in respect to landscape or verse; but the gentry at least, somewhat later in the century, to secure the right forlorn and desolate romantic effect, built ruins,[13] planted dead trees, and erected tombs in gardens. The new poetry had reached them, and fancy they turned into fact. Mrs Radcliffe's mysterious romantic villains, which were the creatures of her inexperience, and in so far as they were not, certainly sprang from the loins of Milton's Satan or his offspring, not out of her experience of eighteenth-century society, came to be, as Sir Walter Raleigh rightly considers, not only the original of Lord Byron's villains but also, in a sort, a model of what the poet himself would be. And the Neo-Catholicism of Pusey and Newman and the Pre-Raphaelitism of Rossetti and his brotherhood led to the esthetic craze, which carried art into life with a vengeance, and was made game of for it by Gilbert. But it is, no doubt, only the upper crust of society that is thus gradually and eventually influenced by literature, whether in the way of eccentric behaviour or in that of indefinable sentiment. Rightly the Victorian period is conceived as sober and strait-laced, though nearly all the great poetry and fiction

---

[13] Some of these ruins, medieval or classical in style, are still to be found in England and on the Continent; and the reader of *Bouvard et Pécuchet* will remember how those worthies consult a work on gardening, in which are described many *genres,* including the *genre mélancolique et romantique* and the *genre terrible,* both of which they diligently reproduce.

written during the period—Browning's, Rossetti's, Swinburne's, Meredith's, Hardy's, Morris', even Tennyson's —were highly romantic; and much of both was inspired by a spirit of protest and revolt.

9.

Of the illusion or fallacy there are many examples upon which we have not touched, and the philosophers we have not called to our aid, nor, for all that he is with us, have we breathed the name of Croce. What we have touched upon is those extremes of comedy or tragedy which by critics and historians have not been remembered as extremes. But even to-day (now that the historical spirit and the doctrines of the human document and the slice of life have arisen, and have more or less entered into all our fiction and even our art) it is only the best novel and (in less degree) the best drama that keep much more discreetly within the limits of the 'modesty of nature,' and are less romantic or remote. Even they reflect our taste, our notions of life as it is, as we would have it, or as we should fear to have it—the free life within us rather than the life which holds us in its indifferent grip. They show us what we are thinking, feeling, fancying, which often is not like what we, or others, are doing and are. They are the stories we would hear or tell; only in part our own story or our neighbours'. They too are not history. The ideas in them are the ideas of the writers themselves and their set rather than of the people.

And the morals in them are not the morals of our time; only by eccentrics are they put in practice; and what a picture would be painted by future historians who, following in the ways of those who have availed themselves for this purpose of the older English and Continental drama, should reconstruct contemporary society from the pages of many who ply the pen audaciously to-day! A more chaotic people we should appear than the England of Restoration comedy. For here is a frankness and irregularity in sexual matters such as, save in jest or pretence, the Elizabethan and Restoration literature kept shy of, but here not in jest or pretence at all, and in novel after novel, in play after play. Mr Kipling's short stories, Mr Chesterton complains, were in England 'not appreciated but believed. They were taken seriously by a startled nation as a true picture of the empire and the universe.' In Ireland, he says, (strangely enough taking up with what is not the only fond illusion that the disillusioned Mr Shaw[14] clings to while he continues to reside in England), the thing couldn't have happened, forgetting as he says it, the big to-do there was over all Home-Rule Ireland and America because the picture of Irish life in *The Playboy of the Western World* wasn't true—or was. Boards of Guardians and Municipal Councils banned it; a Cardinal, Catholic primate, pronounced against it; even the Chicago City Council felt, as an Irish legislative body, called upon to take official action; and one would have thought this play about Irishmen had been written and was played by Englishmen. And in Dublin history has repeated itself of late, at the performance of the plays of Mr Sean O'Casey.

As for the moods nowadays, the swift-succeeding waves of optimism and pessimism, sympathy and cynicism, scepticism and faith, they for the most part agitate only the imaginations of writers and readers, and whether before or after the writing, not a nation, not a city. What city or household could be swept by them and stand? And as for the individual figures, why should the critic or historian look upon drama or novel as more of a human document than painting or sculpture? Unless he steadily remember

---

[14] See his plays, *passim,* and among his essays that entitled *Meredith on Comedy,* for this notion that your Irishman enjoys the 'intellectual virtuosity' of the Frenchman, American, and ancient Greek, as almost no Englishman can. Nowadays, no doubt, Mr Shaw would add 'the German' to the intellectuals—and he lives (though as an outpost) constantly in England, and declines to come to America and see.

that art, all art alike, is much more—or less—than the image of life, he might in the future, as he surveys the un-numbered, innumerable canvases of the neo-impressionists, cubists, futurists, and the rest, think of us in these hum-drum days of ours, not as cave-men, indeed, or 'noble sav-ages,' but as cripples and cretins, goats and monkeys, the degenerate tag-end, rather than a reversion to the begin-ning of the race. That would be like taking, as some do, the Renaissance to be as pagan as its pictures, as if ladies in the Veneto, like Titians and Giorgiones, picnicked with well-clad gentlemen imperturbably in the nude. In art and literature alike we seek out the most primitive subjects and treat them in the most primitive style—Egyptian, Cam-bodgian, Hindu—alien from our own. 'The Spirit of Art,' said Mr Binyon in a lecture, in April, 1926, 'is against the spirit of the age . . . we express our own age by resisting it, by creating something which will outlast its fears and dis-illusions.'

*   *   *

Since writing the above (although the book first ap-peared in 1919) I have come upon Mr Cabell's *Beyond Life*. I am glad to take refuge behind the opinion of an accomplished man of letters, that 'what mankind has gen-erally agreed to accept as first-class art, in any of the varied forms of fictitious narrative, has never been a truthful reproduction of the artist's era.' Mr Cabell points to such as Marlowe, Shakespeare, the Restoration drama-tists, and Dickens. 'Few persons not already under re-straint,' he says, a bit extravagantly, 'would care to deny that Dickens unfailingly misrepresented the life he pre-tended to portray.' And of the Restoration dramatists he writes as follows:

A great deal of queer nonsense has been printed concerning the comedy of Gallantry, upon the startling assumption that its authors copied the life about them. It is true that Wycherley, in this the first of English authors to go astray, began the pernicious practice of depicting men as being not very much better than they actually are: of that I will speak later: but Wycherley had the saving grace to present his men and women as trammeled by the social restrictions of Cloud-Cuckoo-Land alone. And, were there nothing else, it seems improbable that Congreve, say, really believed that every young fellow spoke habitually in terms of philosophic wit and hated his father; and that every old hunks possessed, more or less vicariously, a beautiful second wife; and that people married without licenses, or, indeed, without noticing very particularly whom they were marrying; and that monetary competence and happiness and all-important documents, as well as a sudden turn for heroic verse, were regularly accorded to everybody toward eleven o'clock in the evening.

As for downright wickedness, Mr Cabell observes, what few critics seem to have noticed, that in literature until recently it has seldom been reflected in its reality, whether as of its own day or of any.[15]

Indeed, I question whether wickedness is possible to humanity outside of literature. In books, of course, may be encountered any number of competently evil people, who take a proper pride in their depravity. But in life men go wrong without dignity, and sin as it were from hand to mouth.

. . . . It is only the unscrupulous person who can retain always the blessing of an untroubled conscience. Anyone of us can to-day observe that such is still, and perhaps will be forever, the case in human society. And equally, everyone of us knows that in enduring literature of the first class this fact has always been ignored, and retributive justice, in the form of both gnawing remorse and physical misfortune, has with gratifying regularity requited the evil-doer.

And by means of another postscript I would, if Mr Cabell's fail me, run to cover under the ægis of none other than Mr Lytton Strachey. In a review of Mr Summers' 'Congreve,' in the *New Republic,* November, 1923, he recognizes somewhat as I do above the highly conventional element in comedy, though in tragedy, for the moment at least, he seems to ignore a corresponding conventional element, less considerable, indeed, and of a different sort:

[15] See below, the chapter on Criminals, which as an article appeared in 1912.

Nevertheless, it is plainly paradoxical to find in *The Double Dealer* or *The Way of the World* a faithful presentment of any state of society; it is not in that fashion that real life is lived. What, then, is the explanation of this close resemblance combined with this obvious unlikeness? How is it that we are well acquainted with Mrs Frail, without for a moment supposing that either she or ourselves are figuring in a Congreve comedy?

Perhaps the truth is that pure comedy, unlike tragedy and drama and most forms of fiction, depends for its existence on the construction of a conventional world in which, while human nature and human actions are revealed, their consequences are suspended. The characters in comedy are real; but they exist *in vacuo*. They are there neither to instruct us nor to exalt us, but simply to amuse us; and therefore the effects which would in reality follow from their conduct must not appear. If they did, the comedy would cease to exist: the jealous husband would become a tragic personage; the heavy father a Galsworthy character; the rake would be revealed as a pest, and the old bore as . . . an old bore. By the magic of comedy, what is scabrous, what is melancholy, what is vicious, and what is tiresome in the actual life of society is converted into charming laughter and glittering delight.

10.

Still other aspects of the illusion, seem, as I return to the subject, to demand attention. Tragedy, too, as Mr Strachey would no doubt admit, is conventional, and, until *drame* arose to humanize and mollify it, was subject to a formula which had held for thousands of years, from the time of Seneca and before. The religious and superstitious machinery and atmosphere, the spirit of divine retribution and of personal revenge, the highflown and declamatory speeches—the rhodomontades of the heroes, the lamentations of the heroines, and the curses of both—and the abundant blood and cruelty and the accumulation of deaths at the end,—all this is a picture of no age or country, and of no state of culture, not even of the pagan from which it sprang. And yet critics, particularly the German, have tried to explain the spirit of the vendetta in *Hamlet* as either an historical effort to present the grim times of Saxo or as the reflection of the contemporary *ethos*. On the former explanation we need not waste words; all the enlightened critics nowadays recognize that Shakespeare had nothing of the historian's spirit, and at best, in the later Roman plays, avoids the glaring anachronisms such as he lightly perpetrated in the *Comedy of Errors*. He had the artist's sense of propriety and harmony, not the historian's sense of fact. Nor are we to think that in the England of Shakespeare's time the *jus talionis* was still in force. One may be permitted to doubt if it was in force so fully as it is in certain regions of the United States to-day, where family and clan feuds still persist, and where, in case of the murder of rivals or faithless lovers, is openly pleaded 'the unwritten law.' From Reeves, Stephen, Wordsworth, and Coke himself, it would appear that, whether adultery or murder be the cause, it could not be pleaded before English courts—the right of blood-feud was done away with in Anglo-Saxon times, if indeed it ever existed—nor does the record of events in Elizabethan England indicate that the vendetta was then a custom. 'The Italian vendetta,' says Sir Walter Raleigh, 'of which so many terrible pictures are to be found in the dramatists, came into English literature rather than into English life.' But even so, it came early, and for the most part not through direct contact with Italy but through the pages of Seneca. Just as without the motive of revenge there would have been no Senecan tragedy, so there would have been no *Gorboduc*, no *Hamlet, Titus Andronicus,* or *Richard III*. Law in Shakespeare is, save for phrases and incidental matters or what is taken out of the novel or chronicle he is dramatizing, nothing but stage law.[16] Even the morals

---

[16] So say quite justly both Sir Walter Raleigh and Professor Mackail; and the juristic disquisitions of the Germans on the issue in the *Merchant of Venice* are among the most misguided and wasted of human exertions.— Some passages in this paragraph and the next are taken from my monographs on *Hamlet* (1919) and *Othello* (1916), University of Minnesota Studies.

of marital retaliation, as in *Othello,* are stage morals: and so they are in somewhat later plays which deal with the 'point of honour' in Spain. This the great Lope several times admits. In the Preface to the twentieth volume of his Theatre, he confesses, in reference to his own 'Wise Vengeance,' that its title is absurd, because all revenge is unwise and unlawful.[17] Shakespeare could have said as much. And yet, though he thus expresses himself against revenge, 'it seems,' as Ticknor observes, 'as if one half of Lope's plays go to justify it.' And almost the same might be said of the pious Calderón. In fact, it is only in the present day that Spanish drama has dared to throw over the convention as regards the jealous husband; and even English drama and story kept the revenge convention into the eighteenth century. Drama, says M. Maeterlinck (though in some degree exaggerating) 'est encore plus lent que tous les autres arts à suivre les évolutions de la conscience humaine.'

The very violence and abruptness of the changes in our older tragedy have but moved men to cry, how Elizabethan! So Taine says of Marlowe: 'All this is pretty strong, you will say; these people kill too readily, and too quickly. It is on this very account that the painting is a true one,' etc. But it is a matter of Elizabethan art and taste rather than of character. So Professor Wetz explains the conversion of Leontes and the success of Richard, like the shameful conduct of Claudio (not merely in repudiating Hero publicly but in jesting at Benedick's expense just after the news of her death), all on the basis of Renaissance character,—passionate, unreflective, running and leaping from one extreme to the other. Not in the disposition of the people of the Renaissance does the difficulty lie but in the art with which they are presented—with which they were content. Simpler men, says Wetz, have

[17] Ticknor, *Spanish Literature,* ii, p. 263. But compare to the contrary effect Menéndez y Pelayo, *Calderón y su teatro,* pp. 279-80.

stormy and passionate conversions; but that of Leontes is a recantation rational and complete. He sees, and remedies, the whole error of his course in the twinkling of an eye, whereas, however primitive, a man must, in relinquishing his old beliefs, fumble and grope a bit into the new. Such a man might change by leaps and bounds indeed, instead of step by step, but he would stumble and fall back again into his old ways—his old jealousy—and not put on the new man at once and for ever. The same is to be said of the barons in English historical plays, who yield or renounce their allegiance as occasion demands, and never regret their breach of fealty to their former sovereign until they are disposed to commit a breach of fealty to their present one. Only by a stretch of the phrase can *Edward II* or *Richard III* be called a social document. And Anne, who spits on Richard at the beginning of the scene, plights her troth to him at the end—as, later Elizabeth bestows on him the hand of her daughter—only on the strength of the old convention at the bottom of Iago's intrigue, the omnipotence of dissimulation [18] and the persuasive arts, and another even older—the frailty of woman. It is idle to accumulate historical and psychological lore[19] in order to justify to us a method that the literary historian easily recognizes as customary and acceptable in Renais-

---

[18] Gervinus and Fischer are quite taken in by it, and the latter even declares that Richard does not dissemble! (Wetz, pp. 133-4.) Even Wetz, who demurs, says, 'Es setzt ein sehr grosses Seelenleiden voraus, wenn ein so harter Mann wie Richard zum Weinen und zu hoffnungsloser Verzweiflung gebracht werden konnte.' (p. 125) Richard a romantic soul matches Iago as a kindly one; see chapter vii.—For the convention see my monograph on *Othello,* and below, chapter iii, section 2.

[19] Wetz, pp. 118-126. Such a notion, for instance, as that Anne has a primitive indifference to relatives and spouse, that revenge is incumbent upon her as a duty to herself and her family rather than to the murdered, and that therefore, like Ximena Gomez, she does well to marry and allay the feud. The text of the scene, of all the play, of every Elizabethan play in which revenge appears as a motive, shows how little of these considerations Shakespeare could have entertained. Or, again, such a notion as that she admires his strength as women often admire it in those who maltreat them, and in criminals.

sance art, which had at command none of this lore, but intolerable in modern art, which has it all. What is stranger still is that the critics should on the same basis ground a contrary opinion, and when you complain of the complete consciousness and detached self-knowledge of the Elizabethan criminals [20] or villains, declare that this is Elizabethan too.

Indeed some aspects of what is supposed to be English natural character now—the sang froid and phlegm, the reticence and emotional shyness of Englishmen—both Shakespeare and all other Elizabethan dramatists seem pretty much to ignore. Lovers pouring out their hearts before almost anybody, like Orlando and Rosalind, Antonio, Bassanio and Portia, Romeo, the Claudios in *Much Ado* and *Measure for Measure,* and the Duke in *Twelfth Night;* tragic heroes laying bare their griefs and passions in all their tumult to the world like Othello and Desdemona, King Lear, Antony, the Roman heroes, and the English kings, queens, and nobles,—how un-English they all are. Of the chief characters only those do not act so whose business in hand forbids it, as Iago, Macbeth, or Hamlet; and even they make speeches to confidants and utter soliloquies (or speeches to the audience), in which they do. Among the serious and the highborn, Kent and Brutus (of the men) and Cordelia and the Countess in *All's Well* (of the women), are the principal exceptions. Hotspur and King Henry V, no doubt, are English enough, but they are treated in somewhat comic vein, especially in love matters, where instead of being simply reticent they mock at those who aren't. Are we therefore to infer that English char-

[20] See below, chapter vii, section 18, Professor Schücking's reply to Dr. Wolff.—So with the boastfulness of Elizabethan kings and heroes, which we discuss in chapters iii and vii. It is a tradition of the stage, of Senecan *decorum;* and as Professor Schücking shows (p. 40), the Elizabethans themselves esteemed modesty as much as we do. They were not on the cultural level of the Iroquois or the Pawnees, though the people that produced the *Iliad* and the *Roland* in respect of this virtue may have been.

acter was very different then? Even in *Beowulf* and the *Battle of Maldon* it does not seem different. Nothing is so common in Elizabethan drama as the lamentations of the heroes over their fates or the fates of their friends, and though all unused to the melting mood they weep in fact or mourn and wail as if they wept. Few of Shakespeare's heroes meet their fates blithely, though they are gallant and brave. But Beowulf tells Hrothgar it is better to avenge his friend than to mourn much; and the one Earl in the Battle of Maldon laughs in the face of death, and the other declares that forever shall mourn he that flinches from this sword-play. And that is the spirit in the English and Scottish ballads. Indeed, it would seem that the highly charged emotional character of the speeches of lovers and tragic heroes, in which passion is displayed so abundantly and frankly is mainly owing, not to the fact that such was English character under Elizabeth, but to the fact that it is drama. The characters talk about themselves, describe themselves, instead of speaking only to the business in hand, and of being talked about or described only by others; and the influence of Senecan technique prevails, which had not been sufficiently developed out of the epical and lyrical to permit the character quite to keep his own point of view. They lay bare their passions, even as they expound their own moral qualities,[21] quite unnaturally.

This appears clearly in the mere matter of reticence and taciturnity, which Hotspur and Henry V as true Englishmen are supposed to have, despising those who haven't

[21] See below, chapter iii, section 4, and chapter vii.—Eavesdropping and the reading of others' letters are still other means of exposition or of thickening the plot. It abounds in English and French drama and novel, even into the nineteenth cetury; and yet there is no reason to think either was good manners even in the sixteenth. In the Elizabethan drama the character sometimes apologizes to himself (or the audience) as he listens or breaks the seal; but in the late seventeenth-century novel the *Princesse de Clèves,* by Madame de La Fayette, a great lady at the most polite court in Europe, the hero and heroine and others engage in such business with no apparent scruple. Readers of themselves made allowances.

it.[22] Hotspur, indeed, is testy and splenetic and impatient of pretence as are the characters in later English novels; and Henry V, how English, as I have elsewhere said, he is —so practical, sportsmanlike, moral, and pious; so manly and stalwart and yet free and easy; so self-assertive and yet modest and humble; so fierce against his enemies, and yet merciful towards women and the weak; so serious and yet simple and humorous; and so bluff and downright, and yet hearty and genuine, in the avowal of his love.[23] Both of them, for all that, professing taciturnity and scorning loquacity, talk like a torrent, and yet certainly Shakespeare does not mean to intimate that they do not know themselves, like the cowards who despise cowards, the drunken who call others drunk. Of the inconsistency he seems not aware, and really there is none. The Elizabethan drama is rhetorical, and the principal characters must speak often and at length. The minor characters, who need not be displayed so amply, are free to be in these respects more English, as are Horatio and Benvolio. And those traits of English character with which this self-descriptive, self-expository technique does not interfere—humorousness, eccentricity, all that we mean by the phrase 'a character'— appear in Shakespeare as freely as in Fielding or Dickens. The citizen in *Julius Cæsar,* the gravediggers in *Hamlet,* Casca and Menenius, Polonius and Old Capulet, Juliet's Nurse, Emilia, and Mrs Quickly are a few examples among many.

Sometimes, however, it is not the needs of exposition but of situation that interfere. Hamlet's last words in the first act, 'O cursed spite,' etc., may be thus explained. They motive the delay and prepare us for it. As I have said elsewhere, 'not every word or act of the hero means character, whether in ancient drama or epic or the drama

---

[22] Mr Harris (*Shakespeare the Man*) notices this inconsistency but explains it differently.

[23] My introduction to *Henry V.*

of the Renaissance. We remember the lamentations of
Orestes before the deed, and the wailings of the heroic
Antigone, and of Electra (whether in the *Choephori* or in
any other of the Orestean dramas of the Greeks); the wild
outcries of the Sophoclean Hercules; the fears and apprehensions of the much-enduring Odysseus (and of Æneas
too) at every evil turn of fortune in the tale. Like the
tears of Romeo and the trepidations of Macbeth, they
seem to-day little befitting these heroes' manhood, except
as we bethink ourselves how they serve to mark and measure for us the tragic situation. And Hamlet is not at his
manliest here; for the moment he is supine like Antonio,
and bemoans his fate like Romeo, Troilus, and Antony.
A momentous task faces him; and he is sad and dejected,
like Orlando before the wrestling, like Romeo before he
enters the Capulets' house, and like Brutus as he talks with
Portia on the morning of Cæsar's death. He may be
infected with the pessimism which Mr Bernard Shaw complains of in Shakespeare in general. But it is, rather, a
matter of art. Where in Shakespearean tragedy is there
any one who, in the spirit of Browning and our whole age,
holds life to be a high adventure, welcomes fortune's buffets, and—even out of his love of life—goes forth to meet
his fate? That, in the Renaissance—as in the ancient—
tragedy of terrors, would be to take from the hero's fate
some of its terribleness. Hamlet, to be tragic, must shrink
a bit from his.' [24] In the old ballad, 'guid' Sir Patrick
Spens, when he gets the braid letter bidding him set sail,
cries,

> O wha is this has don this deid,
> This ill deid don to me,
> To send me out this time o' the yeir
> To sail upon the se!

But he loses no reputation with us, any more than should
Macbeth when, on hearing from Macduff's lips that he was

[24] See my *Hamlet*, pp. 73-4.

not of woman born, he declares that he'll not fight with him.   Without that impulsive outcry the effect of the oracle's fulfilment would be lost—and of the shout 'Lay on Macduff!'—'Mak' haste, mak' haste, my mirry men all'— which follows.   Here is art, and stout character as well.

II.

Other aspects of this fallacy are the biographical and the autobiographical.   The writer of fiction is supposed in such or such a character or situation to be depicting a certain contemporary or himself; and the whole mood or spirit of play, novel, or poem is presumed to reflect some particular passage or experience in his life.   Bottom is James VI of Scotland; both Hamlet and Prospero are Shakespeare himself: and *Hamlet* the play reflects the gloom into which Shakespeare settled when his little son and his father died and the Earl of Essex was put to death. Discoveries such as these are the particular bent and delight of the learned or would-be learned, now that philosophy and the study of literature have almost parted company; and it is the unending succession of them that more than anything else nowadays makes the study of literature, both the reading and the writing of criticism, a burden. At times, no doubt, a dramatist or novelist paints himself or another, and at times the mood of novel or play is the present mood of the man; but in the best literature this is seldom the case, or rather when it is the case this cannot be recognized.   Fact, as such, has nothing to do with the world of imagination—fact there is all coloured and transformed.[25]

As for the autobiographical, there is a notable remark

[25] Since finishing this chapter I have come upon two articles in the same number of the *Yale Review* (July, 1925), in which independently this truth is recognized and receives striking illustration.   In the one Professor Tinker shows that certain fine poems of Shelley's and Byron's, which have a definite connection with their mundane lives, are an unfaithful reflection of these; and in the other Mr Read shows that Charlotte Brontë's best work often contains only a nucleus of experience.

on the vanity of this subject of inquiry by Remy de Gourmont, in his essay on Shakespeare.

On n'arrive jamais à prouver que l'homme représente l'œuvre et que l'œuvre représente l'homme. Mais la critique n'accepte pas volontiers l'illogisme des divergences. C'est-à-dire qu'elle modifie l'esprit de l'œuvre pour le mettre d'accord avec les actes de l'homme, ou, au contraire, partant des actes, juge l'œuvre selon leur signification. Racine, réputé doux, tendre, familial et religieux, fit paraître longtemps sous le même jour, et malgré l'évidence, son œuvre pourtant cruelle et passionnée. Récemment, partant de l'œuvre violente, on a dessiné un Racine violent, un Racine "tigre". On l'a plié à la logique. Était-ce nécessaire? J'en suis moins persuadé maintenant qu'après la lecture du livre de M. Masson-Forestier. Les recherches de ce genre sont toujours illusoires, surtout, dirais-je, quand elles aboutissent à l'établissement de coïncidences logiques, pour ce que le génie de l'homme est l'illogisme même et que plus grand est ce génie et moins il est d'accord avec la logique de la vie. Le génie est la révolte; suprême expression de l'humanité, comme l'humanité est la suprême expression du vertébré, il se révolte même contre lui-même, et son œuvre ne raconte sa vie que dans la mesure où il a été dominé par elle. Je sais bien que les efforts de l'homme supérieur pour s'affranchir de lui-même ne réussissent pas toujours, et aussi que, la plupart du temps, il n'y prend point garde et n'y pense même pas; bien plus, se répand naïvement en confidences tout comme un autre.

Of this opinion are all those critics of Shakespeare and Molière, who, like Gourmont, know much about the creative process at first hand—Coleridge, Croce, Middleton Murry, and Quiller-Couch; though, had it prevailed, many books like Brandes's and Harris's Shakespeare could not have been written. Coleridge himself was as subjective and personal a poet as one shall easily find, but he makes it one of the points of genius in Shakespeare that he chose even in his early poems 'subjects very remote from the private interests and circumstances of the writer himself. At least I have found, that where the subject is taken immediately from the author's personal sensations and experiences, the excellence of a particular poem is but an equivocal mark, and often a fallacious pledge, of genuine poetic power.' So Sir Arthur Quiller-Couch, as he considers whether Prospero may be Shakespeare, says, 'let us ever beware how we say of any imaginative author that (as the phrase goes) he has put So-and-So into his book. Dickens, to be sure, did it once or twice—with unhappy result. For in truth it is not the way of the imaginative artist: and if the reader will not take that from me he may take it from Aristotle.' And the better critics of Molière no longer hold that he was thinking of himself as he presented Arnolphe, Alceste, and Dandin,—as indeed they well might, since in reality these were not meant to be as they in the Romantic Age were thought in some measure to be, pathetic or tragic figures. Moreover, as Monsieur Mornet has observed, 'Il n'a pas voulu se confesser ni même se trahir. Aucun auteur [least of all on the stage] n'y pouvait songer à cette date.'

And that is still truer of the more impersonal poet and dramatist, Shakespeare, at an earlier date. He may indeed have revealed himself and his affairs and feelings, almost unconsciously. In *Troilus and Cressida* and *Othello* he may have betrayed 'the madness of his jealous rage'; in *Hamlet*, 'his spirit of revenge against Herbert and his jealousy of Mary Fitton'; and in *Antony and Cleopatra* his passion for Mary Fitton may have found 'its extreme expression.' But apart from the material fact that of such feelings of Shakespeare's for Herbert or the Lady, or even of his acquaintance with them, we know quite nothing, we should, in entertaining these opinions of Mr Harris's, be untrue to that impression, which we like most men have been given, of fairness and serene impartiality pervading all his plays.

12.

Most critics do not conceive it so definitely and personally; but they do incline to the theory of a dark and gloomy period of his life in which he wrote his great tragedies and his 'bitter' comedies, and generally find the reason for it in the personal misfortunes and disillusionments which at this time befell him. Like Mr Harris and Dr Brandes these critics, too, think either that all literature is immediately personal and autobiographical, or else (whereas the contrary is the case) that Shakespeare's plays reveal more of this element than do others among the greatest. But the more we study the bitter comedies, for instance, in the light of other plays, Elizabethan and modern, the more we discover that there is no discernible inward touch. There is humour in them, as Sir Walter Raleigh shows, and much fine and normal human nature, not a spirit of misanthropy or profound sense of sexual evil everywhere pervading; and they quite evidently were not written by Marston or Tourneur, by Wedekind or Strindberg. As in the great tragedies, Shakespeare here still 'holds the balance even.'

From the plays, at all events, the dark period in his life cannot justifiably be inferred. If to these critics the plays seem gloomy and misanthropic, still the man at that moment may not have been. The imaginative mood runs often contrary—is a relief, a counterpoise. Tennyson wrote, *Break, break,* far from the sea, in a Lincolnshire lane; Browning wrote *How they brought the good news,* far not only from Ghent and Aix but from terra firma, on the Mediterranean; Curel's only play written in Paris is, he says, that which breathes most freely of the country air; and tragic gloom and comic gaiety may well be subject to this same *illogisme,* which is within the bounds of the logic of human nature—to this same *révolte,* which is under the ultimate sway of psychological causes. Mark Twain, we know, was not a merry soul in the family; and to one of his friends he once confided that he found life not worth the living. Of a contemporary cartoonist the London *Nation* recently observed that in private his tongue, like that of another great humorist, W. S. Gilbert, was apt to be withering and mordant, but in his art, again like Gilbert, his humour was bland and urbane. And this principle holds in morals too at times, as in the Renaissance, when public opinion offered little resistance. The most prurient dramatists in the Elizabethan age are not the loose-living actors or the roysterers Greene and Marlowe, but the sage and moral Chapman, Marston (who entered the church), and Tourneur; and Aretino, whose name became a bye-word, how clean and pure are the pages of his comedies when compared with those of Archbishop Piccolomini's *Alessandro* and the martyr Bruno's *Candelaio!* And the devotion to duty and the magnanimity and generosity rising above amorous passion, which we often find in Italian and French comedy or tragedy, though not in Shakespeare! How English or 'Nordic'—contrary to the facts! To the author's character, certainly, his art is but a single clue. Much that is known of the private life of Burns and Byron, Carlyle and Ruskin, Tolstoi and Michelangelo, may, indeed, be psychologically harmonized with their writings but could never have been conjectured from them. The writers who can be infallibly recognized in their characters, like Byron and Poe, are universally acknowledged to be self-centered; but even they do not so much reproduce what they are as what they think they are or what they fain would be. 'And it will be found true,' says Stevenson, in his *Humble Remonstrance,* 'that the artist writes with more gusto and effect of those things which he has only wished to do than of those which he has done.' He himself is the great example.

How much truer must this be of him who is rightly considered to be the supremely objective dramatist; and Coleridge's words should hold good, though even more in his later than 'in his very first productions he projected his mind out of his own particular being, and felt, and made others feel, on subjects no way connected with himself, except by force of contemplation and that sublime faculty

by which a great mind becomes that on which it meditates.'
That is, he did as poet what we do as spectator or reader
—entered into the tragic world by a sally of the imagination, and just as our actual lives are not plunged in gloom
as a result of the seeing or reading, so need not his life have
been as the cause of the writing. In both cases it is a
matter of imagination alone; no doubt he had emotional
capacity, a fund of emotional experience within him, but
his imagination was not fettered to the emotion of the
moment; and this fallacy or illusion which the learned follow confounds the things of the imagination with fact and
biography—with facts not only of time (as we have just
seen) but of place, circumstance, and profession, as if the
dramatist had no more imagination than the writer of
the monograph. It is a naïve remark of Gildon's, echoing
the naïveté of popular criticism, in 1699: 'I have been told
that he (Shakespeare) writ the scene of the ghost in *Hamlet* at his House, which bordered on the Charnel-House
and Church-yard'; but it is not unlike the rash identification
in more recent times of John Webster, because of his
sombre and gruesome imagery, as if he had no imaginative
autonomy at all, with the sexton (or undertaker) of St Andrew's, Holborn. John Donne (before he became a parson) must therefore have been one too. And by the same
token Shakespeare and Rossetti must have spent a long
time in Italy (which the latter certainly, and the former
probably, never saw), and the double-dyed romantics and
dreamers Charles Lamb and Mr De la Mare could by no
means have been the business-like clerks that they were.
Some have thought that Shakespeare wrote *King John,* in
which appears the boy Arthur, in 1596, shortly after the
death of his little son Hamnet, aged eleven. 'The supposi-
tion accuses Shakespeare,' says Mr Masefield, 'of a want
of heart, of a want of imagination, or of both wants
together.' And what would they say of *My Sister's Sleep,*
which seems to be written not out of the imagination but

wholly from the heart and memory, though Rossetti at that time had lost no sister or brother either?

Is it not here the same downright literalism, clipping the wings of the poet, which makes the gloom of King Lear to be the gloom of the playwright on the Bankside or in Silver Street, or the vindictiveness of Hamlet against his uncle to be Shakespeare's own vindictiveness against a rival—the same, really, which, because of his abundant particular information, makes of him a lawyer, a doctor, a printer, a schoolmaster, or a Catholic, or because of his superiority to his rustic upbringing and the obscure life he led in London makes of him not the nobody Shakespeare at all but my lord of St Albans and Verulam, or of Rutland, or of Oxford? They that are so minded know not, as he did, how a man could be bounded in a nutshell and count himself king of infinite space.

However objective, Shakespeare, to be sure, was too much alive to remain the same. He had his periods, which the critics have duly noted—he changed not only from comedy to tragedy and back to comedy, but in style and metre too—but a difficulty arises when we relate these changes to his life. He was young, then mature, then—but not for long—old, both as an artist and as a man, and the two went no doubt hand in hand. But they were not one and the same—he was more than himself and his experience added together, in his plays. His look was outward, however much went on within. In his dramas he was not a lyric poet or diarist—he was a 'dramatist by nature as well as by profession.'

He changed, we have seen, because he was so alive, but he had his periods (which to many seem to be those of experience rather than of creation) because he was an artist. On the one hand, an artist must change style not only because his thought and feelings are developing but because in itself the style grows stale and meaningless, both for himself and for his public. On the other, he must for a time keep the new style if it pleases, and as long as it pleases. In the interest of economy of effort and attention, which is in the interest of a mutual understanding—indispensable to artistic effect—he cannot change day by day. The well of emotion that he has happily struck he must let flow generously while it will. The audience eagerly expecting one thing must not be disappointed with another, asking for bread they must not be given a stone. The happy ending befits the play while it continues to mean something to both author and audience, then the gloomy ending; or the abrupt suggestive ending (it may be), then, after a while, the casual, tapering one. Change is necessary to an artistic community but so are periods of repose. And it is quite possible for the truly imaginative dramatist to be as sincere in one ending as in another: indeed he can be more sincere if he does not cling to any too long or in the love of novelty change to another too often. And none of these endings necessarily reflects the life of the time or his personal life. Any of them, however, as he fashions it, can reflect something of the shape and colour of the life he leads in imagination. When it ceases to do that, then is the time for a change. Plays ended happily, not only Shakespeare's but Beaumont and Fletcher's and Massinger's, in Shakespeare's last years. But Shakespeare's endings are not quite like theirs. And Webster's did not end happily at all, and much of the best prose and poetry of the time was darkened with a melancholy like that of Donne.

13.

The biographical or satirical illusion is more potent and prolific still; and, embracing the most tenuous clouds of evidence, teems with chimerical notions. James the Sixth of Scotland, and First of England, is not only Bottom but also (like Shakespeare himself) Hamlet and Prospero, in these latter omniscient days. If true, we must know and face it. But the consolation of those whose duty it is to peruse innumerable similar well-laboured pages is the reiterated proof, unintentionally thus provided, that the world of fact and the world of the creative imagination cannot be one and the same. Unfortunately, however, this disparity in outward semblance, borne in also upon the writers themselves, is to them only proof of their inner identity. The very lack of evidence is evidence, for one who entertains the probability of a satirical allusion and duly remembers that the prudent author must needs veil it and play safe; or for one who entertains the probability of a flattering allusion, and duly remembers that the author must flatter indeed. Once that principle is adopted any satirical allusion can with facility be proved. Malvolio, then, is your Puritan, for all that he so little resembles one! There is (though not much) no doubt some point to this, in the case of a satirical writer such as, in a measure, was Molière, but there is little enough in Shakespeare. And in him, as in all highly imaginative writers, the difficulty lies not so much in the unplausibility and undemonstrableness of the suggestions—James with an ass's head on his shoulders and the Virgin Queen caressing him, or the author of the *Demonology* (now Shakespeare's own sovereign) himself a princely sorcerer, and (of all things!) doubtful of his throne, and both characters presented thus unflatteringly before their own royal eyes—but, as we have seen above, in the poetic and artistic effect. Shakespeare himself as Hamlet or Prospero, though not so incredible, sadly troubles the atmosphere and blurs the outlines of the play. But James! If he is to be our Prospero or Hamlet, we are sorry for it, we and all men are the poorer.[26] Let him be Bottom, let

[26] Since the article was printed I have come upon Mr Machen's book, *Hieroglyphics* (1923), in which, independently, he takes the point of view presented in this essay. 'Pickwick,' he says, 'is in no sense, or in no valuable sense, a portrayal, a copy, an imitation of life in the ordinary sense of "imitation" and "life"; Pickwick, and Sam, and Jingle, and the rest of them are not clever reproductions of actual people (is there any more foolish pursuit than that of disputing about the "original" of Mr. Pickwick?)' (p. 51).

the Weaver, who would fain take every part, play the King.

14.

In a sense this discovery of reality is proper enough; great art should fascinate and grip us; and the author no doubt would be pleased to see us so utterly confound his fiction with the fact. But in pleasing him in that at the beginning we run the risk of pleasing him in the end not at all. At the play it is better to be lost to the world than to be unaffected; but it is best to be subject only to an esthetic illusion, still able to judge as well as to enjoy. Only children and those on a level with children hiss the villain or villainess, or do like the young woman who, as Sir Arthur Quiller-Couch reports, rose from her seat in the gallery and shouted to Othello, 'Oh, you great black fool! Can't you *see?*' The birds which pecked at Zeuxis' grapes were very clever for birds, quite stupid for spectators. The right audience, as Dr Johnson said, long before Gourmont, 'are always in their senses, and know that the stage is only a stage, and the players only players.' The best in this kind are but shadows, without a third dimension; and dramatic art is not mere imitation or acting a deceptive mimicry. And while the author may be pleased enough at our thinking that he gives us the 'real thing,' a 'slice of life,' as so many have thought or pretended to do, he is not likely to take it so well when we limit his powers to his own experience or his friends'.

Nor, if the greatest artist, is he likely to take it well when we make the error discussed in the chapter below, of giving his characters an independent existence.[27] Artists themselves speak mysteriously of their characters at their advent, hear them talking and but record the words, see their faces and but draw their lineaments, or like Michelangelo impetuously set free the form imprisoned in the marble

[27] See pp. 117 ff.

block. Such tricks hath strong imagination. But thus, the dramatist reduced to the bare rôle of biographer or scribe, the characters lead a life concerning which he is but ill informed, whether anterior to the play or subsequent to it, or even within the limits of the play itself. As for the past, had Hamlet seduced Ophelia? Had Ophelia and Laërtes inherited Polonius's moralizing vein? As for the future, will Benedick and Beatrice quarrel, or Celia or Mariana be at all happy? And here, and now, upon this bank and shoal of time, was Lady Macbeth a brunette or a blonde? But though no doubt somewhat troubling to the Bard, these questions would be nothing to those darker and deeper ones which have come up with the new psychology: the real motives of Hamlet, the real motives of Iago, concerning which they themselves were in the dark for all that they had to say about them; whether the Macbeths were not getting even with the world for their childlessness, and Hamlet were not caught in the clutches of a 'complex.' Only one consolation would the dramatist get out of it all and that he would surely disdain—these critics' attributing his every slip to Nature, not his art. That's his character, they whisper, like Mr Puff at the play. If it is in Hamlet we can only endeavour to explain it, and if we cannot explain it, why, that is because we are not equal to understanding him, in fact our failure to understand him only shows us how real he is!²⁸

In Shakespeare's case in particular, says Croce, men praise the 'objectivity' of the representation and the perfect reality of his characters,—things that may be said loosely but must not be taken literally, being figurative; for when we stretch out our hands to these characters, which are nothing else than the creatures of the poet's imaginative passion, and would seize them, if there is not an explosion (as when Faust threw himself upon the phantom of Helen)

²⁸ See Professor Wright's essay, *Columbia Shakespearean Studies* (1916); also my comment, *Hamlet* (1919), p. 20, and Professor Herford's comment (*Sketch of Recent Shakespearean Investigation*, p. 49), either one amazing to the writer of the other. Also see my *Othello* (1916), p. 67, note 2; and, below, chapter iii, section 10 *et seq.*

certainly those figures, in that very moment, collapse and vanish from before our eyes. And then instead of them arise the infinite insoluble questions how to understand or re-establish their solidity and coherence; most appalling of these being those which make up the Hamlet literature, every day on the increase. Round about the Shakespearean figures, which have been detached from the creative centre of the drama and transferred into a pretended objective realm, like persons of flesh and blood, crowd strangers of every sort, —historians, psychologists, gossips, policemen, criminologists, who investigate the characters, their purposes, their thoughts, their affections, their temperament, their preceding life, the tricks they played, the secrets they hide, their relations to family and society; and to the discussion there is no end.[20]

1924.

[20] Croce, *Ariosto, Shakespeare, e Corneille* (1920), p. 201.

I should like to observe, in addition to the discussion (on pp. 45-52) of the Restoration Comedy of Manners as no adequate or veracious picture of Restoration Society, that the standard of morality appears in it even as in the comedy of Jonson and Molière. Only, there that standard is more prominent. Vicious characters like the miser, the hypocrite, or the misanthrope, are presented directly as egregious digressions from the norm of human conduct, with 'the corrective laugh.' Now in the Comedy of Manners the like are treated in much the same way, as well as various shams and affectations; but much room is given to characters whose vices are merely sexual. These personages, in so far as they are genteel, youthful, and handsome, are treated sympathetically, but still comically; and the means whereby this is accomplished is the wit, illustrated above, which turns the received morality upside down. Without this 'code,' or anti-code, which Mr Palmer takes for the one actually followed in life, these particular characters would not be comic figures at all; but what (apart from its phrasing) makes it so comical is obviously, as I have above suggested, the fact that the received morality is, not at hand indeed, but in the background. It is comical by contrast, not only because so witty but also because so different, so wicked. There were a few, no doubt, like Etherege and Congreve in part, and Sedley, Dorset, and Rochester almost wholly, who may be conceived to have followed some such code 'in their serious pilgrimage'; but in ribald rebellion, turning life itself into a joke. There were more who followed no code at all, but merely their instincts and appetites. But that the code was observed or acknowledged by any large number of the subjects of Charles II is about as likely as that the later and more modest one formed upon it, by the modern Congreve, Oscar Wilde, was followed by a considerable proportion of the subjects of 'our dear Queen.' As scholars have observed, the good or edifying books published in his reign far outnumber the frivolous and bad. And Collier's onslaught was almost immediately followed by the appearance of sentimental comedy, which held up virtue to admiration, not ridicule,— a sudden change such as could easily take place in taste but not in the life which drama is supposed to mirror.

CHAPTER III

THE CHARACTERIZATION

ALL felicitous characterization is a mystery; and characterization as practised by the greatest of dramatists may well be more of a mystery than any other. Nevertheless something of the means or method of it may appear. In the greatest art means and methods are generally simple; the mystery and marvel lie in their application—the right touch, at the right time and place; and often we can, in a sense, see how a thing was done which none of us could ever do.

Shakespeare's method at times in tragic or serious work has been well described by the Poet Laureate in his essay 'On the Influence of the Audience,' in the Appendix to the Stratford Town edition:

Having found a story the actions of which were suitable, Shakespeare adopted them very much as they were, but remade the character of the actor. In the original story the actor would be known and judged by his actions: this Shakespeare reverses by first introducing his hero as a man superior to his actions; his art being to create a kind of contrast between the two, which has, of course, no existence in the original tale; and his success depends on the power and skill with which this character is chosen and enforced upon the audience; for it is when their minds are preoccupied with his personality that the actions follow as unquestionable realities, and in the *Macbeth* even preordained and prophesied.

The examples which Mr Bridges dwells upon are those of Angelo, Macbeth, and Othello, presently to be considered. Something of the same phenomenon in Shakespeare has been observed (though to different effect) by other critics, such as Thomas Whately in the eighteenth century and Ten Brink in the nineteenth. Speaking of Macbeth, Whately, with his eighteenth-century inclination to 'the tender' (moral sensibility it might in this case be called) remarks:

Thus in a variety of instances does the tenderness in his character shew itself; and one who has these feelings, though he may have no principles, cannot easily be induced to commit a murther. The intervention of a supernatural cause accounts for his acting so contrary to his disposition.

Nor does he leave out of the reckoning the influence of the man's wife. And the contrast, at least, is recognized by Ten Brink, as he considers Othello and Macbeth:

We here observe that Shakespeare often, especially in his most powerful tragedies, causes the tragic passion, which of necessity springs out of the nature of the hero, to come into decisive opposition to it.

I.

The case of Macbeth is the clearest of these. Independently critics like Mr Bridges and Mr Firkins have had difficulty in comprehending 'how such a man could have committed such actions.' He is prodigiously troubled by his conscience, not only after the murder of Duncan but before it; and his ambition is so lightly touched—'the portrayal of the incentives to the crime is so slight and incidental,' says Mr Firkins, 'and the portrayal of the deterrents is so appallingly vigorous and vivid, that the reader scarcely sees how the thing ever got itself done.' And when the reader compares Shakespeare's story with the chronicle from which it is taken, this effect upon him is only heightened. Not only is the ambition of Macbeth and Lady Macbeth there made clearer but it is given more justification. Duncan had been a feeble, ineffective king, which he is not in Shakespeare. Macbeth, moreover, had claims to the throne, then not strictly hereditary—whereas in Shakespeare he has

aspirations only—which Duncan's act in creating Malcolm
Prince of Cumberland had directly thwarted; and yet not
treacherously and in violation of the laws of hospitality did
he slay the king, for a long time afterward he was (whatever
his motives) not only a vigorous but a righteous ruler, and
he and his lady were munificent to the Church.   Nor is this
the only time that Shakespeare thus simplified—and darkened—the character he recast.   Richard III, also, was a
bad man but a good king (so in the poet's own day John
Webster calls him), yet in Shakespeare's hands, though interesting enough, he is not good at all; and Iago and Don
John originally had motives of thwarted love which somewhat explained and redeemed them, but of which they have
been deprived.   What, then, Shakespeare was seeking was
his contrast, clear and unbroken.   In the case of the villains
mentioned the contrast is between them and the other characters; in the case of Macbeth and Lady Macbeth it is
not only the contrast between themselves and between him
and Banquo or Macduff but also that between the man and
his conscience, the woman and hers.   And, as I show in the
chapter on the Criminals, the conscience is of that external
sort—the voice of a better nature within him, not of the
character's own—which in other plays of Shakespeare, and
earlier Elizabethan plays as well, could, in those days plausibly enough, threaten thus fearfully but vainly before the
deed and torment so speedily afterwards.

Considered psychologically, therefore, but not dramatically, Macbeth proceeds strangely upon his course. His apparent motive, ambition, is not kept before us; and others, such
as resentment for his grievances, do not arise.   Instead, he
dwells beforehand on the thought of the murder, and on his
treachery and ingratitude to a just and beneficent king, in
all their horrors; in his mind's eye he sees the dagger, not
the diadem; he takes no satisfaction in the sweet fruition of
an earthly crown, once he has got it, and neither seeks

beforehand nor discovers afterward a justification in his firmer and wiser wielding of the sceptre that he has seized. He is psychologically—or unpsychologically, rather—reduced to the lowest terms, to the murderer and his conscience; and a conscience not, after its wont, clad in the man's own desires or appetites, and sneakingly lending approval, but rising up in its stark reality to bar the way. Proceed then how can he? Apparently under the external influence of the Weird Sisters and his wife, however quickly he may respond to it. The Sisters have something of the nature of witches also—'supernatural soliciting' are the words he applies to their promptings—and they are not the totally indifferent voices of prophecy; and his wife is not indifferent; and he takes his way shrinking and faltering, but, as has been said, under the spell of a fatal fascination.

2.

That, certainly, is not a naturalistic way, and not the modern way, of motiving a character; but before we take up the matter let us turn to *Othello*. In my monograph on the subject I have endeavoured to show that a process of simplification, both in relation to the source, and in relation to reality as we know it, takes place in that tragedy also, not merely as regards Iago, who is blackened, but as regards Othello, who is ennobled. Despite the efforts of the psychologists to find it, there is no seed or germ of jealousy or distrust in his make-up before Iago plays upon him; indeed, by his friends and acquaintances throughout the tragedy, as well as by himself at the beginning and at the end, he is explicitly and repeatedly declared to be without it; neither time nor place lends colour to suspicion;[1] and by an external influ-

---

[1] Both Mr Bradley and Mr Archer have pointed out how unplausible Othello's acceptance of Iago's charges is in view of the fact that Desdemona has had no opportunity to be unfaithful, having arrived the day before, and having been accompanied by Iago and Emilia, not Cassio; and how easily these difficulties might have been obviated.

ence, again, in this case of a slanderer's arts, he is brought to a pitch of passion foreign, in a sense, to his nature. Instead of breeding the poison as the jealous do, he is infected with it—though he is not asleep in an orchard, it is poured into his ear. The convention of the slanderer believed, by those who have no sound reason or natural inclination to believe him, is in story or in drama, a very ancient one, and has only of late been quite done away with. It is employed, by Shakespeare also in the cases of Claudio in *Much Ado,* Gloster in *King Lear,* and Posthumus in *Cymbeline;* and there, as in Othello, the supreme instance of its effectiveness, it serves the purpose of keeping for the hero the sympathy which an inborn inclination to suspect or hearken to suspicion would somewhat alienate, and of involving him in a closer complication, a sharper contrast. He can at the same time both love and hate more nobly and intensely than if he had come to hate gradually and naturally, of himself. His passion is given depth and volume.

Now though Othello is incomparably the nobler character, and is placed in a very different situation, he and Macbeth are treated somewhat similarly. Both stories are in a sense made more improbable than in the original, and for the sake of the contrast, for the highest dramatic effect. They are made as improbable as those stories which in times ancient or modern have, because of the quality already present in them, been chosen for tragedy and been repeatedly presented since—the stories of Prometheus, Œdipus, Orestes, Phædra, Herod and Mariamme, Faustus, Hamlet, and King Lear, Tristram and Iseult. The material is simplified and little analysed. The apparent propelling force is external—it is Iago, the witches, Lady Macbeth. Motives, whether of ambition or jealousy, do not shine through thought or deed; above all, motives do not meet in a contention or clash. There, whether in the modern drama or in that of Corneille and Racine, now lies the central mechanism of the dramatic method. In *Macbeth* and *Othello* it lies in the contrast between the hero and his conduct—between his murders and his conscience, in one case, between his noble, generous nature and his ignoble, jealous rôle, in the other.[2] There is fluctuation in passion but almost none in purpose: of struggle and debate, such as is usual in French classical drama, there is here little trace. No tradition of the sort was established on the English stage—no technique already developed, and Shakespeare developed none.

Not that the modern method is wholly that of the seventeenth century French. Argument or debate, in particular, such as is to be found in the *Cid,* is unusual to-day. In the last generation or so, much has been made of instinct and impulse, and the struggle now is simple, imaginative, and concrete, rather than intellectual or argumentative. But still, among all the methods (for since we are the heirs of the ages, there are more now than then) and under all the influence of the new psychology, with its self-deceptions and masked movements, brainstorms and 'swoons of the mind,' the method of French classicism prevails, motives perceptibly appear, the mental as well as the emotional integrity and identity of the character are (as far as may be) kept intact, and the man who murders for ambition or jealousy at the end is made discernibly ambitious or jealous from the beginning. Shakespeare's method, strange to say, is, despite the classicism of Corneille and Racine, nearer than theirs to the Greek. The Greeks, too, secured a contrast between character and conduct—the hero, according to the best interpretation of Aristotle, having no 'tragic fault' but committing a tragic error of judgment. Through the agency of fate, and in ignorance, the hero is enmeshed in the toils, and the tragedy lies in his awakening and recognition. And the main difference at this point between the Greeks and Shakespeare lies in the fact that with him, since the whole story,

[2] The likeness, of course, is not at all complete. While Othello is not jealous by nature, Macbeth is ambitious, as appears most clearly when the witches first meet him; and the strange thing is only that in his thoughts afterwards this so seldom appears.

and not the last act only, is presented, and the entanglement, therefore, with or without a struggle, is, when the play begins, not already brought about, the supernatural influence must, as the Weird Sisters in *Macbeth* or the ghost in *Hamlet,* come visibly upon the stage; and, the belief in fatality being weaker (and the sense of individual responsibility stronger) much of the burden of this must be shifted to the shoulders of the hero or a villain. In Greek tragedy, however, the contrast is not so much between character and conduct as 'between the hero's conduct and its consequences —between the favourable expectations raised by his action and the deplorable results that actually ensue from it, as when an act calculated to ensure success is in reality productive of calamity.' This is particularly true of Sophocles, as in the *Œdipus* and the *Antigone.* Man proposes, Fate disposes. In Shakespeare it is the contrast 'between the expectations raised by the hero's personality and the disappointment caused by his subsequent career.' [3] Œdipus and Antigone are good to the end, but Macbeth plunges from shelf to shelf down the abyss; and though Othello is somewhat like a Greek hero kept intact, what a disappointment!

3.

The advantages of these methods are divided. Theatrically, to be sure—at least for the less sophisticated audience —the method of the Greeks and Shakespeare is superior. The contrast—to dramatic art all-important—is more complete and striking; and if the play less satisfies the reason it does what is more necessary—fires the imagination. But that of the French is, in one sense, far truer to life, and better fitted for a story in which decisions and changes must take place before the spectators' eyes. According to it, the seed of the sin or error being from the first in the hero's own bosom, the interest lies in its gradual development, its slower but deadly growth. To understand is to forgive—but, dra-

---

[3] The last two quotations are from Professor Frye's fine essay on the *Theory of Greek Tragedy,* University of Nebraska Studies, 1913.

matically at least, that as doctrine or practice is modern. In another sense it is not true to life, for real people do not analyse themselves or others, or argue with themselves or others, so clearly or so at length. Often they act and know not why.

To Shakespeare and the Elizabethans, however, who had no such technique of analysis and development, and were not inured to it, such treatment would, as I have said, have seemed less sympathetic, or less so at least than their own. To give, from the first, Othello the seeds of jealousy, Macbeth those of ambition, Hamlet those of vacillation and delay, or to let them debate and struggle over the issue, would not have been to hold the attention of the Elizabethans as it does ours. They were not so interested as we are in development, the influences of environment, and the 'point of view.' ⁴ And by this method their compassion would have been weakened, not strengthened, because the contrast would have been obscured. Compare the effect of the unsuspecting, deeply enamoured Othello plunged into wild jealousy, or the brave and honourable Macbeth staggering as in a trance to the murder of his king, with the more gradual and intelligible approaches and developments in Racine's Nero and in the hero of Voltaire's *Zaïre*. And such treatment is also more expeditious, a necessary quality in a popular play—a play that tells the whole story—a story packed with incident, as French tragedy is not. Yet to modern French taste, even since the days of Naturalism and the reign of impulse, the awakening of Macbeth's passion and its consummation are only too sudden and swift:

On voit l'ambition et le crime naître en même temps dans le cœur de Macbeth, sans que rien nous ait préparés à admettre cela. De fait, on le voit, on ne le comprend pas. La femme entre aussitôt dans son dessein, de plain pied, sans une objection, comme si elle eût toute sa vie rêvé ce qui va se réaliser. C'est possible, mais rien ne nous le laisse entendre.—Gourmont, *Promenades*, iv, 314.

⁴ See below the chapter on Shylock, and the chapter on the Criminals.

In point of internal (though not external) preparations the art leaves something to be desired. Comprehend one does not and cannot—one but sees and hears and is swept along.

Shakespeare and his audience being, however, at one, he himself may have had not only no other technique but no other interest. He seems not to have been much inclined to analysis, on the one hand, or to mixed and ambiguous characters or situations (or internal struggles where such are involved) on the other. He presents no studies of love, ambition, pride, or jealousy, though he presents characters powerfully animated by such passions. And upon the causes and springs of action he is often content not to intrude. Almost always the cause of love assigned (if any be) is, as in the medieval romances, merely the woman's beauty; and then it is a love at first sight. The passion presented is a far deeper and bigger thing than that, but such is its origin or basis, whether given at the time or afterward. And it is because of this, no doubt, that in the development of his story he can content himself to employ the medieval substitution (or pretended substitution) of one woman for another, as in the dénouements of *Much Ado, Measure for Measure, All's Well,* and the *Winter's Tale.*

And as for mixed or ambiguous situations, Romeo and Juliet and Desdemona hesitate not for a moment between filial obedience and sexual love. Brutus does not weigh love of country against love of friend. It is intimated that he does do this, as it is intimated that Macbeth weighs his ambition against his fealty, but neither struggle is presented. And why Hamlet feigns madness, or Cleopatra flees from battle, or Benedick exposes himself in his lovesickness to the gibes of his friends, no one will ever know. For Shakespeare there are no questions, no problems, not even the question of questions, the problem of sex. In particular, as long ago Coleridge pointed out, 'keeping at all times in the high road of life Shakespeare has no innocent adulteries, no interesting incests, no virtuous vice;—he never renders that

amiable which religion and reason alike teach us to detest,
or clothes impurity in the garb of virtue, like Beaumont and
Fletcher, the Kotzebues of his day.' Of such art he has not
the disadvantages or the advantages either. In *Measure
for Measure,* as Professor Schücking shows, Shakespeare
was given an opportunity to make of his saintly Isabella a
Monna Vanna, but avoided it. Even in Whetstone's primitive play the pure maiden sacrifices her virtue to save her
brother, and yet pleads for Angelo when in danger of his
head—in a fashion, not only a Monna Vanna but a Ruth
Jordan too. Instead, Shakespeare had recourse only to a
Boccaccian deceit and substitution; and the troubles of his
lovers generally are external—with fathers or uncles, rivals
or tyrants, fortune or circumstance.

And everything else in situation or characterization suggestive of a subtle contradiction or paradox (though nowadays these are continually being discovered in him) he
eschews. For him no honour rooted in dishonour; no Falstaff of the critics, with the constitutional instincts of courage, but without the principles which ordinarily accompany
them; no Othello with such confidence in Iago, who is not
his friend, that he can naturally distrust his innocent friend
Cassio, and the wife of his bosom; no Macbeth such as
Professor Schücking's, prompted by fear of his own courage; no Hamlet such as Mr Clutton Brock's, endowed (or
afflicted) with a 'double consciousness,' who, the more he
tries to force himself into action, the more his unconscious
self invents pretexts to keep him from it.[5] No doubt Shakespeare would have sympathized with Fielding in his preference of good intentions to virtuous performance and of generosity to probity; but even of that easy antithesis and paradox he makes no demonstration in his plays, and at the end
of them at least judges people by their deeds almost alone.

[5] See my discussion, 'Recent Criticism of Hamlet,' in the *Contemporary
Review* 1924, pp. 348 ff. And, on the subject of paradox in general.
pp. 356-7 and, below, the chapter on Falstaff, section 1, and *passim.*

Motives count with him more than with the Greeks but he
does not tamper with them; or pit them one against another.
That, apparently, was his way of thinking, if not of feeling.
Twilight, as has been remarked,[6] is a word used but once
in all his pages. Twilight—wavering outlines and dim intimations, paradoxes and contradictions—is for Donne and
Milton and us of to-day.

4.

How conventionalized Shakespeare's presentation of
Macbeth is, and how wide of the strictly psychological mark,
appears still more plainly when we examine some frank and
honest modern criticism, aloof from the dramatic tradition,
—by foreigners, and by thinkers and psychologists rather
than critics. A coward they think him, a hypocrite or sentimentalist. Most English critics, despite romantic and philosophical inclinations and vagaries, have, like English actors
and audiences, in the essentials not gone wrong; not clearly
understanding the technique or convention, or appreciating
how it removes the object from reality, they have, nevertheless, practically allowed for it, and seen that Macbeth is
meant for a brave man, not a coward, a man actually troubled by his conscience (however little it may be his by
nature), not a hypocrite. Even so subtle and psychologically
inclined an intellect as Coleridge's did not go astray. For
then the poetic tradition of the external conscience was not
yet dead; and like Schiller in Franz Moor, Coleridge himself followed it in his Osorio. But hypocritical and sentimental Macbeth is to Fletcher in 1847, to Flathe the German in 1863, and (much more recently) to Professor F. C.
Sharp, the American psychologist. And no wonder he is.
On unprejudiced, unprepossessed readers, a conscience that
prompts and warns one so clearly and vividly beforehand,

---

[6] Mr Bradley notices this, by the way, in his lecture on *Shakespeare the Man*.

and moves one to lamentations straightway thereupon,
would almost necessarily have such an effect. If conceived
to be only the man's better nature speaking, it cannot appear
very genuine; and small pity can the melancholy and misery
it breeds, inspire. The great passage

> My way of life
> Is fallen into the sere, the yellow leaf . . .

what can it be to them, measuring and judging by the
standards of reality alone, but, as one of them confesses,
'mere poetical whining over his most merited situation?' If
rightly so, however, where is then the tragedy? Macbeth
is bad enough without the whine.

These candid critics are, however, misled only as others
have been, or are, by still other conventional devices and
means of simplification in Shakespeare. There is the device
of deception and slander (already touched upon), feigning
(or playing a part), mistaken identity, or disguise, whereby,
like all other Elizabethans and the Renaissance as a whole,
he constructed his plots. Alfred Berger, the great director
of the Burg-Theater at Vienna, came to the conclusion that
to Shakespeare life was a monstrous bit of play-acting, and
justified passion, as a motive force in drama, was wholly
unknown; and Mr Masefield, in his criticism, dwells on the
sin of treachery and the evil effects of false report in play
after play, as if these constituted the central idea or theme
and the plays were studies of the subject. Dramatic machinery—artistry—is what they are. All the devices mentioned
are means of contrast, of simplification and compression,
which to the psychology of the time gave no offence and of
which the conventional character was not recognized as it
can be now. Effects of compression are in these still more
evident than in the characterization of Macbeth. Various
effects of irony are produced; various lights and colours are
made to play upon a scene or a speech, and scene and speech

are given body and volume. The character says one thing and means another, sees one thing and not another which other people on the stage or in the audience duly see, or (if he hearkens to slander) feels what his inmost nature would forbid him to feel. Such effects of clash and contrast, of simplification and compression, are of course, highly desirable in drama; they are analogous to the compacting of the time which Shakespeare had to bring about when he took in hand the material of chronicle or novella; and however unplausible the means, our own dramatists are, by the lack of them and by their regard for reality, sadly hampered in the making of new plays, as are our critics, on their part, in interpreting the old ones. Indeed, our modern dramatists and novelists endeavour to secure effects somewhat similar as they fall back upon naked character, or character confronted by the situation. Less hampered here, they light upon new moral or emotional problems or antinomies, as in *Monna Vanna* or in *Tess of the D'Urbervilles;* or, in lieu of the irony of disguise or mistaken identity they present the irony of spiritual blindness, as when the Duchess of Fontanges, in Landor's *Conversation,* is confessed by the Bishop though without sense of sin; or they reveal character, as do Ibsen, Chekhov, and Dostoevsky, by apparent contradiction, speech following speech as in some of the post-impressionistic paintings strip borders upon strip of contrasting colour, to produce an harmonious effect only at a distance or when the whole is recalled at the end.

Another example in point is the self-descriptive method, descending from Seneca, which below we examine further,[7] whereby the good characters speak of themselves frankly as good and the wicked as wicked, the brave as brave and the timid as timid. Professor Matthews takes umbrage at the vanity and conceit of Brutus in the Forum, and his complacence and 'abounding conscious rectitude' in the quarrel scene; and so far does Mr Harris misapprehend King

[7] Cf. the chapter on the Criminals.

Henry V in his speech before Harfleur,[8] and Othello when
before the Senate he tells of the distressful strokes which his
youth has suffered, and how he disdains to put love before
duty, as here to find another bit of evidence that when it
came to sheer courage Shakespeare simply hadn't it in him.
Though he could describe it he could not present it. How
much better to recognize in the poet's work traces of a primitive technique than to find in his character or imaginative
sympathy defects such as these!

And there is that further application of the Elizabethan
self-descriptive, or apparently self-conscious, method (also
discussed below), whereby tragic characters in passion speak
of it as if it were as external as a fever—nurse their woes,
declare them greater than all others, or wish themselves but
equal to them—and cry aloud for the sympathy of Nature.
Macbeth, for instance, bids the earth not hear his steps for
fear the very stones may prate of his whereabouts and

> take the present horror from the time
> Which now suits with it.

There Mr Firkins finds 'the mark of what we might almost
call the epicure in crime.' But the like, then, he should find
in King John, when, giving bloody instructions to Hubert,
he 'expresses a wish for the fitting stage effects'—darkness,
the churchyard, and the passing-bell; and in Othello when,
after killing Desdemona, he thinks it should be now a huge
eclipse of sun and moon, and that the affrighted globe should
yawn at alteration. And then what a morbid, degenerate,
fin de siècle set they one and all would be! But Shakespeare that would surely have surprised and pained, just as
it would have done to hear Imogen called self-conscious,
when, about to fall in a faint on the body of him she takes

---

[8] *Henry V*, III, i, ll. 5-17, where the King shows some concern for the
fierceness of look or aspect in the troops he is urging into the breach. It
is quite parallel to Macbeth's and King John's concern for the proper
encompassing horror; and for the moment his eye is not on the object, the
business in hand.

for Posthumus, she bethinks her of her own pale cheek; or Miranda, Arcadian child of nature, to whom sin or temptation is unknown, when she calls to witness her own 'modesty' and 'innocence.' [9]

There is little, I think, approaching the morbid or pathological, or, in the narrower sense, even the psychological, in Elizabethan drama. Hamlet and Jaques are suffering from melancholy; but Jaques is not the hero, and for Hamlet's melancholy there is ample cause; nor is there in him, as we shall see, any indication of weakness of will or other defect. And not only he but the rest of Shakespeare's heroes are, like all the heroes in tragedy and many in comedy of that romantic age, strong and vigorous, in both soul and body. Least of all is there any hero weak of will. Richard II and Edward II are only apparent exceptions. Though pitied and censured by the worthy and serious-minded as Hamlet is not, even by those who are neither the one nor the other, they are not irresolute—are fickle and capricious, easily uplifted and easily cast down, but not pusillanimous or feeble. Neither Edward nor Richard is so tame and weak as to evade or procrastinate. They rush to extremes, instead. There is no great duty or task from before the face of which they shrink or shy away; duties, indeed, do not trouble them. And it is a sign of the health and noble simplicity of the Elizabethans, as of the Greeks before them, that nowhere in their serious drama is there a good character who, squarely confronted with an enterprise, fails to embrace it. They are all quick and gallant spirits. Theirs are sins of commission, not of omission; they make no great refusal; they always take the dare. By the *maladie du siècle,* the disease of a later age—the age of Werther, Coleridge, and Sénan-

[9] Much of this paragraph is taken from an article on 'Drama Old and New', *Modern Language Review* (1925). Professor Schücking has noticed the case of Miranda; but this characteristic of Shakespeare's art was, I think, first adequately expounded by Monsieur Jusserand. Cf. my article on the Criminals, *Modern Philology*, 1912.

cour, in which our Hamlet really had his birth—they are untouched.[10]

The spirit of heroic romance, pervading Elizabethan drama, explains this, but so does the lack of analysis. As with the Greeks the tragedy is not so deep-seated as ours, or is not like ours laid bare. The case of Macbeth is again in point. Surely he too was meant to be an heroic nature. Before the crime no defect—save ambition—is displayed in him, and afterwards only the crime. No flaw is to be detected in the metal, although modern critics have thought there was. Even the latest and most scientific of them discovers in him a diseased imagination or nerves—finds him suffering from 'unmistakable hallucinations of the visual and auditory organs.' How contemporary the diagnosis! And any diagnosis, I cannot but think, is to a Shakespearean character inapplicable. The ghost and the witches, as we show in a later chapter, are genuine and are part of the story. But what of the dagger and the voice that cried, 'Sleep no more'? They are intimations of conscience, which, as we have seen, portend the enormity of the deed beforehand and visit him with nemesis afterwards. Or the dagger may be simply the outward embodiment of the fatal fascination. In either case these imaginative and poetic phenomena but lend weight and emphasis to the crime —but reveal his properly excited state. He has been an honourable man; and a crime he cannot commit without a convulsion. And the ghost, though it is Banquo himself, not the personification of remorse, is the supernatural minister of vengeance, like his very conscience.[11] To interpret these things pathologically seems as alien from

[10] Part of this paragraph is quoted from my *Hamlet*, pp. 27-8. Cf. there also pp. 7-9, 12-15. For further discussion of Hamlet and Richard see below in this same chapter.

[11] See the further discussion of this matter in Chapter v.—For discussion of the more modern craving for psychological unity in a character, touched upon at the end of this paragraph, see my *Othello*, pp. 46-8.

their spirit as to do so to the visions of Orestes. Only one
bit of evidence is there for a constitutional infirmity:

> My lord is often thus,
> And hath been from his youth.

But this, as Professor Schücking admits that it may be, is
only an excuse to put the banqueters off the scent. For a
neurotic certainly Macbeth is prodigiously vigorous; and for
such a temperament early Scottish life, before thanes were
called earls, or even the monarchy was yet settled into the
ways of primogeniture is a strange *milieu* and environment.
Professor Schücking would retort that Shakespeare pays
small attention to *milieu;* but still less attention does he pay
to highly developed or much distorted psychical conditions,
which are its product. The situation in his tragedies is simple, comparatively external. The heroes are such indeed—
sinners sometimes, breakers of the laws of God and man,
but not diseased. They are 'open and generous,' like Othello;
or suffering from melancholy, like Hamlet; or ambitious,
like Macbeth; but they are not spiritually lamed or crippled.
The day had not yet come when every felon was thought to
be suffering from a physical malformation or cerebral lesion,
or even when the root of every misdeed must be thought to
lie deep in the doer's heart from the beginning. Then a man
could be tempted and fall without being already fallen—
Othello, Posthumus, and Leontes could be jealous without
the suspicious nature, just as Chaucer's Cressida could be led
away from Troilus without an artful and designing heart.
That makes them for the unsophisticated taste only the
more interesting. Strong and sound as they are, they are
caught in the traitor's snare, the toils of circumstance, or the
poisoned folds of conscience. The contrast is simple but
most striking: in the hands of either a Shakespeare or an
Æschylus it can fill and hold the stage.

5.

As we turn to other characters we find them to be as simplified, and treated in as concrete and imaginative a fashion.
Lady Macbeth, who, with the Weird Sisters, bears the brunt
at the outset, is not wholly wicked like Iago and yet is no
more analysed than Macbeth, is in fact presented similarly.
Ambition is in her more evident; but, as I show below,[12] she
seeks the favour and benediction of the powers of evil before
the deed, yet experiences no sense of triumph after it, and—
both awake and asleep—is gnawed by the worm that shall
never die. Gourmont aptly remarks:

La scène de la tache et du somnambulisme n'est pas moins saisis-
sante ni moins artificielle. Rien n'est encore expliqué et on a peine
à admettre qu'une femme si hardie dans le crime soit si profondément
déprimée, aux jours mêmes du triomphe.

In her, conscience is still more external than in Macbeth,
more like a nemesis; there is even less that approaches to
sorrow for sin and compassion for the victim—that is, to
repentance—and less, accordingly, that exposes her to our
present-day suspicions of hypocrisy. 'Evil, be thou my
good!' she has as much as said before the deed, whereas
Macbeth, even while he followed evil, has shrunk from it;
but it turns and rends them both. Temptations, then, are
not beautiful;[13] sin, from the very beginning,—even though
both run to meet her—is not sweet. It is a moral process
rather than a psychological one, but in the lady's case the
nemesis is still more evident and notable. For that Shakespeare had prepared, again in a fashion external, by making
her delicate and refined, not brutish, and indicating that she
had forced herself, done violence to her nature. She has to
take wine to brace herself up, shrinks from murder by her

[12] See the chapter on the Criminals, sections 6 and 9.
[13] See below, chapter vii, section 9.

own hand because Duncan resembles her father, faints[14] after it is over, walks in her sleep, and dies before her time. There again is a contrast. Again, in a sense, the character is superior to his actions, whereas in Racine character and actions are almost one and the same.

6.

Angelo, in *Measure for Measure,* is one of Mr Bridges' instances. In a few hours this character is completely changed from a 'hard, cold, austere professor of virtue' to a 'licentious hypocrite, trafficking in crime.' Here is a contrast, but little harmony; the man was all virtue, and now, as he himself well knows, he has no virtue worth the naming. 'The situation might be satisfied,' as Mr Bridges says, 'either with an unprincipled or with a passionate man. Angelo is neither.' He is not a hypocrite before temptation, or a self-deceived soul, who would fain think his lust a holy love, after it. 'And although his self-knowledge began with his temptation, and was complete at his fall . . . he shows no remorse until he is publicly discovered.' The rôle is an effective one and it provides striking ironical situations, but what can be made of the character behind it, so far as causes and developments are concerned? From that point of view, we can only with Mr Bridges 'believe that he has been a solid hypocrite all along; that having no virtue to fall from, he never fell; that the spiritual conflict of his "temptation" could not have occurred; and, as there was nothing in his first character to respond to the call to crime, so now, in the revelation of his second phase, there is—except his demoniacal passion for Isabella—nothing left of him to be pardoned and married to Mariana.' But that he was not a hypocrite at first, for all that we psychologically incline to think so, is

---

[14] This may be a pretence, as in the eighteenth century it was thought to be; though it need not be, in her plight. In the eighteenth century, according to Davies, people laughed, which may be the aboriginal tradition; but it is better that they shouldn't.

made clear by the whole tenor of the presentation, though Isabella's words at the end point either way:

> I partly think
> A due sincerity govern'd his deeds
> Till he did look on me.

Sir Walter Raleigh, to be sure, thinks Angelo 'considerately, even mildly treated' (in the matter of punishment he is, like scoundrels generally at the end of a Shakespearean comedy); and that 'his hypocrisy is self-deception, not cold and calculated wickedness. Like many another man, he has a lofty, fanciful idea of himself.' Sir Walter is referring to Angelo's condition of mind previous to the temptation; but as I have shown elsewhere,[15] there are no unconscious or subconscious self-deceptions in Shakespeare; quite on the contrary, the wicked who in life admit not—even know not—their own wickedness, in Shakespeare know it, like this same Angelo, all too well. Their enlightenment is preternatural, and instead of the real man in Angelo surprising the play-actor in the hour of temptation, as Sir Walter imagines, the play-acting (though not at all to his own deception or much to Isabella's) now first begins. Such a suggestion as Sir Walter's would make the character more consistent, but there is no such deceptive sentimental haze or penumbra about the thoughts of Angelo. A Pharisee at the outset, he is but a whited sepulchre thereafter.

Brutus and Hamlet are further examples of the contrast described, and of the failure to analyse or perfectly to harmonize the character. Hamlet, like Macbeth, is by supernatural influence involved in an enterprise little in keeping with his nature. He is led into it, as (though without supernatural influence) are Brutus, Othello, old Gloster, Claudio, and Posthumus, into theirs. Throughout the play the task hangs over him, and the thought rouses him to rage, whether against his uncle or himself. Yet he does not debate the

---

[15] See my *Hamlet,* chapter iv; and compare the discussion of hypocrites below, in the present chapter, and the chapter on the Criminals.

question, or sway from one alternative to another like a hero of Corneille's or like Wallenstein—he reproaches himself for inactivity but engages in intrigue supposed to advance his enterprise or to checkmate the King.[16] Almost throughout the play, moreover, Hamlet feigns a part, designed (unplausibly) to serve his purposes, which contrasts with the real Hamlet, who in soliloquy or with Horatio, reappears. This, like other feigned rôles, such as Rosalind's, or disguises, such as Kent's, or changes which are not of the character's own seeking, such as the madness of Lear and the jealous rage of Othello, is another means of contrast, striking in effect. Othello before he falls into Iago's toils, after he falls, and after (the worse for it) he escapes them, is one of the great stage-contrasts of all time. Hamlet, in company and out of it, is another. In him, as in Othello, Macbeth, and Angelo, what analysis there is is of moods or emotions rather than of causes and developments; and it appears chiefly by the contrast secured through an improbable situation. His love for Ophelia might have motived his delay—he might have hesitated whether to revenge his father and die or to live and be happy; but that again would have been in the French style; and Shakespeare lets her play no more part in his thoughts than Sophocles lets Hæmon in Antigone's, and keeps his contrast broad and clear.

Brutus is in some measure led into his conspiracy, by Cassius; but the principal thing for us here to remark upon in this character or in Antony or Coriolanus, is, again, the neglect of analysis or motivation. Here is a lack of interest, not in the human but in the political subject, or else (again) a lack of the appropriate technique; and Shakespeare is silent or slurs the matter over. Unlike Macbeth, Brutus, as a republican or lover of liberty, has some reason for killing the head of the state. But from the time of Coleridge many have remarked upon the failure of the dramatist to present it. His republican principles, his sorrows for

[16] See my monograph on *Hamlet,* and in this chapter below.

the fall of the republic—where are they? He is acting from some lofty and solemn sense of duty—he is a reformer, though without a cause or motive [17]—we can see no more. As with Macbeth, again, there is a contrast between the hero and his conduct, though Brutus acts with a good conscience, Macbeth with a bad. His conduct, it seems, is, as conceived by Shakespeare, unjustified; but his character is by every means—his manner and sentiments, his relations to Portia, Lucius, and his friends—made to appear noble and pure. Only by analysis could be laid bare the motive which might justify the deed. And the change in Antony, whereby he deserts Cleopatra and takes up with Octavia, and then to Cleopatra returns, is treated externally, with no explanation whatever. For his return to Cleopatra, indeed, there is ample preparation, in Enobarbus's prediction before and after his marriage to Octavia, and in the soothsayer's warning, which serves Antony for excuse. But in the warning there is no analysis at all, and in Enobarbus's words only an analysis of the charms of Cleopatra. One wonders, not so much at his desertion of the Roman lady as at his marriage to her; but the whole psychological transition or transaction, which for Racine would have furnished forth the play, stands undisclosed. The romantic lovers' passion is a palpitating whole. And how does Coriolanus come to resolve upon the destruction of the city in which his mother, wife, and child all dwell? We are prepared for the change in that resolve when they plead, not only by what we know of his affection for them but by his dutifulness to his mother; but in his speeches neither tie is kept prominent; and before he has come to the resolve both seem to have quite passed out of his mind. Then, when his mother pleads, he yields up his dearest desire, with quite unpsychological though highly filial facility, almost at once. In the one play the

[17] Cf. Mr Frank Harris's *The Man Shakespeare* (1909), pp. 259-61.— The evidence that Shakespeare does not sympathize with the conspirators in the slaying of Cæsar is rather plain, particularly in Cassius' soliloquy on the way he was misleading Brutus, I, ii, end.

conflict—between love and honour—is scarcely engaged; in
the other—between pride and filial piety—it is not laid bare.
Here and elsewhere changes and resolutions are by Shakespeare treated rather externally and summarily, often with
preparations narrative in method rather than (in our sense
of the word) dramatic.

In the cases of *King Lear* and *Romeo and Juliet* there are
contrasts almost as sharp and striking but brought about by
less peremptory means.   There is no omniscient slandering
villain (save in the underplot of *King Lear*) to bring about
the mischief, but the good characters, by their headlong
impatience or unconciliatory imprudence, pull down their
fate upon themselves.   Even where there is a villain Shakespeare calls such qualities into service; and no lady so clever
and charming as Desdemona was ever so tactless, no wait-
ing-woman so loyal and sensible as Emilia ever so faithless
or stupid. [18]   And yet by nature Desdemona is not tactless,
Emilia not stupid, but only for the occasion.   So Lear, Cordelia, and Kent, though devoted to each other, in the first
scene fairly conspire together to contrive their tragedy.
Who could be more uncompromising than Cordelia or more
provocative than Kent, though they know the nature of the
King's other daughters into whose clutches they are thus
throwing him?   Characters so fine and devoted as they and
the King, too, later show themselves to be could not at the
outset have acted so in real life; but so they act to bring
about the complication—grief at the ingratitude of the
favoured daughters mingled with remorseful thoughts for
the one he had loved best, and death at the end from heart-
break for the loss of the child he has recklessly cast away.
In the contrast, in the irony lies the tragedy.

And *Romeo and Juliet*—there the contrast is between the
hatred of the parents and the love of the children.   How
beautiful it is, but how abruptly brought about!   They are
as precipitate in love as in their conduct afterwards.   It is

---

[18] See discussion below, end of section 9 and note 23.

not unnatural that love should arise out of the midst of the hatred, but (though romantic) not natural that there should be so little transition from one to the other, so little trace of struggle, so little memory, even, of the feud save where it practically interferes. They have forgotten not only the quarrel but their parents, both the tyrannous and the indulgent ones. In this respect they are like Desdemona and Othello as regards old Brabantio, and like Hamlet as regards Ophelia and her father's death. But the contrast in this play is not within the character but wholly in the story, between the leading characters and their environment.

8.

These are by no means all the cases; but enough have been examined to show the truth of the observations of Gourmont, Mr Bernard Shaw, and the anonymous early critic of Shakespeare who wrote in 1736 his *Remarks on the Tragedy of Hamlet:*

> The more I read him, the more I am convinced that as he knew his own particular Talent well, he study'd more to work up great and moving Circumstances to place his chief Characters in, so as to affect our Passions strongly, he apply'd himself more to This than he did to the Means or Methods whereby he brought his Characters into those Circumstances.—*Some Remarks,* p. 55.
>
> They (the Elizabethans) could place a human figure before you with perfect verisimilitude; but when the moment came for making it live and move . . . they had to invent some artificial stimulus to make it work.—*Man and Superman,* Epistle Dedicatory.
>
> . . . Je crois qui'il a eu moins d'intentions profondes qu'on ne lui suppose, et qu'il s'attardait moins à la vérité psychologique qu'aux surprises de l'action.—*Promenades,* iv, p. 315.

And the German scholars Wetz and Bulthaupt have much the same to say. It is with plot, certainly, that Shakespeare started—as even now do the dramatists that have any, and as Shakespeare, borrowing a plot, could not but do—and

then invented characters to suit.[19] And the motives often
gave him trouble, but not so much as they well might have
given. In the sources they are often more sufficient and
plausible than in his plays; as for the conduct of Iago and
Don John the slanderers, of Emilia and Margaret who
unseasonably hold their tongues, of Leontes in turning jealous, of Macbeth in killing his king, of Lear in dividing up his
kingdom, of Hamlet in pretending to be mad. Sometimes
he left them out, because they were complicated and embar-
rassing, as in Richard II's relations to Mowbray, and when
he arranges for the combat and then breaks it off before
it has quite begun; or because they were queer and eccentric, like Lear's purpose in the old play to make Cordelia if she loves him most marry a British prince and
stay in Britain. Sometimes he provided new ones perfunctorily, in simple conventional form, as 'love' or
'honour,' and no more, for the hero, or revenge or sheer
love of evil for the rogue; and sometimes he felt the need
for a motive more than he saw the way clear to provide it,
and, hinting darkly, drew the veil.

This last is the case, strangely enough, with Shakespeare's
most intellectual and conscious characters, Hamlet and
Iago. None of his creatures might be expected to know
better or tell more plainly why he does as he does; but
though both have more to say about it than the others they
avoid a clear conclusion. 'I do not know why yet I live to
say this thing's to do,' says Hamlet, in the fourth scene of
the fourth act, after touching on several reasons; and Iago,
though in no doubt at all about his hatred for Othello, gives
various trumped-up reasons to explain and reinforce it. And
so both have been exposed to the probings and surmises of

[19] An opinion on such a subject held by Watts-Dunton, Sir Walter
Raleigh, Mr Bridges, and apparently Sir Arthur Quiller-Couch, I need not
defend at length. To have started with the character, a Hamlet, or a
Lear, and found the story ready made to suit it afterwards is quite unnatural and incredible. And it is dubious if such a process is common even
with those who invent their plots. See my article, 'Recent Criticism of
Hamlet' (*Contemporary Review*, 1924), p. 352.

two centuries. But one thing is evident—that in a tight
place it is an excellent device for a dramatist, serving to
explain (or seeming to) when, on the one hand, a character
for three or four acts has everything to do, or, on the other
hand, for three or four acts next to nothing. Nothing else
dramatically or even psychologically could be so adequate
when your play depends on a villain who sweeps not only the
hero but everybody else in the way into his net, or on a hero
who is bid to seek revenge at the beginning but attains it
(and in the act perishes) only at the end. What motives
would suffice for either, particularly with a poet so little
inclined to analysis? And the device not only serves for the
story but lends the semblance and colour of reality to the
characters themselves. How often, whether we say it to
ourselves and others or not, we too do not rightly know,
whereas in mere stories men do!

The semblance of reality (which despite the large element
of convention in his work Shakespeare most happily
attains) how all-important to the effect of it! Two things
above all else he sought—a striking situation and a vivid
impression of personality; and perfection of structure and
adequacy of motive were secondary. Indeed, it is when the
spectators' minds are preoccupied with the hero's personality, as Mr Bridges says above, 'that the actions follow
as unquestionable realities.' And this effect in turn is produced in part by the 'convincing verisimilitude and richness
of Shakespeare's detail,' in part by the fact that the characters seem to 'live with a larger life than that of the
action,'[20] but above all else, I think, by the manner or quality of their speech. In the place of psychology, with its
analyses and subtleties, the poet had an infinite tact, the
artist's delicate, plastic, life-giving touch. 'The Shakespearean delineation of character owes all its magic,' says
Mr Shaw, 'to the turn of the line, which lets you into the

[20] Cf. above, p. 108, the contrast with Racine. The words here quoted
are Professor Frye's.

secret of its utterer's mood and temperament, not by its commonplace meaning, but by some subtle exaltation, or stultification, or shyness, or delicacy, or hesitancy, or what not in the sound of it. In short, it is the score and not the libretto that keeps the work alive and fresh.' [21] At the moment, to be sure, Mr Shaw is vexed at finding no philosophy in Shakespeare—in whom indeed there is little. But Mr Shaw would agree with Mr Bridges in thinking that it is this reality and individuality of tone and manner, marvelled at by people so different and diverse as Pope and Hugo, which capitivate and bewitch us, and make some think we must explain, or accept without explaining, the inconsistencies within. These in comparison do not greatly matter. Even in our modern dramatists, with their psychological prepossessions, and even in our novelists, who have more play and freedom, such inner inconsistencies—not moral or logical ones I mean but the really psychological— are frequently to be found. What does matter is that there should be a false note—and that is rare in Shakespeare; what matters still more is that the tune or the accents should in the first place be unimportant or unindividual—and that in Shakespeare is rarer still. 'To this life and variety of Character,' says Pope (though somewhat exaggerating, adds Johnson) 'we must add the wonderful Preservation of it; which is such throughout his plays, that had all the Speeches been printed without the very names of the Persons, I believe one might have apply'd them with certainty to every speaker.' By the tone and manner we thus recognize them and forever remember them,—Hamlet, Shylock, Falstaff, and the Criminals, as we shall see, despite the inner inconsistencies which the critics, in explaining them away, have only brought to our notice; and for us should not that

[21] *Dramatic Opinions and Essays* (N. Y., 1906) i, p. 24. The reader may be referred to the close of my *Othello*, pp. 63-70 for some discussion of Shakespeare's characterization by the differentiation of their tone, not repeated here. For the individuality in the turn of the character's speech, see also above, chapter i, section II.

be enough, as it was for the Elizabethans? But it has not been—art is far from enough for philosophers or even for critics. It is this very reality and vitality, no doubt, that has kept the tide of Shakespeare criticism for two centuries flowing; but it is this that has given rise to the mystical illusion, or superstition, that Shakespeare's characters are verily alive, not merely the figments of art. It is an artistic effect and triumph, that Shakespeare should succeed in making us think it[22]—though it is likelier to be owing to the superstitious regard into which great reputations degenerate—but even he would not have us think it in truth and soberness, for good and all.

9.

This is the great and continually recurring error in Shakespeare criticism, which I discuss above, in the last section of the preceding chapter, and which I must beg leave to recall to the reader's attention as we consider the question of psychological consistency, and the analysis that may properly be applied. The *locus classicus* of the illusion, is, as Mr. Walkley has pointed out, a passage in Maurice Morgann's *Essay on Falstaff*, in 1777:

If the characters of Shakespeare are thus whole and, as it were, original, while those of almost all other writers are mere imitation, it may be fit to consider them rather as Historic than Dramatic beings; and when occasion requires, to account for their conduct from the whole character, from general principles, from latent motives, and from policies not avowed.

Thus, whether under Morgann's direct influence or not, 'the strange habit was acquired,' as Mr Walkley says in his essay on *Professor Bradley's Hamlet,* 'of considering the personages of Shakespeare's plays as actual flesh-and-blood people instead of fictitious inventions'; and the 'distinction ignored between nature and art, realities and appearances.' And though recognizing the naturalness of this confusion

[22] But see Johnson and Gourmont above, chapter ii, page 87.

and even its desirableness as the momentary effect of any
particular fiction or play, Mr Walkley rightly insists that
'deliberately to import this confusion into criticism is quite
another matter. For it is the object of criticism not to
flatter the fancy but to understand, to trace results to true
causes, to see the thing as it really is.' Yet he points out
that not only in the Romantic Age, the age of the Shakespeare cult, but also to-day the best work of our Shakespearean commentators is 'constantly vitiated' by it, even
the work of Dr Bradley. This great critic is puzzled by the
insensibility of the Court in the play-scene in *Hamlet;* and
'his delightful naïveté is merely the result of his considering
the Court in *Hamlet* as a real Court and not a stage-crowd
put there to manœuvre in a striking theatrical situation.'
The 'stupidity' of Emilia (otherwise shrewd and clever
enough), in not taking the hint from Othello's to-do about
the handkerchief and clearing the matter up, is another
instance. 'Stupidity'[23] critics also of the rank of Brandes
and Stopford Brooke have found even in Othello. It is the
right word, were he flesh and blood. A stupid hero, introduced into tragedy intentionally, is, even in our day of
universal indulgence—even in Russian art—hardly possible; and in the high romantic days of Elizabeth one weak
of mind was still more impossible than one weak of will,
as Hamlet in the nineteenth century was generally made
out to be.[24] Even the realist Bacon would have said so.
'Therefore,' he declares at the end of a great passage in
the *Advancement of Learning*, 'because the acts or events of
true history have not that magnitude which satisfieth the

---

[23] See my *Othello,* pp. 31-44, especially p. 34. This is owing of course
to their failure to make allowance for the convention of the slanderer believed, discussed at the beginning of this chapter. As for Emilia, no
intelligence, as Mr Bridges says, was needed. Iago has snatched the handkerchief from her; she has begged him because of her mistress' anxiety
to hand it back; and now she is present at the excited inquiry. And there
is no reason for her presence, as Mr Bridges observes, save to 'increase
the tension of the spectators' anxiety' (p. 332).

[24] See section 4 above.

mind of man, poesy feigneth acts and events greater and
more heroical.'

10.

One would think that Mr Walkley's essay should surely
have killed the error—nay, 'one would have thought it,'
as he says himself, 'almost superfluous to point out the
fallacy of a critical method which works on the assumption
that a dramatist's characters are real people.' On the
contrary, he has but scotched the snake, not killed it, and
(under cover) it still wriggles. Shakespeare criticism continues to be a cult, a mystery—is not critical. Professor
Herford in his *Sketch of Recent Shakespearean Investigation (1893-1923),* saying with satisfaction that a modern
psychology, by its disclosure of the phenomena of dual and
multiple personality, 'has eased the path of those who find
real inconsistency in any of Shakespeare's characters,' takes
up anew the standpoint of Morgann in the passage above—
latent motives, policies not avowed—adding an anachronism
of his own. In his zeal (but, as it seems to me, in the
teeth of his better knowledge) he would, in these latter
days, out-Morgann Morgann, or applaud the high emprise
in others. Hamlet, according to him, is independent of his
creator, and people may feel free to discover (which the
moment that this new notion was out they had of course
proceeded to do) a dual or multiple personality within him,
as they may in a patient at the psychopathic clinic. Hamlet
is but a 'case,' the play but a document, the critic a psycho-
analyst. But 'a real person,' says Mr Walkley again, 'is the
resultant of his will, hereditary circumstances, environment,
and millions of causes entirely beyond his control. A
dramatist's personage is a mere projection of one man's
mind, limited by his powers of observation and imagination,
and can utter nothing, think nothing, be nothing, outside
the range of the dramatist's own nature and mental vision.'
En art il n'y a que d'exprimé. Outside the range of William

Shakespeare's vision, we may be sure, lay the new psychology as well as any means for presenting it dramatically. If Shakespeare criticism has been a bye-word, nothing has so clearly made it such as has this initial and fundamental misconception—of misconceptions so fruitful —which Mr Walkley has not killed and to which Professor Herford would lend life anew.

And for special approval he picks out a conspicuous instance of it, in Professor E. H. Wright's essay on 'Reality and Inconsistency in Shakespeare's Characters.'[25] 'Mr Wright recognizes with perfect clearness,' says Mr Herford, 'that our sense of a man's reality not merely does not depend upon our being able to reduce him to a formula, but is even heightened and quickened when we find our efforts to do so futile. And Shakespeare's persons impress us as real for the same reason.' If Mr Herford meant no more than he may seem to mean we might here agree with him—for into a formula what great character can be put?—but he quotes admiringly Mr Wright:

> No critic has made one perfectly comprehensible man out of Hamlet. And there is no question of his reality—no one denies it— there is only a question whether we can grasp him as an entity, whether we can put him in a definition. We *know* Hamlet in much the same way as we know our friends, in spite of the fact that we cannot explain him. Or rather it is the meaning of this essay that we know him in this way partly *because* we cannot explain him.

The writer's are the italics; he seems to mean, comprehensible and at the same time true to the text; but just above he has said that it is doubtful if such a character can ever be made out of him. The word *know*, then, is used somewhat mystically—we know without understanding, as do the faithful; or, if that seems too simple, by the old metaphysical sleight of hand a reason is snatched out of

[25] *Columbia Shakespeare Studies* (1916).—I dwell upon this essay because in it is presented the central problem, with a rare and genuine effort to establish in a scholarly fashion what seems to me an unscholarly, untenable point of view.

unreason, and the *Verstand* bows before the unanswerable
but irresponsible *Vernunft*. *Credo quia incredibile est;* for
theology and literary criticism have had much in common.
There has been the same juggling in both.

II.

'Law is common sense'—and so (at least in some measure) criticism should be. The reality of a friend and of a
character in a play are, as has already been explained, essentially two different matters. That of a friend you are not
free to doubt—unless you be a thoroughgoing disciple of
Berkeley—and it does not depend upon your understanding
or misunderstanding. Understand him or not, he is there,
—a fact, like the stone against which Dr Johnson, to refute
Berkeley, struck his foot. That of a character does so
depend; not a fact is he but an image or simulacrum, real
or not real only according as he has effect upon us. And if
it be true—it is not altogether, otherwise Mr Wright and
Mr Herford would not be here pleading—that Hamlet's
reality is doubted by nobody, it is simply in the sense that
nobody doubts his individuality of utterance and manner
(which we have discussed above and eagerly acknowledge)
or his consistency in point of view and sentiment, not in
conduct. That everybody doubts—everybody is concerned
to prove.

The inveterate and besetting fallacy, then, of the confusion of art and life is here again manifest. There is a
mystical turn, we have seen, to the interpretation, but there
is a literal turn as well. The dramatic character, though
a mystery, is also supposed to be a 'copy' of life—the 'astral
body' of it, shall we say?—and you may pass lightly from
the one to the other, since they are equally real, are almost
commensurate and equivalent. Mr Wright practically
frames this syllogism: Real people are baffling from their
complexity and inconsistency; Shakespeare's people are the
purest copies that we have of real people; hence they too

are baffling. That is, a mystery in life is the same thing as a mystery or puzzle in the representation of it, or a bore in reality should also be a bore upon the stage! By such reasoning any character can be made to pass the test. But what troubles me particularly is the fundamental conception, alien, as it seems to me, to a sound esthetic theory. Just above Mr Wright remarks on Shakespeare's characters being 'copied with so little alteration by the poet from the population of the world.' I doubt if to Mr Herford such a remark can be wholly agreeable; it is very parlous praise, and if there be any point to the later Shakespearean investigation or to our previous and our subsequent discussion, it does not apply.

The mystical and the literal are, however, only different aspects of one bent. Either way it is implied that as regards Shakespeare's characters we must renounce the right of criticism or reason. 'Hands off,' they of this persuasion seem to say, if not, *favete linguis*. If you cavil at a contradiction they fall back upon life, of which their poet's every line must be the transcript, or appeal to the light within—within him and them. They do not realize that the position is a dangerous one, and at bottom implies that these plays are not the product of art at all, but the record of a camera, 'which does not lie,' or else the vision of a seer. The latter, to my mind, is their ultimate opinion —that this greatest of dramatists, seeing life steadily and whole, was free to cast off the trammels of artistic method and classical logic and introduce what matter he pleased. 'Der Hinweis darauf, dass es ähnliche Widersprüche in der Wirklichkeit gebe,' says Creizenach very justly, 'kann in solchen Fällen zur Rechtfertigung des Dichters nicht genügen.' Yet it must be added that on the following page the great scholar himself shows leanings toward the mystical, romantic point of view of Grillparzer—'dass wir bei Shakespeare an die Möglichkeit nicht denken, weil die Wirklichkeit vor uns steht.' And he even quotes Schlegel:

'Wissen wir doch in unsern . . Bekannten, wenn sie einige
Tiefe und Umfang des Charakters haben, nicht immer
mit deutlichen Gründen darzuthun, warum sie sich jedesmal
unter besonderen Umständen so oder so benehmen, ohne
dass wir darum an dem Bestande ihrer Persönlichkeit irre
würden.' This now timeworn argument sounds a bit like
that of the apologist for religion, who, when you cannot
accept his miracles and dogmas, reminds you that you
cannot comprehend the law of gravitation or the flower
in the crannied wall. But he and Schlegel and the score
of critics who have quoted and echoed him must themselves be reminded that your friends uncomprehended differ
from either an incredible doctrine or an unplausible work
of art in the very material respect that these latter, *ipso
facto,* correspond to no reality, have no claims upon our
attention whatever.[26] The credibility—the plausibility—
is what is just in question, and the question is thus emphatically begged.

To the baffling character of a friend, moreover, there
is a key, whether we can manage to lay hands upon it (and
make use of it) or not. There is to him some unity, however loose—he is an organism, an entity, he is in short
there! To that of Hamlet there may be none, Mr Wright
suggests, even in the mind of the author. 'For Shakespeare
may have had in mind some further explanation for the
delay, or he may have had none; he may conceivably have
thought out some reason in psychology for Hamlet's not
acting, or he may never have dreamed of any one such reason; and according as he did or did not, there is an explanation or there is no explanation for Hamlet' (p. 401).
And yet (inconsistently, to be sure, with his general point
of view) Mr Wright had just said that Shakespeare's
'Hamlet is the only Hamlet there is.' Is it not clear, then,
that to Mr Wright and Mr Herford knowing a character

[26] The latter part of the paragraph is quoted from my *Othello,* p. 67,
note.

is not the ordinary sublunary process, to which understanding, or even there being anything that can be understood, is indispensable;—Hamlet is there, and is to be accepted!—or else that it is (though that conclusion they would abhor) simply and merely equivalent to the perception (as we too have perceived it) of Hamlet's individuality residing not in psychology at all but in his tone and manner? In either case, it would seem that for anything like a discussion of Hamlet's motivation and internal consistency there can be between them and some of us no common ground. With those who bear within them the chief evidence of their faith, a discussion of the evidence is impossible.

Yet, as I suggest above, Mr Wright does not really mean that Shakespeare's Hamlet is the only Hamlet; like many critics he and Mr Herford conceive him as a free and legitimate subject for a psycho-analysis of which Shakespeare knew nothing, and not as inconsistent but as a 'copy' of the inconsistency that is in human nature, for which, as they think, there may be a key or not. As for the former, the impropriety of psycho-analysing, as though they were real persons, literary characters created before that process was invented, becomes, if not already sufficiently apparent, quite glaring under the fire of Mr Chesterton's recent ridicule; and the double consciousness which Mr Clutton Brock discovered in that strange, strange trio— Hamlet, Jesus Christ, and Julius Cæsar,—may for aught I know have been present in the last two but in the drama could not be, and would have ruined the drama for the stage if it could. Such a conception is owing to the modern critic's taste and bent, which in the case of a great old poet assimilates what it cannot well reject. The feigned rôle of Hamlet having furnished a sharp contrast of merry madness with sad sanity (and thereby a magnificent opportunity for dramatist and actor but a pitiful one for a psychologist), Mr Clutton Brock practically ignores the feigning; and the character as a whole he turns into a case of double consciousness, or mental disorder, and his madness in company into a tendency to misexpress himself under a compulsion which he does not understand. But, alone, Hamlet is at once as right as a trivet, and though company may make a man crazy it will not leave him sane; and if the young prince had not misexpressed himself pretty thoroughly, under a compulsion which both he and his audience understood all too well, he would hardly have got off with a sea-voyage or returned to tell the tale.[27]

As for the latter—the inconsistency which is in human nature—that is too big a question here to embark upon, as is indeed the scarcely smaller one of Hamlet's character as a whole. All I can undertake to say is that to me it is grossly improbable that the great popular Elizabethan dramatist deliberately undertook to present inconsistency, a riddle in character, at all. Even to-day there is not much chance for that sort of thing on the stage: on the stage things must needs be fairly clear and plain. No such riddle —no such bundle of subtleties and contradictions, held together in the subconscious life alone, is to be found in Ibsen himself, for an audience, comparatively, of intellectuals, or 'highbrows.' How much easier of comprehension is Hedda Gabler or Peer Gynt than the psychologized Hamlet of the nineteenth century! Yet even by them, even by the single consciousness, the spectators' powers of attention are sufficiently taxed. Would Shakespeare have attempted to present such a character to an audience which in tragedy demanded melodrama, in comedy farce, and, as the best Shakespeareans admit, always got somewhat of what they demanded?

The very contrary, indeed, is the whole impression of Shakespeare's dramatic art. It is explicit rather than implicit, in so far as to make frank modernists like Mr

[27] Some sentences in the paragraph are reproduced from my article 'Recent Criticism of Hamlet,' cited above.

Shaw complain of its 'eternal unsuggestiveness." Above we have amply seen how he simplified rather than further complicated the characters he took from his sources, and instead of tampering with the subconscious as even nowadays your dramatist can hardly do, made his characters (both good and bad) unnaturally and unnecessarily frank and aware. Motives, when not merely neglected or intentionally slurred over, come boldly to the light of day, instead of betraying themselves casually and unconsciously as in life or in some present-day drama; and so far (in the theatre at least) are poet and people from a notion of the relative and unconscious that the motives appear, not in the dim and subdued colours in which they are seen by the soul itself, but in the black and white of vice and virtue, as if a cherub saw them. They are plain and clear like the plans and purposes of the characters, duly announced and confided to the audience; and like the whole course of the action, for that matter, which is duly marked and fingerposted with comment upon the characters or their conduct, with anticipations (by means of omens or forebodings, predictions or curses) instead of surprises, with whole scenes given over to explanation (as that at the end of *Romeo and Juliet* and two in *Macbeth* and two in *King Lear*)[28] and the very jokes made transparent as the day. (Only the smutty ones can be entrusted to the hearers' wits unaided.) And all this is that he who runs may read, that he who nods or chatters in the pit may understand. Indeed, when the dramatist thinks the psychology a bit difficult he lets the character himself or another explain it; as when Desdemona stops in her badinage with Iago, while they wait on the quay, and remarks that she beguiles the time to seem more merry than she is, or when Enobarbus explains Antony's affectionateness with the servitors as one of those odd tricks which sorrow

[28] The scenes between Kent and a Gentleman, in this play; and those between Ross and an Old Man and Lenox and a Lord, in the other.

shoots out of the mind.   When a character does deceive
himself, it is he himself in soliloquy—as Hamlet when he
falls a-cursing like a very drab, or Iago when for the
moment he dallies with the notion that he is not playing
the villain—that catches himself and detects it.   'Why,
what an ass am I!' cries the one; 'Divinity [that is, *theology*] of hell,' jeers the other.   And when Othello replies
'Not a jot, not a jot!' to Iago's remark 'this hath a little
dashed your spirits,' he either is deceiving himself only
as the angry man does when he denies that he is angry,
or else is too proud to confess the truth.   'I' faith, I fear
it has,' is Iago's rejoinder; and his opinion, together with
the obvious and unmistakable evidence of Othello's speeches
just before and after, makes it ours.   There is no mystery
here; the audience is not left in the dark for more than a
moment.

12.

Yet there is Hamlet, so real, though not to be understood.   But even by dint of much subsconscious self-deceiving,
of which as a dramatist (at least) Shakespeare knew
nothing, this character has truly not been made a 'perfectly
comprehensible man.'   He is beyond our present powers
of analysis, some even say, though if that be true, except
as it is true of any character whatever, he is not a work of
art.   A work of art incomprehensible, save to the angels
only, is a chimæra, a myth.   And what is an incomprehensible character, created for the public stage by a popular
dramatist, save as it should turn out such inadvertently?
As I have shown elsewhere,[29] however, he was comprehensible enough to the Elizabethans, to the seventeenth and
eighteenth centuries, and until the Romantic critics arose,
who, however they knew Shakespeare the poet, knew not
the dramatist or his stage.   Down to the days of Henry
Mackenzie, the Man of Feeling, no one, though many intel-

[29] In my *Hamlet*, chapter i.

ligent persons had written about him, suspected a mystery
in him or any fault at all. The mere fact that the play
is, as the Earl of Shaftesbury says, 'that piece of his which
appears to have most affected English Hearts, and has perhaps been oftenest acted of any which have come upon our
Stage,' is sufficient proof, if of popular audiences we know
anything, that to them it was not a puzzle or riddle. The
puzzle or inconsistency was discovered as men began to read
and ponder, instead of seeing, the play, and to consider
more curiously than by the dramatist they were intended
to do. It is there, to be sure, if so pondered and considered
—if so misread,—but it arises out of the refractory and
highly improbable old story, out of the lost old play, the
structure of which, with many fragments clinging to it,
reappears in the new, though it is not exposed or dwelt
upon but as far as may be slurred over and concealed.[30]
It is in the art, not in the character.

There lies the difference—the modern novelist or dramatist who has an inconsistency to present, presents it,
clearing up what he can, adumbrating what he cannot, and
Shakespeare would have done the same. Upon the passage,
'I do not know why yet I live to say this thing's to do,'
which, says Mr Wright, 'is for the theory of this essay
priceless,' he lays, as might have been expected, an incom-
mensurate emphasis. Above I have explained it as an
artifice employed in an improbable plot. In this last
soliloquy, as in that at the end of Act II, the main course
and tenor of Hamlet's thought is that of remonstrance and
exhortation. Neither here nor anywhere else, whether by
Hamlet himself or by Horatio, is it suspected that there
is any mystery about him or within him; and for the others
there is any only as regards his madness. It is quite contrary to the spirit of Shakespeare's popular technique that
there should be a mystery intended and yet no more be
made of it, so dark a mystery, above all, as this. But

[30] See my *Hamlet,* chapter iii.

making much of the priceless 'four words' *I do not know,*
by the same mincing, finicking methods with which much
has been made of Hamlet's reference to

> The undiscovered country from whose bourn
> No traveller returns,

Mr Wright discovers behind them the inscrutable mystery
of the living soul.   These are the dark and cryptic ways
of psychological exegesis; but Shakespeare, playwright for
the Globe, seems only to be availing himself of the familiar
fact that the most practical person in the world may some
time or other say, 'I don't know why I haven't done that,'
and no more.

How different is the method of Meredith with Diana
when she betrays her lover's secret, to which Mr Wright
turns for comparison.   Here is mystery in human character
but not in the art whereby it is presented.   Here is inconsistency intended by the writer rather than by him not to
be avoided—brought to light, not obscured—and what,
more deeply considered, is, in the circumstances, not an
inconsistency after all.   That is, when we allow for the
undercurrent—a counter-current, for the most part—of the
instinctive and subconscious, in a 'swoon of the mind'; and
because the author allows for that himself.   He has prepared for her conduct by her marrying Warwick—'voluntarily, quite inexplicably.   Voluntarily as we say.   But there
must be a spell upon us at times.   Upon young women there
certainly is.'   And yet we are made to see clearly how
both the earlier and the later spell descend.   'Unwelcome
attentions' prompt her in the first case; in the second case
the explanation is ample.   Her reason is for the time suspended under the sway of her financial distress, her sense
of being down and out, with nothing but stale news (upon
which Tonans has just taunted her), and her sense of
degradation and loss of sovereignty at Dacier's having
dared to embrace her.   Now she has news that is news:

now her fortunes and her sense of self-respect and importance may be restored together. And throughout this
scene she 'went like a bullet; she was mad.' For instinct
knows no delay, undergoes at the time no scrutiny. She
acts like a criminal, as you shall find him in Dostoevsky or
Tolstoi, a prey to impulse as she is. And at the end she
sinks asleep without a dream, and has no twinge of
remorse next morning. To her treason she awakes only
when Dacier brings it home to her. Now whether in his
making the inconsistency consistent—that is, in keeping
Diana the same woman through her changes—Meredith
has or has not been successful, that at least has been his
deliberate intention, and he and Shakespeare here are little
alike. The one has the ample expository latitude of the
novel, to be sure, the other only the narrow limits of the
drama; but of similarity whether in purpose or in method
there is no trace. In Hamlet the mystery is not solved—
is apparently not even envisaged.

Above I have explained this drawing of the veil as an
artifice of construction. It is not to hide a psychical mystery
or problem but to mask the great improbability of the plot,
which is the price of the precious contrast the poet has
secured. As I have repeatedly shown, a critic has no right
to explain so much by character, and a comparison with
other plays proves it. Even in this chapter we have seen
how character has as an image of reality been manipulated
for dramatic purposes, particularly in Macbeth. Mr
Bridges rightly points out the 'veiled confusion of motive':

Judging from the text, [Shakespeare] does not wish us to be
clearly determined as to whether Macbeth's ambition had preconceived and decided on the murder of Duncan; or whether the idea
was chiefly imposed upon him by a supernatural devilry; or whether
he was mainly urged to it by his wife, and was infected and led by
her.

Definiteness and explicitness, which the dramatist generally

desires, is as Mr Bridges shows, avoided because it would
blur the picture of nobility impressed on us by Shakespeare
and essential to his drama.   It would break in upon the
contrast sought:

> It would not be untrue to the facts as presented by Shakespeare
> to precede the drama with a scene in which Macbeth and Lady Mac-
> beth should in Machiavellian composure deliberate together upon
> the murder of Duncan; but plainly such a scene would destroy the
> drama.

The drama, the struggle of the noble nature in the toils,
the magnificent effect, is what concerns the poet, not the
psychological reality or entirety. 'This is not nature,'
as Mr Bridges says, 'in the sense of being susceptible of
the same analysis as that by which the assumptions of science
would investigate nature.'   Nor is this the only place in
this play or in others, where Shakespeare for his purposes
takes liberties.   To retain our sympathy for Macbeth—
though this makes no difference as regards the reality, the
fact and the guilt—he lets such a previous Machiavellian
deliberation be not described, indeed, but hinted at; lets
the murder itself be not presented before our eyes, but
imaginatively suggested or reported; and envelops both
hero and heroine with an atmosphere of poetry incompatible
(in a sense) with their conduct.   He in a way glorifies
a pair of traitors and murderers.   He holds our interest
at some cost to truth.   So other artists do, a painter, for
instance, who makes his snow not white but yellow in order
not to lose the effect of the radiation of light.   And so,
before and since, other dramatists have done—Æschylus,
Euripides, and Racine.

So with this 'mystery' in Hamlet, and how can we press
behind it?   In him and in Iago too it is a result of manipulation and adjustment, both to secure the striking dramatic
effects of situation and also to preserve the plausibility of
the character.   Both mention various reasons for their

conduct—Hamlet seeks them, Iago makes them up—but none of them applies. As I have shown elsewhere,[31] Shakespeare handles gingerly in *Hamlet,* as well he might, the queer old plot. He drops out the motives for feigning madness—and there for the critics is another mystery —because they will not do. A poor explanation only creates a need for explanation. To save the story, he lets the hero heap upon himself reproaches for his inaction; to save the character, he contradicts the effect of these by his own words, those of others, and the whole impression of his conduct. And by nearly all the changes he introduces into the Second Quarto and the Folio, he omits or tones down such details as might call attention to his inaction or detract from the effect of his manliness. He adds a touch here, or removes one there, much as a painter or sculptor—not by the reason but the promptings of genius—brings his work to completion: and all this in order to produce a certain effect for the whole, not to pen a document; in order to conform the image he is tracing to one in his mind's eye, not to reproduce any object that is or might be in nature.

13.

The decisive thing, it seems to me, is that if the inner inconsistency or self-deception were by the poet intended and expressed—and if the inconsistency be not intended and expressed, it is of course not in the character but only in the poet's method—it must needs be by a different technique. No one thinks Hamlet a hypocrite, but since there are no other parallels (save the sentimental Richard whom we consider below) the hypocrites must in so far as they are self-deceivers serve for such; yet Angelo, Richard,

[31] See my *Hamlet,* especially chapters ii and iii. At this time (1919), I had not read Mr Bridges' essay; and the similarity of his impression to mine of Shakespeare's methods and purposes in *Othello* and *Macbeth* gives me greater confidence in mine in regard both to these plays and to *Hamlet.*— For Iago's pretexts, see chapter vii, section 14.

and Iago, hypocrites all, deceive not themselves but other
people, and so unctuous and egregious are they in their
demeanour that by La Bruyère and Marivaux they would
have been treated more disdainfully than was even Tartuffe.
Morals count here for less than psychology, and a dramatist
who attributes no self-deception to hypocrites on the stage
is not likely to be found attributing it to them that are none.

In fact, the hypocrite who deceives himself unconsciously
makes his appearance in the drama—in the novel he
appears a trifle earlier—not, so far as I know, before the
days of Becque, in *Les Corbeaux* (1882) and *La Parisienne*
(1885). Here, at last, as a writer in the *Quarterly
Review*[32] observes, 'are hypocrites wholly concealed from
themselves.' And what is the method with these? There
are soliloquies, but not for the purpose of self-revelation;
and the thing is done by the familiar dramatic devices
of contrast and repetition, and by other means of emphasis,
guided a little or given point by the comment of others.
There is the contrast between the words of the speaker
and his conduct, or between his criticism of the conduct of
others and similar conduct of his own. The situations at
the same time are so contrived and arranged that the
fairly clever audience shall be in no doubt concerning the
hero's motives, whether through the comment of others or
in themselves. Hialmar Ekdal, the sentimentalist, in
Ibsen's *Wild Duck* (1884), is treated somewhat similarly,
but more obviously, with such repeated comment—not by
the self-deceiver himself (save with his proper bias) but
by Relling and others—as no audience could possibly
mistake.

Now of all this there is next to nothing in *Hamlet,*
though the critics have proceeded as if there were. The
contrasts or parallels with the Player and Fortinbras are
drawn by the hero himself, for the purpose of exhortation
and amendment, and that effect they should have alone.

[32] April, 1922, p. 337, Mr Garnet Smith.

With Laërtes he draws only a sympathetic parallel—'by the image of my cause I see the portraiture of his'; and, as I have pointed out elsewhere,[33] he should in the comparison not be made to suffer. The contrast that may be drawn by others, moreover, is moral rather than psychological; and how much better it is to revenge like Hamlet, any spectator must think, however tardily! But this is neither here nor there. The contrasts supposed to betray Hamlet in his besetting sin are not telling enough to do that—are neither sharp enough nor sufficiently repeated or otherwise emphasized to affect an audience now, still less an audience then. Contrast is the grand dramatic device and resource, but like the blockade in war it must be effective.[34] At the end of *Les Corbeaux* old Teissier, who has fleeced the Vignerons and brought them to such a pass that to save the others from starvation the daughter of the house consents to marry him, turns, once he has her word, and frightens away another harpy who is seeking to prey upon them, or what is left of them. A thief to catch a thief, or drive others away, now that he is in the family! But he himself does not take it so. The play ends with his naïvely compassionate words:

Vous êtes entourées de fripons, mon enfant, depuis la mort de votre père.

And the whole effect is secured (without other comment

---

[33] See my *Hamlet*, p. 38, especially the note.

[34] Shakespeare's contrasts are particularly bold and striking, but some that have been discovered in his text would have been ineffective, unnoticed, on any stage. Of those in *Hamlet* I speak below; others for instance are: that, in respect to jealousy, among Othello, Iago and Bianca; and that, in respect to sentimentality, between the Duke and Sir Toby. Iago, indeed, says that he is sexually jealous, but he does not act like a jealous man (see below p. 387), and his ambitious jealousy (though by an accident of language the name is the same) is a totally different feeling. And though of the same general class, Bianca's petty and venal affection can nowise put us in mind of Othello's passion. As for the Duke and Sir Toby—that is another contrast that occurs to one only in the study. On these points I am constrained to differ with the great scholar M. Feuillerat (Introduction to *Merchant of Venice*, p. 35).

from the self-deceived than of such indirect and inadvertent sort) by the cunning juxtaposition of situations, by the unconscious aptness of a remark, by the speciousness or transparency of a motive, in short, as I have said, by ironic contrast and repetition.

14.

By Mr Wright, however, and by others before and after him it is supposed that effects somewhat similar are to be found in *Hamlet*. The hero receives the command of the paternal ghost but feigns madness; he upbraids himself for failure to act but resolves upon a play; he undertakes the play, but next appears soliloquizing on suicide and saying not a word of play, ghost, or revenge; he gives the play at last, but after it, though now convinced, spares the king at prayer and 'goes softly to his mother';[35] and thereupon he upbraids and exhorts himself in soliloquy once more, but embarks for England. Yet it is merely as we edit and gloss the dramatic text, or, so to speak, rewrite the score, that any such effect of contrast can be attained. Here is no sharpness, no speciousness, no bleak ironic light, nor the repetition that we think to find. For the Elizabethans, as I have shown,[36] familiar with the old story, the old melodrama which Shakespeare was rewriting, and with popular Senecan tragedy on their stage, these motives and conduct, so queer to us, were natural enough, in those uncritical days. Hamlet doubts the ghost hon-

[35] Mr Wright, *op. cit.*

[36] In the monograph cited, especially chapter iv, is to be found the evidence for this statement and the following ones.—If Shakespeare had meant to convey the impression that his own revenge play was essentially different from the others, and the hero evading his duty and deceiving himself, he would, of necessity, have had recourse to comment by some one like Horatio, as I suggest below, section 15. Hamlet's own reproaches are not sufficient; Kyd's Hieronimo reproaches himself too. Imagine a playwright to-day rewriting a stage-play of ten or twenty years before, like other plays still on the stage or alive in men's memories, and undertaking to give his own play a very different turn and his hero a 'complex,' without being more explicit with his audience.

estly and legitimately, because according to the received
opinion of the day he may be the devil; he undertakes
madness as a revenger's artifice and the play as another,
both of these being in the drama then not uncommon; and
he spares the king at prayer because when he kills him it
must be according to the strict principle of the vendetta,
an eye for an eye, a soul for a soul. And exigencies of
plot as well as of common sense require that he shall not
speak of the play in hand or of revenge to follow when
two men—one of them his enemy—are behind the arras
eaves-dropping—for by the laws of the Elizabethan stage
they would overhear even the soliloquy—and shall apparently acquiesce in going to England in order to beat the
king at his own game. Not to go to England, as not to
feign madness, would have been quite to change the popular
old story, and also to rob it of that spirit—characteristic
of revenge plays, and (save to the critics' eyes) prominent
in *Hamlet*—of crafty and cunning intrigue almost for its
own sake:

> They [Rosencrantz and Guildenstern] must sweep my way
> And marshal me to knavery. Let it work;
> For 'tis the sport to have the enginer
> Hoist with his own petar; and 't shall go hard
> But I will delve a yard below their mines,
> And blow them at the moon. O 'tis most sweet
> When in one line two crafts directly meet!

All this craft, however, has been turned into a pretence,
as is his strength into weakness, and the play itself from a
conflict of persons (which every Elizabethan play is) to 'a
conflict within the mind of Hamlet', and every detail of
the story into a revelation of his soul.[37] All is turned
inward, illegitimately to satisfy our own spiritual cravings.
These seeming contrasts, picked out by the commentators,
lie embedded in the story, and are so softened down not
only by motivation (as we have seen) but also by prepa-

[37] See my article, 'Recent Criticism of *Hamlet*,' p. 351.

ration (as we shall now see) that they are no contrasts at all. The hero spares the king because he must be struck down like his own father, with all his imperfections on his head, as the ghost has taken the pains to reveal; he goes to his mother because he has been called, has promised to go, and indeed was on his way already; and a trip to England must be his lot because the king has twice designated it, and Hamlet, even before he has been actually informed of it, has, in speaking to his mother, taken it for granted as settled.

Now on the stage, even more than in life, pretences and excuses should appear to be lugged in or snatched at, and evasions should look like evasions, as indeed for two centuries Hamlet's (if such they be) did not. And what of the repetition, which should enforce them? If he spares the king at prayer, vowing, 'This physic but prolongs thy sickly days,' at the next chance, in the next scene, to kill a man whom he thinks the king, and now indeed about some act that hath no relish of salvation in it, Hamlet keeps his word by killing him; and to an audience not otherwise instructed no other impression can be given than that. Indeed, what other impression could be given when, after going off to England, with 'bloody' thoughts, of 'hoisting with their own petar,' [38] he is next heard of as sending Rosencrantz and Guildenstern to their deaths, boarding the pirate, and, with but a brief 'interim' before him till the news shall be out, recklessly returning? Such conduct

---

[38] 'Thoughts,' he says, not deeds,—'my thoughts be bloody or be nothing worth;' but it is, again, a niggling criticism that makes anything of that, and unbefitting a stage-play. The emphasis is on blood, on revenge. Yet the criticism can be answered on its own ground, and the contrast is in Hamlet's favour; he is better than his word. See here my *Hamlet*, pp. 38-40; particularly Professor Lewis's suggestion that the last soliloquy, the words, quoted above, about hoisting with the petar and craft meeting craft, and the incident of the pirate capture in which Hamlet takes his fate into his own hands and cuts loose from his companions instead of being without a reason set by his companions ashore (all lacking in Quarto 1) have been inserted by the dramatist into Quarto 2 to give Hamlet's inaction the most favourable colour—to protect him against the eventual misconception!

is not nerveless, such promises not idle. Here are the only opportunities for contrast between promise and fulfilment, and contrast there is none. There is repeated emphasis instead, to impress us, not with weakness of character, but strength. These effects, however, have for us been blunted or obscured by various subtle interpretations, as if only on the spur of the moment could Hamlet kill his man, not eye to eye, not face to face. The arras is become a symbol, as if in Yeats or Maeterlinck. But, without more of a clue to guide them, all that an audience, then or now, could have made out of that would be that he was a coward. He that is anything of a man, according to the rough-and-ready logic of the theatre (as of the world) can face his foe.

15.

The technique of Becque, which we have been discussing, involves, almost necessarily, an ironic, well-nigh satiric or comic treatment, like the contrasts between the big pretence and little performance of the coward or miser, considered in following chapters; and the nearest approach to them in Shakespeare's serious drama is in *Richard II*. Richard himself in fact is the nearest (but, as we have seen, not a complete) approach to what the critics conceive Hamlet to be—morbid, vacillating, impotently reflective and emotional, and but dimly aware of this. His resolutions collapse before the task, his emotions fluctuate from despair to exultation and from exultation to despair. When he sets foot on his native soil he luxuriates in affection for his country, and in the thought of being a king and having Heaven and the angels on his side. But hearing Salisbury say his soldiers are dispersed, he at once gives up. 'Comfort, my liege,' says Aumerle, 'remember who you are.' 'I had forgot myself, am I not King?' he answers like an echo; 'awake, thou coward majesty! thou sleepest.' But in a trice he droops again, and presently he is for their all sitting down on the ground together and telling sad stories of the death of kings, which he himself then does.   And the same facile and shallow emotions, widely, impotently fluctuating, reappear, both in this scene and in the following ones.   This is a much clearer and more evident contrast than any provided by the intentions and conduct of Hamlet, but that even this the audience may not fail to perceive there is the explicit comment or counsel of Aumerle and Carlisle; and, besides, continually repeated, there is the clear contrast, of which Richard himself is not conscious, between him and Bolingbroke.   Thus in these early scenes is produced an effect unheroic and mainly alienating to the sympathy of the audience; and that it does not become so entirely, and comic as well, is owing not only to the immediate tragic consequences but to the dramatist's speedily hedging—his relinquishing this technique, and his remembering both the pitifulness of a king brought so low and the ruthlessness of his rival who has brought him there.   But in *Hamlet* only through the spectacles of the critics can be discerned anything approaching such an ironic effect; and a satiric or comic they would have abhorred.   Yet if a contrast betraying an inherent weakness, such as they presume, had been produced upon the stage, this last effect, I think, would, upon that sturdy audience have been the almost inevitable result.   Hamlet is not a king of England and not a victim; there is lacking in this situation some elements that would, in the audience, have changed contempt for his impotence to pity.   But even the merely ironic effect would not only have run counter to the whole spirit of the play (in which Hamlet is uniformly treated with respect and admiration, and his acts are great and heroical) but have made impossible the long popular success of it.   The very accent and manner of Richard, moreover, betray him; his heroic words, quoted above, ring false and hollow.   Hamlet's, if any man's, do not:

I'll tent him to the quick; if he but blench
I know my course.

It will be short; the interim is mine.

And they prove sound and true in the sequel; in the case
of the former speech only a further consideration, of a
more perfect vengeance, not mere 'hire and salary', delays
the fulfilment.

A technique of ironic contrast, moreover, accompanied
with only favourable comment and quite out of harmony
with it, would have sadly baffled the wits and troubled the
sympathies of an ordinary audience in Shakespeare's or in
any day. And it would have been without reason, and
altogether unlike Shakespeare elsewhere. The comment of
others is one of Shakespeare's chief means of characterization, employed in every play, and also in this, as regards
not only Hamlet but the other characters, both King and
Queen, Polonius and Laërtes, Ophelia and Horatio, Rosencrantz and Guildenstern. Horatio could have commented
critically, in the fulness of knowledge; and others, who
were not in the secret and had not the key to Hamlet's
character, could at least have made such unanalytic but
appropriate judgments—to guide, or at any rate not mis-
lead, the audience—as are to be found in the words
of the Bishop of Carlisle to Richard:

My lord, wise men ne'er sit and wail their woes.

But here, where (if the critics be right) for two centuries—
until arose Morgann and Mackenzie and the Romantics—
the audience sorely needed leading, there was no help at all.
There was misleading, instead. To no one in the play is
Hamlet known to have a defect; and no one ventures to
speak of him or to him either slightingly or critically. Why
does not the king, Laërtes, or Fortinbras, who at the end
declares he would have been a kingly king, despise him for a
scholar and dreamer at least—for a college man—instead
of speaking, indeed, quite to the contrary, and taking him

as they all do for the worthy son of his warrior sire?
Elsewhere Shakespeare has not thought it beneath his
dignity to furnish comment on the tragic fault, if there
be one, or on the self-deception. He is far less restricted
in his appeal, less exacting in his demands upon the attention and understanding, more popular, in short, than Ibsen.
But with what elaborate repetition and variation of situation, with what cunning contrast between character and
character or between character and circumstance, and with
what plenitude of comment, Ibsen presents to us the self-
righteous self-deception of Helmer in the *Doll's House,* the
sentimental self-deception of Hialmar in the *Wild Duck*
and the hedging and dodging of *Peer Gynt!* In the *Doll's
House* comment is provided through Nora; in the *Wild
Duck* through Relling and the comically—pathetically—
mistaken Gina, Gregers, and Hedvig; in *Peer Gynt,* not
only by the hero himself but by the Dovre King, the Lean
One, and the Button-Moulder. Thus upon the self-deception in the two plays and the 'going roundabout' in the
other many rays of light converge; but in *Hamlet* it is
otherwise,—*Hamlet* which has held the stage for three
centuries, and which, if there be real self-deception in it,
was a prodigious innovation in its day.[39] And this cannot be,
as we have seen, because Shakespeare's art is more reticent.
In his work everything comes to light or is given a voice,—
motives, all the vague stirrings and impulses of the soul,
and the sympathetic throes of dumb nature itself. 'Genug,
das Geheimnis muss heraus,' as Goethe said, 'und sollten
es die Steine verkünden.' That is, if there be one.

16.

The big and serious inconsistencies in Shakespeare, then,
arise mainly, as we have seen, out of the improbable but

[39] See further discussion and evidence in my *Hamlet,* as pp. 24 and 60.
Cf. especially the case of Wallenstein, who doubts, hesitates, and pro-
crastinates, but not escaping the enlightened comment of four other characters in the play.

striking old plot he employed, or out of the simplified treatment of such a plot and the contrasts which he sought deliberately, or out of inadvertence or hastiness in workmanship. But that does not mean that Shakespeare had not a wide and liberal view of the range and Protean changes of human nature—the widest. If he had no apparent knowledge of the dark and furtive flights and evasions of the human spirit which modern psychology has discovered and modern fiction disclosed, he knew enough not to keep her strictly fettered to a rôle. He was not troubled by—does not trouble us with—psychology, but in tone and opinion no other poet's creatures change colour so freely while remaining the same. His characters are not always serious or humorous, not always stately or simple, not even always fixed at the same point of view, and neither rules of *decorum* nor principles of logic are there to limit them. His characters are the sons of nature—'we are the sons of women, Justice Shallow,' said Falstaff; while those of Corneille and Racine belong to court or camp, if not rather indeed to the stage. The human heart contains four chambers, not one; the human brain is folded into a thousand wrinkles and convolutions; and Shakespeare gives us something of the variety of life itself. To him man is not a fiddle with one string, as he often is in French tragedy or comedy, but a harp provided with many; and he fingers and sweeps them all. What a gamut is run in *Hamlet* alone—love and tenderness, grief and melancholy, hate, scorn, rage, despair, humour and irony, scepticism and awe. Faulconbridge—even Cloten—rises to a pitch of dignity, when as an Englishman he faces the foreigner; Shylock, when he defends his race; Coriolanus, the oaken-garlanded hero, flushed with victory, must—as in life he some time or other would—go wash. Lady Macbeth, at the supreme moment when Macbeth comes before her, his hands stained at her bidding with the blood of their guest and King, speaks the language of barest commonplace but tensest passion, 'My husband!' nothing more. Again contrast counts: he is her husband still, nay—through the blood—as he had never been. Macduff breaks silence with a Humph! when he hears of his wife and children's murder. Lear, the great King, in the throes of heart-break, groans, 'Pray undo this button,' which is the humblest of prayers or services. Queen Cleopatra, having already chosen death as the better part, does not even then forget her cunning, but endeavours like a sharper to cheat Cæsar out of her jewels and treasure. And though Schlegel (*in vieler Hinsicht kein Mann*) was, for all his learning and insight, not the one to appreciate how Emilia, speaking lightly and loosely of the marriage tie, could yet to her mistress be staunchly true, it is not among the least of Shakespeare's glories that the like cannot be said of him. And though of late Professor Schücking has found the aria on Queen Mab to be out of keeping on the smutty lips of Mercutio, Shakespeare, Aristophanes, the poets of the Restoration—Titania herself—well knew that the lyric gift and a faery fancy are not incompatible with a sort of gay and gleeful indecency, and would have detected the fantastic vein running all through him. But this liberty of his characters to unbend and disport themselves, to step down from poetry to prose, and from seriousness to humour, or from the humdrum to rise to the heights, is nothing to their liberty to be both one and the other at the same moment. Human emotion is a complex, a multiple mixture, and in French tragedy the serious element is abstracted—extracted one might say—and alone presented. But Hamlet jeers and gibes when his heart is breaking; Mercutio dies scolding but jesting still; Othello smiles as he faces the bright swords and with words that would have blunted them defends himself in court; and Juliet, finding the poisoned cup in her dead lover's hand, speaks to him, when at the moment perchance of rejoining him, with a pitiful flicker of the gaiety that she had shown while

they had been together: 'O churl!' she murmurs—'bad
boy!'—

> O churl! drunk all, and left no friendly drop
> To help me after.

Death is a word lovers are slow to learn, and even now
she is speaking to Romeo, not of him. And Cleopatra
on her deathbed is still the amorous intriguing, wrangling
Queen, jealous of Iras who may meet Antony first—for
without kissing what would Heaven be?—but tickled at the
thought of outwitting by her death great Cæsar, 'ass unpoli-
cied!' [40]

[40] I agree with Mr Herford (*op. cit.*, pp. 49-50) in his criticism of Professor Schücking as he finds Cleopatra a heartless coquette and courtesan in
the first half of the play, only a devoted lover and noble queen in the second;
though I would not go so far as to call him and others like him rather
wooden-minded. As it seems to me Mr Herford is quite right in finding
her even now, as through her sorrow for the loss of Antony and fear of
being led in triumph she rises above herself, Cleopatra still. But the essential unifying element in the character is, I think, overlooked by both critics.
It is, as I have pointed out in section 8 above, rather in the speech, the
identity of tone, than in the deeper psychological structure or the mental
attitude. It would take many words for me to show this—there are so many
facets to her glittering figure—if indeed I could show it at all. There are
glimpses of her humour, for instance, not only in her death scene but at
Antony's death. And her spontaneous explosiveness appears when she calls
Dolabella a liar and vents her rage on Seleucus, as when she called Antony
one, raved against the Messenger, and threatened Charmian with bloody
teeth. She is not wholly sublime and ideal as Professor Schücking takes
her now to be. She abuses the gods and rails at Fortune when Antony
dies, as she has always done at whatever thwarted her. She remembers
Octavia continually and vindictively, with her modest eyes and her dulness.
But above all she keeps her vivacious manner when excited. 'Note him,'
she had said in the first Act to Charmian; 'Note him, good Charmian, 'tis
the man; but note him.' Again and again this dancing repetition recurs,
as after Antony's death:—

> What, what! good cheer! Why how now, Charmian,
> My noble girls! Ah women, women, look,
> Our lamp is spent.

> He words me, girls, he words me, that I should not
> Be noble to myself.

And how from beginning to end, through all her fits and starts she keeps
her languorous, voluptuous manner—

> Give me some music, music, moody food
> Of us that trade in love—

I need not undertake to show. (See above, chapter i, section 11.)

That is Shakespeare's vein and not another's. His mind was creative and accretive, we have seen, not critical; synthetic, not analytic; and it comprehended human passion in all its mysterious amplitude. No one ever depicted it so truly, even in its changes and phases, as it waxes or wanes, or starts and quivers like a living thing. Hamlet, Othello, Mercutio, Juliet, however different, are always indubitably before us. But it was the passion as a whole that he presented; he laid nothing bare. It was the result of the change that interested him, not the internal mechanism, not the cause or motive which produced it. His touch seldom failed him, though his reasoning sometimes did. He made few discoveries or disclosures; there is little in his characters that is surprising and at the same time (as we must instantly realize) indisputably true. What is surprising is generally not true, or, else, like Cleopatra's cheating (taken from the source), left unexplained; and he has no characters like Diana of the Crossways, Manon Lescaut, Monna Vanna, Carmen, Stendhal's Duchess of Sanseverina, Dostoevsky's Liza or Stavrogin, and some of the characters of Browning. The good man Ivan, after he slew the woman, was found unconcernedly playing with the children, by the village elders who had sat in judgment on him. In all Shakespeare, I think, there is nothing like that. We have seen above that he had little casuistry in him, and dealt not in deep moral incongruities or paradoxes, in contentions or entanglements, keeping to the plain high road of life, as Coleridge said. An artist may be much interested in such things as questions and problems, and yet keep to the high road himself; but to be a discoverer he must in imagination venture to leave it, shift his mental and moral latitude or longitude, and go boldly out into the bush. There people live their own lives, and hold by their own values, not only for themselves, but for others, as they do not, we have seen, in Shakespeare. But though he knew not their lives and opinions, he had heard and caught the accents of their voices, and had powers within him to reproduce them, as has done no one before him or since.[41]

[41] The theory, touched upon above, pp. 104-5, that Hamlet is not a pathological case, though suffering from melancholy, has, as it appeared in my monograph (1919), been attacked by Miss O'Sullivan, *Mod. Lang. Pub.* (September, 1926). She points out the fact that in T. Bright's *Treatise* (1586) an indisposition to action is a symptom in certain extreme forms of the disease. But drama, of course, then as now, and above all purely popular drama like *Hamlet,* was not a document, a vehicle for learning; and so important a matter, upon which the whole play would then depend, would according to the principles discussed above, or any principles of artistic construction, demand comment. Not only does drama deal with the familiar, but when a point is important dwells upon it. A symptom not generally recognized (since it does not appear in the other treatises) would not have been familiar even to the learned. And how strange a dramatic method, for Hamlet to wonder whether the sight of the ghost was not owing to his melancholy, but when it comes to his procrastination to say he 'does not know;' and for others—Horatio at least, who is in the secret—not only not to speak up and explain but fail to notice the indisposition to action at all! To Miss O'Sullivan it seems to be enough simply that Shakespeare should have read the Treatise—then the play is explained. To me it would not be enough if she could prove that everybody in the audience had read it too. How could they be counted on to note this particular symptom, and recognize in Hamlet this particular variety of the disease? But that even Shakespeare had read it is not made probable: the evidence is only a few words and phrases current in that day.

CHAPTER IV

THE COMIC METHOD

WHEN an Anglo-Saxon, brought up under the shadow of Shakespeare, first comes to know Molière, he at once enters a different world. As different, one might be inclined to say, as are seventeenth-century London and seventeenth-century Paris, only there is not much of the actual London or England, either, in the one, or of Paris or France in the other. The main difference lies in the personalities of the two dramatists, both in themselves and as representatives of two great peoples, and as regards temperament, taste, and art. The subject as a whole is here (if not indeed anywhere) beyond me: I shall touch only on the difference in comic art, and what I shall dwell upon is the matter of comic repetition and variation.

This last is a bit of technique rare in Shakespeare, and in English comedy generally except Jonson and Fletcher, though abundant in Molière and French comedy before him and since. By comic repetition and variation I mean such artistic processes as resemble those in music, a theme or *motif* repeated with variations—so in a comedy is repeated and varied a *motif,* a situation or device. The situation may, as in *George Dandin,* be repeated from act to act, throughout the play, the hero catching his wife in misconduct and calling upon his wife's parents to come and witness it, while his wife gives him the slip and leaves to him the apologizing, three times over.[1] Or it may be confined to a single scene, as when

[1] Cf. Bergson, *Le Rire* (1913), to which I am in this chapter much indebted.

147

Don Juan fobs off his creditor, Monsieur Dimanche, keeping him by solicitous inquiries for his health and welfare from coming to the point. I do not mean, however, another sort of repetition, also comic in effect, much commoner in Shakespeare and rarer in Molière. This has to do mainly with character and with mental processes, whether it be a particular favourite word or phrase to which the person is addicted, like Nym's 'And that's the humour of it,' or the trait and trick of repetition in general, highly significant in people so different as Falstaff, Shallow, or Mrs Quickly. Or if it have to do mainly with situation, it is, unlike the devices of Molière described above, simply the same phrase repeated after considerable intervals to mark and punctuate stages in the story. Of such *mots de situation* Ibsen in recent times made very cunning use—witness the word 'triangle' and the phrase 'one cock in the basket' in *Hedda Gabler*—and the device was imitated and worked to death by English and American dramatists after him. What is most like it in Shakespeare and the Elizabethans, as well as Molière, is the ancient trick of twitting, older than drama itself, as when the tables are turned on Shylock in the judgment scene, or when on Malvolio the whirligig of time brings in his revenges. But these do not here concern us; the particular quality of that art of repetition in Molière and his predecessors and successors which we are undertaking to discuss is its approximation to the condition of music, the working out of a *motif* or theme rhythmically. That quality in these *mots de caractère* or *de situation* is generally lacking; though in Ibsen's hands the particular *mots de situation* of which we have spoken, being used seriously, not comically, and having to do with character and central idea as well, approach, as in some scenes between Hilda and Solness in the *Master-Builder,* the antiphonal or amebean. That is in tragedy, however, and the art of repetition is, though seldom, exquisitely employed in tragedy by Shakespeare. But of French comedy, as we shall see, it is a special characteristic, both in Molière's time and before and after, and not at all of the English or Teutonic.

I.

In Molière this repetition with variations takes many forms; and not a play, not an act, and often not a scene, is without it. The whole structure of the play, I have said, may involve it, as not only in *George Dandin* but in the *École des femmes* and the *École des maris*. Yet in the play the rhythmical, dancing quality of the movement is not so perceptible as in the scene. The phrases (to use the word in its musical sense) are too long for that, their recurrence is at too great intervals: in the scene or series of scenes it is another matter. Something of the same situation and method as in the scene between Don Juan and his creditor is found again in that between Sganarelle and his rival, where the latter's repeated compliments and courtesies stave off the message the former would convey;[2] and with the situation slightly different, the method is employed again and again, as when Doctor Pancrace, professionally incensed, babbles on and will not vouchsafe Sganarelle a hearing, in the *Mariage forcé* (sc. iv), and when Arnolphe, abstracted, not to say distracted, is deaf to the notary, in the *École des femmes* (IV, ii).[3] Another method is that of the catalogue or inventory, with comments, as when the valet (or the master himself) runs down the list of the master's debts or his loves, or the lover that of his mistress' points or of his grievances against her, to the accompaniment of the comments of his valet, as does Cléonte in the *Bourgeois gen-*

---

[2] *École des maris,* II, ii. The device holds the stage at least down to Musset's *Chandelier.*

[3] Cf. the last scene of *Le Sicilien*, where Le Sénateur will not listen to Don Pèdre and talks only of the dance; and Regnard's *Légataire Universel*, II, xi, where Clistorel, in his tiff with Géronte for contemplating so unsalutary a measure as marriage at his age, won't listen to his explanation that he has already given the project up.

tilhomme with Covielle.[4]   Still another is that whereby the
character, in a self-absorption and with a *raideur* beyond
that of Pancrace and Arnolphe, hearing indeed the words
but not heeding their purport, plants himself in his obstinacy
or shuts his eyes in his infatuation; as when Sganarelle [5]
pities and embraces his deceitful and successful rival, or
Bélise, in the *Femmes savantes*,[6] persists in her notion that
Clitandre is in love with her and but feigns to be in love with
others.   But this method is more varied in movement and
richer in effect when the chief character says or does the
same thing over and over, his eyes set in his head as it were,
his utterance reduced to the laconic squeak of a mechanical
toy, and his action to that of the jack-in-the-box (with which
M. Bergson compares him) while the variations are kept
for the lips of others.   Here is the effect of simplification
and of a heightened contrast.   Orgon, as he attends to the
long tale of his wife's illness, three times interrupts Dorine
with inquiries concerning the health of Tartuffe instead,
ejaculating after each reply, satisfactory as heart could
wish, 'le pauvre homme'; Harpagon, asking Valère to judge
whether he is not right in accepting as a husband for his
daughter the old man Anselme, who will forego a dowry,
has, to all the various considerations diplomatically urged
upon him, no answer still but 'sans dot'; and Géronte, when
he hears from Scapin that his son is held in a Turkish
galley for a ransom of five hundred crowns, responds to
Scapin's importunities and the horrors he paints of a
Turkish slavery, one moment with the shriek, 'What, five
hundred crowns!' and the next with the wail, 'But what
was he doing then in that galley?'   Or there may be no
verbal repetition at all, but, with equal effect, the mere trait
of avarice, or amorousness, or cowardice, or what not, constantly reappearing in various forms and at various junc-

[4] Regnard's *Joueur; Bourgeois gentilhomme*, III, ix.
[5] *École des maris*, II, ix.
[6] I, iv; II, iii.

tures, whether in the scene or in the play as a whole. To this technique Molière's method of portraying one predominant vice or folly in a character lends itself quite admirably. But even when the principal character is not so concerned, and no particular vice or folly is in question, this method of repetition and variation—in the score, so to speak, if not in the text—is apparent in scene after scene: as when Maître Jacques again and again stumbles and recovers himself in accusing Valère of having stolen the casket;[7] or when Éraste palms himself off on the simple soul, M. de Pourceaugnac, as an old acquaintance whom he had forgotten, and proffers, with mingled gingerliness and audacity, the fitting (but unfitting) inquiries with respect to his various relatives and their well-being (I, iv); or when, as in the *Bourgeois gentilhomme,* the lover and his valet quarrel, the one with his mistress and the other with her maid, the two men at first playing indifferent while the women plead with them, and then the women playing indifferent in turn. This last goes like a quadrille or minuet. In the whole play, indeed, as Monsieur Donnay notices (and of others of Molière's it might be said as well), there is the movement of music or the dance; and concerning this particular scene he adds:

Les quatre personnages semblent véritablement danser le pas de la brouille et du raccommodement. Leurs répliques sont croisées, mêlées, alternées de façon à former des figures symétriques.—*Molière,* p. 317.

2.

Now 'all art,' says Pater, 'constantly aspires towards the condition of music. For while in all other works of art it is possible to distinguish the matter from the form, and the understanding can always make this distinction, yet it is the

[7] *L'Avare,* V, ii.—The quantity of repeated *motifs,* not only in the comedies cited but in every other of Molière and most of his successors, is never so fully appreciated as when one sees them on the stage. Often there is *même jeu* without the stage direction.

constant effort of art to obliterate it.' To defend that thesis
would carry us too far afield; yet not in comedy only but in
tragedy—witness the last scene of *Othello*—it seems to
hold good. To comedy, however, the musical method and
movement—repetition and variation—are particularly congenial. Everyone has noticed for himself the fact that a
good story-teller is prone to repeat the last few words of his
story, whether from sheer relish in the repetition or from
artfulness in producing his effects. As Stendhal remarks,
'S'il sait son métier, s'il a l'art charmant de n'être ni obscur
ni trop clair, la moisson de rire est beaucoup plus considér-
able à la seconde répétition qu'à la première.' For comic
effect resides in a momentary shock of incongruity, and as
a single shock upon the spectator is often bewildering, and
of itself may produce rather the effect of surprise or pain
than of the comic or ridiculous, the comic artist takes to
repetition almost instinctively and perforce. If he fail of
his effect at the first attempt he may get it at the second,
for the mere repetition suggests not only the comic intent
but also a comic quality. Mere repetition of an effect suggests that mechanical *raideur* and automatic responsiveness
—as of the puppet or jack-in-the-box—which is of the
essence of comedy. Done once, the thing may seem natural,
and not funny and mechanical at all. Or, if the artist get the
effect at first, he is doubly sure of it in the repetition, just
because of the resemblance, noticed by the spectators, to
that at which they had laughed before. Herbert Spencer's
principle of economy of attention, which Professor
Matthews and Mr Hamilton have applied to the drama,
clearly operates here. It is a pleasure, moreover, to laugh
at the same thing again, not only for those who do not know
why they are laughing but for those who do.

Comedy, furthermore, is to farce as tragedy is to melodrama; and farce, as is well known—whether on a large or
a small scale, whether in a three-act play or in vaudeville—
runs to repetition, inversion, and variation of a *motif,* as

melodrama does not.   It has been truly said that there are
few good farces in English save those borrowed from the
French; though they that say so forget those colossal farces
The Silent Woman and *Bartholomew Fair,* in which such
a technique is employed; and forget Gilbert, whose texts
were not only penned according to a musical technique but
also set to music.   But neither Jonson's art nor Gilbert's
was essentially a native growth.   And comic opera (French
or Italian in origin), where repetition in both score and
text abound, is ordinarily a happier union of the arts than
tragic opera, not merely because it is less in danger of turning out comic without intending to do so but also because
it is ordinarily more harmonious in itself.   I know of no
texts in tragedy that approach the condition of music as do
those of Molière or Regnard in comedy.   And that these
are in verse is not to be wondered at, despite the practice
of the Italians in comedy and the prescription of the Renaissance.   Verse is the halfway house on the road.[8]

Whether this musical method be the final and ultimate
perfection of comedy or not, it is certainly an exquisite
method.   By it form is made to count for much—by it the
utmost possible is made of the content.   Of a particular
situation, such as Éraste's scraping acquaintance with M.
de Pourceaugnac, groping and stumbling and recovering
himself as he pursues his intimate inquiries, every comic

[8] About a third of Molière's comedies are in prose, the latter third, when
he no doubt found time and energy failing. This bent for repetition in
Molière and his predecessors, as in the old farces, demanded verse; and
such was then the predilection for it in comedy that *Don Juan* and *L'Avare,*
in prose, were at first failures. That in the Renaissance prose was pre-
scribed for comedy was owing partly and chiefly to the false notion that
Plautus and Terence employed that medium; partly to the realistic character of comedy and the disposition of the Renaissance to widen the chasm
between it and tragedy. In the same direction, though for different reasons,
modern criticism inclines; and to prose Mr Middleton Murry allots at
least the comedy of manners, because of its intellectual and critical character. But comedy (see the third paragraph below) has its emotion too:
and when in the comedy of manners, as in Molière, this prevails to the
point of taking on the musical forms of repetition and variation, it may
happily, as in Molière, take on the form of verse as well.

aspect is brought to view. Not a flicker of the comic spirit
is suffered to escape us, and there is the effect of perfect
logic and fitness, of economy and a rounded whole. The
matter is not only introduced but something is made of every
bit of it: the theme is not only proposed but developed;
and the rhythm gets under way, is not interrupted, and
comes to a satisfactory and fitting close.

3.

With Shakespeare it is a different story. Save in his
earliest comedies—and even there one finds of it but little—
there is next to no technique of the sort. Form, complete
development count for less with him, matter for almost all.
Economy is not the impression he makes, but that of prodigal abundance and God's plenty. Instead of repetition and
variation he often has riotous accumulation, as in Mercutio's
account of Benvolio's quarrelsomeness or of the pranks of
Queen Mab. 'La plus grande marque de stérilité spiritu-
elle,' says Balzac, 'est l'entassement des faits. La sublime
comédie du Misanthrope prouve que l'art consiste à bâtir
un palais sur la pointe d'une aiguille.' But that is the
judgment of the French, based on one half the truth. Mr
Masefield's remark upon Biondello's description of Petru-
chio's horse, which represents the English judgment, is based
on the other half. 'It has the abundance,' he says, 'of the
great mind'; and his words apply not only to Shakespeare's
descriptions but to those of Rabelais—and Balzac! Seldom
in one of Shakespeare's scenes is there as in Molière's a
single situation worked out to the end, but a cluster of situations; not one character—or rather one trait of a character
—put under every light and viewed from every angle, but
many traits, and many characters. Seldom in one of Shakespeare's plays—never save in the Latin *Comedy of Errors*
—is there but a trio or a pair of situations repeated, still
less a single one. Situation, character, scene, and play as a
whole, in fact, are often more than merely comic. Comedy

in Shakespeare's hands is blent with fantasy, with sentiment
—even with tragedy itself.

For his genius, as we have seen, is synthetic, not analytic,
and his thought concrete, not abstract—both being different
from Jonson's and Molière's. Only two or three of Shakespeare's comedies are comic fairly all through—the others
are fantastic, romantic, or tragic, as well; while Jonson's
and Molière's are comic essentially and entirely, in so far
as great works of dramatic art may be.[9] What is more, this
same mingled web or complex may in Shakespeare be found
in the same scene, situation, or character; while in Molière
scarcely at all. Emotion, Monsieur Bergson [10] avers, is alien
and repugnant to comedy; but though he does not say so he
would surely except that inverted emotion out of which
springs laughter;—and truly, save this, emotion appears
but meagrely in Molière and the chief comic writers of
France, on whose practice his theory reposes. But not so
in Shakespeare, or Sterne, or Lamb. Though in different
ways, Juliet's last words to Romeo,[11] Cleopatra's playful
fancies with the clown and with the baby at her breast, and
Mrs Quickly's report of Falstaff's death, bring tears to our
eyes and smiles to our lips at once and together. And if
Shakespeare's heroines die so, it is because they have lived
and loved so, and even their romantic passion—Juliet's,
Rosalind's and Cleopatra's alike—finds play in wit and
humour. The tragic heroes, too, like Hamlet, must give
vent to their wit and their irony in the midst of their
sufferings—still waters run deep but not so deep as a
fountain; and also into the presence of suffering may
intrude, when in ignorance or innocence, even the merriment
of others—that of the gravediggers in *Hamlet,* the Porter
in *Macbeth,* the Clown in *Antony and Cleopatra.*

[9] As for Molière cf. Sarcey, *Essai d'une Esthétique,* section 5, where he
admits indeed that not all the scenes are comic, but holds that at least they
are in harmony with such an effect.

[10] *Op. cit.,* pp. 6, 142.

[11] See the preceding chapter, p. 144.

4.

In Molière and Jonson, on the other hand, situation and character are wholly comic and are fully worked out as such. They can be neither separated nor even conceived apart. By themselves, the characters would lose their comic quality, for in themselves they have none: in Harpagon the miser or Alceste the misanthrope there is no fun at all. The contrary is the case in Shakespeare. In *Much Ado,* for instance, the comic situations are limited to the Benedick and Beatrice scenes and the Dogberry scenes; and the comic elements in these and the others are owing mainly to the humorous or witty characters, who would be funny anywhere. And how much less is made of the comic possibilities of the misunderstanding between Benedick and Beatrice, or of Orlando's misunderstanding when he and Rosalind play at wooing, than would have been made by Jonson, Molière, or Lope, though the passages are bright with the gaiety and humor welling up from their hearts! In their hands the lovers would a dozen times oftener have been at cross purposes or have skated on the thin ice of discovery; and comic they would have been rather than droll or witty. For in Shakespeare's comedies there is not what there is in Molière's or Jonson's—the all-pervading critical 'comic spirit' and a plot wholly to fit and suit. His characters make fun, breathe fun, seldom are made fun of. He has clowns as Molière or Jonson has none, and even his other comic characters are often products of the same direct comic method,—are humorous, witty, full of mirth rather than the objects or agents of it. In Molière's and Jonson's theatre there is an immense amount of laughter, but most of it is in the audience alone. In Shakespeare's it is also on the stage [12]—the audience laugh in sympathy or by contagion rather than in condescension, censure, or retort. In

[12] Not in the text, of course—see below, the chapter on Falstaff, notes 136, 137.

Molière or Jonson there is no Rosalind or Beatrice, Falstaff or Mercutio, all in fine fettle and at high jinks. Indeed, aside from the happy ending, the chief difference between Shakespeare's best comedy and tragedy is often the mere fact that in the former the characters are more kindly, light-hearted, and humorous, on the one hand, and more fortunate, on the other. Structurally, and in point of content, as Miss Woodbridge has shown, the *Two Gentlemen of Verona,* might, with some changes toward the end, have been a tragedy, *Romeo and Juliet* a comedy. Even as they stand, both alike contain comic scenes and characters and also serious ones, and there is no fundamental difference in the conception and treatment of character or situation save in the shadow of necessity and death thrown over the one play and not the other. But in Jonson or Molière, as in ancient comedy, such changes would have been impossible. The difference between the comedy and the tragedy which they wrote (or would have written) is not, as it is with Shakespeare, one of degree, but of quality, in which the two species are totally opposed.

5.

Of such comic repetition and variation as we have been discussing, the best examples in Shakespeare are in his early work. In *Love's Labour's Lost* there is something of it in the parallel grouping of the three lords and three ladies, the King at the head of the one group, the Princess at the head of the other, and in their concerted action as they woo or repel. They advance, bow, and retreat, as in a cotillion or quadrille. Here is the influence of Lyly's ceremonious formality of arrangement; and in Lyly in turn, as Professor Keller shows, is that of the Court Masque, in which song, dance, and mimicry were united. But the most marked and highly developed example of the technique is in the scene where the King and his three lords, one after the other, betray in one another's presence their love-sickness, and the breaking of their vows to which it has brought them; Biron, who had witnessed the others' fall and jeered at them, being, through the miscarriage of a letter, exposed in the end himself. This situation, too, may have been imitated from one in Lyly's *Gallathea;* and certainly another, in the *Two Gentlemen of Verona* and the *Comedy of Errors,* that of the character running through the catalogue of his sweetheart's points, was taken from Lyly's *Endymion.* Since, as we have seen, we find it in Molière, it, like Leporello's catalogue of Don Juan's loves in divers cities, may have come down to him and Lyly alike from the *Commedia dell' arte.* In *A Midsummer Night's Dream,* another example of the Court Comedy created and cultivated by Lyly under the influence of the Masque, there are less striking illustrations of repeated *motif* in the changes wrought by the magic juice upon the lovers; and there is more of it in the mistakes and entanglements of the two pairs of twins in the *Comedy of Errors,* imitated, though with further developments which increase the confusion but lessen the effect of repetition, from Plautus.

Later this element of repetition diminishes and disappears. Yet in the *Merchant of Venice* is to be found the most marked example of the device in Shakespeare—the scene where Shylock shrieks now in grief for the loss of his ducats or his daughter, now in glee at Antonio's ruin. As I observe in a following chapter, Shylock is here the puppet and Tubal pulls the strings; and this device of alternation, which is like that in the similar situation in Marlowe's *Jew of Malta,* may, though it appears also in the vacillations of Jack Cade's rabble, have come down from the old play of the Jew, seen before 1579 by Gosson at the Bull. With its mechanical oscillations it looks as if it had actually belonged to the repertory of the marionettes and of the *Commedia dell' arte,* even with the stock character of the miser attached. For there is much the same situation in Molière's *L'Avare,* when, at the end of Act II, Harpagon repeatedly *prend un air sérieux* and thereupon *reprend un air gai,* according as Frosine, the go-between, hints at the need of money to aid her in her lawsuit, or, changing tune, tells him how tickled Marianne will be to see him. The device of Gratiano's twitting the Jew in the judgment scene, whereby his own words are, like Malvolio's, cast in his teeth when the tables are turned, may also have been inherited, although for this a definite source was less needed. And the same may be said of the scene where Falstaff pretends to deafness with the Chief-Justice, talking volubly beside the point; a situation similar, again, to many in Molière,[13] and to few in Shakespeare. The tricks played upon Benedick and Beatrice are alike and parallel; but the two processes are in time and place so far removed, and the effect on the two characters is so far contrasted (rather than made parallel), that the comic quality lies more in either incident itself than in the device of repetition. In the *Merry Wives,* probably written a bit earlier, there is something of the same technique as in the *École des femmes,* that of the alternation of scenes in which tricks are played upon a character with scenes in which that character, through mistaken identity or disguise, receives the confidences of him who played them. The exact source of the play is not known; but a similar succession of mishaps befalling a foolish gallant in intrigue is to be found in Italian novels, and hints of the dramatic technique, so like Molière's, probably came from Italy too. This is another case, however, where the repetition is only on the larger scale; and while it is far more noticeable than in *Much Ado,* and contributes more to the comic effect, it does not much partake of the rhythmical or musical quality to be found sometimes in Jonson and often in Molière.

To this technique, no doubt, whether as illustrated above or elsewhere, Shakespeare was not much inclined. Not applying it with perfect skill, he must have been a little im-

[13] See above, p. 149.

patient with it as more form than matter. 'Reich an Stoff,' says Goethe of German art; and Shakespeare was Teutonic in so far as he was rich in matter if any artist ever was. He must have thought the artifice mechanical and dehumanized, too much that of the puppet-show generally, as even in his own hands it became in the depicting of Shylock's griefs. But such an effect is not out of keeping with Jonson's or Molière's esthetic purposes. Presenting in the chief rôle not a rounded character but an angular and purely comical one, a character pretty much the embodiment of a single trait, they found such a technique fit to their hand for portraying that very quality of a man's nature when, according to Bergson, as we have seen, it is essentially comic—out of harmony with circumstances or society, stiff and mechanical like the jack-in-the-box. Touch the spring and up he jumps with a squeak, or, to use the vulgar phrase, you take a rise out of him. Something of that, indeed, is in human nature generally, but particularly when the hobby is set going, the ruling passion touched. Yet such a process, several times repeated, is (quite apart from the fact that it is in their case more delicately manipulated) manifestly much more appropriate to the presentation of a Géronte or Harpagon than of a Shylock, though we find it in all three. The last-named is so much more than a mere miser that we should hardly expect him to furnish the required reaction again and again. And so with Falstaff.[14] Really he is too well balanced and clever to let his cowardly boastfulness run away with him as it does, his lies mounting palpably while the Prince and Poins jeeringly lead him on. What is more in Shakespeare's vein is the thoroughly human, unabstracted comedy, when Falstaff, after chasing Pistol out of the lodging, tastes again and again his pitiful triumph and fights the battle over.—'A rascal, to brave me!—A rascally slave! I will

[14] See below, chapter viii, page 436 f.

toss the rogue in a blanket—A rascal bragging slave! The
rogue fled from me like quicksilver!' And his right reward
he has in his lady's favours, in Doll's caresses. Here the
repetition, though a matter of situation, not an idiosyn-
crasy or trick of speech, is as human as it well can be.
Though comical, it has little of the mechanical—or the
musical, either—about it, and is not developed for its own
sake. The same may be said of the riotous accumulations
of Mercutio's fancy, mentioned above, or of Falstaff's own
as he dwells on his slenderness when a youth. All this presents a character, rather than a comic idea set free and
logically and completely, musically and rhythmically worked
out, and does not remind us of Jonson or Molière. Indeed,
almost the only instance in Shakespeare of that kind of repetition—in the character's words, involving a comic idea
worked out logically and in rhythm—are the outcries of
Shylock and Jack Cade's rabble, mechanical, as we have
seen, in the extreme. The others have to do with incident—
with coincidence, as in English comedy generally. They are
like that of the naval lieutenant in Shaw's *You Never Can
Tell,* who is first reported to have proposed to the elder
daughter, then the younger daughter, then the mother
herself.

6.

Of repetition such as Jonson's and Molière's, fine, musical,
and various, Shakespeare has less in comic than in sentimental or tragic vein; yet even of that there is not much,
though it is masterly. Sometimes the repetitions are lyrical,
sentimental or romantic, such as are to be found in Lorenzo
and Jessica's talk in the moonlight at Belmont, and in
Romeo and Juliet's dawn-song and farewell. But here serious or tragic drama simply passes over into the lyric; it does
not, as in the last scene in *Othello,* remain truly dramatic
and yet in its fulness and intensity fuse with the lyric too.

On this scene in *Othello* I have touched above, and dwelt at length elsewhere.[15] The *motifs* of the sword and of suicide, of his pride in the past and his thought for his name in the future, recur and intertwine as in music, and prepare us for the end.

But the chief use to which Shakespeare turns the art of repetition is in connection with that blending of the comic and the tragic—the emotional complex—of which I have treated at the end of the preceding chapter. That this may be accomplished felicitously the droll human participants are made unconscious of the tragic issue, their voices becoming almost as the voice of Nature or of fate, and the comic blends with the tragic even as irony does, the device of repetition heightening the harmonious effect. In the Gravediggers' scene in *Hamlet,* the First Clown, digging a grave for Ophelia, who is not known to him, sings the stanza which ends:

> O, a pit of clay for to be made
> For such a guest is meet!

and Hamlet, as he inspects the skeletons, talks on ironically about this fine revolution, from dust to dust, and then asks idly, 'Whose grave's this, sir?' not knowing as we know. 'Mine, sir,' the Clown answers, quibbling, and thereupon croaks out the two lines again, as unconscious of their import in this particular connection as the wind is of its wailing. 'Clay to clay, dust to dust,' mutters the bruised but calloused world, and from force of habit sings it. And an equally fine example, though different, is in the Porter scene of *Macbeth*. The Porter's half-drunken fancy, to which he clings, that he is keeping hell-gate, in the name of Beelzebub, seems a voice out of the mouth of dumb Nature herself. He speaks more wisely than he knows. How wisely not only his words but the repeated knocking brings home to us. He has been carousing till the second cock; he has been made drunk, we recall with a shudder, along

---

[15] In my *Othello,* pp. 60-61.

with Duncan's grooms. And the knocking which goes on at intervals until he turns the key, and which he mimics— 'knock! knock! knock!'—as a boy mimics a dog barking or a horse neighing (for drink restores us to the dominion of impulse)—it has begun in the scene before, striking terror to our hearts as to the murderers'. Never was stage device more pregnant and inspired. In the preceding scene it brings the tragic emotion to the highest pitch, and now it furnishes the transition from that height to this earthy level. It casts a lurid light over the Porter's words, and they make it dance and flicker. We have been trembling, but now we cannot quite laugh, for the emotion is mingled. Something of the same effect is produced by the Fool's babblings in *King Lear* and by the repeated counsels which the Clown imparts to Cleopatra, as he hands over the basket. They too speak more wisely than they know; they sing, and repeat the song, as the voices of Nature do. The dehumanizing effect of musical repetition, which repelled Shakespeare elsewhere, here served his purpose.

Without the comic turn, in Lady Macbeth's sleep-walking there are echoes from the murders—the clock striking, Macbeth's alarms, the knocking at the gate, their whisperings about the nightgown and hastening to bed—and repeated allusions to blood and the washing of hands. Even in these internal repetitions it is the voice of Nature, again, asserting herself. And there is much musical effect in connection with the prophecies of the Weird Sisters and their fulfilment. The predictions, like the incantations which precede them, are repeated as in a ritual; and the various reiteration of the phrases about Birnam Wood coming to Dunsinane and about not fearing man of woman born, as Macbeth again and again clutches the comfort to his bosom and fate piecemeal wrests it from him, develops all the possibilities of irony. Without this musical development the dénouement would be but the redeing of a riddle. The repeated appearances of the Weird Sisters themselves, like those of the ghost in this play and in *Hamlet,* and of Ophelia with her mad songs, are, as it were, Wagnerian *leitmotive*. When the fourth act begins—

Thrice the brinded cat hath mewed,

and thus for the third time Fate appears and is given utterance, the lines profit by all those that have been uttered before, and the effect is cumulative, as at the third sounding of the trumpet. *Macbeth* in particular is the tragedy which most approaches to 'the condition of music'; though repetitions elsewhere in Shakespearean tragedy, as in the scene of the supernatural music in *Antony and Cleopatra,*[16] are so fine that we can only wish there were more of them. In tragedy too, as well as in comedy, he is surcharged with matter.

7.

So is Jonson, to be sure; and yet in many ways, as we have seen, he is like the light-armed, light-footed Molière. Not only has he something of the repeated *motif* and rhythmical movement, but above all he has the abstract method of characterization, the ruling passion shown in every light and from every side. There are no scenes in Shakespeare like that in which the jealous Kitely is on the point of leaving the house but fears to do so; undertakes to confide his secret to Cash his man but fears even to do that; and in a panic or paroxysm confides it to him after all, anxiously pretending and protesting the while that this is not the secret that he meant. Or like that in *Volpone* where Mosca, apparently absorbed and abstracted in his cares, makes up, item by item, with malicious delight, the inventory of his supposedly defunct master's valuables, while in swoop the legacy-hunters, one after the other, each in turn gloating over the precious items as mentioned, in the thought that they are already, not the others', but his own. In such scenes and many in the *Silent Woman,* you have repetition and variation of *motif,* inversion and transposition, and comic art

[16] IV, iii; cf. chapter v below, pp. 231-32.

approaching that state considered by Pater to be the perfection of art—that of music—as elsewhere you shall find it only in the supreme *maestro* of comedy himself.

Voltore.   How now, my Mosca?
Mos. (*writing*) 'Turkey carpets nine'.—
Volt.   Taking an inventory! that is well.
Mos.   'Two suits of bedding, tissue'—
Volt.   Where's the will?
          Let me read that the while.
                    (*Enter Corbaccio in a chair.*)
Corb.   So set me down
          And get you home.
                                        (*Exeunt servants.*)
Volt.   Is he come now to trouble us?
Mos.   'Of cloth of gold two more'—
Corb.   Is it done, Mosca?
Mos.   'Of several velvets, eight'—
Volt.   I like his care.
Corb.   Dost thou not hear?
                    (*Enter Corvino.*)
Corv.   Ha, is the hour come, Mosca?
Volpone. (*from behind a traverse.*) Ay, now they muster.
Corv.   What does the advocate here,
          Or this Corbaccio?
Corb.   What do these here?
                    (*Enter Lady Politic Would-be.*)
Lady P.   Mosca,
          Is his thread spun?
Mos.   'Eight chests of linen'—
Volp.   O
          My fine dame Would-be, too!
Corv.   Mosca, the will,
          That I may show it these, and rid 'em hence.
Mos.   'Six chests of diaper, four of damask'—There.
          (*Gives them the will carelessly, over his shoulder.*)
Corb.   Is that the will?
Mos.   'Downbeds and bolsters,' etc.

As they read the will and bother him, Mosca now and then interrupts his sing-song with a deprecation, double-barbed:—

'A perfum'd box'—Pray you forbear
You see I'm troubl'd—'made of an onyx'—

And when they insist, he lays down his pen and roundly
reviles first one and then another, until all but Voltore, who
now thinks more than ever that he alone is the heir, slink
away.

Volt. Now, my faithful Mosca,
I find thy constancy—
Mos. Sir!
Volt. Sincere.
Mos. 'A table
Of porphyry'—I marle you'll be thus troublesome. . . .

And here, after the digression, the main rhythmical movement is resumed, as in an opera or a sonata. But in Jonson
so finely elaborated an effect as that is rare. After all he
is an Elizabethan. Abstract in method, he is concrete in
material, copious and abundant in detail, and has far less
in him than has Molière of repetition and rhythm, but gives
his characters, though abstract too and not more real, much
more of the colour and flavour of reality.

8.

What now of the origins? From Jonson, of course,
Molière no more learned his art than from Shakespeare or
Lyly—the influence and the very names of all three alike
being to him unknown. And it would seem that in its begin-
nings this flowing and ample comic art must be Latin, not
English. The only other Elizabethans to exhibit traces of
it are Lyly, who taught Shakespeare, and Fletcher, who was
taught by Jonson, both influenced by classical and Italian,
if not French and Spanish, drama. The comic drama before
Shakespeare—the interludes and farces—has, so far as
I know, none of it; and the same may be said of English
comedy since, the only exception down to the present being
the Comedy of Manners of Etherege, Wycherley, and Con-

greve, under the direct influence of the French. But of French comedy the contrary is to be said. Such art is to be found in the old farces, in Molière and Regnard, in Beaumarchais as in Rostand. And with less effect of rhythm, it appears in Italian comedy of the sixteenth century and even in Plautus. To show just who in this respect influenced whom would be difficult, and is not my purpose; it may even be difficult to show, as is my purpose, that this art in comedy is Latin, not English, for that would seem to be limiting—clipping the wings of—genius. Frontiers art does not acknowledge, and so simple a device as repetition ought not to need to be imported like orchids and apricots. In the lyric and epic that may be true, although the repetition and amplitude of Spenser in epic style are directly owing to Ariosto and Tasso. But the drama is different. It is rooted in the tastes and prejudices of the public, and not lightly does it put up with bold innovation. It is a striking fact that Jonson, who, in the respect discussed, most closely approximates the comic art of the Continent, was not highly acceptable to the London public. And Shakespeare, who even in his early plays approached it not so closely as to present difficulties to an unaccustomed audience, was then under the influence of Lyly, the poet of the court.

It is with Plautus, in so far as the Renaissance is concerned, that abstract characterization began, particularly in his miser and his braggart soldier. Euclio is the model, not only for all later misers, but also for Jonson's jealous Kitely and other characters, who, in changing lights, exhibit every aspect of a monomaniac vice or folly. And the repeated *motif* on the larger scale, somewhat as in *George Dandin* and the *École des femmes,* is employed in a play like the *Menæchmi,* source of the *Comedy of Errors.* The visiting *Menæchmus* falls in with each one of his twin-brother's associates after the latter has left them with some business in hand or with some project started—his wife, the parasite, the courtesan, her cook and her maid-servant,—

and the twin-brother thereupon falls in with them in turn, and
also with his father-in-law (whom in the play he had not
seen but who had seen the visitor) and with the visitor's
slave: and all this occurs in a way which at each repetition
arouses expectations of mirth from the confusion and fully
satisfies them.   And here and in that other comedy which
altogether depends on doubles and mistaken identity, the
Amphitruo, there is such repetition and variation, combination and permutation, that the comic possibilities are completely worked out and expressed.   Rightly considered,
either play contains one situation only, repeated and varied;
and all the changes are rung on the theme of Sosia's and
Amphitruo's bewildered wondering whether they are themselves or other men.   In comedies, such as the *Bacchides*
and the *Epidicus,* there are repeated intrigues of the slave
which result in a structure somewhat like that in the *École
des maris* or the *Fourberies de Scapin.*   And now and then
within the scene itself there is worked out pretty fully such
a situation as the teasing of the eager questioner by speaking
beside the purpose, to be found in the *Mercator,* the *Curculio,* and the *Phormio,*[17] as in *Romeo and Juliet* when the
Nurse complains of head and back and inquires whether they
have dined at home.   But of repeated *motifs* on the smaller
scale, within the scene itself, and with verbal or phrasal
recurrence, there is little.

9.

There are good instances of this, however, in sixteenth-
century Italian comedy.   It appears in Ariosto, Aretino,
Bentivoglio, Sforza d'Oddi, and in Giordano Bruno towards
the end of the century it becomes prominent.   One wonders
whether this is not the influence of the Comedy of Masks,
so near at hand, upon the literary drama; and Molière
(although subject to another influence also, one home-
grown) must, since his contact with the Italian drama and

[17] *Mercator* I, ii; *Curculio* II, iii; *Phormio,* ll. 850 ff.

stage was so close and immediate, have felt its influence both in its popular and also in its learned form.

In Ariosto's *Scolastica*, IV, v-vi and V, iv, there is the device of the repeated ingenious lie, evasion or retort (each time after an interval of suspense), produced to save one from difficulties or to carry away the honours—a *motif* employed in the Comedy of Masks, no doubt, as by Beaumarchais,[18] and by Rostand in *Cyrano,* where four times De Guiche thrusts, and as many, to the delight of the Gascons, Cyrano parries.[19] Bartolo, the father, too soon returning, hears the host, Bonifacio, called by his own name, and it is for Accursio the servant, as best he can, to explain it; then hears his son Eurialo mentioned—no, it is a mistake, 'tis another name; and then hears that he has just married, and with the consent of his father. Later, face to face with Bonifacio, he four times asks him whether he be really Bartolo, and four times Bonifacio evades the question. This certainly is like the technique of the Comedy of Masks, which was a comic technique for its own sake, as it were, a repertory of *lazzi* like that of the messenger's repeated returning for trivial or irrelevant information. And in V, ii, Claudio insists on telling his story of good fortune in love to the old woman Veronese, who takes no interest in it and is intent only on seeking safety from her enemies.

In Aretino's *Ipocrito* (1541), supposed to be a source of *Le Tartuffe,* there is a good deal of comic verbal repetition in the trick of Liseo's speech after he has learned indifference; but, having to do with character rather than with situation, it lies beyond our scope. There is much cunning abstract characterization, however, in the vice of the hypocrite and the obsession of Liseo, such as may have influenced Jonson or Molière. In Bentivoglio's *Il Geloso* (1545) comic repetition is provided by the jealous physi-

[18] *Mariage de Figaro,* II, xxi. It also appears in the *Barbier de Séville;* and in both plays there is a good deal of repeated *motif,* which fairly cried out for the score of Mozart and Rossini.
[19] IV, iv.

cian and the young man who disguises himself in the old man's likeness to gain access to his niece. In the one it is by what the character does; in the other it is by what is done to him. All too well disguised the lover finds himself, and is beset by the doctor's patients (who will not take no for an answer) one after the other. In Sforza d'Oddi's *Morti vivi* (1576) the hero, Tersandro, long supposed to be drowned, returns when his wife is about to marry. A suitor has planned to stop the marriage, at the last moment, through a fake Tersandro; but this has leaked out, and the real Tersandro is taken by every one for either a joke or a ghost. His steward, however, on whom he has been counting but who really is in the plot, acknowledges him indeed before a slave and the clown as his master, so that he thanks and praises God, but, on their departure, turns about and congratulates him on his success as an impostor, and assures him that if he had not known better he should have taken him for Tersandro himself.

That Italian comedy, however, which most fully exemplifies the technique in question is Giordano Bruno's *Il Candelaio* (1582). This fantastic and lively play is inspired by the Comedy of Masks if any is. There is Bartolommeo, the naturalist, who relates his love-affair according to the formula of a declension—nominative, genitive, and so on. There is Manfurio, the Pedant, who, having told Ottaviano which were his favourite affirmative and negative expressions, *utique* and *nequaquam,* has them then, to his disgust, thrown at his head, when he asks Ottaviano's opinion of his verses. This is like Lavache with his 'O, Lord, sir' in *All's Well* (II, ii); but it is much more variously and cleverly used, is introduced less arbitrarily, and (though not on the Countess) here produces an effect on the person spoken to. It is like the Shepherd's Bé, bé, in *Maître Pathelin,* which he used as he was taught to do at the trial but also when the lawyer would have his fee. And there is Bonifacio, trembling in anticipation of his meeting with Vittoria the courtesan; and Manfurio, required to turn over his remaining money or else take a certain number of blows either on hand or rump. He chooses the former as less shameful, but before he has taken the fourth blow turns to the latter as less painful, and then, before he has taken the seventh of these, recollecting that he has some scudi left, offers to pay up instead. Then, for his duplicity, he must needs have seventy instead of fifty, and since he counts the blows too fast the tale must begin all over to make sure of no mistake.

Behind these literary dramatists, however, is, as we have said, the Comedy of Masks, which in this respect exerted an influence upon them, and (through the travelling Italian troupes) upon Molière himself, more potent probably than any. Theirs was an art much depending on improvisation, and hence in some measure (almost inevitably) on repetition, though from the meagre text of the *scenari,* very naturally, this can little appear. If certain tricks and jokes were successfully repeated (as we know they were) in play after play, how much the more would certain master-strokes in a joke or trick be repeated in the play itself. If what the audience wanted in a play of improvised speech was 'not the pain of taking in new jokes but the pleasure of recognizing old ones,' [20] how much the more does that hold good of the part than of the whole, of the kernel than of the shell, and in the selfsame play and not another. And that such was the case appears sufficiently from Flaminio Scala, who wrote the *scenari* down; from Gozzi, who was strongly under their influence; or from those situations out of the popular unprinted drama which the actor Riccoboni cites [21] as Molière's originals. There is that in *Il Dottor bachettone,* where the usurer, like Harpagon, in lending money insists on including at a high price a ridiculous lot of odds

[20] Quoted from an article of Mr Walkley's, *The Times,* September, 1924.
[21] See *Observations sur la Comédie* (1736), pp. 190, 192, 194, etc. (Despois et Mesnard).

and ends as part of it. The list in itself is comical, and (though of things valueless instead of things precious) like Leporello's list of Don Juan's loves or Mosca's inventory. Another is that in the *Case svaligiate,* where Pantaloon gives money, as Harpagon in the same situation bestows thanks, each time he hears of his praises being sung to the lady whom he loves. And still another is that in *La Cameriera nobile,* where Scapin twice intervenes between Pantaloon and the Doctor, as does Maître Jacques between Harpagon and his son, patching up a truce by secretly and falsely telling the one and then the other that his rival has given up his claim to the hand of the lady in question.

10.

Yet though the comedy of the Italians, both the literary and the improvised, shed an influence on Molière, it probably, as I have intimated, did not act alone. The plays above-mentioned have little of the verbal repetition or contagious rhythm which approach the effect of opera; and these may have come to him from a native source. The abstract characterization, and the repetition in the main outline of the plot and in the development of a single situation, descended from the Italians and from Plautus and Terence; but the musical form resembles that in the old French farces, so different in this respect from the English. How this reached him I do not know. In Desmarets de Saint-Sorlin's *Visionnaires* and Cyrano de Bergerac's *Pédant joué* the essentials of Molière's art already appear, but there is much less of the musical method. Rotrou has more. But that it reached him, indirectly, through these or others like them, or through the vulgar theatre, there can be small doubt, for his public took to it as readily as did he.

The farce of *Maître Pathelin* we have already cited, but the musical method is more marked elsewhere, as in the equally famous *Farce du cuvier.* Jacquinot is domineered over by his wife and his mother-in-law, and is bid take down on a scroll the manifold household duties expected of him, item by item. Then he goes ahead with one of these, helping with the washing. In the midst of it his wife falls into the tub and calls to him for help—to do this or that or at least the other—in her distress. But to her, and afterwards to her mother who arrives upon the scene, his only reply is to say

> Cela n'est point à mon rollet,

or to recite at length the duties that are there. Only when a new bargain is struck will he save her. And through the whole story there is a swing or lilt to the movement that is much nearer to that of Molière than anything I know in the Italian.

The same and more may be said of the *Farce de deux jeunes hommes*,[22] and especially of the *Farce des femmes*,[23] which reads as if it were meant to be sung. The maid recounts her own experience to a neglected lady, who, not unlike Orgon or Harpagon, three times exclaims in the intervals of the tale:

> Helas! C'estoit un beau plaisir!

And later the maid herself, who had not been neglected, three times exclaims as admiringly, while she tells what a man it was:

> Il ne luy chault à qui il paye,
> Mais qu'ilz soient quitz.
> ### La Dame
> Midieux, non.
> Ce n'est point une morte paye;
> Il ne luy chault à qui il paye.
> ### La Chambriere
> Ha, quel bon payeur, saincte Avoye!
> ### La Dame
> Au moins en a-il le renom.

[22] Picot et Nyrop (1880).
[23] Viollet-le-Duc i, p. 111f.

La Chambriere
Il ne luy chault à qui il paye,
Mais qu'il soit quite.

Similar triads are to be found in the *Farce de Colin qui loue et despite Dieu en ung moment.*[24] It is the old story, like that of *Our Goodman,* no. 274 in *Child's Ballads,* of the husband after long absence returning to his house and finding changes, many pleasant, but one unpleasant and hardly to be borne. To the question where she got this fine thing or that his wife answers,

Colin, de la grace de Dieu.

And it is an answer that stands her in good stead when he finds a baby in the cradle. Until he comes upon that he gives God thanks, but she makes so bold as to bid him thank God still:

Car cecy n'a rien de nouveau;
C'est le dict de chascun quartier;
A la vache est tousjours le veau.

Colin
Ou mol ou dur comme un mortier,
C'est le dict de chascun quartier.

Femme
C'est trop exposé le psaultier;
Ne vous chault qui soit le toreau.

Colin
C'est le dict de chascun quartier:
A la vache est tousjours le veau.

This too goes like singing, and there are others that do. In the *Farce de Colin Filz de Theuot le Maire*[25] there is less of this—more variation than repetition, more recurrence of similar thought than of phrase. Colin (not the same as the above) is treated somewhat like Euclio and (in another way) like the Miles Gloriosus, in the ample depiction of his traits of petty roguery and cowardice. The Mayor

[24] Viollet-le-Duc i, p. 225.
[25] Viollet-le-Duc, ii, 388.

expects his son's return like the lion that he is. An old woman comes and complains that someone has stolen her hen, killed her cock, eaten her goose, and forced her maid. Suspicion points to Colin, but it yields to certainty when he appears. Then ensue a series of disclosures—of his exploits, which turn out to be shams, of his justifications for loss or failure, which are pitiful excuses—constantly interrupted by the old woman's complaints.

II.

Turning from the farces, we find in *Les Visionnaires* of Desmarets de Saint-Sorlin (1640), a play known to Molière and imitated by him in the *Femmes savantes,* much of his manner immediately before his time. A whole scene is developed out of a single situation, or out of one or two traits of a single character, or out of two characters contrasted with each other; and though without verbal or phrasal repetition, such scenes are so full of the recurrence of trait or trick that, as where Don Juan fobs off his creditor, the rhythm of movement is quite apparent. One of the best scenes Molière imitated not merely in form but in substance,—the scene in which Hespérie, like his Belise, is of the same opinion still that Phalante, like all other males, is in love with her, not with Mélisse, who endeavours to convey to her the contrary; and that he pursues Mélisse only from want of prowess for the loftier emprise, or else Mélisse is deceiving her now only to get a more favourable occasion to persuade her to accept him. Another is that in which Artabaze boasts one moment and breaks into exhibitions of cowardice the next, dancing again and again through this figure. It is from Plautus and the Italians, no doubt, that the method in some measure comes; but there is *Colin le Filz de Theuot le Maire* in France itself; and of such rhythm there is, so far as I know, little in the drama of Italy.

Cyrano de Bergerac came before Molière, and was both

his friend and his literary creditor.   In his *Pédant joué*
there is more verbal repetition than in the *Visionnaires,*
whether it be due to the influences of the farces or of the
Italian comedy, learned or popular.   He writes in prose, and
hence sacrifices one means employed by Desmarets, as by the
writers of the farces, to heighten the effect of rhythm; but it
is there for all that, both in content and in verbal and
phrasal recurrence.   The most striking instance is the scene
of the Turkish galley (II, iv), imitated in the *Fourberies
de Scapin*.   In Molière the rhythm is better managed, but
in Cyrano there is greater *vis comica* in the climax.   Much
has been said about paying a ransom, but the exact sum
has not yet been mentioned.   The curmudgeon of a father,
having no notion of the size of it, has made several meagre
offers, such as that the son should hand over to the Turk
the residue of his pocket money, or that the servant should
go sell the doublet of the master's father for the purpose;
and then with a clap comes the demand for a hundred
pistoles.

> Cent pistoles!   Ha! mon fils, ne tient-il qu'à ma vie, pour con-
> server la tienne?   Mais cent pistoles!   Corbineli, va-t'en luy dire
> qui'il se laisse pendre sans dire mot; cependant qu'il ne s'afflige point,
> car je les en feray bien repentir.

An admirable example of that method, peculiar to Italian
and French, and also Spanish, comic art, of working out
the situation by repetition or variation to the end!   Sometimes, as even in Molière, this seems, in the spirit of mere
virtuosity, to be comedy for comedy's sake, a little at the
expense of character, or logic.   *Même jeu—même jeu—*at
the wave of the *maestro's* bâton, the instruments sound, the
puppets trip or dance.   Earlier in the play, for instance, the
Pedant tries to get his rival, his own son Charlot, out of
the way by packing him off to Venice.   Charlot refuses to
leave his love.   Finding him obdurate, the Pedant takes it
into his head to consider him a madman, and calls upon

his pupils to bind him, in order to feed him with hellebore.
No, he will not go.   Then they tie him and handle him
roughly.   'But, Father, why do you treat me so?   Is it only
a matter of going to Venice?   I am ready to do that.'
'Hands off!' then cries the Pedant, turning to his pupils.
'Yes, Father, I promise to obey you in everything, but as
for going to Venice it must not be thought of.'   'What,
you drones, must of my bread, gangrene of my substance,
this stubborn chap has no hobbles yet on his feet?   Quick,
more fetters than Xerxes hurled into the ocean,' etc.   'Ah,
Father, don't bind me, I am quite ready to go.'   'Ha! I
knew that my son was too well brought up to give way to
a frenzy.   Go, my Dauphin, my Infante, my Prince of
Wales. . . . I vow to love you a hundred-fold, once you
are down there.'   'Where, Father?'   'At Venice, son.'   'At
Venice? Me? I will die first.'   'Catch him, catch him, don't
you see how he foams at the mouth!' . . . 'Again? Why do
you lay hold of me?' he asks the pupils.   'Because you won't
go to Venice.'   'I won't? You are made to think so.   Why,
Father, all my life I have wanted to see Italy, the garden
of the world.'   'Why then, my son, you have no more need
of hellebore.   Your head is as sound as a headed cabbage
after a frost,' etc.   The changes are amusing, but they
would be more so if there were more reason or occasion
for them.

Another instance is in a later scene, where the coward
Chasteaufort, as he talks with the country-fellow Gareau,
is beaten by him for insolence, and gives reason, designed
to do himself huge honour, for not striking back.   Again
and again he is beaten, but only more and more ingenious
and farfetched are his excuses.   Working the theme out to
its limits, though highly comical, leads to preposterous conclusions psychologically; as it does at times with Sosie and
Harpagon, for instance, in Molière and Plautus.

Desmarets, then, has more of the abstract method and
full rhythmical development; Cyrano has more of the verbal

repetition; but though both have more of the musical quality than have the Italians, neither has it in such measure as Molière, and Molière himself has it not in such measure as the farces. I am not trying to prove that the influence lay here or there but only that the art in question was Latin— Italian, French, or Spanish—rather than English or Germanic. That, at least, seems clear. It was not for naught that the supreme comic literature of the modern world has been the Latin—Boccaccio and Ariosto, Gozzi and Goldoni, Lope and Cervantes, Rabelais and Molière. The glory of the North—dark, true, and tender—is tragedy,— is Shakespeare and Schiller, Goethe and Ibsen,—and tragic are even the Sagas and the Northern popular ballads and epics. But perfection of form, in either art, is the fruit of the South, above all in the art which there flourishes. It was not for naught too that on Latin soil arose opera— comic or serious—not to say modern music itself. It seems also sufficiently clear that comedy without music attending upon it, but itself half turned to music, is especially French. In France, at any rate, it took on its ultimate development. Whether Molière ever came in direct contact with the farces or not he inherited their spirit. That had no doubt lingered on upon the *tréteaux* and in the *foire*—both he and his audience were predisposed. In Rotrou's *La Sœur* (1647), from which—for the *Bourgeois gentilhomme*— Molière also borrowed, there is not only the verse form, as in Saint-Sorlin, but verbal repetition more like that in the farces than it generally is in Molière, and even the repeated *sans dot* of Harpagon before his time, as well.[26] Molière developed and perfected the harmony and rhythm of comedy.

12.

The Englishman nearest akin to these, we have seen, is

[26] See the *Molièriste,* x, p. 46 f. an article to which my attention has been directed by Professor Searles.

Jonson. How he came in *Volpone* and the *Silent Woman* thus to anticipate Molière it is difficult to say. What he shares with Plautus and Terence needs no discussing, and it is of course a possibility that having gone so far with them hand in hand he might have gone the same road to a musical perfection independently. But it is not likely. Few artists go far alone—Molière himself, a greater artist, drew heavily, we have seen, not only upon the ancients and the Comedy of Masks, but upon his immediate predecessors, and must have come into contact with the spirit of the farce as a tradition on the vulgar stage. Why should not Jonson have come in contact with it too? At least he must have known something of the Comedy of Masks and the Italian drama. In the *Conversations* Drummond of Hawthornden reports of him that 'he neither doth understand French nor Italiannes' [*Scotice,* for the language]. Yet just before that he reports Jonson's judgments on Petrarch and Guarini, and on Perron's translation of Virgil and Ronsard's odes. By Drummond's standards he may have known little, but the presumption in the case of one so learned and intellectually inquisitive is that he knew a good deal. According to Drummond himself he had been in the Low Countries and (though so late as 1613) in Paris; and it is unthinkable that he should not have learned the French tongue and both seen and read French plays.

13.

As for Shakespeare, he, we have said, took hints in regard to this kind of art from Lyly or Plautus, or from the Italian novels, or from odds and ends of stage tradition. Troupes of Italian players had been in the English court as early as 1573, 1576, and 1577;[27] and in some such way it comes that a few of their *lazzi* appear in the *Comedy of Errors* and the *Taming of the Shrew.* And farce being, if not in fact, by right of nature French, it is, appropriately, when

[27] See Schelling, and Miss W. Smith, *Commedia dell' Arte,* pp. 173-5.

Shakespeare wrote farce, as in the *Comedy of Errors* and the *Merry Wives,* that he made his nearest approach to the French technique. But it is only in his early years that he did this; and the element of comic repetition and rhythm in his work, and, indeed, of a separate and special treatment and technique for comedy, rapidly diminished. This is natural in one who cultivated both comedy and tragedy, and was interested in life more than in either, and not in esthetic theory at all. Thought is free—is *one,* as life is. Tirso, Lope, and Calderón are here kindred spirits; but Jonson, Corneille and Racine—and Molière too—kept the two types distinct and apart, and followed the rules. The highest imaginative genius perhaps does not do that, any more than the sea hearkened unto King Canute, or than Nature generally respects the paths we lay or barriers we build. She will still be wandering.

And, as I have intimated, the comic bent in Shakespeare was not the predominant or fundamental one, which indeed would appear from the mere fact that his comic art did not attain so complete and perfect expression. Dr Johnson and other English critics have thought it was predominant; but in Johnson's case at least that opinion was owing partly to his classical prejudices and sense of decorum, partly to the greater simplicity of Shakespeare's comic style. The incursion and intrusion of comic elements into Shakespeare's tragedy struck him as more sweeping and startling than that of tragic elements into his comedy. And in a certain sense this may be. There is more of jesting in his tragedy than there is of tragic seriousness in his comedy; and the one intruder may be more surprising and seemingly incongruous than the other. And that more commonly he is simple and correct in his comic style there can be no question, though the elevation or inflation in tragedy was according to the example of Seneca and the precept and practice of his time. Yet in his greatest moments in tragedy he is simple again.

But when we consider the quality of the thought rather
than the quantity, or look to the source of it in the mind
of the author, we remember that the essential thing for
comedy, the critical spirit, of which in Rabelais, Cervantes,
and Molière there is abundance, is not abundant in Shakespeare.[28]   He stands aloof, indeed, but not to judge, or
at least not to judge and castigate, all in the same lightning
flash of laughter.   His judgments are moral and serious
rather than social and merry, and his impartiality is not so
much that of a judicious amusement or indifference as of an
all-embracing tolerance and sympathy.   His criticism is
applied only to the most obvious objects—to the gross and
enormous stupidity of clowns and bumpkins, the glaring
affectations of a Malvolio or Osric, and such notable follies
and vices as jealousy, cowardice, and miserliness.   And
even of these there are no careful full-length studies.   Such
are in farce, as the *Merry Wives,* and none of them is the
leading character.   His high comedy is all romantic, fantastic, and sentimental; and when he is critical he really is
not much more than chary of his sympathy, and readily runs
into vast exaggeration and burlesque.   His satire is not fine
or delicate.   And instead of that comic irony which arises
from the exhibition of a vice or folly he has, more commonly, that which arises from circumstances—disguise,
feigning, or mistaken identity—literally not skin-deep.
Instead of essentially comic situations, or essentially comic
characters, indeed, such as we judge and laugh at, he often
made characters somewhat like himself, full of high spirits,
riotous in fantasy, prodigal of wit and verbal dexterity, who
both judge not and are not judged.   They are harsh enough,
to be sure, by our standards, laughing without judging—
almost without thinking—but having all merry England, not
merely the *beau monde,* on their side.[29]   Sound sense and
healthy instincts they have instead of a critical faculty, and

[28] Cf. R. M. Alden, *Shakespeare* (1922), p. 327.
[29] Cf. chapter vi below, section 16.

they can be serious too at need.   And often the irony appears
in medieval style, springing not out of the situation but from
the lips of the character himself.[30]   Falstaff and Benedick
are examples.

14.

And that irony which we call tragic lacks in Shakespeare
the note of mockery apparent in modern authors.   In
Ghosts, or the *Wild Duck,* or *Hedda Gabler* 'some one is
laughing' at the end; but in Shakespeare there is no 'ironic
tragedy of disillusion.' [31]   His irony is the irony of fate—
the work of justice (or retribution) unforeseen or ignored.
From the time of Schlegel it has been the custom of the
critics to find irony in him where he gives no hint of it.   Mr
Yeats thinks that Shakespeare looked ironically upon Henry
V, as upon a fine animal, for all his royal blood and show.
And Professor Trench thinks ironical the remarks of Fortinbras upon Hamlet's making a good king had he had the
chance (though most critics indeed, to be consistent, should
take the words as so meant at least on the part of the poet).
But these and similar interpretations are instances of that
hearkening for the overtone which comes of reading
wholly modern plays and stories and modern criticism.
And they are prompted by modern idealistic philosophy, as applied by the Fichtians, Schlegel and Tieck, who
conceived all art to be inspired by irony, to be a transcendental farce; [32] or as applied by the Hegelians, Professors
Dowden and Bradley, who heard in *King Lear* or *Othello*
a transcendental note of reconciliation and a faint far-off
hymn of triumph, a *Stimme von Oben* or *chorus mysticus,*
so to speak, at the end.   So a play is interpreted on
the rebound or by its echo.[33]   How different are the endings of Shakespeare from those of Ibsen or Hervieu!   They

[30] See below, chapter viii, sections 21, 22, etc.
[31] See Mr Alden, *Texas Review,* Oct. 1916.
[32] Croce, *Estetica come Scienza* (1922), p. 324.
[33] Cf. my *Hamlet,* p. 23.

are on a note of sorrow, of resignation or despair, it may
be, but not of consolation or of mockery at all. At least
there is an effect of calm and repose, in instinctive but
unwitting sympathy with the art of the Greeks. And the
end of the individual in the tragedy is like it. No noble
or respectable character of his drama dies jesting or laughing; no noble or respectable person, for that matter, consciously or unconsciously speaks lightly of death or the
dead. The poet's own personal humour, it would seem,
did not sally across the confines of the frivolous or profane.[34] But the writers with whom to compare Shakespeare
are those nearer to him. In all his plays there is no suggestion of such comic irony as in Boccaccio's tale of Alatiel,
bride of the King of Garbo; or that of Ser Ciappelletto,
a mere child of sin and unregenerate limb of iniquity, whose
remains, being mistakenly entombed as those of a saint,
wrought miracles and healed multitudes; or as in Machiavelli's rank comedy *La Mandragola*. Here poet and
spectator both have wry faces, or are exchanging waggish
glances, as they part.

Still less is there of that modern sense of humour which,
allied with the modern sense of time and space, eternity
and infinity, almost makes our world totter or shrink up.
To him this might have seemed impious or frivolous; yet
there is scarcely anything in him even of that form of
humour which springs out of sheer courage when face to

---

[34] Cf. my article 'Anachronism,' *Modern Philology* (1910), pp. 572-73—
Dowden's and Bradley's interpretation has had wide acceptance, for it
is unto edification—whether it be founded is a minor matter; and thus
King Lear becomes a book of consolation like *In Memoriam*. 'What happens to a being like Cordelia does not matter—all that matters is what
she is:' if that be the sentiment of Shakespeare, his play should be by
our bed's head, with the prayer-book. But as I was not definitely aware
when I first called the interpretation in question, this *arrière pensée* and
ulterior sentiment is almost pure Hegel. It is since then that I have read
Croce and W. Mac. Dixon's *Tragedy* (cf. pp. 172, 176). That the idea
is Hegel's both Dowden and Mr Bradley would no doubt have eagerly
acknowledged; but without losing faith that it also lies embedded in
Shakespeare.

face with death or disaster, such as there is in the *Njal saga* or the *Grettir saga,* or on the lips of Englishmen 'before action' (or in it) to this day. 'Those broad spears are now in fashion,' mutters Atli as he topples down under the stroke of one; but Falstaff, thwarted and rebuffed, does *not* laugh till the welkin rings as Mr Beerbohm thinks he fittingly might. In fact Mr Harris is not far wrong, and of the courage high-uplifted beyond hope, the resolution springing from despair, as we find it in the sagas, in *Béowulf* and the *Battle of Maldon,* in Milton and Bunyan, Shakespeare has little. His heroes like Hotspur and Henry V drink delight of battle; and even bid their companions rejoice that as against the enemy they are so few; but in the presence of death they are depressed and melancholy, not defiant; and they are none of them great rebels, men of iron, Uebermenschen sympathetically treated, such as Cæsar or Cromwell in a play should be.[35] But it is mainly a matter of cosmical outlook. The rim or confine of things, the brink of the abyss, was to Shakespeare dark and terrible altogether, lit up by no grim or ghastly ray of laughter, however the inner humdrum round may have been warmed with sportiveness and mirth. His greatest plays are tragedies, we know; which is as it should be, fitting into the harmony of the poet's nature. Is not life a comedy to him who thinks, a tragedy to him who feels?

So it comes that there is in him no scepticism or cynicism such as Boccaccio's or Machiavelli's, no 'divine irony' of indifference such as Croce finds in Ariosto. Another reason (than those above mentioned) that Shakespeare is more tragic than comic is that he and the English people had kept the fear of God and his law, of fate, of chance or of fortune—that is, the fear of life itself—as the southern

[35] It is remarkable that Cæsar, Octavius, and Bolingbroke are treated without sympathy or understanding for their large iconoclastic political plans or their determination in executing them. And Aaron, Richard, and Iago—these are his rebels and Uebermenschen.

sons of the Renaissance had not done, and as, in our scientific knowledge, we do less and less ourselves. Wicked are his sceptics and cynics and all their works, not so much doubters of the good as its enemies; and of the indifferent—of Oxford men or Cambridge men if then there really were any—he has none. As an idea or principle *Jenseits von Gut und Böse* was no doubt foreign even to Ariosto. 'A great writer,' as Mr Murry says, 'does not really come to conclusions about life; he discerns a quality in it.' A tragic poet is not a pessimistic philosopher, however sternly some critics may insist on treating him as one, nor does an ironical poet fetch precepts from the cynic's tub. But in fact or in feeling, no doubt, Ariosto, as Croce says, 'transcends good or evil, retaining interest in them only on account of the rhythm of life, so constant and yet so various.' And certainly it is true (what he says of Shakespeare) that he 'transcends all individual emotions, but he does not transcend, on the contrary he strengthens, our interest in good and evil, in sorrow and joy, in destiny and necessity, in appearance and reality; and the vision of this strife is his poetry.' [36] Not to him is one act or one opinion as good as another; and the strife or antagonism does not rise, or sink either, into a harmony. Evil is not turned to good, or good to evil. Rightly Mr Bradley protests against Swinburne's words about *King Lear*: 'Here is very Night itself'; but when he himself insists on the evil in the play being merely destructive and negative, on calamity or the malice of others being powerless against man's soul, and on it not mattering what happens to Cordelia,—he is thinking of what, however true, the dramatist was not thinking, and for his tragic effect would have us think not so much. [37] Transcendentalism, optimistic or pessimistic either, there is in him none—and of indifference no more.

[36] *Ariosto,* etc. p. 94; cf. the chapter on Criminals below, pp. 340-45 (first published in 1912).
[37] Cf. my article, 'Anachronism in Shakespeare Criticism,' *Modern Philology* (1910), pp. 571-73.

'The good,' or virtue, in Shakespeare is without doubt stronger than evil and vice, not because it overcomes and resolves the other element in itself but simply because it is light opposed to darkness, because it is the good, is virtue; by reason, in short, of its special quality, which the poet discerns and seizes in its original purity and truth, without sophisticating or weakening it.[38]

And here still less is it a matter of philosophy or Weltanschauung; for of the two, Ariosto decidedly is the one who thinks and smiles, Shakespeare the one who feels, and when he also smiles, it is how differently! Not only does he laugh as all England laughed but he believes as all England believed, and no more of the critical spirit is there in him than must needs be in one so well-balanced and sane. That is reserved for individual cases; and not a single ideal, ethical judgment, or custom of his time does he question, thus losing a great source of comedy indispensable to the dramatist of our day. And where it stands unquestioned, the individual confronted with it in his blindness,—the Duchess of Fontanges, Louis XIV's favourite, at confession, or Villiers' demoiselles de Bienfilâtre, who charge the fee, virtuously contemning their sister for her romantic, unprofessional weakness,—Shakespeare misses such irony too.[39] His failure to keep for the individual his point of view as regards his own moral worth—the self-descriptive technique or apparent self-consciousness which we have mentioned[40]—interfered. Indeed there is no sign that he took any such special delight in what critical faculty he had as Molière or Ariosto, Voltaire or Mr Shaw, took or takes in his, and as we all take in whatever is our own particular gift, or what we fancy to be such. By choice he accepted life; and his imagination comprehended more than it discriminated, though not indifferently. His imagination was an embrace.

[38] Croce, *Ariosto*, p. 92.

[39] Of such spiritual blindness, treated ironically, there is, indeed, a rare example in Shylock's attitude to the contract, touched upon below, chapter vi, section 22.

[40] See above chapter iii, p. 102.

CHAPTER V

THE GHOSTS

ARE the ghosts in Shakespeare real, the ghosts of superstition? Under the influence of nineteenth-century philosophical criticism they have generally been taken to be hallucinations or symbols; and in recent years this belief has
received the sanction, more or less complete, of such scholars
as Professors Herford, Moorman, Moulton, Schelling, and
latest of all, Dr W. W. Greg. Some of these (though not
Dr Greg) make an exception of the ghost of Hamlet's
father; others, like Professor Schelling, make an exception
of this ghost only when on the platform; still others, such
as Professor Bradley and Professor Thorndike, may be said
to suspend judgment; only a very few in the last two or
three years, as Dr Whitmore and Professors W. W.
Lawrence and H. A. Doak, have declared for their reality
without reserve. The historian of the Elizabethan stage,
Mr W. J. Lawrence, however, took this point of view in
an article in the *Gentleman's Magazine* as long ago as 1887.

The question is of no small importance as regards not
merely the history of ideas or the constitution of the poet's
mind, but (still more) the interpretation of his artistic
method, whether in the plays in which the ghosts appear
or in others. If Cæsar's ghost is real, and ranges for
revenge, we have one sort of play; if he be merely the
'embodiment of Brutus' sense of the egregious mistake he
has made in slaying Cæsar and of the approaching overthrow of republicanism,' we have another. And if it be
allegory or symbolism here, it may be the one or the other
also, as some indeed have thought, in the *Tempest*. My

own opinion is that all the ghosts in Shakespeare are as
real as the ghost (on the platform or off it) in *Hamlet,*
and are not different in superstitious character—though
vastly superior in artistic effect—from the other ghosts in
Elizabethan drama.

Far from being subjective or allegorical, the ghosts of
Elizabethan drama, like the ghosts of folklore, were, as
Mr Lang has observed of the latter, 'ghosts with a purpose'. They were not used recklessly, as in some modern
drama and fiction, for mere uncanny and melodramatic
effect.[1] Groan and gloat, curse their enemies and harrow
the senses of their friends, as they might, they came, first
and last, to effect a definite end. That, above all, was to
wreak revenge by appearing either to the victim or to the
revenger; or it was to protect some loved one;[2] or it was
to prophesy;[3] or to crave burial;[4] or simply to serve in the
capacity of an omen of death.[5] These purposes were from
of old those of the ghost of folklore. All except the one
before the last are represented, as we shall see, in Shakespeare; but the paramount purpose of ghosts in the four
plays, *Hamlet, Richard III, Julius Cæsar,* and *Macbeth,*
is revenge.

As regards motive,—and for the moment we beg the
question and speak of motives—Shakespeare's ghosts are
to be classed with the ghost in *Hamlet.* They differ from
it in that they appear not to the revenger but to the victim
of revenge. Here it is, perhaps, that readers have stum-

---

[1] In the decay of the drama, indeed, in Shakespeare's *Cymbeline* and *Henry VIII* and in Webster (see the writer's *John Webster,* 1905, pp. 120-1, 150-1) the supernatural begins, under the influence of the Masque, to be treated without much meaning, spectacularly. See below.

[2] The second appearance of the ghost in *Hamlet,* to protect Hamlet's mother. Cf. the Friar's Umbra in Chapman's *Bussy* and the friendly service of Jack's ghost in Peele's *Old Wives' Tale.*

[3] Marston's *Sophonisba,* ghost of Asdrubal.

[4] The *Second Maiden's Tragedy* (1611), ghost of the Lady.

[5] Webster's *White Devil,* Brachiano's ghost, Chapman, etc. It is a wide-spread superstition that ghosts—the ghosts of friends—come to fetch the souls of those left in the land of the living. Cf. Frazer's *Golden Bough.*

bled; the ghost in *Hamlet,* appearing to the revenger to incite him, is not open to subjective interpretation; those of Cæsar and of Banquo, appearing to the murderers, in some measure are. One has disclosures to make and exhortations to deliver; the other may accomplish its purpose merely by its presence—by its gestures and bloody wounds, and by the fate which its mere appearing bodes. In short, one has to make for itself a hearing; the other may appeal to a witness and advocate dwelling within the victim's breast. When the latter is so treated, accordingly, without such crasser and more material features as speaking or as appearing to more than one person, it is but natural for a present-day critic to interpret it as an embodiment of conscience, or, as the merely ominous becomes more prominent, even as a presentimental hallucination. But such an idea did not occur, and was not intended to occur, to the Elizabethans themselves. Speaking and appearing to more than one person made, as we shall see, no difference; apparently, at least, all these ghosts were the ghosts of superstition, most of them seeking revenge like the ghosts in Seneca; and though in later developments there is a tendency both in Shakespeare and in the Elizabethan drama generally to restrict the range of the ghosts' communicativeness and visibility, that does not imply that they are meant to be less real. The ghosts in the prime of the drama serve a functional purpose, like other forms of the supernatural, such as the Weird Sisters;[6] they both impel the action and influence it; and, like other artistic devices, they soon began to lose their functional character and sink into decoration or spectacle. The unplausible character of the convention of itself led to the elimination of speech or other mortal doings. But it was the incessant advance

[6] This has been best shown by Dr Whitmore in his elaborate review of the whole subject in his monograph *The Supernatural in Tragedy* (Cambridge, Mass., 1915). To this work, eight years subsequent to my article on the ghosts in the *Modern Language Publications*, I am here considerably indebted, as I try to indicate below.

towards greater refinement in method of presentation that caused the change rather than any inclination to turn the ghost into an hallucination or symbol.

To trace this development, whether in Shakespeare or the Elizabethan drama generally, is not our present affair. Thus much has been said of it to explain the difference in effect between the ghost in *Hamlet* and Shakespeare's other apparitions—to show why they talk less and do less and stand more aloof; but in order to prove that they were none the less the ghosts of popular superstition we shall turn to other considerations. Beginning with the crucial instance, Banquo's ghost, we shall, instance by instance, endeavour to prove this from the situation itself, from the evidence of folklore and of a comparison with other Elizabethan and classical ghosts of certainly objective character and from Shakespeare's attitude towards the abstract, the supernatural, and the occult in general.

Macbeth

In *Macbeth* the mere situation lends itself to our interpretation. Banquo has been invited to a feast by his would-be murderer; and when his murderer, among the guests, believes that he now bides safe for ever in a ditch, Banquo stands before him. He has been bid—ironically —not to fail our feast, and with irony for irony he keeps the word he pledges. Such a situation is personal, concrete, objective, Elizabethan, if any be. So it is understood by Macbeth, it seems to me, and so it would be understood by the audience. Indeed, as Professor Keller observes, 'it is an ancient popular belief that the dead take part in the feast to which they are invited'; and that they may do it as here, ironically and vindictively, appears from the old monkish tale of Don Juan and the Statue, presented dramatically a few years later than *Macbeth* by Tirso in Spain. At first Macbeth seems not to see the ghost—he finds the table full. It is only when Lennox points to the

chair that he recognizes him. 'Which of you,' he then
cries, 'have done this?' What he means by 'this'—the trick
of filling up the table, the making of an effigy representing
Banquo, or the actual killing of him—it is hard to say.
Probably the last, and forthwith he snatches the opportunity of warding off such an imputation from himself.
For to him at least the Ghost's errand is plain: it is prophecy, retaliation, vengeance. He sits in Macbeth's royal
chair as a token that none the less his seed shall sit there
hereafter. He shakes his gory locks at the King in wrath,
and perhaps as a dark menace of the nemesis that awaits
him. And he makes other pantomimic signs of a sort that
drive Macbeth to desperation—'what care I?'—and to a
challenge to speak and out with it. As the ghost retires,
Macbeth vows that hereafter 'the monuments of his victims shall be the maws of kites'—the body annihilated, that
is to say, so that the ghost may not walk.[7] Easily recovering himself thereupon, he calls for wine, and in the teeth
of this experience, drinks to Banquo's health. Equal to
Macbeth's presumption, or *hybris,* however, is the ghost's
ironical rancour, and he reappears. This time Macbeth's
fear and rage are well-nigh frenzied; but the ghost gone,
he is himself again. Everything, then, in the scene com-
ports with objectivity—the completeness and abruptness
of Macbeth's changes on the one hand and the spirit of
merely personal antagonism in both parties on the other,
the unremorseful fear and defiance of the murderer and
the ironical vindictiveness of the ghost. Macbeth hears
no cry from a conscience such as we know, never thinks of
brushing the reality of the ghost aside as he does that of
the dagger, but himself comprehends, in that day of the feud
and vendetta, the purport of his errand very well:

It will have blood, they say; blood will have blood.

[7] Cf. Nash, *Summer's Last Will and Testament,* Hazlitt's *Dodsley,* viii,
p. 77; the mutilation of Agamemnon's corpse, *Choephori,* 439.—The interpretation originates, I surmise, with Professor Kittredge.

Even more objective, even more evidently revengeful, is the ghost's second—or perhaps we should call it third— appearance. This, at the Witches' Cavern, takes place, like the appearance of the shade of the prophet Samuel at Endor, and that of the spirit Asmath in *Henry VI*, by dint of conjuring; and one is as little susceptible of rationalistic interpretation as the other. Banquo plays a part like that of the most material and vindictive ghost of the Kydian Tragedy of Blood, Marston's Andrugio;[8] or like that of Heywood's Agamemnon,[9] taunting Macbeth with his 'blood-boltered' smile as he points at the line of kings-to-be 'for his.'

This interpretation, moreover—that Banquo's ghost is but a disembodied person seeking revenge—restoring to us the effect of ironical reversal (lost under a rationalistic or allegorical interpretation), fulfils Shakespeare's manifest intention. Banquo is bid, sardonically, not to fail the feast, nor does he. In the folly and hypocrisy of his homicidal success Macbeth gives voice to a wish that Banquo were present, and turns to find him—father of a line of kings—seated on the throne. Macbeth had called Banquo 'our chief guest,' and there at the head of the table he sits, a ghostly kill-joy, the proverbial death's-head at the feast literally reproduced and outdone. To the Elizabethan audience all this meant that Banquo—that fate— was getting even, and how could it have such a meaning if his ghost was merely a figment of Macbeth's imagination? It is but the simple, objectively ironical nemesis which, in the *Knight of the Burning Pestle*,[10] Beaumont, recalling possibly this very scene, makes Jasper, entering with face mealed as his own ghost, threaten against his enemy:

[8] *Antonio's Revenge*, V, i,—'tossing his torch about his head in triumph.'
[9] See below, p. 199. He points to his wounds.
[10] As the *Knight of the Burning Pestle* was acted in 1611, it is almost contemporary with Forman's notice. See below, p. 215.

When thou art at thy table with thy friends,
Merry in heart, and fill'd with swelling wine,
I'll come in midst of all thy pride and mirth,
Invisible to all men but thyself,
And whisper such a sad tale in thine ear,
Shall make thee let the cup fall from thy hand
And stand as mute and pale as death itself.—V, i.

Such a reversal, with its abrupt, sensational irony, and its personal revenge for nemesis, is characteristic of the Elizabethan drama. Whirls of the wheel like this occur not infrequently to overthrow the fatuous or presumptuous. Such are the solutions of the witches' enigmas in this very play, Birnam Wood coming to Dunsinane and Macduff confronting Macbeth as one not of woman born; such is Hamlet's letter announcing his return at the moment when Claudius was on the point of telling Laërtes how he had forestalled the latter's revenge; such, still more exactly, are the condemnation out of his own mouth of the much-warned, headlong Hastings, and the fulfilment of Buckingham's jesting prayer.[11] In the case in question the irony is accentuated by Macbeth's wish that Banquo were present and by the health he drinks to him, either of which coincides with an entrance of the ghost. These have been interpreted, according to the law of the association of ideas, as provocatives of the hallucinations; but thus the irony—the Elizabethan meaning—is obliterated, and the *motif* of superstition explained away. He comes because he is called. 'Ghosts never appear unless

[11] Cf. such irony in the fulfilment of Anne's curse of herself, *Richard III*, I, ii, 112 and IV, i, 72-85, and of Buckingham's conditional prayer that his friend may be faithless, II, i, 38-40 and V, i, 12-21:

That high All-seer, which I dallied with,
Hath turned my feigned prayer on my head
And given in earnest what I begged in jest.

And compare in point of ironical abruptness of reversal: *Romeo and Juliet*, V, i, 17 f, news of Juliet's death; *Lear*, IV, i, 10, Edgar's seeing his father blinded; etc.

sent for,' runs a proverb in Lean's *Collectanea;* [12] just as 'they never speak'—witness the Dane—'till spoke to.' Speak of the Devil and he will appear. Even now no superstition is commoner than the aversion against naming the dead, and it once had a quite definite cause and practical basis. Really the words of Macbeth are words of impiety, of a classical Infatuation and Insolence,[13] and as such they are answered from the other world. They fly in the face of Heaven, and, like those of Hastings and Buckingham, are, in fulfilment, hurled back upon the speaker's head. Macbeth is like Don Juan, who invites the statue to supper and also drinks to his health before he comes; and like the statue, the ghost comes even at that moment.[14] And the dramatist is writing the language, not of psychology, but of the stage.

Other instances quite parallel to this in Shakespeare there are perhaps none, but there are plenty in the other dramatists. It is no uncommon thing on the Elizabethan stage for ghosts or the heavenly or the infernal powers to answer words of appeal, defiance, or blasphemy with outcries or with thunder and lightning;[15] and in the passage below cited from Massinger we have a remarkable instance of ghosts, objective as one could wish, answering the murderer's challenge, much to his amazement, on the spot. The situation may be presented as a whole because it is parallel to that in *Macbeth* in more ways than one. It is Malefort, the murderer of wife and son, that speaks:

[12] III, 471.

[13] Ἄτη. ὕβρις

[14] Coleridge cites the passage in full where this occurs in the *Ateista fulminato, Works* (Shedd) iii, 566; in Tirso there is the invitation, but the health is drunk in his presence. His hero has still more *sang froid*.

[15] Marston's *Sophonisba*, V, i, the ghost of Asdrubal in answer to the challenge; Tourneur's *Atheist's Tragedy*, II, iv; *Revenger's Tragedy* (Mermaid ed.), pp. 411, 428-9, thunder three times in answer to appeals to God, or as a mark of his approval. Cf. Chettle's *Hoffman*, ll. 11 f.

Though this centre
Labour to bring forth earthquakes, and hell open
Her wide-stretched jaws, and let out all her furies,
They cannot add an atom to the mountain
Of fears and terrors that each minute threaten
To fall on my accursed head—
[*Enter the Ghost of young Malefort, naked from the waist,
full of wounds, leading in the Shadow of a Lady, her face
leprous.*]
                    Ha, is't fancy?
Or hath hell heard me, and makes proof if I
Dare stand the trial? Yes, I do; and now
I view these apparitions, I feel
I once did know the substances. For what come you?
Are you aerial forms deprived of language,
And so denied to tell me, that by signs
                    [*The Ghosts use various gestures.*]
You bid me ask here of myself? 'Tis so:
And there is something here makes answer for you.
You come to lance my sear'd up conscience; yes,
And to instruct me, that those thunderbolts,
That hurl'd me headlong from the height of glory,
Wealth, honours, worldly happiness, were forged
Upon the anvil of my impious wrongs,
And cruelty to you! I do confess it;
And that my lust, compelling me to make way
For a second wife, I poisoned thee . . .

    .   .   .   .

                    Yet, thou being my son,
Wert not a competent judge mark'd out by heaven
For her revenger, which thy falling by
My weaker hand confirm'd—[*Answered still by signs.*]
                    'Tis granted by thee.
Can any penance expiate my guilt,
Or can repentance save me?—[*Ghosts disappear.*]
                    They are vanish'd!
What's left to do, then? I'll accuse my fate,
That did not fashion me for nobler uses;
For if those stars, cross to me in my birth,
Had not denied their prosperous influence to it,
With peace of conscience, like to innocent men,

I might have ceased to be, and not as now,
To curse my cause of being—
> [*He is killed with a flash of lightning.*]
> —*Unnatural Combat,* V, 2.

Equally Elizabethan and far more Shakespearean is the conception, according to our interpretation, of nemesis as a personal revenge. So in Shakespeare (though so the critics do not interpret it) nemesis is generally conceived. Hamlet's father, old Gloster, Cæsar, and the infinite villains and victims of the *Richard III* and *Henry VI* trilogy, are avenged, as the parties concerned themselves make clear, in a blood-feud. Hardly one of the dozen or more of princes and peers who fall under Richard's axe fails to recognize that his fate is due to Queen Margaret's curse;[16] and these and all the others, be they guiltless or be they guilty, crave Richard's blood, in turn, as ghosts on Bosworth Field. Here blood will have blood, regardless of considerations of law or even of guilt; and not the vague powers of nature, society or justice take order to that end, but, in the body or out of the body, the murdered one himself. The Richard III and Henry VI cycle, however, are early plays, crudely Senecan, and curses and blood-guiltiness are there visited upon men more indiscriminately than afterwards; yet even in the political drama *Julius Cæsar* the nemesis is still highly personal. Not only does Cæsar's ghost actually appear to Brutus on the eve of battle, but, as Brutus and Cassius severally at the end confess,[17] and Antony had prophesied, it was his ghost—and by that is

---

[16] Queen Anne (*v. supra*) suffers from her own curse; this is classical, as in the *Œdipus.*

[17] V, iii, 45; V, v, 17-20, 50; V, iii, 94-6. Anthony's prophecy, III, i, 270 f.:

> And Cæsar's spirit, ranging for revenge,
> With Ate by his side come hot from hell,
> Shall in these confines with a monarch's voice
> Cry 'Havoc!' and let slip the dogs of war;
> That this foul deed shall smell above the earth
> With carrion men, groaning for burial.

meant, not the *spirit of Cæsar*, as we should say, but his indignant shade, 'mighty yet' and 'ranging for revenge,'— that 'turned their swords in their own proper entrails.' The nemesis does not take the form of society outraged, a mob devoted, after all, to absolutism, the spirit of the times revolting against republican conservatism, or any form whatsoever that philosophical critics have devised, but, as both Antony and Octavius avow,[18] that of a vendetta.[19] Macbeth himself falls not merely as a usurper, a foe to liberty or justice, but, at the hands of Macduff, explicitly to appease the ghosts of the latter's wife and children.[20] The nemesis which Shakespeare delineates is direct and simple, an even-handed justice that strikes the

[18] Cf. the whole tenor of their words in the parley, V, i, especially ll. 50-55.

[19] The impression is confirmed by a passage of like tenor in *Antony and Cleopatra*, where Sextus Pompey says to Octavius and Antony:

> To you all three,
> The senators alone of this great world,
> Chief factors for the gods, I do not know
> Wherefore my father should revengers want,
> Having a son and friends; since Julius Cæsar,
> Who at Philippi the good Brutus ghosted,
> There saw you labouring for him, etc.
>   And that is it
> Hath made me rig my navy . . .
>   . . . with which I meant
> To scourge the ingratitude that despiteful Rome
> Cast on my noble father.—*A. and C.*, II. vi, 8ff.

And the passage testifies as well to the objectivity of the ghost of Cæsar and the revengefulness of his mission.

[20] *Macbeth*, V, vii, 15:

> If thou be'st slain and with no stroke of mine,
> My wife and children's ghosts will haunt me still.

This is the true spirit of the vendetta, still stronger in the remarkable passage which precedes this:

> *Malcolm.* Let's make us medicines of our great revenge,
>   To cure this deadly grief.
> *Macduff.* He has no children.—IV, iii, 214 f.

'He' is Macbeth; and Macduff, like the bloodiest of the Kydian revengers, may be meditating in the strain of an eye for an eye and a tooth for a tooth. The Clarendon Press Editors soften this interpretation a little; Professor Bradley and others reject it; and I myself would not insist upon it. 'He cannot know my love, my grief'—but never before or after was Shakespeare so laconic.

human breast from without rather than from within, and takes, not by preference so much as in instinctive sympathy with the age, the primitive, popular form of a personal, or supernaturally personal, vengeance. It is retaliation as well as retribution, and of such a nemesis Banquo's ghost is but a capital instance.

Not that these larger and higher aspects of justice and retribution are to Shakespeare unknown, or by him unexpressed. The swords of Richmond, Macduff, and Hamlet bear the sanction of fate, of heaven, or of an outraged humanity. But always, as here, there is the sword, a concrete and human agent or minister; the dramatically effective vendetta and the cause of justice are one. There is in the text no evidence at all of that philosophical notion, which arose in the nineteenth century, of a conflict and clash between the revenge desired by Hamlet's father and a higher justice, not so personal. In this play, too, they are one and the same. Indeed, it is not improbable that Shakespeare, for a time at least, accepted the scriptural (and classical) superstition of the sins of the fathers visited on the children even to the third generation.[21] Nor is Shakespeare oblivious of the retribution within the human bosom, or of that visited upon a man by society. Lady Macbeth suffers from the one, Macbeth—as he laments the loss of honour, love, obedience, troops of friends—more especially from the other. But these too are simple and direct. The sufferings of Lady Macbeth, who has no compassion or remorse, though spiritual, are almost as external as Macbeth's in the banquet scene, as the sufferings of the reprobate in the Bible and in Dante, —the worm that never dieth or that fire which Bunyan declares was let down into Mr Badman's conscience from

---

[21] He accepts it, in imitation of the ancients, as the constructive principle in the Richard and Henry Cycle; and even Henry V prays before battle that the sin of his father may not be visited on him and his people. Cf. Brandl, *Shakespeare* (1894), pp. 74-7, 93.

heaven.[22] And of the vague and devious visitations of an
alienated environment there is nothing at all. The mob in
Julius Cæsar or in *Coriolanus* is as solid and individual as
a person.

What now are the arguments adduced in favour of the
contrary interpretation with which we are contending?
Professor Bradley has tabulated them,[23] though he does not
definitely accept or reject them:

1. *Macbeth has already seen one hallucination, that of the
dagger; and Lady Macbeth would remind us of it here.*

The main answer to this, as to all the other arguments
here quoted, is that as the stage-directions in the first edition
of the play, the Folio, indicate, and the account of the play
in Forman's Diary proves, the ghost was represented, and
was meant to be represented, on the stage; whereas the true
hallucinations, the air-drawn dagger and the voice that cried
'Sleep no more,' were not. The dagger and the voice Macbeth himself acknowledges to be the creation of his fancy,—
'methought I heard a voice,' 'there's no such thing.' Of
the ghost, despite the testimony of all his guests, he is certain—

> If I stand here, I saw him—

and he remains so, despite all, almost to the end of the
scene. And as for the authority of Lady Macbeth, are we,
against the witness of Hamlet's eyes and ears and of our
own, to accept Queen Gertrude's explanation—

> This is the very coinage of the brain?

or, in the case of the ghost in Heywood's *Iron Age* (an unmistakable instance, as Professor Bradley points out, of objectivity), Clytemnestra's similar explanation to Orestes—

> Thy former murder makes thee mad?

[22] For this matter of the external conscience see the chapter on the
Criminals, and chapter iii, sections 1 and 4.

[23] See Bradley, pp. 492-3. In quoting him I sometimes take the liberty
of condensing his language.

Those who in accordance with the traditions of folklore (as we shall learn) are not privileged to see the ghost, must of course have their say; but we the audience are wiser—know that Banquo is dead, dead by Macbeth's hand, and are now vouchsafed the visible though intangible evidence.

The argument from character, moreover, has been in this matter of little—perhaps no—force. For if Macbeth sees ghosts by dint of imaginative leanings, why do Richard III, Brutus, and dozens of other persons in the Elizabethan drama see them without such leanings? And even apart from these pressing considerations, what on its own merits can be made of the psychology? The esthetic critics hold that the strength of this hallucination, in which Macbeth believes, is a logical and inevitable development from the previous hallucinations, in which he did not believe. But if things have gone thus far why do they go no farther? Nay, why do they come to a pause and leave Macbeth henceforth hallucination-free? The scene itself, moreover, does not bear out such an interpretation. The murder done, Macbeth expresses his complacency, but at finding it after all but half done he chides. Of that half he assures himself, however, and after appointing another meeting with his mercenary he turns, cheerfully enough, with a conventional table-greeting, to his guests, and, with the instinct of a host and hypocrite, wishes for Banquo's presence. He is not at all in the same spiritual state as he was when he saw the dagger or heard the voice which bade him sleep no more. When he sees the ghost, fear—pure fear and horror—overwhelms him; but when it is gone he is himself again: and the experience is repeated at the ghost's return. The conclusions which Macbeth then reaches are: the wonder of the apparition and of the guests' not seeing it, the wisdom in such a business of making assurance doubly sure by dismembering the body, and the impossibility of keeping murder hid. In all this there is no real remorse, nor much concern for the crime as such. And there is conscience only as the victim of his crime, breaking out of the other world to have vengeance, would naturally be the minister of a conscience visited upon him.[24] There is indeed something of what Mr Moorman discovers—a deep sense of insecurity; but it appears rather when the ghost is present, and it is not half so much fear of being proclaimed a murderer, or fear of Fleance proving father of a line of kings, as fear of the ghost before his eyes, the hideous, horrible shade that dogs him. A subjective cause, then, has not been indicated by the poet, nor has an adequate subjective cause been suggested by the critics.

To us, no doubt, except as we remember the Elizabethans, a ghost following (in order of time) an air-drawn dagger and a spectral voice must seem only another creation of Macbeth's feverish brain. For we plant ourselves in the mind of the character, and interpret the story all through his eyes. But the Elizabethans, we know, did not; nor did Shakespeare expect them to do so. Dagger, voice, and ghost, moreover, are to an Elizabethan not phenomena of the same description, as indeed the stage representation indicates. One with disordered brain might see or hear what is not, but a ghost he saw only when it appeared. To be sure, one with disordered brain might see a ghost as well, but an Elizabethan would then need a hint such as that put into the mouth of the Duke Francisco;[25] for that it should be an hallucination is not the Elizabethan's foremost thought as it is ours. Scepticism as to ghosts in general went, in his day, only so far as to attribute ghosts to the imposture of the evil one, as we shall see below.

2. *The ghost seems to be created by Macbeth's imagination, for his words:*

> Now they rise again
> With twenty mortal murthers on their crowns—

[24] For this matter of the External Conscience and the question of the psychological interpretation discussed in this paragraph and the next, see chapter iii, sections 1 and 4.

[25] Webster's *White Devil*, III, iii, Isabella's ghost. See below, p. 214.

describe it, and they echo what the murderer had said to him
a little time before:

> Safe in a ditch he bides
> With twenty trenched gashes on his head.[26]

Taken as Shakespeare would have us take it, this is not a
matter of psychology but of story-telling, of narrative fact.
To be sure, Macbeth does not count the gashes—twenty is
only a round number—and he merely echoes the murderer's
words; but with the gashes' getting there neither murderer's
words nor his own imagination has the least thing to do. He
sees the twenty gashes because they are there. For by the
laws of folklore the world over and the usage of literature
ancient or modern, a ghost in outer semblance is no more
than the corpse revivified. It is pale, livid, or blood-bespat-
tered; it is leprous and tettered from poison; or it is
befouled with the dirt of the death-struggle or the dust of
the grave; and always it shows its wounds. So with the
ghost of Hector in the *Æneid:*

> raptatus bigis, ut quondam, aterque cruento
> pulvere, perque pedes traicetus lora tumentis.
> Ei mihi, qualis erat, quantum mutatus ab illo
> Hectore, qui redit exuvias indutus Achilli,
> vel Danaum Phrygios iaculatus puppibus ignis,
> squalentem barbam et concretos sanguine crinis
> volneraque illa gerens, quæ circum plurima muros
> accepit patrios;

so with the shades whom Odysseus visits in the underworld:

and many there were, wounded with bronze-shod spears, men slain
in fight with their bloody mail about them (*Odyssey,* xi, 40);

so with the ghost of Clytemnestra as she rouses the
Eumenides:

---

[26] The same objective point of view is taken by Professor Moulton,
Moral System, p. 261. Indeed, he seems bent on taking no other point of
view: the very blood on First Murderer's face as he appears at the door
he makes out to be in Macbeth's imagination.' Is Duncan's there too?

See these sword-wounds of my heart, from whom they came;

so with Eurydice in Hades, who advances at a slow pace, by reason of her wound.[27] So, too, with the ghosts of Laius and Hector in Seneca, one showing his bloody limbs, and both their matted hair;[28] with the murdered in Chaucer's *Nun's Priest's Tale*:

> And atte thridde tyme yet his felawe
> Cam, as him thoughte, and seide, 'I am now slawe;
> Bihold my blody woundes, depe and wyde!'

and with the ghost of Agamemnon in Heywood's *Iron Age* as he appears to Orestes pointing at his own wounds, that of the Host in the *English Traveller,* that of Alonzo, in Middleton's *Changeling,*[29] and the ghosts of Malefort's Son and Lady, cited from Massinger above. Shakespeare himself had previously recognized the superstition and made similar dramatic use of it in *Henry VI,* Part II. In Act III, scene ii, Warwick, when describing Duke Humphrey's corpse, dwells on the state of his hair—upreared and sticking to the sheets in which he was strangled. And then, in scene iii, the spirit thus appears to the dying Cardinal:

> Comb down his hair; look, look! it stands upright,
> Like lime-twigs set to catch my winged soul.[30]

Banquo's ghost, therefore, rises with twenty mortal murthers on his crown, not because Macbeth remembers the words of the murderer and visualizes them, but because

---

[27] Ovid. *Met.* x, 49.

[28] *Oed.* 624-5; *Troades,* 449-50.

[29] II, ii, a false report, Mostellaria fashion; but made as plausible as possible—'His body gash'd and all ore-stuck with wounds.'—The ghost of Alonzo, *Changeling,* IV, Dumb Show, 'showing him [the murderer] the hand whose finger he had cut off.'

[30] For the above reference to Ovid and one to the *Æneid,* vi, 495, see Professor Kittredge, *Am. Journ. Phil.,* vi, 163-5. Additional references on this subject:—*Eumenides,* l. 103; Spenser, *F.Q.* II, xi, 20; *Kalevala,* quoted by Butcher and Lang, *Odyssey* (1887), pp. 416-17; Fletcher's *Faithful Shepherdess,* II, ii, 102, 109, 113; Calderón's *Principe Constante,* III, xi and xiii, where Don Fernando, a real ghost certainly, appears in the mantle of his Order, in which he had begged to be buried; and Tylor's *Primitive Culture* (1871) i, 450-2.

the ghost must needs be like the corpse. It is no matter
of psychology or symbolism, but the exceedingly simple
matter of a story hanging together.

3. *It vanishes the second time on his making a violent
effort and asserting its unreality:*

> Hence, horrible shadow!
> Unreal mockery, hence!

*This is not quite so the first time, but then too its disap-
pearance follows on his defying it:*

> Why, what care I? If thou canst nod, speak too.

So, apparently, the dagger vanishes when he exclaims,

> There's no such thing!

The unreality of the ghost is asserted by Macbeth, not,
certainly, in the sense of its subjectivity but only in the
sense of its being unsubstantial as a shade.[31] Immediately
after this he wonders that the others can keep the natural
ruby of their cheeks when his are blanched with fear. As
for defying it, that of course is quite another matter, on
which I, in these pages, would be the last to spend words,
but with which the passage quoted for comparison, where
the dagger is dismissed as an illusion—

> There's no such thing:
> It is the bloody business which informs
> Thus to mine eyes —

has nothing to do. Elsewhere [32] Professor Bradley quotes
to the same purpose Brutus' words to Cæsar's ghost—

> Now I have taken heart thou vanishest;

but would Brutus have it vanish? In the next line he cries
after it,

> Ill spirit, I would have more talk with thee,

just as Macbeth himself cries to the witches,

[31] And also, in the words 'Unreal mockery', in a sense discussed below,
p. 215.
[32] P. 493.

> Stay, you imperfect speakers, tell me more;

and Brutus's first utterance is no more than an outburst of
mystified vexation.   The situation here is only that to be
found in ghost-stories and folklore the world over—the
oracle breaking off at the tantalizing moment.   Quite
otherwise is it in *Macbeth*.   The ghost makes no disclosures—his vengeance is the horror and menace of his presence, and of this the murderer is but too glad to be rid.
That, however, he himself does this, by will-power, is far
from having been proved, and certainly the burden of
proof is on the shoulders of the asserter.   Indeed, the
assertion itself depends for proof upon the proposition
that Banquo's ghost is an hallucination, which it was
adduced to prove.

4. *At the end of the scene Macbeth himself seems to
regard the ghost as an illusion:*

> My strange and self-abuse [33]
> Is the initiate fear that wants hard use.

There is force in this argument as in none of the others;
but granted that in folklore and the Elizabethan drama a
ghost may appear to one person only in a multitude (as
below we shall see that granted it must be), these final
words of Macbeth's become, I think, the most natural reaction from such an experience.   No one has seen anything;
the queen has rated and taunted him and cast his former
hallucinations in his teeth; and his guests have tried to
overlook his passion as the fit of a moment.   The case is
different from that of Hamlet—there the ghost speaks,
and Hamlet has only one witness, his mother, against him,
but on former occasions Francisco, Bernardo, Marcellus,
and Horatio for him; and how can Macbeth stand out
alone against his sarcastic queen and the whole table?   Be
that as it may, there are instances in the Elizabethan drama
of the most unquestionably real ghosts being received, even

[33] 'Self-deception.'

by one person when alone, with equal incredulity.[34]   In
the present play, after the indubitable witches have taken
flight, Banquo asks Macbeth,

> Were such things here as we do speak about,
> Or have we eaten on the insane root
> That takes the reason prisoner?

Likewise, after their second appearance, Macbeth questions, fruitlessly, his lord-in-waiting, Lennox. For your
subtler dramatist must have a way of distinguishing the
natural and the supernatural, particularly when, as on the
Elizabethan stage, both are represented in a form equally
substantial and corporeal. Wonder and doubt are the
natural means.

This seems to me a thoroughly adequate explanation for
Macbeth's conduct at this juncture; as well as for that of
Brutus and Posthumus in a similar situation, not to mention Hastings, Cæsar, Antigonus, and the numerous others
who doubt or seek to verify the portents, oracles, or
dreams sent to warn them.[35] If ghosts be, and do appear,
how else would the ghost-seer conduct himself, once the
horror is departed? Would he not rub his eyes, pinch
himself, ask questions, doubt the whole experience, call it
his melancholy, like Hamlet and Webster's Flamineo, or
his fancy, like Macbeth? Particularly, if this be the ghost
of the murdered and he have a sense of guilt? But above
all by this means, by this clearly marked transition of
wonder or bewilderment and of doubt, the dramatist brings
home to us the difference between the intangible and the
tangible—makes us realize that it *was* a ghost, a being
from another world. *We* do not doubt it, because the
ghost-seer does; we do not doubt it, because we are not
asked by the dramatist to believe that the ghost-seer, at

[34] Tourneur's *Atheist's Tragedy*, II, vi; III, ii; Massinger's *Roman
Actor*, V, i; Webster's *White Devil*, V, i. See also below, pp. 207-8,
notes, and *Cymbeline*, V, iv, 30-151, in particular, 130-151.

[35] For Brutus, see below, p. 225; for Posthumus, *Cymbeline*, V, iv, 30-151;
for Antigonus pooh-poohing his dream, *W. T.* III, iii, 39.

the moment when he naturally would, did not.   His doubts are to satisfy our artistic cravings, not our intellectual. They make the ghost more real, not less.

The whole matter becomes clearer when we consider the same method in other dramatists and poets.   To be sure, the doubts and questionings of Charlemont in Tourneur's *Atheist's Tragedy,* of De Flores in Middleton's *Changeling,* of Cæsar in Massinger's *Roman Actor,* and of Flamineo in the *White Devil,*[36] may be owing to Shakespeare's example.   But the device is wide-spread and seems to have been generally recognized as one of the means specially fitted for the purpose.   One of the most exquisite examples is the return of the lovers to the workaday world in *Midsummer Night's Dream:* they wake, and think the night has been a dream, with all its marvels.   And Theseus, when he hears their story, will not believe it—'the lunatic, the lover, and the poet,' quoth he—though his wife, who has her indefeasible last word, sees that their story is more than a figment of the fancy, however strange.   Then Bottom, the weaver, who alone of mortals had seen the fairies, but only when enchanted, thinks too that this is all a dream, though it isn't.   Something of the same way of doing, as Dr Whitmore[37] observes, is to be found, even in the days of faith unquestioning, in the York *Transfiguration* and the Towneley *Prima Pastorum*—

> now fares all as fantasye,
> For wote not we how thai are went;

and in the anonymous *King Richard II* (c. 1596), where Woodstock doubts the ghosts who had come to warn him of his danger.[38]   And it is a very common way of present-

---

[36] *Atheist's Tragedy,* II, vi; III, ii; *Changeling,* V, i; *Roman Actor,* V, i; *White Devil,* V, i.

[37] Pp. 159, 166.—This explanation of the ghost-seers' doubts, proposed in my article, is by Dr Whitmore richly illustrated and amplified; and to him I am here indebted.

[38] *Jahrbuch,* xxxv, p. 108.

ing the supernatural in Spanish plays. The ghosts in Tirso and Lope and the Demon in Calderón's *El Magico Prodigioso* are as real and unquestionable as any to be found; and yet after their disappearance those visited make inquiry of others and endeavour to explain the phenomena away, much after the fashion of Brutus and Macbeth, as an illusion[39]—as either the creature of their fears or an imposture.[40]

It is to be observed, however, that the dramatist does not leave the ghost-seer to his doubts in the end. Charlemont is the most obvious case—

> O, pardon me, my doubtful heart was slow
> To credit that which I did fear to know.

Justina, in *El Magico,* doubts the reality of the apparition, but on questioning the others, who had not seen it, she turns round and asserts its reality. Generally, however, the dramatist, having to do with an audience unbiased by rationalistic prejudices, depends, on the one hand, on the ghost's actual appearance before their eyes and, on the other, on the ghost-seer's manifest unwillingness, for personal causes, to accept it. He doubts, but drops the subject. In Tirso's *Infanzón,* the ghost appears three times; the first and second times the King denies his reality, but the third time not. So in the Witches' Cavern Banquo appears once more, and there is no doubt or questioning then.

The same method has been employed by Shakespeare and other dramatists, whether before the appearance of the supernatural or after, to make the transition from the tangible to the intangible, as well as from the intangible to the tangible again. 'Horatio says, 'tis but our fantasy,' says Marcellus: 'Tush, tush, 'twill not appear,' chimes in

[39] *El Magico,* III, vii and viii; Lope's *Lealtad en el agravio,* t. viii, (*Acad.* 1895), p. 513. Lope's *Las Paces de los reyes* (*ibid.*), p. 546.

[40] Tirso's (or Lope's) *Infanzón de Illescas, ib.,* t. ix, I, pp. 483-4 (a trick of his brothers' or the Queen's); II, p. 504.

Horatio for himself. But when the dreaded sight appears, Horatio is indeed convinced, and so perforce are we. Reasoning or argument, quite rightly, there is none. Horatio is not a sceptic on principle [41] but simply a man of enlightenment and common sense, who, having never yet seen a ghost, is not disposed to believe that there is one hereabouts, till he has seen it. Horatio and the audience do not disbelieve in ghosts—all that the dramatist needs to do is to make Horatio and the audience believe in this.

What concerns the dramatist here, before as well as after a ghost's appearance, is to bridge the chasm, to make the most unreal of things real, and the apparition plausible, not intellectually or philosophically, but as a matter of art; and by the cajoleries and sorceries of the imagination to bring about 'that willing suspension of disbelief for the moment which constitutes poetic faith.' He does the thing quickly, dramatically, by the impression on the witnesses at the ghost's appearance and disappearance; the poet who wrote the words just quoted, himself did it more slowly and poetically, by events and by changes of scene; and 'the skeleton ship, with the Spectre-woman and her death-mate, is ushered in by all the silences and wonders of a tropical sea, by loneliness and dreams.' [42]

Scepticism prepares the way for the supernatural; and breaks it to us gently, we might say, as does indeed another psychological element which has been similarly misunderstood. If there is a Horatio there is a Hamlet, and he is as ready and eager to see the ghost as Horatio is indifferent; sees his father in his mind's eye before he sees his purgatorial shade; and at the first revelation, imparted to him by it, cries, 'O my prophetic soul!' 'Good Sir,' says Banquo to Macbeth, 'why do you start and seem to fear,

---

[41] Antigonus is, it seems, as regards both ghosts and dreams; yet presently he says that he does not believe Hermione dead and that Apollo wishes him to follow the ghost's words. And in a moment the ghost's words concerning his own fate come true. *Winter's Tale,* III, iii.

[42] Sir Walter Raleigh.

Things that do sound so fair?' As both Professor **Bradley** and Sir Walter Raleigh have remarked, the supernatural is placed in closest relation to character; and the Queen of Denmark cannot see the spirit of her husband as does her son, because she does not hold him in her heart as her son does in his. Thus even in the case of his one unquestioned ghost Shakespeare raises and spiritualizes the phenomenon. He gives it psychological appropriateness and meaning, but thereby comes no nearer to making it a vision or hallucination; he makes it poetical but not a symbol. Professor Bradley[48] rightly compares the incident of Athena, descending to stay Achilles' hand in the council, though Achilles was already debating in his mind whether to draw his sword or to curb his soul. Athena is no symbol, either, though goddess of wisdom, invisible to the others.

5. It does not speak.

This is no real difficulty, whether from the point of view of folklore or of the drama. A ghost, says Brand, need not speak at all, and generally does not till bidden. Banquo's ghost, though bidden, does not speak, simply because he has nothing to say. Unlike Hamlet's father he has no message to impart, necessary to the action. And unlike the ghosts of Richard's victims or the ghost of Cæsar, he cannot cry, I will meet thee on Bosworth Field, or at Philippi; for revenge is in the hands of others than his friends and kin—Malcolm and Macduff—and is for other causes. Obviously there would be no point in his denouncing a retributory death which should come at the hands of Macduff, not Fleance, and to appease the ghosts of Macduff's wife and children. His program is to push the usurper from his stool and plague him with a blood-boltered presence and inscrutable menaces, and at the Witches' Cavern to taunt him with the show of a line of kings stretching out to the crack of doom. Silence and gestures, moreover, were now getting to be the approved

[48] *Shakespearean Tragedy,* p. 348.

demeanour for spirits on the stage. The talking ghost
taxed men's credulity; those few ghosts that hereafter
tread the stage—Webster's, Massinger's, and Heywood's
—point, nod, or beckon, but hold their peace; and Massinger's [44] and Webster's,[45] at least, awe and plague their
victim much as Banquo's does. No one is so fine and delicate in the treatment of unearthly things as Shakespeare,
for all that he keeps firm hold on the material reality of
superstition; and if for no other reason, Banquo holds his
peace because there is a crowd. No ghost in Shakespeare
is heard to speak by more than one person; Hamlet's
mother does not hear the ghost; the 'swear, swear' comes
from the cellarage; and both Richard and Richmond on
Bosworth Field are asleep. Indeed, in all Elizabethan
drama I know of no case of a ghost appearing before a
crowd and speaking; and here fine and delicate treatment
and superstition itself are at one. Even the Lord spoke
unto Moses or the prophets alone, not to all Israel gathered together before him.

6. *It is visible only to Macbeth.*

It is strange that with the scene between Hamlet and
his mother in mind Professor Bradley and other critics [46]
should in this matter find cause for question; for I cannot
take seriously the opinion of a few that the ghost in the
bedchamber is not the selfsame spirit of Act I. From the
point of view both of folklore and of classical and Elizabethan epic and dramatic practice—the only points of view,
I must think, to take,—it is quite regular. 'Now Athena
stood in presence manifest to Odysseus over against the
doorway of the hut; but it was so that Telemachus saw
her not before him and marked her not; for the gods in no
wise appear visibly to all.' So in Book I of the *Iliad*, as
we have seen, she appears only to the enraged Achilles.

[44] *The Roman Actor, The Unnatural Combat.*
[45] *White Devil*, Brachiano's ghost.
[46] Fletcher (Rolfe's *Macbeth*, p. 216) and others.

At the close of the *Choephori* the Eumenides appear only to Orestes, not to the chorus,—'Ye see not these forms, but I behold them'—though in the following drama of the trilogy they are actually represented. With one consent authorities on folklore like Reginald Scot and Brand[47] declare that most commonly a ghost appears to one person only, even when that person is in company with others; and so it appears in Chapman's *Revenge of Bussy D'Ambois*,[48] Heywood's *Iron Age*, and *King Edward IV*,[49] and the late play Sampson's *Vow-Breaker*,[50] as well as in *Hamlet*,[51] in all of which cases the objectivity is beyond cavil. Even in a modern play, Grillparzer's *Ahnfrau*, a real ghost, which appears to many of the characters separately, is, when it appears to Jaromir, invisible to Berta:

> Es ist nichts, Geliebter, nichts,
> Als die wilde Ausgeburt
> Der erhitzten Phantasie.
> Du bist müde, ruh' ein wenig.—II, i.

[47] Reginald Scot's *Discoverie of Witchcraft* (Nicholson's reprint, 1886), p. 449: 'Also they never appear to the whole multitude, seldome to a few, and most commonlie to one alone. Also they may be seene of some, and of some other in that presence not seene at all.' Hazlitt's *Brand* (1905), i, 270: . . . 'rarely visible to more than one person, although there are several in company.' Lavater, *Of Ghosts and Spirites* (London, 1596), p. 89: 'It commeth often-time to passe, that some one man doth heare or see something most plainly, when another, who standeth by him, or walketh with him, neither seeth nor heareth any such matter.' *Remarks on the Tragedy of Hamlet* (1736): (discussing the ghost in the closet-scene) 'the poet had also an eye to a vulgar notion that spirits are only seen by those with whom their business is, let there be never so many persons in company.' It was not merely a notion of the learned, then.

[48] Bussy's ghost appears to Cleremont, p. 206 (Shepherd's ed.), without being heard or seen by Guise, although, p. 209, he is visible to others.

[49] *Works*, London, 1874, iii, p. 423; i, pp. 163-4.

[50] Published in 1636 (Whitmore, pp. 275-76).

[51] Mr J. H. Hudson and Professors Schelling and Moulton, after accepting this ghost as real at his first appearance, are inclined to refuse him that quality at the second. This the Elizabethan historian cannot justifiably do. If the ghost was real at the first appearance, how to the audience, as he comes and speaks at length to stay Hamlet's wrath and whet his purpose, can he, without any hint on the part of the author, lose his reality? If the ghost was a ghost when he appeared in person to command, he is just as much one now that he appears to reiterate his command. It is by such obvious logic as this that an audience is guided, and should be guided.

It is quite clear that Berta's testimony is no more to be accepted than Queen Gertrude's. Here, indeed, in the exigencies of dramatic art, not in the notions of superstition, evidently resides the chief and fundamental reason why dramatists make an apparition visible to one character and not to another. Like the doubts of him who sees it, this is a means of bringing home to the audience the supernatural character of the phenomenon.

For it appears to the person in question *and the audience*. The last circumstance is, I think, the crucial test of the objectivity of any Elizabethan ghost. Whatever, under the load of outworn traditions, may be the occasional practice nowadays, then the audience was never made a prey to an illusion. Shakespeare, as usual, has here provided against all mistake on the part of the sensible spectator by giving him the key to the situation, just as he provides one for misunderstandings and mystifications such as those in the *Comedy of Errors* and the *Midsummer Night's Dream,* or those in the *Tempest* where Stephano, Trinculo, and Caliban are being beguiled by the invisible Ariel;[52] and nothing could be more stupid of the spectator than not to take it but insist on putting himself on a level with the characters on the boards. The case of Ariel, indeed, is one much in point: not only in the scene mentioned but invariably he is invisible either to all but the audience or to all but the audience and the person or persons to whom it behoves him to appear—visible and audible to Prospero alone when in company with Miranda or others, and to Prospero and the three criminals alone when in company with Gonzalo, Adrian, and Francisco.[53] Indeed, with Shakespeare, as with the Elizabethan dramatists generally, it may be taken as a rule, fairly absolute, not only that whatever is represented by him on the stage is actual

[52] *Tempest,* III, ii.
[53] *Tempest,* III, iii, 52-82. It is possible, but not probable, that here Ariel, like Prospero (stage-direction, l, 18), is visible to the audience (and Prospero) only, and to the criminals merely audible.

and objective, but that what is unobjective is not so represented. Thus it is with Lear's lunacy, and with Macbeth's dagger and the voice that cried to him, 'sleep no more.' Still, there are exceptions, though these are perfectly clear and explicit. One is Cardinal Beaufort's deathbed vision of the ghost of Duke Humphrey, whom he had murdered.[54] The ghost is real, though not represented, for the simple reason that Vaux's words in the scene preceding, and the Cardinal's in this, as well as the whole situation and context, make representation unnecessary. 'They are oftenest seene,' says Scot, 'by them that are readie to die.' The dying—witness the child in the story of the Erlkönig—were supposed to see what the bystanders could not see, even the future; in Shakespeare they prophesy;[55] and a murderer at death, if never before, was expected to see his victim's ghost. And Isabella's ghost in Webster's *White Devil* is, though represented, not real, for the simple reason that the audience must lend credence to his words as Francisco summons up her image—

> how strong
> Imagination works! how can she frame
> Things which are not!

In both cases the words of the text are clear.[56]

That it was Shakespeare who provided that Banquo's ghost should appear on the stage cannot be disputed. The

[54] *Second Henry VI*, III, iii. That Beaufort's vision is of Duke Humphrey's ghost appears from sc. ii, ll. 171 and 372-4, and from l. 15 of sc. iii. In the original of *Second Henry VI*, the *Contention betwixt the Two Famous Houses of Yorke and Lancaster*, the treatment of this ghost is similar, but the identifying of it with Duke Humphrey's is still more explicit. See Hazlitt's *Shakespeare's Library*, Pt. II, vol. i, pp. 479, 482, where both Vaux and the Cardinal himself roundly declare the figure seen to be Duke Humphrey's ghost; and compare Seneca's *Medea*, ll. 962-3, where the heroine sees, unrepresented, the ghost of her brother.

[55] See Dyer, and the historical plays *passim*. *Richard II*, II, i, 31-2; *1 Henry IV*, V, iv, 82-3; Henry VI prophesying at his death, *3 Henry VI*, V, vi, 56-7; *Merchant of Venice* I, ii, 30-31. Cf. Berzeviczy, *Surnaturel*, pp. 66-7.

[56] See Whitmore, 259-260, 281. Dr Whitmore is right.

two entrances, with the corresponding exits, and the seating of the ghost are indicated in the earliest text. To the
contemporary acting, moreover, there is the witness of Dr
Simon Forman (1610)—

And as he thus did, standing vp to drincke a Carouse to him,
the ghoste of Banco came and sate down in his cheier be-hind him.
And he turning A-bout to sit down A-gain sawe the goste of banco,
which fronted him so, that he fell in-to a great passion of fear and
fury, Vttering many wordes about his murder, by which, when they
hard that Banco was Murdred they suspected Mackbet—[57]

as well as the very definite testimony of Beaumont, quoted
above, and that of the anonymous play called the *Puritan*—

Instead of a jester we'll have the ghost in the white sheet sit at
the upper end of the table [58] —

to the acting of such scenes in general.

In one sense to be sure (but still a superstitious one)
the ghost of Banquo is an illusion; and that is probably
what Shakespeare means when he lets Macbeth cry,
'Unreal mockery, hence.' The ghost is not the veritable
manes of Banquo but a phantom in his likeness, created by
the devil, or (in that likeness) the devil himself. 'Take
any shape but that' he had adjured the spectre just before;
and if Banquo's it really be, he could, of course, take no
other. Shakespeare is here abreast of the Protestant
opinion of his day; [59] and this is not the only place in which

[57] If Forman here is right, he is describing the second entrance and a
second seating of the ghost. This took place from behind—not before
Macbeth's eyes like the other—and, by bringing him within an ace of
sitting in the horror's lap, must have produced a tragic sensation well
over the verge of the comic. It would be like the Friar's Umbra frightening
away the murderers of Bussy.—For the actual representation of the ghost as
late as 1686, see Higden, cited by Munro, *Mod. Phil.* (1916), Jan., p. 532.

[58] This passage has been used to determine the date of *Macbeth*—the
Puritan was published in 1607—but the context proves that it has no necessary reference to that or any play.

[59] Spalding, pp. 55-62; Creizenach, v, 423; cf. also my *Hamlet*, pp. 47-8.
In addition to these references, the first-hand evidence of Sir Walter
Raleigh, *History of the World*, I, xi, 6; Cranmer, *Remains* (1833), iv,
p. 204; John Deacon and John Walker, *Dialogical Discourses* (1601), pp.
121, 124, etc.

he has given expression to the opinion. Hamlet has generally been thought to be deceiving himself when he fears the ghost may be the devil, at the end of Act II; but both he and Horatio had thought of that before. Horatio has it in mind when he questions the spirit:

> What art thou that usurp'st this time of night,
> Together with that fair and warlike form
> In which the majesty of buried Denmark
> Did sometimes march?—(I, i, 46);

and Hamlet, when he balances the alternatives:

> Be thou a spirit of health or goblin damn'd,
> Bring with thee airs from heaven or blasts from hell
> —(I, iv, 40);

for such alternatives, of course, would not present themselves in relation to his sire. And when thereupon Horatio tries to dissuade Hamlet from following the ghost, he speaks, as Spalding has shown, exactly according to the tenor of James I's words about the devil's motives for appearing in a ghost's semblance, in his *Demonology* (1597), III, ii:

> What if it tempt you toward the flood, my lord,
> Or to the dreadful summit of the cliff
> That beetles o'er his base into the sea,
> And there assume some other horrible form,
> Which might deprive your sovereignty of reason
> And draw you into madness?

The one is the tinsell of their life, by inducing them to such perrilous places at such time as he either followes or possesses them; . . . The other thinge that hee preases to obtaine by troubling of them, is the tinsell of their soule, etc.

And that is the last thing to be expected of Hamlet's father, whether in the flesh or out of it. But Shakespeare does not cling to this opinion and consistently keep to it. Though the alternative is duly and frequently considered, Hamlet's father's ghost is decidedly not the devil; and

Banquo's ghost is by Macbeth sometimes addressed as if he were not, either—

> Or be alive again
> And dare me to the desert with thy sword.

The case, then, seems very clear: Banquo's ghost is real. Many Shakespeare questions, more obscured than illuminated by criticism and the traditions of criticism, are best answered by an appeal to the Elizabethans and the foremost judges on the Continent—not the scholars and philosophers there, with intellectual prepossessions, but the poets and dramatic critics, such as Mézières, Lemaître, Gourmont. If they and the Elizabethans agree we can feel fairly secure. There is Grillparzer, the dramatist and poet:

> Wenn ihr mir sagt, diese Hexen seien der eigene Ehrgeiz des Helden, so antworte ich euch: tut die Augen auf. Was ihr da vor euch seht, das sind Hexen und nicht der Ehrgeiz; so wie das Gespenst Banquo's ein wirkliches Gespenst ist, weil ihr es mit euren eigenen Augen seht, indes der Gedankendolch vor dem Morde nur ein Gedankendolch ist, denn nur Macbeth sieht ihn, ihr aber nicht.— *Shakespeare-Jahrbuch,* xviii, 118.

And there is Gourmont, the acute and pellucid critic, to the same effect:

> La scène du spectre est saisissante, pourvu que l'on croie aux fantômes et qu'on ignore les jeux de glaces. M. Maeterlinck veut que l'on y voie comme une projection de la conscience, une hallucination morale. Voilà bien de l'ingéniosité. C'est un fait matériel que voit Macbeth, et cela seul peut expliquer son trouble.

For the Belgian dramatist is a symbolist.

Richard III

The ghosts which appear to Richard in a dream on the eve of battle are easier to interpret. Much that has been said of Banquo's ghost may be said still more emphatically of these. They are the ghosts of Richard's victims, seeking his blood and tormenting his spirit; and anyone who with a thorough knowledge of contemporary Elizabethan drama had read the preceding portion of the play might feel the inevitableness of their appearance before the curtain fell. To satisfy Elizabethan poetic justice it is not enough that Richard should fall and die.

In the way of this interpretation there are, to be sure, two slight stumbling-blocks—the dream and Richard's doubts. In general, dreams are treated by Shakespeare objectively, in the superstitious fashion, unsusceptible of psychological explanation, to be found in poetry, folklore, and tragedy from time immemorial, as the avenue of occult information to the soul; and in this same play Clarence, even though he has dreamed of Gloucester's murderous perfidy, refuses at first to believe the witness of the cutthroats before his eyes. So with Duke Humphrey, Stanley, Romeo, Posthumus, Calpurnia, and the poet Cinna [60]—they dream more wisely than they can know or think. In folklore, moreover, which knows nothing subjective, dreams are treated not only after the fashion just mentioned but as the special medium for ghosts, just as they are for ghosts in Homer, Æschylus, and Virgil, and in the Bible for Gabriel or 'the angel of the Lord.' [61] 'For the mind in them that slumber,' declares Clytemnestra to the slumbering Eumenides, herself a ghost at that moment,

[60] 2 *Henry VI,* I, ii; *Richard III,* I, iv; III, ii and III, iv, 84; *Romeo and Juliet,* V, i, 6-10; *Cymbeline,* IV, ii, 346; V, iv; V, v, 425 ff; *Winter's Tale,* III, iii, 16 ff; *Julius Cæsar,* II, ii; III, iii, 1-4. Cf. Andromache's, *Troilus and Cressida,* V, iii, 10 and 63; Balthazar's, *Romeo and Juliet,* V, iii, 138, etc. In tragedy all Shakespeare's genuine dreams are fulfilled, even in the rare cases where, as in that of Duchess Eleanor (if genuine hers be), they flatter the subject in his folly; for it is an old saying that dreams go by contraries. Stanley's dream, in *Richard III,* is not fulfilled because, unlike Hastings, he does not scoff but gives heed, as in stories men seldom do.

[61] So the messengers of Zeus appear to mortals; so Patroclus's ghost appears to Achilles and Hector's to Æneas. Subjective, of course, none of these can be. As conceived by the primitive mind, indeed, the dreams are a state in which the soul is out of the body, roaming about, collecting information, communicating or being communicated with; and the question of subjectivity is here simply not in point.

'hath the clearer vision. A narrow outlook is our portion in the daylight.' Whatever the philosophy of it, appearing in a dream does not—in drama and epic, ancient or modern —rob the ghost of reality; it is the same spirit that appears to the waking. In the seventh book of the *Æneid* Alecto the Fury visits both Amata and Turnus, the one when awake and the other when asleep. In the *Octavia* the ghost of Agrippina comes calling for revenge with a flaming torch in her hand,[62] and similarly she afterwards appears in a dream to Poppæa. So in Jodelle's *Cléopâtre* the ghost of Antony at the beginning treads the stage, and also, as we learn from report, appears in a dream to the heroine.[63] And so in the Elizabethan drama generally and in the case before us. There are few ghosts less unsubstantial than that in Tourneur's *Atheist's Tragedy;* he appears to one person, then to two persons at once, then to one person again, and once he stands fire for his pains: and yet it is in a dream that he makes his first appearance.

Another instance, still less dubious, is that in Massinger's *Roman Actor,* where, as Cæsar dreams, the ghosts of his victims, Rusticus and Sura,

> Although their ashes were cast in the sea,
> Were by their innocence made up again,
> And in corporeal forms but now appear'd,
> Waving their bloody swords above my head,
> As at their deaths they threaten'd. And methought
> Minerva, ravish'd hence,[64] whisper'd that she
> Was, for my blasphemies, disarm'd by Jove,
> And could no more protect me. Yes, 'twas so,
>   [*Thunder and lightning*]
> His thunder does confirm it, against which,
> Howe'er it spare the laurel, this proud wreath
> Is no assurance.   —(V, i.)

Nor do subjective interpretations of the dreams in Shakespeare square with the characters of the persons who have

[62] Whitmore, p. 102.
[63] Creizenach (1901), ii, p. 441.
[64] A statue had been carried off by the ghosts in his dream.

them. This becomes clear when applied to still another
instance in a later and more finished Shakespearean play
—Queen Katharine's dream in *Henry VIII*:

Sad and solemn music. Enter, solemnly tripping one after an-
other, six personages, clad in white robes, wearing on their heads
garlands of bays, and golden vizards on their faces; branches of bays
or palm in their hands. They first congee unto her, then dance;
and, at certain changes, the first two hold a spare garland over her
head; at which the other four make reverent curtsies. Then the
two that held the garland deliver the same to the other next two,
who observe the same order in their changes, and holding the garland
over her head; which done, they deliver the same garland to the last
two, who likewise observe the same order; at which, as it were by
inspiration, she makes in her sleep signs of rejoicing and holdeth up
her hands to heaven; and so in their dancing vanish, carrying the
garland with them. The music continues.

Shall we interpret these spirits as the figments of Katharine's imagination? It would mean monstrous complacence, and it would altogether defeat the poet's intention
of signifying heaven's recognition of her saintly character.
They are but a stage-device,[65] of course, yet they are not
subjective; they are—operatically, unreligiously conceived
—'spirits,' 'angels of the Lord.' And shall we, more
justly, interpret these ghosts, so rancorous against Richard
and so propitious to Richmond, as the figments of his conscience? What has he, a thorough Machiavel, lineally and
immediately descended from Aaron the Moor and Barabas
the Jew, to do, before this or after, with conscience or
remorse?[66] The word as he uses it must mean something

[65] As a stage-device compare the masque-like dream of Posthumus,
Cymbeline, V, iv. Nothing could be more objective—Jupiter descends with
a tablet, the oracular contents of which are read by Posthumus on awaking.
But the marvel is without the sincerity or the meaning of the ghosts in
Hamlet and *Macbeth*. Jupiter and the apparitions of the Leonati make mere
dramatic machinery.

[66] With one accord they, as Elizabethan Machiavels, scoff at conscience.
Cf. Meyer's *Machiavelli and the Elizabethan Drama* for the evidence, and
Richard's own words,—

   Conscience is but a word that cowards use—(V, iii, 309).
But see the chapter on the Criminals.

very external; and they are without him, voices of an Elizabethan Nemesis, ghosts shrieking for his blood and his eternal reprobation, bidding him 'despair and die!'

Richard himself, however,—and this is our other stumbling-block—may seem, as Mr Moorman says, to explain away the ghosts as the figments of conscience in his subsequent soliloquy. It is not clear that in his awkward and obscure speech he means that; but it is clear that he is trying to shake off the great dread that has seized him. Such questionings and explainings arise in the Elizabethan drama, as we have seen, after the appearance of the most indisputably objective ghosts [67]—especially when they have appeared in dreams—as is but to be expected of human nature. This, like the scepticism of those who have just seen a ghost when awake, is his instinctive 'defensive reaction,' and at the same time an artistic device. Who would not cry 'I but dreamed' if else he must think that in the fray of the morrow eleven ghosts were to 'sit heavy on his soul?' But it is now dead midnight—cold fearful drops stand on his trembling flesh—the lights burn blue.

All three are signs unmistakable and authentic. Ghosts come at midnight, everybody knows. Coleridge remarks that in 'all the best attested stories of ghosts, as in that of Brutus, of Archbishop Cranmer, of Benvenuto Cellini, and the vision of Galileo communicated by him to Torricelli, the ghost-seers were in a state of cold and chilling damp.' The truth of the statement I have not been able to confirm; but such is the state of Æneas when he wakes from his vision of the Penates,[68] of Don Juan in Tirso's *El Burlador de Sevilla*,[69] of Beatrice in Middleton's *Changeling*,[70] of Cæsar in the *Roman Actor*, and of

---

[67] See references to the *Atheist's Tragedy* and the *Roman Actor*, above, pp. 206, 219, especially the remarkable parallel, the dream of Posthumus, who doubts the reality of his vision with the tablet, or book, in his hand!

[68] *Æn.*, III, 175: 'Tum gelidus toto manabat corpore sudor.'

[69] III, xv.

[70] V, i—'has left a shivering sweat upon me.'

Almanzor in the *Conquest of Granada.*[71] And the lights
burning blue are a phenomenon 'so universally acknowledged,' says Grose [72] in 1773, 'that many eminent philosophers have busied themselves in accounting for it, without
once doubting the truth of the fact.' 'How ill this taper
burns,' mutters Brutus to himself just before his eyes are
fixed on Cæsar's ghost. 'My mother would often tell mee,'
says Raffe the miller's son, in Lyly's *Gallathea*[73] (c.
1585), 'when the candle burnt blew there was some ill
spirit in the house.' This is one of the many superstitious
circumstances of ghost-lore which by Shakespeare are
naturally, almost piously, reproduced, like the ghost's
appearance at midnight, fleeing the morning air, blasting
you if you crossed it, appearing to one and not another,
speaking only when spoken to, and bearing all the wounds
that the body had received at death. As no one else's are,
Shakespeare's ghosts are 'full, material, and circumstan-
tiated.'

This second stumbling-block, however, has not been
removed, and it must be admitted that the evidence, particularly in view of Shakespeare's sources, is somewhat
ambiguous. In some of the chronicles and in the *True Tragedie of Richard III* the hero is represented as haunted by
remorse—like Marlowe's Faustus, as Professor Churchill
suggests, rather than like the Machiavels; and even in
Shakespeare Richard harks back at times [74] to this earlier
conception. It may possibly be, then, that Shakespeare
meant these ghosts to be no more than a dream, no more
than pangs of conscience. Even so our thesis holds, for he
has not succeeded. They are objective still. Not only do
the ghosts tread the stage and lift up their voices, but—
unmistakable, immemorial token—the lights burn blue.
Moreover, at the same time these ghosts appear and
prophesy to Richmond, and by him too are recognized,

[71] Pt. II, IV, iii.
[72] Brand, iii, p. 69.
[73] II, iii, 63.
[74] As, I, iii, 222; IV, i, 85.

though not doubtingly as they are by Richard, as the 'souls whose bodies Richard murdered.' [75] The same dream —the same figments of conscience and imagination, there-fore—for two men, murderer and avenger, at once! A con-venient stage-device, one may answer; but surely not one to which a poet would have recourse who had been given a higher light than had his fellows.

In short, the genius of the poet cannot belie itself. The mind of the Elizabethans—and theirs was Shakespeare's—like the mind that informs folklore, or, for that matter, the mind that made all poetry and drama before the Eliza-bethan and much of them after, either was far from clear in regard to the distinction between subjective and objective or in poetry and drama ignored it. Posthumus in *Cymbeline* doubts the reality of the vision which has brought him the book in his hand. Even Duke Humphrey's ghost, consid-ered above, is, though invisible to the bystanders, very evi-dently not a figment of conscience and imagination but a ghost, as Vaux declares. However much emphasis is thrown on the facts of conscience and crime, neither the personality of the relation between murderer and murdered, as then commonly conceived, nor the traditional reality of an aveng-ing presence is obscured. His hair stands upright and his eyes are blinded by the dust of the grave. These two details, even though the former had been noted by the Cardinal as a fact, are, in this connection, external, superstitious touches; and by the Elizabethan audience would certainly be taken not to be the effect of memory in one case or of a frenzied anticipation in the other, but, however invisible to the bystanders, to be the features of the actual ghost—like Hector's shade, the image of the very corpse itself arisen. Here at work is but the same poetic, instinctive materialism, the same inability or unwillingness to discriminate things subjective and things objective, that in the popular mind and popular literature, as we have already seen, lends an ear

[75] V, iii, 230.

to dreams as to presages and oracles, peoples them with veritable angels of the Lord or with the souls of the departed, or out of the digestive and sexual operations creates fiends like the nightmare and the incubus or succuba.

Into this undiscerning, mythopœic way of thinking Shakespeare lapsed, when, in dealing with the pangs of Richard's conscience, he represented them (if that really be what he represented) as the hauntings of menacing ghosts. And that too, except for dramatic effect, without any need. In the *True Tragedie* Richard when in the throes of remorse simply declares that the ghosts of his victims throng him night and day, gaping for revenge, and in the chronicles of Holinshed and others he dreams before the battle that he is haled by devils to hell: out of hints so slight [76] Shakespeare makes up his scene of eleven individual ghosts, amid blue lights, each crying vengeance, in conventional melodramatic fashion, for his particular wrongs, and vowing to have it, too, in battle on the morrow.[77] Surely, whatever Richard on awaking says about all this, and however Shakespeare himself may have intended it to be, there is little in it that can be called illusory or subjective.

Julius Cæsar

Of this ghost we have already treated. It speaks—and not in a dream, if that remain a difficulty—and Brutus does

[76] Compare Professor G. B. Churchill's *Richard III up to Shakespeare* for the contributions to the Richard legend by chronicler and by poet.

[77] Professor Churchill, though somewhat non-committal on the question of subjectivity, insists on a difference between these ghosts and the ghosts of the ordinary revenge plays (p. 516). And, as we have been admitting, a difference there is: not only are they interpreted by Richard as the advocates of conscience, but they avoid the words *revenge* or *vindicta,* and they threaten the pains of despair quite as much as those of defeat and death. Nevertheless I cannot admit that these ghosts do not appear, as do the revenge ghosts, 'to satisfy themselves.' Each one recounts his wrongs, curses Richard's sword and lance in battle, and foretells his death. Prophecy, perhaps, is their main office, as often in the Elizabethan and the Classical drama; but, as there again, it is the prophecy of the injured and resentful.

not undertake to doubt it. He questions his men, indeed,
as Macbeth does Lennox at the Witches' Cavern, whether
they had seen or heard anything or themselves had made
an outcry; but their negative answers, like Lennox's, only
go to prove the supernaturalness of an undeniably real
appearance. Cæsar's ghost is, as the confessions of the
dying conspirators and the corroborating testimony of Sextus Pompey, quoted above,[78] conclusively show, only what
by its own words, the stage-direction,[79] and Brutus's subsequent remark to Volumnius it purports to be; and it is but
our present-day prepossessions and philosophizings that
have dissolved that famous apparition into an 'embodiment
from its own words, the stage direction,[79] and Brutus's subsequent remark to Volumnius it purports to be; and it is but
licanism.'[80] That is our present-day equivalent to the
medieval 'allegorical' or 'anagogical' interpretations of the
Bible or of a classical text, and equally repugnant to the
meaning.

How actual, how concrete and personal, on the other
hand, is Shakespeare's conception:

> O Julius Cæsar, thou art mighty yet!
> Thy spirit walks abroad, and turns our swords
> In our own proper entrails.—V, iii, 94.
>   [*To Volumnius*]
> The ghost of Cæsar hath appear'd to me
> Two several times by night; at Sardis once,
> And, this last night, here in Philippi fields.
> I know my hour is come.—V, v, 17.
>   Cæsar, now be still,
> I kill'd not thee with half so good a will.—V, v, 50.

Political drama that this is, it, like the rest of Shakespeare,
has little politics or statesmanship in it,—how much better

---

[78] See above, notes 17-19, and below.

[79] *Julius Cæsar,* IV, iii, 274—*enter the Ghost of Cæsar.* This is in the first
edition, the Folio.

[80] F. W. Moorman, *Modern Language Review* (1906), pp. 195-6.

a play it is than any that has more!—and really it is conceived and wrought out as a thoroughly Elizabethan murder and revenge play, the latter half of it, like *Hamlet,* containing a ghost to preside over the revenge. The other interpretation does violence to the clear and simple meanings of the passages cited, as well as to passages where Antony speaks of the spirit of Cæsar as now looking down upon them and ranging for revenge;[81] and thus it breaks in upon the unity of the play.[82] The eponymous hero does not drop out of the plot in Act III, after all.

The dramatist's deliberate deviations, moreover, from his source, North's Plutarch, leave us no room for doubt. There it is 'evill spirit,' 'ill Angel,' or 'this spirit' simply, but never 'Cæsar's ghost'; but, while Shakespeare's reverence for history will not permit him to tamper with the text where the ghost is speaking—'Thy evil spirit, Brutus,' are the words—still for him it is a ghost and no more, both in his stage-direction and in Brutus's explicit remark to Volumnius afterwards. The 'genius' or 'demon,' guardian angel good or bad, attending upon one throughout life, was a familiar and living superstition in Shakespeare's time as well as in Plutarch's; several times Shakespeare uses it both in its classical and its Christian form;[83] and yet, though this superstition would have lent itself more readily to the modern allegorical interpretation, as more closely identified with the hero's own thought or personality than another man's ghost, he steers straight away from it. What is more, Brutus and Cassius' last words, in recognition of Cæsar's

[81] III, i, 195, 270.
[82] Cf. Creizenach, v, p. 120, who recognizes the improvement in changing from Plutarch's spirit to the ghost, discussed in the following paragraph.
[83] See *genius* in Bartlett; and *angel,* in such passages as *Othello,* V, ii, 208—'curse his better angel from his side.' The classical form lasts as late as Clarendon. See Variorum *Macbeth* (1822), p. 142: 'When Cromwell refused the crown many were of the opinion that his genius at that time forsook him and yielded to the King's spirit, and that his reign was near its expiration.'

vengeance as fulfilled, and Brutus's words about Cæsar's spirit walking abroad, and visiting him at Sardis and Philippi, are entirely Shakespeare's own. Even the spirit of the ancient tragic vendetta is his, not Plutarch's; and it is the self-same sword, as Cassius says,—

> Cæsar, thou art reveng'd
> Even with the sword that killed thee—

just as it was with the axe with which they had felled Agamemnon that Clytemnestra and Egisthus were slain. And whilst Shakespeare adds these unequivocal speeches and circumstances, he, as significantly, suppresses others. In North's Plutarch Brutus tells Cassius of the spectre; and Cassius in turn imparts to him his Epicurean scepticism,— melancholy, fatigue, the delusion of the senses—explanations highly desirable if really the dramatist had had a mind to serve the purpose of a psychological or allegorical interpretation.

* * * * * *

I have shown, I hope, that Shakespeare's ghosts are all real and external, like other Elizabethan ghosts; and that those here discussed, though performing a different function, are as objective, if not so material, as the ghost in *Hamlet*. Though they appear to the victim instead of the revenger, and though they arise, in one notable instance —that of Banquo's ghost—at a time when an effort was making to divest the ghost of its cruder and more material qualities, they never melt away, as we moderns think they must, into the subjective or abstract. They are neither hallucinations nor poetic personifications: they are the murdered appearing to the murderer. Their motive is revenge, and their errand is to menace, torment, or forebode. They are the concrete representations of Nemesis, after the world-old conception of it by our forefathers as a blood-

feud carried beyond the confines of the grave; and as such
they are the products of an art and a culture widely different from our own.

A naïve and literal art—for all the refinement and
subtlety in the handling—but the art that is Shakespeare's.
We have seen how he conceived of Nemesis as a personal
blow-for-blow—even when by the hand of God [84]—rather
than as the vague, devious, impersonal retribution that we
nowadays discern in nature, and in human experience and
history, and try to body forth in our drama and novels;
and we have seen how superstitiously, how unpsychologically, he conceived of curses and dreams. The same may
be said of all else in Shakespeare—and there is much else—
that borders on the supernatural and occult. It is altogether supernatural, altogether occult,—it is nowise ration-
alized, or allegorized, after the fashion of modern authors
such as the German. His witches are the witches of James I,
who ride on a broomstick and sail in a sieve, boil unspeak-
able cauldrons, call up spirits and familiars, and raise
storms; and in *Macbeth* even the 'goddesses of destinie'
become in Shakespeare's hands Elizabethan witches, not
the authentic fates themselves but the 'instruments of
darkness' or limbs of Satan, though lifted by his imagination to a loftier plane. 'They are of another jurisdiction,'
says Lamb, than the sheriff's. His conjuring and magic
in the Second Part of *Henry VI*, in *Macbeth*, and in the
Tempest is the real conjuring and magic of his Elizabethan,
half-medieval age, introduced to satisfy the superstitious
love of the wonderful and marvellous in his audience (for
the imagination of the dramatist must kindle his spectators'
imagination or it deserves not the name); and on the heath
near Forres it is an incantation or witches' Sabbath such
as they had heard of, and is calculated to meet their expectations to the full.

[84] *Richard III*, V, i, 20 f.

And his portents and omens,[85] his prophecies[86] and presentiments, are all of the same description. They are no mere fanciful or poetical embroideries, but signs and tokens, literal, objective, binding. Portents like those at the birth of Richard III and the death of Henry IV, that of the horses devouring one another in Glamis Castle, that of the Lion stalking by the Capitol, or that of the slave holding up his hand to burn, itself unscorched, like twenty torches, are in Shakespeare as actual and unmistakable as in Plutarch or Holinshed. Such things stand forth as unreasoned, prodigious facts; they are history, the staple and stuff of the plot. So even with his presentiments. They are always fulfilled unless they are cheerful and flattering; and, whether that or not, they are the promptings of occult wisdom—wisdom beyond the reach of the wit of man—sent to warn or to deceive and cajole. Many of them, of course, are of constructional import; but some of them are not, and all of them, as well as every soothsayer's word or augur's omen,[87] Shakespeare fulfills and substantiates without a trace of modern attempt at sub-

---

[85] *Richard II*, II, iv; *Hamlet*, I, i, portents before the death of Cæsar; *Macbeth*, II, iii, at the death of Duncan; at the birth of Glendower (see below, p. 245) and of Richard III, *3 Henry VI*, V, vi, 44. Comet and three suns in *1 Henry VI*; five moons portending the death of Arthur, *John*, IV, ii, 182; bloody sun and roaring wind, *1 Henry IV*, V, i; omens of the King's death, *2 Henry IV*, IV, iv, 121-8; *Richard II*, II, iv, 6-17. Some of these, appropriately, are reported by humble and ignorant people.

[86] The list of references is too long to reproduce. Such appear in the English historical plays *passim;* in *Macbeth, Julius Cæsar, Winter's Tale, Cymbeline, Troilus and Cressida, King Lear* (Gloster's 'prediction'); and all come true. 'Before the alteration and chaunges of kingdomes and in the time of warres, seditions, and other dangerous seasons, ther most commonly happen very strange things in the aire, in the earth, and amongst living creatures, clean contrary to the usuall course of nature. Which things men call wonders, signes, monsters, and forewarnings of matters to come. There are seene in the aire, swords, speares, and suche like innumerable; there are heard and seene in the aire, or upon the earth whole armies of men encountering together, etc.—Ludwig Lavater, *Of ghostes and spirites walking by night* (1596), pp. 80-81.

[87] *Antony and Cleopatra*, I, ii; *2 Henry VI*, IV, i, 33 f.

jective interpretation. Most remarkable in this respect are the curses; as treated in *Richard III*[88] and the other 'histories' nothing was ever more literal, more superstitious, more unillumined by a ray of reason. Not only do the curses hold, but, as in the most benighted byways of folk-lore, they hold by the letter only and to the last jot and tittle. Queen Anne and Buckingham unwittingly curse themselves; the fiendish Queen Margaret, herself bowing under the curse of the dying York, curses eight princes one after the other; Richard is cursed condignly not only by everybody else but by his mother herself;[89] and of all these every particular syllable comes true as if the gods kept books. 'Va, va, le ciel n'est pas si exact que tu penses.' But in such matters Shakespeare knew not reason or symbol, where we moderns would know nothing else.[90] He heard no call to press beyond the veil of seemingly supernatural phenomena to a natural fact or a human meaning; to him the phenomena themselves were both meaning and fact; and so far from ever evincing discontent with that meaning or doubt of the fact, he betrays at times a primitive, ceremonial preoccupation with the mere form and letter.

While that is true, it is not all the truth. The historical plays are early and comparatively crude; and Shakespeare has, as we have seen, also spiritualized superstition—this is especially true of his later work,—and generally given dramatic and psychological appropriateness to the ghosts. Though not welcome, these visitors often are, so to say, 'expected,' and no wonder that the uninitiate modern reader

---

[88] It is noteworthy that the curses are deliberately introduced by the dramatist into his fable, without authority in his sources, as a convenient, though highly conventional and superstitious means of giving a local habitation and a name to nemesis.

[89] *Richard III*, IV, iv, 182-195.

[90] Of a dozen themes or more once written for me by freshmen on the old ballad of the *Wife of Usher's Well,* almost all explained the return of the drowned men to their mother as a dream or an hallucination. See below, p. 251, note, for the classical criticism.

has taken them for hallucinations or symbols. Banquo's
ghost is a real ghost; but such is the skill of the dramatist,
and the power of his poetry, that none can deny it a moral
and philosophical significance. The murk of popular superstition is in his hands shot through and through with light.
And the same is true, in another way, of the portents and
omens. Unlike Tourneur and others, Shakespeare does not
let his comets or his five moons appear upon the stage
but has their appearance reported; and not as seen by
anyone and everybody, but generally by those supposed to
be naturally superstitious,—by Welshmen, by common people, by old men and women; and often they are reported
remotely, at second hand. Hubert tells King John that
'they say five moons were seen tonight'; Casca in his own
person describes the St Elmo's lights and the owl hooting
at noon-day in the Capitol; but when it comes to the men
all in fire walking up and down the streets he himself saw
only a heap of ghostly women, transformed with their fear,
who swore they saw them. So on the platform Horatio
says he 'has heard' that at the cock's warning ghosts hie
to their confines; and Marcellus thereupon commences
another superstitious tale, in a similar way. And the scene
in which subterranean music betokens that the god Hercules is forsaking his minion Antony, is introduced by a
mysterious intimation of a rumour:

> 2 *Soldier.* Heard you nothing strange about the streets?
> 1 *Soldier.* Nothing. What news?
> 2 *Soldier.* Belike 'tis but a rumour. Good-night to you.
> 1 *Soldier.* Well, sir, good-night.

By such means, as also by the scepticism and wonder of
the ghost-seers before and after the apparition, Shakespeare lends the supernatural that subjective colouring and
that dim and wavering uncertainty of outline which the
finer poetic imagination in the presence of the supernatural
in every age requires, even when it is as yet not matter for

enlightened doubt. And by most of these artistic devices
he himself has prepared the way for the treatment of the
supernatural, in our age of incredulity, at the hands of
Hawthorne, Henry James, Maeterlinck, and such foreign
writers of ghost stories as are represented in the volume
of George William Curtis. They contrive more gingerly
the transition from the natural to the supernatural; and
employ not only scepticism and report, but even the remote-
ness of report within report, and above all the testimony
of the ignorant and the psychologically predisposed. But
no modern has in so few words given the effect of vague
and mysterious awe as has Shakespeare in the scene from
which I have quoted the four lines above. The simplicity
and brevity, the repetitions and echoes, the wondering questions, and the commonplace perfunctory utterances betraying a thought that is all astray—these things, no doubt, have
served for a lesson to Maeterlinck. And this vague and
brooding treatment of the supernatural, in Shakespeare's
later work, is in keeping with the dimmer outline of which
we have taken notice in his later imaginations in general."[91]

Did Shakespeare Believe in Ghosts?

It is by comparing Shakespeare with such writers, moreover, that we best learn the difference not only between his
apparitions and theirs but also between his and their beliefs.
Inferences here are, no doubt, dangerous. The things of
the imagination and of the intellect are incommensurable:
poetic faith and the faith by which we walk are by no means
one and the same. Neither Shakespeare in *Macbeth* nor
Maeterlinck in *L'Intruse* is teaching anything, or asserting
anything, or committing himself one way or the other—
either is simply giving his own imagination the rein and
taking possession of ours. Still, intellect and imagination
are not things apart, but one is the avenue or vestibule to
the other; and we can perceive something of the poet's

[91] See chapter i, page 24.

intellectual belief and his audience's (which, in the drama
at least, are one and the same) as he enters the dim chambers of his imagination.   There all is belief—Death in
L'Intruse is as real as the ghosts of Banquo and Hamlet's
father—but disbelief had barred the way.   It is a willing
suspension of disbelief for the moment, as Coleridge says,
that constitutes poetic faith; and just there lies the difference between Shakespeare on the one hand and the modern
writer on the other.   Shakespeare has only *poetic* disbelief,
if we may so say, to cope with, or the state of imaginative
apathy.   The modern writer has not only that but positive
intellectual incredulity as well.   He must make his creation
'convincing,' as we say, and he must do this in a double
sense.

For lack of material a comparison is difficult.   In drama
nowadays there is hardly a ghost for our purpose; both
the superstition and the convention are so thoroughly
exploded that when, like Bishop Nicholas's in the *Pre-
tenders,* he does come on the stage, he has to be treated
rather comically, grotesquely.   But the other supernatural
element in Ibsen will serve, as in *Little Eyolf* and the *Lady
from the Sea.*   In both, as Mr Archer, quoted by Dr
Whitmore, notices, 'he pursues the plan, which was also
Hawthorne's, of carefully leaving us in doubt as to whether
and how far any supernormal influence is at work.   Everything is explicable within the limits of nature; but supernatural agency is also vaguely suggested, and the reader's
imagination is stimulated, without any violence to his sense
of reality.'   It is otherwise with Shakespeare.   He does no
violence, indeed, to the sense of reality in a reader or spectator who can enter into the spirit of Elizabethan art, and
yet he does not leave him dubious.   It is by awe and wonder
rather than by dubiety that the effect of the spiritual and
supernatural is procured, and in the end the doubts of
Macbeth or Brutus or Horatio, and therefore of the audience also, are set at rest.   The supernatural music in

Antony and Cleopatra is, for comparison with Ibsen, a case more in point; doubt there is confined to whether the music be in the air or under the earth, or bode well or ill; and these doubts heighten the unsubstantial effect without raising at all the question of the phenomenon's reality. And when in default of drama one turns to modern stories such as those of Henry James, one sees at once how very carefully and considerately the writer both disarms and appeases the jealous intellect,—providing all the psychological preparations, not only in the mind of the reader through report within report, distance of time and place, and scepticism or superstitiousness in the teller, but also in the excited and predisposed mind of the ghost-seer; and often, as in the *Turn of the Screw,* intimating a symbolical interpretation for the phenomenon, if the reader be inclined to it, besides. Here is provided every inducement to believe if he can, every loophole of escape if he cannot.

The age of credulity and the age of incredulity—Shakespeare seems to belong to both, and one wonders (and will not easily content oneself within the narrow confines of a scientific suspense of judgment) whether Shakespeare actually believed in the supernatural character and significance of the portents and omens, prophecies and presentiments, dreams, magic, curses, witches and ghosts, to which he gives so large and important a place in his plays. Only by inference and indirection can one discover; since Shakespeare speaks only through his characters, and often a character contradicts another, one has to rely on the evidence of the dramatist's general method and attitude, and on what he does not make his characters do or say as much as on what he does. Such evidence is often of the best, indeed, if only it can be interpreted rightly; it is unconscious and inadvertent. The difficulty is that in matters which have to do with the supernatural people are particularly inconsistent, and the orbits of their thoughts erratic and incalculable. The cleverest and most enlightened of men may cling to some dark superstition or other, or cherish a faith and support a creed which to others is absurd; and the most orthodox and regular of minds may some day strike out into an unheard-of audacity of doubt.

THE AGE

What of Shakespeare's Age,[92] first of all? For though the poet may have been ahead of his time he certainly was not behind it; and would he have been behind it if he had held to such superstitious beliefs? We are apt to consider the age of Elizabeth only as that of the Renaissance. We think of the poets and philosophers, scientists and discoverers, and of illumination after medieval darkness. But the thoughts of men widen not with the process of the suns but of cycles: such books as Lecky's *History of Rationalism* and Andrew White's *Warfare of Science and Religion* convince us of that. Seldom can the mind of even the boldest individuals, much less of a whole people, pass beyond the pale of ignorance and superstitious prejudice in a generation or even in a century. A single fact of itself illustrates this. The Copernican theory was promulgated in 1543, but a full century passed before it can be said to have been accepted in England. Giordano Bruno, who visited Oxford in 1583, was disgusted at the prevailing ignorance of it or prejudice against it; Bacon, of all men, scornfully rejected it;[93] Sir Thomas Browne, a man of science too, later did the same;[94] and Shakespeare, so far as we know, went down into his grave absolutely unaware, not only that the sun did not really rise and set, but that there were sensible men who thought it did not. And an array of

[92] It is impossible without unduly prolonging this chapter to reproduce a tithe of the evidence of superstition in the age and in the poet which has come into my hands since my article was printed in 1907.

[93] See *The Advancement of Learning* (Oxford, 1900), pp. 127, 129, 299, reference in note.

[94] Johnson's remark (Browne's *Works,* 1834, i, xxviii): 'he never mentions the motion of the earth but with contempt and ridicule.'

similar facts might easily be drawn up. It was the day when—of high degree or of low degree—devils and demons, like angels, were numbered up into the hundreds of thousands, and every man, like Marlowe's Faustus, was attended by his own;[95] when sickness was even by physicians held to be a sort of demoniacal possession;[96] when one of the controversies raging was, not whether ghosts appeared or miracles took place, but whether the former were devils or souls from purgatory, and whether the latter were the work of heaven or of hell;[97] when witches, by storms and contrary winds, impeded the progress of royal personages and were discoursed upon and legislated against by the king[98] on the throne and the dignitaries and worthies of the nation; when sovereigns so enlightened as Elizabeth and Charles I consulted magicians and astrologers like Dee and Lilly, and their courts fell into a panic at the appearance of comets; and when so trifling a circumstance as a jackdaw's entering the window of Westminster Hall actually found record in the minutes of the House as a sign from heaven.[99]

SEVENTEENTH-CENTURY BELIEF IN WITCHCRAFT AND OTHER SUPERSTITIONS

Then everybody[100] believed in ghosts; and it is probable that the more advanced thinkers among Englishmen would not have been even so sceptical as to ascribe them to the

---

[95] Spalding's *Elizabethan Demonology*, pp. 34-6. Scot gives names for seventy-nine, and Shakespeare mentions twenty. The Good Angel and the Evil Angel in *Faustus*, who contend for the mastery of the hero's soul, are not allegorical, as, in their prepossessions, most critics take them to be, but are as substantive—as substantial one might almost say—as the hero himself.

[96] Spalding, pp. 64-6; 80.

[97] See above, p. 215, note.

[98] See Lecky (N. Y., 1914), p. 123, for an account of James presiding over the horrible tortures of Fian.

[99] Spalding, p. 31; it was during the discussion of the Statute against Witchcraft in the reign of James I.

[100] Scot, *Discoverie of Witchcraft*, book vii, chap. 15.

deception of the devil were it not for the fact that, like other Protestants, they were concerned to leave no basis or pretext for the dogma of a Purgatory. But witchcraft, because of its practical issues and present terrors, was a more absorbing question. Shakespeare wrote *Macbeth* when the rage of witch-hunting had fairly begun, though the full cry did not arise, we know, till later, in the time of the Protectorate, and in America later still. What the mob and rabble thought and did, does not, of course, for our argument much matter; but with mob and rabble the leaders of thought were for once in sympathy. An immense literature still exists, though as much more, and particularly the juristic part of it, must, being quite worthless, have perished. Up to 1677 there were no thorough-going dissentients from the prevailing view. The sceptics like Reginald Scot, in his *Discoverie of Witchcraft,* in 1584, Samuel Harsnett, in his *Declaration of Popish Impostures,* in 1603, and John Webster, in *The Displaying of Supposed Witchcraft,* in 1677, all were careful not to deny the existence of witches *in toto.*[101] What they condemn is certain silly and preposterous notions concerning their practices and the extent of their powers. And the list of them that, as we happen to know, explicitly avowed their belief in witchcraft is long and (in itself) illustrious: Thomas Nash, King James I, Bacon, Raleigh, Coke, Thomas Heywood, Edward Fairfax, Robert Burton, Sir Thomas Browne, James Howell, Sir Kenelm Digby, Jeremy Taylor, Thomas Fuller, Sir Matthew Hale, John Aubrey, Henry More, Meric Casaubon, Glanvil, Dr George Hickes, Isaac Barrow, Richard Baxter, and, bringing up the rear, half a century behind his time, in words of solemn protest against its innovation and error, John

---

[101] See W. Notestein, *History of Witchcraft* (1911), under the names in the index; for Webster, the most explicit, see pp. 300-301. The statement above concerning vanished witchcraft books and tracts I owe to the Rev. Montague Summers, in a popular lecture (1924).

Wesley.[102]   Yet he was only following in the footsteps of his betters—Luther, Melancthon, and Calvin.   Selden, Hobbes, and Sir Robert Filmer were sceptical; but the first two said little, and none of them denied the existence of witches altogether; and Bacon, though sceptical and constantly inclined to explain the reported practices of witches by recourse to mental or natural causes, either clung to vestiges of the superstition or else did not tell all that he knew or thought.

Shakespeare's Style Saturated with It

Belief in witchcraft was the grossest, cruelest, and most momentous form of superstition in this epoch; life and limb and the soul's eternal welfare were at stake; and where it prevailed there was no likelihood of the disappearance of a belief in mere magic and astrology, portents and omens, soothsayings, imprecations, presentiments, and apparitions. All these superstitions are abundant in Elizabethan drama, and particularly in the most concrete and specific of writers, Shakespeare.   How amazingly full of this material (some of which we have already discussed) Shakespeare's text is, can be appreciated only as one takes up such works as Spalding's and Dyer's and the many others in the bibliography of Schelling, Jaggard, Whitmore, or the Cambridge History; comprising fairy-lore, witch-lore, devil-lore, and dream-lore; the popular mythical lore of beasts, birds, and plants; the symbolism of flowers and the transformation into animals or trees; and those more human

---

[102] This list is in the main compiled from Lecky, Professors Kittredge and Notestein (to Mr Notestein I am principally indebted), and others. Ben Jonson does not avow his belief; but though he has much to say of witches he never denies their existence. Mr W. S. Johnson (*Devil is an Ass*, pp. lxiii-iv) seems to me not at all to be justified in ranging him along with Scot. See Creizenach also (iv, p. 136). For Nash see McKerrow's ed., index; and Dodsley, viii, p. 65.   There is no reason to think that Dekker, Ford, and Middleton, who present witches superstitiously, were not of the same opinion; though the two first-named are in sympathy with the accused, as with one driven into the practice.   See Creizenach, iv, 135-6.

matters of the hatred of the bearer of evil news, the
prophetic powers of the dying,[103] the high spirits which
presage death, the bleeding of the murdered in the presence
of the murderer, the lucky or unlucky times and seasons,
or stars and planets, and the poison that drips from the
moon.[104] The striking thing is that it comes in so naturally
and spontaneously. Shakespeare had no doubt read King
James and Harsnett—from the latter he took names for
his demons—but he did not 'get up' the subject as Jonson
did that of alchemy, and there seems to be little that is
laboured or learned about it. He had unconsciously
absorbed, and he now reproduced, the living superstition
of his time. The very warp and woof of his phrase is
coloured with it. 'In his work', as Dr Whitmore has
observed, 'allusions to the supernatural occur incidentally,
evidently because they are a perfectly normal part of their
author's thought.' [105] Similes, metaphors, and other figures
are drawn from the world of superstition as they are drawn
from the visible world of man and nature. 'And he will
look as hollow as a ghost,' says Constance of Arthur; and
in *King Henry V* the night 'like a foul and ugly witch doth
limp so tediously away.' 'Should she kneel down in mercy
of this fact,' cries the Duke to Mariana,

> Her brother's ghost his paved bed would break,
> And take her hence in horror.
> —*Measure for Measure,* V, i, 440.

Here unmistakable differences are to be noted between
Shakespeare and the modern Romantics. Coleridge, Scott,
and Southey were not superstitious men—under the spell
of the medieval revival, they took to superstition sympathetically but imaginatively, for the purposes of poetry.
Shakespeare might conceivably have done so too in *Mac-*

[103] See above, p. 214, note.
[104] See Dyer for all this, table of contents, and index.
[105] P. 225.—See these and other examples; and see *witch* or *witchcraft* in
Bartlett.

beth or the *Tempest*. But that would not explain this incidental outcropping of superstitious and supernatural elements in historical plays, where the supernatural was not the subject in hand. Similes and metaphors of such a character are to be found in the Romantics, too, no doubt; but they are not spontaneous—they are esthetic, decorative, literary; they occur in the lyric or ballad, not in the speeches of sensible men in a play. These poets, moreover, were the heirs of the ages, particularly of Shakespeare himself; whereas Shakespeare had for these things comparatively few literary sources, and drew most of this superstitious lore and phrase, not like Spenser from books and romances, but out of the air and soil, so to speak, in which he had been nourished. The language of his ghosts or of those who speak of them does not echo Seneca,[106] but is the speech and imagery of Stratford and Warwick, distilled and concentrated.

An argument for Shakespeare's belief in the supernatural which he represents might be drawn from his supreme success in the undertaking. No one in drama, probably no one in all literature, has done it so well. Here and there above we have seen how deftly and skilfully he approaches the subject, with what art he sinks the gulf between the natural and the supernatural triumphantly to span it. And as perhaps no other poet ever did he gets the true ghost-seer's shudder:

> Thy bones are marrowless, thy blood is cold.

> Most like: it harrows me with fear and wonder.

Had he at some eerie moment seen one, in Stratford or Cock Lane? There are critics who exalt the medieval artists in verse or in paint because they believed in what they portrayed. These were of the age of faith, and wrought in a sad sincerity. But a fallacy, as it seems to

---

[106] Dr Whitmore shows that other Elizabethan dramatists in their superstitious and ghostly imagery do echo him.

me, lurks there, that confusion of literal faith and the poetic which we have touched upon above. The one may lead to the other, but unless it does, the art produced is only for believers. The poetic depends on the imagination alone, and that, as we have seen in chapter ii, is not fettered to experience. In this particular case, it depends, not on the faith or superstition of the writer, but on his cunning appeal to the faith and superstition of his audience. His ghosts are better than those of Dryden or Voltaire because they are not literary devices but the spirits the audience have heard of—the ghosts they dread to hear or see.

Superstition Involved in the Structure of His Plays

Much of the superstitious element has, we have seen, a constructional import—the omens and forebodings, the soothsayings and oracles, the curses and the vows in which curses are involved; and these means of anticipation and preparation in tragedy (and in comedy too, for that matter) Shakespeare adopted quite in the spirit of the Ancients and of the Renaissance. What dramatist even to-day would, in his pride of intellect, have passed by 'Beware the Ides of March' in Plutarch or the witches' threefold 'All hail!' in the chronicle? But one wonders that he did not experiment a little, and, in the use of forebodings, sometimes deliberately refrain, in the sequel, from producing the substance in its every circumstance. In comedy at least he might have done so, and for once given Londoners a refreshing esthetic surprise by presenting this disconcerting world as it is, where all signs and prophets fail. In construction generally, to be sure, Shakespeare is not an audacious innovator; but every soothsayer's syllable and every secret internal misgiving come true. Is it not incredible that the foremost dramatist in history should uniformly, even at the height of his powers, employ a fundamental structural device which he did not consider to have a basis in reality? And then there is much that has no constructional import whatever. Why do corpses bleed when the murderer draws nigh?[107] For stage effect, no doubt. But why do messengers with evil tidings deprecate the hatred of their hearers? Why are ghosts and witches explained as the agency of the devil? And why, time and again, do the characters, in all confidence, throw the blame for their mischances on sorcery or witchcraft, fortune or the stars? There are those who will explain it all historically, and have us understand that Shakespeare is making the sentiments suit the earlier times with which he deals; but of such historical criticism we have already had too much. We know that Shakespeare did not think historically; he had no Kulturgeschichte, as Professor Bradley says; and while, in dealing with Roman and pre-Christian times, he avoided topical allusions and the grosser anachronisms of playwrights like Heywood, he did this in a rather negative and general way, not with a scholar's insight but with a poet's tact. He does not put really Roman sentiments into his Romans' mouths; though he does make them stern and heroic, and, unlike Corneille, dispenses, in the Republican era, with the alluring motive of romantic love. And in the early heathen British plays almost the only means he employs to give his text historical flavour is the substitution, for the Trinity and the Saints, of the classical deities.

SHAKESPEARE'S PERSONAL ATTITUDE

All these considerations establish a presumption in favour of Shakespeare's belief in much of the superstition which he presents. That is, in favour of his acceptance of it, for to speak of his belief in such a connection would be mis-

---

[107] See the incident on the stage, *Richard III*, I, ii, 56. The sceptics, Lavater (1570), Scot (1584), p. 303, and Webster (1677), all believe in this (Notestein, pp. 68, 301). So King James in his *Demonologie* (1603), p. 79, and Bacon (*Works*, Spedding, 1857, ii, 660) do not reject it as superstition. Dyer (*Folklore of Shakespeare*, pp. 486-88) shows how widespread the superstition was, even in the seventeenth century.

leading: such matters he must simply have taken for granted. His art—his method of thought and expression —was the spontaneous and unconcerned utterance of himself and his age. It was an age of faith and—by our standards—of very little scepticism; and Shakespeare reflects the one and not the other. He himself was, as I have reiterated, not an analyst, an abstract thinker, and he has no philosophy, no political or religious creed, that differs from that of his time and social environment. And he puts, as we have seen, no scepticism into his plays.[108] On the stage, 'he never,' as Ruskin has observed, 'permits a spirit to show itself but to men of the highest intellectual power—to Hamlet, to Brutus, to Macbeth, to Richard III.' Except momentarily, and, as we have said, by way of artistic preparation or adjustment, it is only the villains that give expression to doubts; it is only the blinded, foolish, or impious, that ignore supernatural warnings or scoff at the stars and their influence. Edmund does; honest and admirable Kent and Lafeu do not; and the latter observes:

They say miracles are past; and we have our philosophical persons, to make modern and familiar, things supernatural and causeless. Hence it is that we make trifles of terrors, ensconcing ourselves into seeming knowledge, when we should submit ourselves to an unknown fear.

The observation goes much further, certainly, than the occasion—Helena's cure of the King—demands; but we cannot make capital out of the remarks of single characters. The impressive fact is that all doubt and scepticism in the presence of the supernatural turns out in the end unwarranted, unfounded; those who follow such counsels suffer or are punished; and the sceptics are only villains or scamps. Even they do not go far; they are sceptical about the reality of human virtue rather than the reality of the supernatural and its powers. Iago, not unreason-

[108] See above, chapter iv, pp. 185-86.

ably, refuses credence to Othello's tales of men whose heads 'do grow beneath their shoulders,' though the supposedly free-thinking Raleigh had recently told of them as found in Guiana; and Edmund, not unreasonably, mocks at those of us who 'make guilty of our disasters the sun, the moon, and the stars, as if we were villains by necessity, fools by heavenly compulsion, knaves, thieves, and treachers by spherical predominance, drunkards, liars, and adulterers by an enforc'd obedience of planetary influence, and all we are evil in by a divine thrusting on.' But he is not contradicting his father, though he may think he is doing so, for Gloster had avowed no belief of the sort; and he himself does not deny that the stars have an influence, which Gloster takes for granted and Kent solemnly affirms.[109] For all his scoffing, cynical tone, he does not demur to the doctrine, but to the way in which it is applied; somewhat as one Calvinist might jeer at another who ascribed his own personal backslidings to predestination.

Even Hamlet, despite the way that he allays Horatio's wonder,[110] has, in the sceptical nineteenth century, been reckoned a sceptic, though under a misapprehension. As I have shown above and elsewhere,[111] his doubt that the ghost may be the devil and his words concerning the undiscovered country from whose bourn no traveller returns, were, the one, a fairly old and very acceptable idea in Shakespeare's time, the other, an ancient and natural turn of phrase. Undiscovered country—no traveler returns— what Christian nowadays contemplating either death or suicide might not say or write the like, as did Seneca, who was not Christian, and Chaucer and Caxton and Du Bellay,

---

[109] *King Lear*, I, ii, 112 f.; IV, iii, 35: 'It is the stars, the stars above us, govern our conditions.' Here the expression does not seem to be used metaphorically as it might be to-day.

[110] 'And therefore as a stranger give it welcome.
There are more things in heaven and earth, Horatio,' etc.

[111] *Hamlet*, p. 35.

who were?[112] And the chief respectable sceptic in Shakespeare, Horatio, doubts, not on principle, we have seen, but only in single instances; and his attitude in general appears in the discussion after the ghost's departure, as he tells how a little ere the mightiest Julius fell the sheeted dead did squeak and gibber in the Roman streets, and (on Marcellus' recounting of the marvels that happen every year, some say, in Advent) replies that he too has heard and does 'in part believe it'. Some do happen—he would not say, quite all.

No skeptics, and there are no superstitious people, either. Though Edmund jeers at him Shakespeare treats Gloster sympathetically; and the very prediction he speaks of, like all others in Shakespeare, comes true. Glendower is jeered at openly by Hotspur, but everybody—the King, Westmoreland, Mortimer, his son-in-law, Hotspur himself [113]—speaks of him as a redoubtable warrior; [114] and Hotspur's own complaint is not that he is a fool or a fraud but to him a bore. And when taken to task by Mortimer and Worcester, he has no other objection to make and promises to treat him better. Afterwards, on the eve of battle, he wishes for his presence—'Would Glendower were come!' Indeed, the Welshman is spoken of as great and formidable, not only because of his wisdom and valour, but also, apparently, because of his magic; the King declares that Mortimer durst as well have met the devil alone as Owen Glendower for an enemy; [115] and the wonder that he promises of music made by spirits a thousand

---

[112] See below, note 119.—It is an obvious thing to say, but the only thing. The news is still that there is no news. We all have a heathen way of talking. 'To think I shall never see him again;'—and we do not hastily and priggishly add, 'in this world.'—Catullus' and Ronsard's names should be added.

[113] *1 Henry IV*, I, iii, 101. Falstaff (II, iv, 405) tries to scare the Prince with the names of his enemies—'that fiend Douglas, that spirit Percy, and that devil Glendower,'—as if they were of the same calibre.

[114] See *Glendower* in Bartlett.

[115] *1 Henry IV*, I, iii, 116.

leagues away is duly performed on the stage, no one doubting it.

No superstitious people, and though there are many magicians, conjurors, prophets and soothsayers [116] in Shakespeare, there are no frauds. All such characters in Shakespeare, as well as their deeds and words, are treated sympathetically and without indignity. With him, moreover, the supernatural plays no comic rôle as it does with Greene, Marlowe, Middleton, and Dekker.[117] Comic treatment is not, of course, incompatible with belief in the supernatural—the mysteries show that; but in an artist less naïve—infinitely more refined—it would be more likely to imply, as in the case of Burns, raillery or burlesque.

THE APOLOGISTS

We are loath to put Shakespeare back into his own age and niche; we would if we could keep him for our fireside and bosom; but apologies and advocacy in the long run do only damage, and Shakespeare does not profit by being treated as an unreasonable and prodigious exception. Professor Creizenach, recently dead, performed this doubtful service; though out of the abundance of his knowledge he freely recognized that Shakespeare and the Elizabethan drama generally were wholly unaffected by the more advanced thought of the day—the Copernican theory, Giordano Bruno's missionary work in Britain, and the questioning spirit of Montaigne.[118] He could not but recognize that Shakespeare's ghosts are altogether real, yet, recalling Hamlet's words about the traveller,[119] he was

---

[116] Bolingbroke the conjuror in *2 Henry VI;* Peter of Pomfret, the prophet in *King John;* soothsayers in *Julius Cæsar* and *Antony and Cleopatra;* Glendower and Prospero the magicians; the witches in Macbeth.

[117] Gibson, *Shakespeare's Use of the Supernatural,* chapter v; Whitmore, p. 267. As Mr Whitmore says, it is only a mock ghost that in Elizabethan drama is treated comically, and in Shakespeare there is none.

[118] IV, 129-32.

[119] See my *Hamlet,* pp. 34-7, for reasons which explain Hamlet's not making an exception of the ghost. Nothing could be more unjustifiable than

quite certain that Shakespeare himself did not believe in them; surmised that Shakespeare's opinions concerning astrology were those of Edmund, not those of the Earl of Kent;[120] and declared the grossly superstitious presentation of the witches was only to please King and people.[121] He found it difficult, he said, to bring this delusion into harmony with Shakespeare's independent and lofty conception of life.[121]

But the impression we have of Shakespeare is one of tolerance, geniality, common sense, imaginative power and fervour, rather than of extraordinary enlightenment; it is like that we have of Sophocles, who believed in oracles, curses, dreams, and an overruling fate, rather than that of Voltaire or Goethe; and it is with the superstition of the time—though without zeal, cruelty, or gloom—perfectly compatible. He had common sense, but the common sense of his day, not ours—in the seventeenth century the sensible, enlightened Reginald Scot was called ridiculous— and he was above all humane. The impression of this last quality is impaired by Creizenach's defence. If Shakespeare presented witches and witchcraft (as he did) fully or inci-

---

to take a single casual expression like this, in soliloquy, with two men behind the arras, as evidence of Hamlet's scepticism or of Shakespeare's. Hamlet is not speaking of revenge, but of the evils after death—which we know not but, once in their midst, cannot escape, since no traveller returns; and must he now add a parenthesis of exception and admit that he knows of one? Professor Feuillerat, indeed, finds no inconsistency—no traveller returns *with news*. But as usual when the loose texture of Shakespeare's thought is tightened, it only tangles. M. Feuillerat cites the words 'But that I am forbid to tell the secrets of my prison-house.' The ghost is, then, in Hamlet's and Shakespeare's mind, and with the audience they should have been more explicit; particularly since the ghost has, for all that, told secrets enough to 'puzzle the will' of any suicide.

[120] Creizenach, iv, 131. See above, p. 244, where I show that there is no real opposition between their views. What is more, Shakespeare never sides with the villain as do romantics like Byron. And Cicero's 'sceptical words' (as Creizenach calls them) on hearing from Casca about the portents at the Capitol (*Julius Cæsar,* I, iii, 34) seem to me not sceptical at all. Instead of questioning the report of the wonders, he questions the interpretation. As for astrological influences and portents, whether in the heavens or on the earth, they always come true. Cf. Gibson, p. 40.

[121] Creizenach, iv, 136-7, 138-9.

dentally in play after play, from *Henry VI* at the beginning
to the *Tempest* at the end, but to please King or people,
though all the time in his heart knowing better, he stands
convicted before all posterity on this point as a man without
principle or scruple. The complimentary reference, in the
same play, to touching for the king's evil, or scrofula,
is a different matter.[122]   When *Macbeth* was written
the champion witch-hunter had just come to the throne,
with the memories of the tortures of Fian and the great
hunt in Scotland after the royal voyage home from Denmark, clinging to his name. Shakespeare had read of these
incidents in the *News from Scotland;* and he alluded to
them, Creizenach thinks, only in compliment to the
King.[123] No doubt he did; but if we know the man, every
fibre of his being would have revolted against paying such
a compliment to James, at this juncture, and in such a
connection, unless he accepted the prejudice and superstition too. To us, without the superstition and prejudice,
the *News from Scotland* seems too horrible to read; and
to us, without the superstition and prejudice, the part which
James plays in it seems utterly benighted and barbarous.
Moreover, fresh and fierce legislation had at the King's
instance just been introduced, whereby it was necessary
no longer to prove that the suspected old woman in question had committed murder but only that she was keeping
familiar spirits; and the great Protestant inquisition, with
its terrors and horrors, had now begun. How much
simpler and pleasanter for us to think Shakespeare
ignorant and superstitious as the age than to think him
more unprincipled, more heartless! There is no sign
of inhumanity in him. The mutilation in *Titus Andronicus* and *King Lear* is in the story, not in life itself,

[122] Creizenach (iv. 137) compares the two cases as similar. There is
no evidence that Shakespeare was incredulous here, either; but if he was,
no serious moral issue is at stake.
[123] See Stevens' notes, *Variorum* (1822), sc. 1 and 3, which put the blot of
such a compliment, without the superstition to justify it, on his name!

and it awakens only indignation and pity in them that witness it.

In any case, to be sure, Shakespeare was not the man to begin a crusade of enlightenment; though doubtless both a Protestant and a Churchman, he left the Catholics and the Puritans in peace; but neither was he the man to follow the rabble, even with a king at their head, in a cruel undertaking, if against his better knowledge. He might not have opposed it, but he would not have joined in it. Always he kept off debatable ground, and the mere fact that Shakespeare dealt with witchcraft so freely would of itself be an indication that on that subject there was then no recognized difference of opinion. And if Shakespeare believed in witchcraft, and could with a good conscience present to the already inflamed imagination of king and people all the provocative details of the prevailing horrible superstition—the raising of tempests, sinking of ships, killing of swine, opening of locks, gathering of venom, boiling of human flesh and the limbs of children, keeping of imps, and holding of carnal intercourse with the devil [124]—I can believe him altogether capable of the other innocuous superstitions such as belief in ghosts or omens. At such gnats he would not have strained.

Be that as it may, this notion of truckling and complimenting, constantly at hand to save Shakespeare's fame, must in all conscience be used with greater restraint. The favour of the groundlings or of the Queen or King the critic has ever at his elbow to explain away Shakespeare's every divagation in sentiment or art. The foremost man

[124] See Spalding pp. 97-117 and Notestein. Both the Pucelle in *Henry VI*, Pt. I, and the Weird Sisters have imps or familiar spirits (Graymalkin, Paddock, Harpier). Even the beards, choppy fingers, and skinny lips, the vanishing in the air and making their victims dwindle, peak, and pine, are according to current report in Shakespeare's day (Spalding, p. 117). The carnal relation seems explicitly intended in *1 Henry VI*, V, iii, 18. And in *Macbeth* such a connection with the devil is repeatedly assumed I, iii, 107; V, v, 43; V, viii, 19.

of all the world could not, I suppose, wholly suppress himself. It is of the greatness of a popular artist that he can please himself in pleasing the people; the people and he are at one. Not always, indeed, did he think of pleasing them as a whole—witness his contemptible mobs and repeated utterances of aristocratic condescension. And since in his pages there is not the faintest echo of the scorn of Scot, the sarcasm of Harsnett, or the sceptical philosophy of Plutarch or Montaigne, and all the abundance of Elizabethan superstitious lore appears in his text with never an ironical accent or lifting of an eyebrow, one can only conclude that the poet either believed in much of it or was hardly a man at all. How strange a being the critics would make of him as they uplift and exalt him, a god or idol who sees and hears but opens not his lips, and leaves the people to their dark and cruel delusions! But Shakespeare was a man, an Elizabethan.

Omniscience and omnipotence are preserved to him at the expense of principle. Creizenach, the scholar who has written upon Shakespeare with widest knowledge, faces this alternative; and insisting that he could not have believed in witchcraft, admits (though he puts it rather mildly) that according to our ideas he ought to have shrunk from flattering the vain pedant on the throne even though he thereby secured a good stage effect. But it was ever the case that if the omniscience and omnipotence of the divinity could be preserved to him, a way would be found to keep the morals. Creizenach excuses Shakespeare by pleading the Renaissance custom of compliment and flattery for kings; it was not for the King's player to speak up when Bacon and Hobbes were so cautious; and scarcely could he be expected to feel his responsibility for so doing in a day when the King was flattered in his delusion even by the free-thinking Raleigh. Everything by this legerdemain is saved. Shakespeare both basks in the enlightenment of today and keeps the manners and morals of 1600. His

thoughts are our thoughts, but his ways are not our ways.
Yet the evidence is as fallacious as the case is unreal.
Small likelihood is there that Bacon or Raleigh was here
flattering the King—Hobbes, at that particular time, had
no king to flatter—though it does not much concern us if
they were.   Bacon suspends judgment, and Raleigh
expresses the same views as do dozens of others;[125] but
neither makes any reference to James's pet ideas or achievements as a witch-finder, or (in a treatise) runs the risk of
fanning the smouldering passions of the multitude into
flames.   And why all this manœuvring and mystery-mon-
gering, this creating of a need for an explanation and then
producing the explanation to fit?   Simply because of the
inability of a scholar or critic to conceive of an art as immortal in which the ideas involved are local and temporary,
or to conceive of an immortal artist who is not also a
prophet or seer.   Even classical scholars, we have noticed,
have been doing the same with Æschylus.[126]

The decisive case is *Macbeth;* if it were not for the
witches we might possibly, though with a wrench, entertain
the thought that Shakespeare took up with superstition, and
concealed his skepticism, only for artistic reasons.   In that

[125] See references in Spalding's indices under *witchcraft*. Raleigh, showing far less of Bacon's scientific discrimination and reserve, explains witchcraft as well as ghosts and dreams as the work of the devil.   The only
place where Bacon can justly be thought to accept the orthodox and official
opinion obsequiously is at the end of the second book of the *Advancement
of Learning,* where he is addressing the King; there he simply calls the
practice idolatry.   In general he thinks the witches are deluded.   For
Hobbes see *Works* (1839) vi, p. 96 (referred to by Creizenach).

[126] No doubt under the influence of Shakespeare criticism.   Some of
the great classical scholars, not to be outdone, have of late seriously held
that the Furies in the *Choephori* are only the conscience of Orestes, and
the Ghost of Clytemnestra in the *Eumenides* only the personification of the
thoughts which torment the Furies in their sleep; and others think that in the
Hercules and *Bacchæ of Euripides* the gods who appear are a dream in the
one case, a fraud in the other. Wilamowitz-Moellendorff, *Cultur der Gegen-
wart* (*Gr. und Lat. Lit.*), pp. 73, 80. So in his translation of the *Choephori*
he goes so far as to make l. 1010 an expression of doubt on Orestes' part
concerning Clytemnestra's guilt.   Contrast H. Weil, *Drame antique,* p. 49.
And see for Euripides, Whitmore, pp. 79, 86, controverting Verrall and
Norwood.

play Shakespeare did not need to bring in witches or witchcraft at all—in Holinshed the Weird Sisters are but the
goddesses of destiny; did not need to strike every tense
and tingling superstitious chord or memory in his audience;
did not need to allude, in this day of fresh cruel legislation, to the witches recently tortured by the King. He
must, then, have done it with a good conscience, or at least
with no enlightened scruples against it. And if that be so,
certainly there is no reason to think he did not unques-
tioningly and without reserve accept many of the other
superstitions he presented so vividly and abundantly. The
power of creation, imagination, and expression, even in its
highest form, does not imply in the poet unusual analytic
or scientific power, any more than it does in other artists—
painter, sculptor, or musician. Like them (and as a popular dramatist still more than they) he reflects, gloriously
shapes and colours, the ideas and sentiments of the time,
does not create new ones. He reproduces the forms of
art then prevailing, and creates new varieties of these; he
reflects things and thoughts already reflected, and things
and thoughts never reflected before. But he does not ordinarily discover truth—extend the boundaries of knowledge
or penetrate the all-embracing darkness. He gives expression only to the knowledge accessible in his day; and by
no means to all of it, for the sceptics Copernicus, Scot,
and Harsnett, might, so far as Shakespeare is concerned,
just as well have never been born. He thinks in images,
poetically; and not only is belief to him more grateful
material than unbelief—such it is to all poets—but unbelief
seems to have no meaning. And apparently such beliefs
and superstitions as we have been considering Shakespeare
took up into the net of his great art without a cavil or
scruple, like an Elizabethan, like the 'soul of the age' that
he was. As did his fellow-playwrights, he represented
ghosts, witches, omens, dreams, and the like, all as frankly

and simply as if he believed in them, and his belief there
is not much more reason to question than theirs.

SHAKESPEARE NOT SUPERSTITIOUS

Yet Shakespeare is not what even to-day should be called
superstitious. I have above compared him to Sophocles,
untouched by the spirit of zeal, cruelty, or gloom. Inherited creeds or beliefs do not make a man or break him.
The Greek religion was not highly moral or spiritual, but
Æschylus and Sophocles are as pure and noble of soul as
any who have written since. Even now many people carry
their beliefs lightly enough, though—since the days of
Bunyan and Wesley—they have been living in the days of
evangelicalism. In outward creed and belief, when we stop
to think of it, Shakespeare hardly differed from Cotton
Mather. What is the difference between the Churchman
and the Puritan save that the latter took his beliefs to
heart? And the time for taking them so, including the
immemorial belief in witchcraft—the belief not only in the
power of God but in that of the devil—did not fully come
till after Shakespeare's death.

Shakespeare was no Puritan; like his generation, he was
of the world, worldly. It is of the essence of superstition,
I suppose, that the supernatural should crowd in upon a
man's worldly life, to warp and distort it, making him look,
not to himself, or to natural causes, but to something
hostile or arbitrary, which it is his business to circumvent
or deceive, and letting darkness in upon that little stretch
of path which, before almost every man, shines fairly plain
and clear. But it did not crowd in upon Shakespeare's
life or that of his characters. Fate is appealed to—Fortune and the stars—but the human will does not cower
under it, lean upon it, or seek cunningly to shun it. Ghosts
and witches, though heeded, vanish—Wenn Geister spuken
geht er seinen Gang,—and do not blight the spirit of Brutus

or Hamlet, or even of Richard or Macbeth.   There is in
Shakespeare no brooding sense of the supernatural,
whether hostile or benign.   Religion itself is relegated
to the critical or dying moments of a man's life, if it appear
at all.   Imaginatively, Shakespeare entered into his superstitious creations as never did man before; but he exalted
them; and in reality his mind and spirit must have had
little in common with the dark, gross, and silly notions that
gave them birth.   Supreme art in dealing with the supernatural is compatible with belief in it, but depends on a
measure of detachment from it as well.

1907

CHAPTER VI

SHYLOCK[1]

His beard was red; his face was made
Not much unlike a witches;
His habit was a Jewish gown,
That would defend all weather;
His chin turned up, his nose hung down,
And both ends met together.

So Shylock was made up, according to the report of the old actor Thomas Jordan in 1664, on a stage that was still swayed by the tradition of Alleyn and Burbage. Macklin kept all this—nose and chin enough he had of his own—when, in the forties of the eighteenth century, he restored to the stage 'the Jew that Shakespeare drew'; and he ventured a red hat in early Venetian style for the old 'orange-tawney',[2] into the bargain. 'By Jove! Shylock in a black wig!' exclaimed a first-rater as Kean, seventy years after, appeared in the wings of Drury Lane for his first performance. And the part was played by Sir Henry

[1] In the general outlines of the conception of this character, and in some of the arguments, I discovered, when on the point of printing my article in 1911, that I had been anticipated by Mr W. H. Hudson, and, after the printing, by Mr George Woodberry. I refer to both eminent scholars below. Similar views have been expressed independently by Mr William Poel, and by Professor Creizenach in the fourth and fifth volumes of his *Geschichte des Dramas*. These discussions are more important than those referred to on the next page. Swinburne, too, in his *Three Plays of Shakespeare* (first published in 1909), with which I have just become acquainted, thinks Shylock 'less sinned against than sinning, not less grotesque than piteous;' and the opinion nowadays seems to be turning in that direction. An external sign in America is the fact that the Jewish Anti-Defamation Society is more and more successful in its endeavours to keep the play out of the schools.—Possibly Shylock's make-up is but Jordan's own invention.

[2] Usurers should have orange-tawney Bonnets, because they doe Iudaize:—Bacon's Essay of *Usury* (Furness).

Irving, in our day, in a grey beard and black cap. Changes in costume (on the stage at least) are but the outward and visible tokens of change. Macklin's grotesque ferocity gave place to Kean's vast and varied passion; and it, in turn, to Macready's and Irving's Hebraic picturesqueness and pathos. Taste had changed; and racial antipathy, in art if not in life, had faded away. Macklin, in an age when a part must be either comic or tragic, and no longer both together, dropped the butt and kept the villain; and this he played with such effect that the audience visibly shrank from him, and during the play and after it, King George II lost sleep. Kean made the Jew an injured human being, an outraged father. And Macready and Irving lifted him, in the words of Edmund Booth, 'out of the darkness of his native element of revengeful selfishness into the light of the venerable Hebrew, the martyr, the avenger.'

With this movement criticism has kept pace, or has gone before. Macklin's conception is in sympathy with Rowe's; Kean's with Hazlitt's and Skottowe's; and Macready and Irving take the great company of the later critics with them in their notions of racial pathos, and despite the declarations of a Spedding, a Furnivall, and a Furness,[3] in their plea for toleration. Few critics have recognized the prejudices of the times, the manifest indications of the poet's purpose, and his thoroughly Elizabethan taste for comic villainy. The few are mostly foreigners—Brandes, Brandl, Creizenach, Morsbach, and Sarcey. Others take account of this point of view only to gainsay it. 'We breathed a sigh of relief,' says the New York *Nation* (as if the worst were over) in a review of Professor Baker's book on Shakespeare, 'when we found him confessing his belief that Shakespeare did not intend Shylock to be a comic character'[4]; and

[3] See Furness's *Variorum Merchant of Venice*, pp. 433-5.
[4] August 15, 1907.

the distinguished critics Professors Bradley and Raleigh may be supposed to have done the same. As much as fifteen years ago Professor Wendell expressed the opinion, which Professor Matthews has of late reasserted, that Shylock was rightly represented on the stage in Shakespeare's time as a comic character, and rightly in our time as sympathetically human; but the dramatist's intention he left in the dark. Undertaking, perhaps, to abolish this antinomy and to bridge the gap between Shakespeare's time and ours, Professor Schelling perceives in Shylock, quite subtly, a grotesqueness bordering on laughter and a pathos bordering on tears.

I.

The dramatist's intention—that, I must believe, together with his success or failure in fulfilling it, is the only matter of importance. A work of art is not merely a point of departure for the mind which perceives it, like the preacher's text. It is not a sacred relic, a lover's token, a fetish, which conjures up more or less irrelevant spiritual or ecstatic states, though such it is ordinarily taken to be. 'A work of art is what it is to us,' wrote a distinguished man of letters not long since; 'not what it was a hundred years ago, or two hundred years ago, or even to its author. His view of it does not concern us except as a scientific curiosity. Does it move us, does it help us, does it delight us here and now? If not, it has artistically no value.' Certainly, as for the last; but the fact that it does move us, help us, and delight us, is not all that determines artistic value. If it were, many qualities and distinctions that are the substance of criticism, would fade away. The unique quality of a work of art, the thing which the impressionistic critic is supposed above all to seek to ascertain,—wherein does it reside if not in the author's intention as cause, in our bosom only as effect? Moreover, the critic who is unwilling to be delighted to-day with that at which others shall be offended to-morrow, will not disdain to look narrowly, in the light of history, to see whether his delight has a cause, or whether, proceeding only out of his own bosom, it is irrelevant and vain. It may possibly be, as M. Anatole France insists, that critical truth, like other truth, is but what each man troweth; but metaphysics aside, we are all reasonably aware, in principle if not in practice, of the difference between getting an idea from an author and getting it from ourselves; and if the author is to say one thing, that his Shylock is a villain, having, according to his word, already made him such, and we are to take it that he says that Shylock is a martyr and an avenger, it matters little, it seems to me, who it is that is helping, moving, and delighting us, Shakespeare or Kotzebue. Our passions and preconceptions overwhelm the poet. And he now is Dowden, Swinburne, Bradley, Raleigh, indeed, no longer himself. But who cares, or ever cared, to read the sonnets of Michelangelo's brother's grandson? Given to the world as the poet's own, they were an adaptation to the taste of a later age. Scholarship, half a century ago, rescued for us the poet himself. Let us have the grandnephew, to be sure, if his be really the better poetry; but we now see that we had been led astray as to that— chiefly his name and fame had led us to accept it—while here is both the great Michael whom we knew and better poetry besides, and the taste of the ages adapts itself to him.

Professedly, to be sure, the intention of the author has for long been the 'guiding star of criticism.' What has the writer proposed to himself to do? Goethe asked; and how far has he succeeded in carrying out his own plan? 'From Coleridge to Pater, from Sainte-Beuve to Lemaître,' says Professor Spingarn, 'the answer to this question is what critics have been striving for even when they have not succeeded';[5] and I could add the names of other critics so

[5] *The New Criticism* (N. Y., 1911), p. 17.

different as Professor Lipps, Mrs Edith Wharton, Mr
Clutton Brock, and Alexander Pope, who for themselves
have avowed it. Only now and then have critics frankly
denied it, and declared that the purpose of the author has
only an historical interest. That way, they seem to see, if
not madness, chaos lies. For thus a work of art means anything, everything—that is, nothing,—and what is the use of
discussing it? It ceases to be a means of expression or communication,—it is a relic, a token, a fetish which conjures
up more or less irrelevant spiritual or ecstatic states, and
starts one off upon a reverie or tangential rapture; and it is
these states, then—this reverie or rapture—that must pass
for criticism. Yet actually and practically criticism of the
great idols, Shakespeare or Cervantes, has oftenest been of
just that nature, and the sound principles so frankly recognized are as freely disregarded. There has been little
patient endeavour to discover the author's intention, and
less fidelity to it when found. Heaven and earth have
been moved to establish the true text, to interpret a now
forgotten phrase or track down an obscure allusion; but
of the larger meaning, the conception of a character, and
the scope and significance of the whole, each man feels
(or writes as if he felt) pretty free to think what he
pleases. His impression, not the author's discoverable
intention, is his standard; his feelings, not the author's
fairly discernible feelings, are his guide. Throughout
Professor Bradley's fine book on *Shakespearean Tragedy*
the supreme authority recognized seems to be the experience of the reader. 'The reader should examine himself
closely on this matter,' he repeats in various forms as he
discusses 'tragic fate' and the 'substance of tragedy'; and
so he frequently arrives at conclusions that on the one hand
neglect the practical and conventional aspects of Shakespeare's dramaturgy, and on the other hand overwhelm
Shakespeare's concrete, dualistic way of thinking with our
prevailingly abstract, monistic one. Examine himself!

Look in thy heart and write, as the poet was bidden!' In a measure, and in due course, to be sure, however historical and scholarly the endeavour. But the case of the critic is just that of the actor, whom, in France at any rate, the critic does not hesitate to take to task. 'Il le joue à contresens,' is a judgment that has not only point but substance. So Sarcey complained of Mounet-Sully as the Cid. But 'C'est comme cela que je sens le rôle' is, he says, your actor's answer. 'Eh! malheureux! il ne s'agit pas de le sentir mais de le comprendre.' And if that be so, then, as the dramatist M. de Curel would have it, 'Il n'y a qu'une façon de comprendre un rôle, celle de l'auteur.' [7]

Not that we are to think of the artist's intention, however clear it may seem to us, as necessarily clear and conscious in him; or that he keeps to it without changing. It is well known that the lineaments of Don Quixote, Sancho, and Parson Adams alter somewhat in the course of the long stories, and that the Falstaff of *Henry IV*, Part I, is not quite the same man in Part II and in the *Merry Wives*; and the like may have happened to Shylock. But then (if indeed it happened) it was altogether of the dramatist's own doing; it was a change in his purpose but a change that he (however unconsciously) made himself, and not one that took place in the character independently. Critics, as I show both above and below,[8] darkly intimate the contrary, and speak of a character taking the bit between his teeth and running away with his author, that is, saying and doing things—getting drunk, even [9]—without the author's permission or knowledge. Thus, seizing upon a common illusion of the artistic temperament, they make a pretext of it for

[6] A fuller discussion is to be found in my article 'Anachronism', *Modern Philology*, 1910, from which some of the above sentences are taken. For the matter of emphasis or context as determining the author's intention see above, chapter ii, section 4, and below, in the present chapter, sections 15 and 16.

[7] *Année psychologique* (1894), p. 141.

[8] See chapter iii, sections 9-11.

[9] See Wendell's *Shakespeare* (1894), p. 171.

running away from the author themselves and setting up
an interpretation of their own. Always the character 'runs
away', very properly, into the fold of our modern sentiments and prejudices, alien from his maker's. He knows
where he shall be welcome, where he is really at home. But
this autonomy and independence of a character is all a
mere delusion and nothing more, thanks to the externaliz-
ing power of the creator's imagination,—it is Michelangelo's freeing of the statue from the block as he carves it,
Rousseau's removing of veil after veil from the landscape
as he paints it, or Blake's drawing of eyes or mouth as if
the figure were there sitting to him for a portrait, just as
author after author, penning his dialogue, professes to be
merely recording the words he hears.[10] It is noteworthy
that only a Michelangelesque figure was by this sculptor
ever set free, only a Rousseau-like landscape by this painter
ever unveiled, and that none of these characters in drama
and fiction, so external and masterful, ever spoke, as in true
spirit-writing they are expected to do, in accents foreign to
the medium's. We are glad the author or artist has cause
to give such a report of the lively vigour of his creatures,
but logic and common sense assure us that the report is
wrong. A character is as much the author's means of communication to the public as a phrase or sentiment; surely
anyone can recognize the impropriety of an interpretation
such as Mr Palmer's above,[11] whereby Sparkish's opinions
are taken as modern and serious, not as a bit of seventeenth-
century irony and raillery on the part of the author—and
when he does so the character comes right as well. And
a convention or dramatic device, though now outworn, is as
important a means of such communication as the wording
of the text. With this we nowadays acknowledge that we
have no right to tamper, but neither have we the right to

[10] See above, chapter ii, section 14. Cf. for other instances Professor F.
C. Prescott's *The Poetic Mind* (N. Y., 1922), pp. 188-200,—Stevenson, Sully
Prudhomme, Scott, Dickens, etc.

[11] See above, chapter ii, section 4.

ignore the others. If we follow the wording only and ignore the old undramatic convention of comment and description, then Mr Firkins' interpretation [12] of Macbeth, at the moment of his anxiety lest that moment should lose its present horror, as an epicure in crime, is quite legitimate, though so far from Shakespeare's. And then Shakespeare's is a 'scientific curiosity.' And then, however he meant them all, the Ghosts are hallucinations, Shylock is a tragic character, Falstaff a courageous and pathetic one, and Cervantes, Molière, and Rabelais himself, if we will, have tears in their eyes.

2.

To get at Shakespeare's intention (after a fashion) is, after all, not hard. As with popular drama, great or small, he who runs may read—he who yawns and scuffles in the pit may understand. The time is past for speaking of Shakespeare as utterly impartial or inscrutable: the study of his work and that of his fellows as an expression of Elizabethan ideas and technique is teaching us better. The puzzle whether the *Merchant of Venice* is not meant for tragedy, for instance, is cleared up when, as Professor Baker suggests, we forget Sir Henry Irving's acting, and remember that the title [13]—and the hero—is not the 'Jew of Venice' as he would lead us to suppose; that this comedy is only like others, as *Measure for Measure* and *Much Ado*, not clear of the shadow of the fear of death; and that in closing with an act where Shylock and his knife are forgotten in the unravelling of the mystery between the lovers and the crowning of Antonio's happiness in theirs, it does not, from the Elizabethan point of view, perpetrate an

[12] See chapter iii, section 4. And compare for further discussion, section 23 in the present chapter.

[13] No great weight, of course, can, with justice, be given to this circumstance; but it is significant that modern critics and translators object to the title as it stands.—On the subject of Shakespeare's impartiality compare, above, p. 18, and, below, the discussion of the criminals.

anti-climax, but, like many another Elizabethan play, carries to completion what is a story for story's sake. 'Shylock is, and always has been the hero,' says Professor Schelling. But why, then, did Shakespeare drop his hero out of the play for good before the fourth act was over? It is a trick which he never repeated—a trick, I am persuaded, of which he was not capable.

Hero or not, Shylock is given a villain's due. His is the heaviest penalty to be found in all the pound of flesh stories, including that in *Il Pecorone,* which served as model for the play. Not in the Servian, the Persian, the African version, or even that of the *Cursor Mundi,* does the money-lender suffer like Shylock—impoverishment, sentence of death, and an outrage done to his faith from which Jews were guarded even by decrees of German emperors and Roman pontiffs. It was in the old play, perhaps, source of the present one; but that Shakespeare retained it shows his indifference, at least, to the amenities, as regards either Jews or Judaism. In not a single heart do Shylock's griefs excite commiseration; indeed, as they press upon him they are barbed with gibes and jeers. Coriolanus is unfortunate and at fault, but we know that the poet is with him. We know that the poet is not with Shylock, for on that point, in this play as in every other, the impartial, inscrutable poet leaves little or nothing to suggestion or surmise. As is his custom elsewhere, by the comments of the good characters, by the methods pursued in the disposition of scenes, and by the downright avowals of soliloquy, he constantly sets us right.

As for the first of these artifices, all the people who come in contact with Shylock except Tubal—among them being those of his own house, his servant and his daughter—have a word or two to say on the subject of his character, and never a good one. And in the same breath they spend on Bassanio and Antonio, his enemies, nothing but words of praise. Praise or blame, moreover, is, after Shakespeare's fashion, usually in the nick of time to guide the hearer's judgment. Lest at his first appearance the Jew should make too favourable an impression by his Scripture quotations, Antonio is led to observe that the devil can cite Scripture for his purpose; lest the Jew's motive in foregoing interest (for once in his life) should seem like the kindness Antonio takes it to be, Bassanio avows that he likes not fair terms and a villain's mind; and once the Jew has caught the Christian on the hip, every one, from Duke to Gaoler, has words of horror or detestation for him and of compassion for his victim.

As for the second artifice, the ordering of the scenes is such as to enforce this contrast. First impressions, every playwright knows (and no one better than Shakespeare himself), are momentous, particularly for the purpose of ridicule. Launcelot and Jessica, in separate scenes, are introduced before Shylock reaches home, that, hearing their story, we may side with them, and, when the old curmudgeon appears, may be moved to laughter as he complains of Launcelot's gormandizing, sleeping, and rending apparel out, and as he is made game of by the young conspirators to his face. Here, as Mr Poel has noticed, when there might be some danger of our sympathy becoming enlisted on Shylock's side because he is about to lose his daughter and some of his property, Shakespeare forestalls it. He lets Shylock, in his hesitation whether to go to the feast, take warning from a dream, but nevertheless, though he knows that they bid him not for love, decide to go in hate, in order to feed upon the prodigal Christian. And he lets him give up Launcelot, whom he has half a liking for, save that he is a huge feeder, to Bassanio—'to one that I would have him help to waste his borrowed purse.' Small credit these sentiments do him; little do they add to his pathos or dignity. Still more conspicuous is this care when Shylock laments over his daughter and his ducats. Lest then by any chance a stupid or tender-hearted audience should not laugh but

grieve, Salanio reports his outcries—in part word for word
—two scenes in advance, as matter of mirth to himself and
all the boys in Venice. It is exactly the same method as that
employed in *Twelfth Night*, Act III, scene ii, where Maria
comes and tells not only Sir Toby, Sir Andrew, and Fabian,
but, above all, the audience, how ridiculously Malvolio is
acting, before they see it for themselves. The art of the
theatre, but particularly the art of the comic theatre, is the
art of preparations, else it is not securely comic. But the
impression first of all imparted to us is of Shylock's villainy
—an impression which, however comical he may become,
we are not again allowed to lose. In the first scene in which
he appears, the third in the play, there is one of the most
remarkable instances in dramatic literature of a man saying
one thing but thinking another and the audience made to see
this. He prolongs the situation, keeps the Christians on
tenterhooks, turns the terms of the contract over and over
in his mind, as if he were considering the soundness of it
and of the borrower, while all the time he is hoping, for once
in his life, that his debtor may turn out not sound but bank-
rupt. He casts up Antonio's hard usage of him in the past,
defends the practice of interest-taking, is at the point of
stipulating what the rate this time shall be, and then—
decides to be friends and take no interest at all. He seems,
and is, loath to part for a time with three thousand ducats
—' 'tis a good round sum !'—but at the bottom of his heart
he is eager.

And as for the third artifice, that a sleepy audience may
not make the mistake of the cautious critic and take the
villain for the hero, Shakespeare is at pains to label the villain by an aside at the moment the hero appears on the
boards :

> I hate him for he is a Christian,
> But more for that in low simplicity
> He lends out money gratis, and brings down
> The rate of usance here with us in Venice.

Those are his motives, later confessed repeatedly;[14] and either one brands him as a villain more unmistakably in that day, as we shall see, than in ours. Of the indignities which he has endured he speaks also, and of revenge; but of none of these has he anything to say at the trial. There he pleads his oath, perjury to his soul should he break it, his 'lodged hate', or his 'humour'; further than that, 'I can give no reason nor I will not,'—for some reasons a man does not give; but here to himself and later to Tubal—'were he out of Venice I can make what merchandise I will'—he tells, in the thick of the action, the unvarnished truth. As with Shakespeare's villains generally—Aaron, Iago, or Richard III—only what they say concerning their purposes aside or to their confidants can be relied upon; and Shylock's oath and his horror of perjury are, as Dr Furness observes, belied by his clutching at thrice the principal when the pound of flesh escapes him, just as is his money-lender's ruse of [15] pretending to borrow the cash from 'a friend' (avowed as such by Moses in the *School for Scandal*) by his going home 'to purse the ducats straight.'

His arguments, moreover, are given a specious, not to say a grotesque colouring. Similar ones used by the Jew in Silvayn's *Orator* (1596), probably known to Shakespeare, are there called 'sophisticall'. But Hazlitt and other critics [16] strangely say that in argument Shylock has the best of it.

> What if my house be troubled with a rat
> And I be pleas'd to give *ten* thousand ducats
> To have it ban'd?

[14] *M. V.* I, iii, 43 f.; III, i, 55 f., 133; III, iii, 2—'the fool that lends out money gratis'; and compare Antonio, line 22 f.:—
> I oft delivered from his forfeitures
> Many that have at times made moan to me:
> Therefore he hates me.

[15] In Silvayn's *Orator* (Furness, 311); *L'Avare*, II, i; and it is employed also by Isaac of York.

[16] See, for instance, below, p. 324 f.

This particular rat is a human being; but the only thing to remark upon, in Shylock's opinion, is his willingness to squander ten thousand ducats on it instead of three. 'Hates any man the thing,' he cries (and there he is ticketed), 'he would not kill!' Even in Hazlitt's time, moreover, a choice of 'carrion flesh' in preference to ducats could not be plausibly compared as a 'humour'—the Jew's gross jesting here grates upon you—with an aversion to pigs or to the sound of the bag-pipe, or defended as a right by the analogy of holding slaves;[17] nor could the practice of interest-taking find a warrant in Jacob's pastoral trickery while in the service of Laban; least of all in the day when Sir John Hawkins, who initiated the slave-trade, with the Earls of Pembroke and Leicester and the Queen herself for partners, bore on the arms[18] which were granted him for his exploits a demi-Moor, proper, in chains, and in the day when the world at large still held interest-taking to be robbery. Very evidently, moreover, Shylock is discomfited by Antonio's question 'Did he take interest?' for he falters and stumbles in his reply—

> No, not take interest, not, as you would say,
> Directly, interest,—

and is worsted, in the eyes of the audience if not in his own, by the repeated use [19] of the old Aristotelian argument of the essential barrenness of money, still gospel in Shakespeare's day, in the second question,

> Or is your gold and silver ewes and rams?

For his answer is meant for nothing better than a piece of complacent shamelessness:

> I cannot tell: I make it breed as fast.

[17] See IV, i, 50, 55-60, 90; and compare (above and below) his jest about baiting fish with his pound of Antonio's flesh, III, i, 54.

[18] See Hawkins in the *Dictionary of National Biography.*

[19] Cf. Antonio's later words in the scene:
> For when did friendship take
> A breed of barren metal from a friend?

Only twice does Shakespeare seem to follow Shylock's pleadings and reasonings with any sympathy—'Hath a dog money?' in the first scene in which he appears, and 'Hath not a Jew eyes?' in the third act—but a bit too much has been made of this. Either plea ends in such fashion as to alienate the audience. To Shylock's reproaches the admirable Antonio, 'one of the gentlest and humblest of all the men in Shakespeare's theatre,'[20] praised and honoured by every one but Shylock, retorts, secure in his virtue, that he is just as like to spit on him and spurn him again. And Shylock's celebrated justification of his race runs headlong into a justification of his villainy: 'The villainy which you teach me I will execute, and it shall go hard but I will better the instruction.' 'Hath not a Jew eyes?' and he proceeds to show that your Jew is no less than a man, and as such has a right, not to respect or compassion, as the critics for a century have had it, but to revenge. Neither large nor lofty are his claims. The speech begins with the answer to Salanio's question about the pound of flesh. 'Why, I am sure, if he forfeit, thou wilt not take his flesh. What's that good for?' 'To bait fish withal,' he retorts in savage jest; 'if it will feed nothing else it will feed my revenge;' and he goes on to complain of insults, and of thwarted bargains to the tune of half a million, and to make a plea for which he has already robbed himself of a hearing. Quite as vigorously and (in that day) with as much reason, the detestable and abominable Aaron defends his race and colour, and Edmund, the dignity of bastards. The worst of his villains Shakespeare allows to plead their cause: their confidences in soliloquy or aside, if not (as here) slight touches in the plea itself, sufficiently counteract any too favourable impression. This,

[20] Cf. J. W. Hales, *English Historical Review*, ix, p. 652, f., especially p. 660 for an accumulation of the evidence for his goodness and amiableness. 'A kinder gentleman treads not the earth.'

on the face of it, is a plea for indulging in revenge with
all its rigours; not a word is put in for the nobler side
of Jewish character; and in lending Shylock his eloquence
Shakespeare is but giving the devil his due.[21]

3.

By all the devices, then, of Shakespeare's dramaturgy Shylock is proclaimed, as by the triple repetition of a crier,
to be the villain, though a comic villain or butt. Nor does
the poet let pass any of the prejudices of that day which
might heighten this impression. A miser, a money-lender,
a Jew,—all three had from time immemorial been objects
of popular detestation and ridicule, whether in life or on
the stage. The union of them in one person is in Shakespeare's time the rule, both in plays and in 'character'-
writing: to the popular imagination a money-lender was a
sordid miser with a hooked nose. So it is in the acknowledged prototype of Shylock, Marlowe's 'bottle-nosed'
monster, Barabas, the Jew of Malta. Though far more

---

[21] It is in these passages, no doubt, that, according to Mr Hudson (*v,
ante* p. 255), the racial feeling rises superior to Shylock's greed and personal
ferocity, and Shylock becomes an impressive, tragic figure. I dislike to
disagree with a critic with whom I have found myself, unawares, so often
agreeing; but I think that at this point Mr Hudson has not quite shaken
off the spell of the *Zeitgeist,* of which, as he himself confesses, it is hard
to rid the mind. As I show below, *passim,* these appeals did not reach the
hearts of the Elizabethans as they reach ours. Mr Hudson explains them,
like Professor Wendell, as moments where Shylock 'got too much for
Shakespeare,' and said what he liked. But that dark saying I cannot comprehend—not in itself and still less on the lips of a critic who protests, so
justly, against treating the characters of Shakespeare as if they were real
people in a real world (cf. above, p. 117 f). What else are Mr Hudson
and Mr Wendell doing when they let the poet be inspired by those whom
he himself had inspired, and so say things in a spirit of racial sympathy
beyond his ken? 'Shylock spoke as Shylock would speak'—not Shakespeare
—'spoke so simply because of the life which had been breathed into him.'
Granting that, Mr Hudson surrenders all the ground he had gained
for historical criticism. Shylock is thereupon free to say, regardless of
his maker, whatever it comes into the head of the critic to have him say;
and here is the entering in of the wedge for all those modernizing tendencies
which Mr Hudson, like a scholar, abhors.

of a villain, he has the same traits of craft and cruelty, the same unctuous friendliness hiding a thirst for a Christian's blood, the same thirst for blood outreaching his greed for gold, and the same spirit of unrelieved egoism which thrusts aside the claims of his family, his nation, or even his faith. If Barabas fawns like a spaniel when he pleases, grins when he bites, heaves up his shoulders when they call him dog, Shylock, for his part, 'still bears it with a patient shrug', and 'grows kind', seeking the Christian's 'love' in the hypocritical fashion of Barabas with the suitors and the friars. If Barabas ignores the interests of his brother Jews, poisons his daughter, 'counts religion but a childish toy', and, in various forms, avows the wish that 'so I live perish may all the world', Shylock has no word for the generous soul but 'fool' and 'simpleton',[22] and cries ('fervid patriot' that he is, 'martyr and avenger') : 'A diamond gone, cost me two thousand ducats in Frankfort! The curse never fell upon our nation until now. I never felt it till now.' Such is his love of his race, which, Professor Raleigh says, is 'deep as life'.[23] And in the next breath he cries, as 'the affectionate father' : 'Two thousand ducats in that, and other precious, precious jewels. I would my daughter were dead at my foot, and the jewels in her ear . . . and the ducats in her coffin.'

This alternation of daughter and ducats itself comes from Marlowe's play, as well as other ludicrous touches, such as your Jew's stinginess with food and horror of swine-eating, and the confounding of Jew and devil. This last is an old, wide-spread superstition: on the strength of holy writ the Fathers (with the suffrage in this century of Luther) held that the Jews were devils and the syna-

[22] Cf. III, iii, where the word, as Cowden-Clarke remarks, is significant. 'This is the fool that lent out money gratis;'—'In low simplicity he lends out money gratis.'
[23] *Shakespeare* (N. Y., 1907), p. 150: 'More sinned against than sinning,' which Swinburne, in 1909, rightly contradicts.

gogue the house of Satan.'[24] In both plays it affords the standing joke, in the *Merchant of Venice* nine times repeated.[25] 'Let me say Amen betimes,' exclaims Salanio in the midst of his good wishes for Antonio; 'lest the devil cross my prayer, for here he comes in the likeness of a Jew.' And in keeping with these notions Shylock's synagogue is, as Luther piously calls it, *ein Teuffels Nest*, the nest for hatching his plot once he and Tubal and the others of his 'tribe' can get together. 'Go, go, Tubal,' he cries in the unction of his guile, 'and meet me at our synagogue; go, good Tubal, at our synagogue, Tubal!'[26] In any one such eagerness for the sanctuary is suspicious; but all the more in those times, when the congregation was of Jews and the business of a Christian's flesh. These sly and insinuating Oriental repetitions would of themselves have given the Saxon audience a shudder.

It is highly probable, moreover, that Shylock wore the red hair and beard, mentioned by Jordan, from the beginning, as well as the bottle-nose of Barabas. So Judas was made up from of old; and in their immemorial orange-tawny, high-crowned hats and 'Jewish gabardines,' the very looks of the two usurers provoked derision. In both plays the word Jew, itself a badge of opprobrium, is constantly in use instead of the proper name of the character and as a byword for cruelty and cunning.

[24] See *Jewish Encyclopædia*, article 'Church Fathers'. Prynne in his *Short Demurrer* (1656 pt. i, p. 35), quotes Matthew Paris and Eadmerus, in passages where the Jew is identified with the devil. In the cases cited here and below, *devil* is not used loosely as the equivalent of *villain;* Shylock is a devil because he is a Jew.

[25] Bartlett's *Concordance,* 'Jew', 'devil'.

[26] There is a medieval picture of such a meeting to be found in Lacroix, t. i, fol. viii, *Conspiration des Juifs*, a miniature in *Le Pélerinage de la vie humaine*. How they lay their heads together! For the unrealistic red hair and beard put upon Judas and the Jews in medieval literature and art, and lingering on in popular lore, English, French, and German, to the present day, there is a deal of evidence, too bulky for me to reproduce. There are, of course, Jews with red hair, but they are not common.

4.

Now a popular dramatist, as I have shown in the first chapter and elsewhere, even more than other artists, cannot play a lone hand, but must regard the established traditions of his art, the rooted sentiments and prejudices of his public. In other Elizabethan plays the Jew fares still worse. Few instances have come down to us; but in Abyssus in the anonymous *Timon*, Mammon in *Jack Drum's Entertainment*, Pisaro in Haughton's *Englishmen for My Money*, and Zariph in Day's *Travels of Three English Gentlemen*, are to be found, in various combinations, usurer and miser, villain and butt, devourer of Christian blood and coin, and limb of the devil,[27]—all big-nosed,[28] or (in accordance with the vulgar error)[29] foul of breath, in some fashion or other egregiously 'Jewy'. In Mammon and Zariph, who are manifestly done under the influence of Shylock, prominence is given to outcries of avarice and of gloating revenge; while in Pisaro and Abyssus it is the nose, enormous and fiery, that bears the brunt. All these figures, the monstrous births of feeble poets, which owe all the humanity they have to Barabas and Shylock, are nevertheless of the same class, and show the same traits, an exaggeration of the same comic spirit. If they are travesties, they are such unconsciously, inevitably.

In two other plays, which certainly antedate the *Merchant of Venice*, and probably the *Jew of Malta*—Wilson's *Three Ladies of London* (1583) and the anonymous

[27] *Jack Drum*, ll. 53 f.; l. 91, etc.
[28] *Ibid.* pp. 140, 142, 143, etc.; *Englishmen for my Money*, Hazlitt's Dodsley, x, pp. 481, 522; *Timon*, Hazlitt's *Shakespeare's Library*, pt. ii, vol. 2, pp. 396-7. In neither of the last named plays is the usurer expressly stated to be a Jew. Cf. Nash, *Pierce Penilesse* (1592), McKerrow, i, p. 163, for usurer with an enormous nose; *Jack Wilton* (1594), *ib.*, ii, pp. 304 ff. for the Jews Zadock and Zacharia, big-nosed, covetous, stingy, treacherous, revengeful, bloody-minded, addicted to poisoning and (like Barabas and Shylock) to casting up to Christians the inconsistency of their lives; *Search for Money* (1609), Percy Soc., ii, 19.
[29] Much is made of this in *Timon*. See below, p. 284.

Selimus (1588)—the Jew has not developed so far. In the former play there is the single instance in the Elizabethan drama of an honourable Jew, one who forgives Mercatore a debt rather than let him go the length of abjuring his faith and turning Turk to escape it. But this episode is one with a purpose, that of satirizing the foreign merchants who are ruining England; and the Jews are painted fair only to blacken these. Gerontus is not held up to admiration as a whole, for his lending at interest is a practice bitterly attacked in this very play;[30] but intent as he is on recovering only interest and principal, he serves admirably as a foil to a love of lucre that knows no bounds. That Wilson is no advocate of the race appears from his crediting to Usury, in his next play, *The Three Lords and Three Ladies of London,* a purely Jewish parentage.[31] In the character of the usurer in Butler's and Overbury's collections, however, and in Rowley's *Search for Money* (1607), the usual conception prevails—that of one who lends money at interest, hoards it, skimps both himself and his dependants, and is an egoist and an atheist without either virtue or conscience. Butler and Overbury do not call him a Jew, but Rowley is sufficiently explicit in giving him a nose like the 'Jew of Maltae's,' a foul odour, and Satan for patron. And the collections of medieval *exempla*[32] abound in stories of usurers who are fonder of gold than of their own souls and have given them up for it to the devil.

In the English mysteries which have come down to us few traces are to be found of a ludicrous treatment of the Jew. Like much of the other comic matter, it may have been such as does not appear in the dialogue—improvisations, gestures, noses, orange-tawny hats. Judas, with his

---

[30] Dodsley, vi, p. 332 f. Usury, robbing Love and Conscience of their house, sets them on the downward path; and he assassinates Hospitality.

[31] Dodsley, vi, p. 457.—Cf. Dr Fernow's *Programm,* Hamburg, 1885, to which I am here indebted.

[32] Those of Jacques de Vitry, for instance, ed. by T. F. Crane, *v.* index.

red hair, red beard, and beetling brows, was no doubt comical; for these features the later drama never forgot, and there is a farcical scene in the York Plays where he is by Pilate's Porter refused admittance at sight. From medieval mysteries elsewhere, however, the omission may be supplied. By the Germans, who, unlike the English after 1290, had the Jews always with them, they are made ridiculous like the devils. Their looks, dress, speech, and proverbial greed are not spared, and the Jews' Song in double dutch is the standing-dish at the feast of fun. This blunt and boisterous satire goes the length, still attested pictorially, of representing them as drinking wine or beer as it gushes out of a sow or a calf.[33] In the Carnival plays, the newly converted are in a state of eager expectancy of the forbidden sausage; and once Hans Sachs delighted the audience by letting the devil, driven out of his patient by a physician, enter into a pair of Jewish usurers.[34] The Italian *carri*, popular plays presented on wagons drawn by oxen at the Carnival through the streets of Rome, were also called *giudate,* because in them the Jews played the main part—were abused and mocked, and, in the end, hanged, choked, impaled, and burned.[35] And to similar derision they were exposed among the Spanish.[36]

The closest parallel to Shylock and Barabas that I have seen is the Giudeo in Aretino's *Marescalco* (1526). He too is sly, fawning, and spiteful; and he even seems to have something of Shylock's trick of thought and speech.[37]

In the Elizabethan drama and character-writing, then, the Jew is both money-lender and miser, a villain who

---

[33] V. Flögel-Ebeling, *Geschichte des Grotesk-Komischen,* Tafel 20; Creizenach.

[34] For the German plays, *v.* Creizenach (1893), i, pp. 205, 406, 419.

[35] Klein, *Geschichte des Dramas,* iv, 239-40.

[36] Creizenach (1903), iii, 199-207, for the Portuguese.

[37] Orsù, dieci scudi e quattro sesini vi costeranno le maniglie, vi dono la fattura, che sarà mai? guadagnerò con qualche miserone' (III, ii). Shylock:—'What of that? Tubal, a wealthy Hebrew of my tribe, will furnish me' (I, iii, 57).

hankers after the Christian's blood, a gross egoist, even
an atheist (though charged with dealings with the devil),
and at the same time a butt, a hook-nosed niggard. And
a similar spirit of rude caricature and boisterous burlesque,
with even less of characterization, prevails, we have seen,
in the treatment of the Jew in early popular drama on the
Continent. Such is the soil from which the figure of Shylock grew; for almost everything in Shakespeare is a
growth, and strikes root deep in the present and in the past,
in stage tradition and in the life about him.

5.

The tradition having been examined, it now remains to
examine the opinions, or antipathies, of the time,—a sorry
tale to tell. Critics have wondered at the knowledge of
Jewish character displayed by Shakespeare; but Sir Sidney
Lee some years since[38] showed that although banished from
England in 1290, and not re-admitted until the latter days
of Cromwell, Jews were then not unknown. 'Store of
Jewes we have in England,' to quote *The Wandering Jew
Telling Fortunes to Englishmen* (1640); 'a few in Court,
many in the Citty, more in the Countrey.' In 1594, shortly
before the *Merchant of Venice* was written, one of these
Jews at court made something of a stir. Lopez, the
Queen's physician, was tried for conspiracy against her
life. Sir Sidney Lee has shown the bitterness of feeling
which it provoked, and the weight that was given to the
fact that the offender was a Jew by prosecutor, judges, and
people. 'The perjured and murderous Jewish doctor,'

[38] *Gentleman's Magazine,* 1880, p. 187 f.; *Academy,* May 14, 1887; *Transactions of New Shakespeare Society,* 1888. Commonly they followed the
trade of old-clothes dealer, it appears from a passage quoted by Sir Sidney
Lee from *Every Woman in her Humour* (1609), and from Rowley's *Search
for Money,* p. 15,—as both now and in the days of St Jerome. Creizenach
quotes Heywood's *Challenge for Beauty* (1635) on their character: 'Your
English Jewes, they'le buy and sell their fathers, prostrate their wives, and
make money of their own children, the male stewes can witnesse that.'
(*Works,* vol. v, 26.)

cried Coke, 'is worse than Judas himself'; and 'of a religious profession,' he said again, 'fit for any execrable undertaking.' Even his judges spoke of him as 'that vile Jew.' Though no longer a Jew by faith, when he protested from the scaffold that 'he loved the Queen as he loved Jesus Christ,' such words 'from a man of the Jewish profession,' says Camden, were 'heard not without laughter'; and 'He is a Jew!' men cried aloud as the breath passed from his body.[39] 'And what's his reason?' asks Shylock in the play; 'I am a Jew!'

Of itself this incident is enough to show that although there was by no means a Jewish peril in Shakespeare's day, the race-hatred of Angevin times had not burned out. Race-hatred, indeed, or the desire to profit by it, may have prompted the writing of this play, that Shakespeare's company might in the present excitement compete with Henslowe's in their *Jew of Malta*. Even the Reformation, in England as in Germany, had done little to quench it:[40] only the later Puritans felt any relentings towards the chosen race. Hebrews of the Hebrews themselves, it was small wonder. The visionaries, the Fifth Monarchy men, the Root-and-Branch men, often looked almost kindly upon the Jews as they made the Jewish Sabbath henceforth and for ever the British Sabbath, contemplated surrounding Cromwell with a Sanhedrim of seventy councillors, and urged on Parliament the establishing of the Torah as the law of the realm. But the nation as a whole was not so minded; with it race-hatred went deeper than religion. Cromwell admitted the Jews in 1655; but it had to be, as Graetz remarks, by the back door, for the Commission designated to sit upon the measure was under the necessity of being admonished and dissolved like Parliament itself. Prynne, who for his own faith had lost his ears, wrote

[39] *Annales* (ed. 1635), p. 431. All the evidence used in the paragraph is Sir Sidney's.
[40] H. Grætz, *History of the Jews* (1891), iv, pp. 540-2.

what was, measured by his own professional Dissenter's standard, a *Short Demurrer,* in Two Parts, in which, like Luther a century before him, he raked up all the charges against the Jews that had ever been made, including usury, coining, cheating and oppression, crucifixion of children, blasphemy and sacrilege, malice towards man and God, the murder of Christ, obstinacy and hardness of heart. 'Do not I hate them, O Lord, that hate thee?' he cries, with none to contradict him, in his zeal; 'I hate them with a perfect hatred.' And others there were like him, as appears from the petition to Parliament of Robert Rich, surnamed Mordecai, in 1653, on behalf of the Jews of England, Scotland, and Ireland: 'Ever since 1648, it was hoped that persecution for conscience' sake would cease and truth and mercy take its place, but contrary thereto, these three last years hundreds in England have been cast into dungeons and prisons, some have perished, and others endured whippings, stonings, and spoilings of goods for matters concerning their law and conscience,' etc. Even after these persecutions had, under Cromwell's iron hand, been allayed, and the Jews admitted to the rights of worship, it was upon a precarious basis. The doors of the first synagogue were threefold and double-locked. In 1660, a remonstrance upon their usurious and fraudulent practices was made by the Lord Mayor and Aldermen to the King, praying for the imposition on them of special taxes, seizure of their personal property, and banishment for residence without a license.[1] Even after the Revolution, in 1689, a bill specially to tax the Jews was introduced into Parliament.

6.

Such were the disabilities under which the Jews laboured for a century after Shakespeare's day. What is the recorded opinion of his contemporaries? Coke, Solicitor-

[1] For this and the above see *Calendar of State Papers; Domestic.*

General, is comprehensible in abusing Lopez, but he is hardly so as, no longer Solicitor but a jurist, ex-Chief Justice of the King's Bench, he abuses the Jews in his *Institutes of the Laws of England.* 'Odious,' he calls them in his commentary on the Statute De Judaismo, 'both to God and man;'—'these cruel Jews, wicked and wretched men.'[42] Bishop Joseph Hall, writing to Samuel Burton, Archdeacon of Gloucester, in 1607, rejoices that 'our church is well rid of that accursed nation, whom yet Rome harbours . . . while instead of spitting at, or that their Neapolitan correction whereof Gratian speaks, the pope solemnly receives at their hands that Bible which they at once approve and overthrow.' He hates Rome for her tolerance and indulgence, forsooth. 'The subtlest and most subdolous people,' writes James Howell in 1633 to Lord Clifford; 'the most hateful race of men.' Jeremy Taylor thinks it is a wonder how the anger of God is gone out upon that miserable people.'[43] And Robert South, the greatest preacher in England a century after Shakespeare's death, declares, in a long and virulent passage, that it was appointed as the bitterest humiliation of Christ's life on earth that he should be born of the race of the Jews, 'the most sordid and degenerate upon the earth.' 'And to this very day,' he continues, 'how much are they disgusted in all those kingdoms and dominions where they are dispersed! They are like dung upon the face of the earth; and that not so much for their being scattered as for being so offensive.' [44]

Nor is it a legal or theological prejudice merely. Popular literature, like the drama, is, as we have already seen, imbued with it; and dozens of ballads, like *Hugh of Lincoln* and *Gernutus,* still handed it down orally from generation to generation. Enlightenment prevailed not against it. Many people think Shakespeare too free a

[42] *Second Part of the Institutes,* pp. 506 ff., where there is more of this.
[43] *Of the Probable Conscience,* bk. i, ch. 4, rule 2, § 28.
[44] *Sermons* (London, 1865), ii, p. 228.

spirit to have entertained it himself; but the freest spirit
of Shakespeare's day, who, in a short life, cast from him
more hearsays and superstitions than any Englishman up
to the time of Hobbes, still clings to this. With not a
thought of their damnation or of the wrath of God upon
them, Giordano Bruno yet calls the Jews a generation so
'pestilente, leprosa, et generalmente perniciosa; che merita
prima esser spinta, che nata;—gente sempre vile, seruile,
mercenaria, solitaria, incommunicabile, et inconuersabile
con l'altre generationi, le quali bestialmente spregiano, et
da le quali per ogni ragione son degnamente dispreggiate.' [45]

Here is a hint at the real cause of Jew-baiting the
world over—the ways and manners of the Jews, their
mores as Professor Sumner would have said, those traits
and customs which keep them to this day a nation, though
of exiles. History is in accord with this. The ancients—
Greeks, Romans, Syrians, and Egyptians—hated them, and
at times persecuted them, with no pious scruple to justify it,
almost as heartily as the medieval Christians. [46] The
frightful persecutions, the Jew-burnings, which at times
of great emotional exaltation or depression raged through
Europe in the thirteenth and fourteenth centuries, were
almost always popular movements, not instigated or
directed by the church; and princes, kings, emperors, popes
like Clement VI, even fanatics like Saint Bernard, the
Dominicans and the Franciscans, had, time and again, to
interpose between the Jews and the violence of the mob. [47]
Converts fared little better than the faithful. And it was
not the priest-ridden countries but those which first attained

[45] *Spaccio della bestia,* ed. Lagarde, p. 500; *Cabala del cavallo Pegaseo,*
p. 576.

[46] *V. Jewish Encyclopædia,* 'Diaspora,' for an account of the horrible mas-
sacres and manifold persecutions at Seleucia and Alexandria, in Syria and
Mesopotamia; and for the almost universally unfavourable opinion of them
held by the ancient writers. Cf. Graetz, ii, pp. 178-9; Mommsen (N. Y.,
1891), iv, p. 642; South, *Sermons,* ii, p. 288.

[47] Lacroix, *Moyen Age et Renaissance,* t. i, *Juifs,* fol. 5; Green's *History*
(1881) i, p. 338; Graetz, *passim,* from whom a long list of rulers might be
made. For the next following statement see Lacroix, fol. 16.

to a consciousness of national unity—England, France, Spain—as Wellhausen has shown, that expelled the Jews from their borders. In Italy, hard by the papal throne, they enjoyed greater security. In England, in the twentieth year of Henry III, the inhabitants of Southampton petitioned the king for a like privilege with the men of Newcastle, that no Jew should dwell amongst them,[48] and Parliament granted Edward I a fifteenth in return for the favour of expelling the Jewish community as a whole.[49] If, then, the hatred of Jews is at bottom a racial and social, rather than a religious, prejudice, and not Protestantism, not even the free thought of the Renaissance, but only Puritan fanaticism, late in the seventeenth century, availed, in any measure, to dispel it, why should we refuse to recognize it in Shakespeare, who, more than any other poet, reflected the settled prejudices and passions of his race?

7.

To the Middle Ages, in the dearth of Jews and contemporary references to Jews in Elizabethan England, we must turn for illustration,—but medieval is the sentiment of this comedy. Most readers and critics nowadays resent the despoiling of Shylock at the end. Indeed, where is there another instance of a villain in a Shakesperean comedy, with such cause for his villainy, coming off so ill? But even a century later, as we have seen, a sense of justice did not keep the government from the consideration of measures of confiscation and extra taxation; and all the European history of the Jewish race for a thousand years before is made up of such measures, put, without consideration, into effect. In the days of Titus, and afterwards in every nation and principality of Europe, they were *servi cameræ;* and, in return for the slight protection they thus received, they were pillaged and plundered, legally or ille-

---

[48] Tovey, *Anglia Judaica,* Oxford (1738), p. 105.
[49] Green, i, p. 340; *Annales De Dunstaplia* (Rolls Series), p. 362.

gally. Of his Jews every feudatory-in-chief spoke as of his
serfs or his hounds;[50] and he sold them, or bought them,
or mortgaged them, or, like William Rufus waxed furious
in defence of them, according to his needs.[51] The king
took possession of all the real property of which a Jew
was seized, in case of his 'death, outlawry, or departure
hence' [52] (or, in some parts of Europe, as soon, apparently,
as he was known to have purchased it) ; and, in defiance of
the fourth Lateran Council, of all property whatsoever, as
the fruits of usury, on his conversion.[53] 'Judæus vero nihil
proprium habere potest,' says Bracton (and the principle
prevailed far beyond the Channel) ; 'quia quidquid acquirit
non sibi acquirit sed regi, quia non vivunt sibi ipsis sed aliis,
et sic aliis acquirunt et non sibi ipsis.' [54] 'They are doomed
to perpetual servitude,' writes Saint Thomas Aquinas, 'and
the lords of the earth may use their goods as their own.' [55]
'The curse of the Patriarch rests upon the descendants of
Ham,' declared in 1851 the Supreme Court of Georgia,
with reference to another subject race; 'the negro and his
master are but fulfilling a divine appointment.' [56] A
medieval sentiment, but alive in Shakespeare's day and not
totally extinct in our own.

Nor were men content with injustice that was legal. Not

[50] Lacroix, op. cit, fol. 8.
[51] Du Cange, sub. voc. Judæi; Tovey. Matthew Paris (Du Cange)
makes a medieval jest of it when Henry III mortgages the Jews to Earl
Richard, his brother, ut quos Rex excoriaverat Comes evisceraret. The poor
Jews were back within a year or two on his hands, to be then made over
by deed to Prince Edward and by him assigned for two years to the Cahor-
sins! Cf. 'Lettres par les quelles le Roi donne un Juif à son frère—achète
un Juif.' Recueil général des anciennes lois françaises, ii, p. 709.
[52] Prynne, Demurrer, pt. ii, pp. 39-65, citing a preamble of a writ of 34
Henry III. Cf. Du Cange.
[53] A. M. Hyamson, The Jews in England (1908), p. 29; Du Cange, etc.
[54] De Warrantia, cap. vi. 6. To the same effect, the Leges Anglicanæ,
Hoveden (Rolls Series) no. 51, ii, p. 231: 'Judæi et omnia sua regis sunt.'
Leges Edwardi Confessoris (earlier version, c. twelfth century) cap. 25.
Du Cange, Judæi.
[55] Van Bruyssel, Histoire de commerce belge, i, p. 239, letter to Alice of
Burgundy (Lecky).
[56] Neal vs. Farmer, Georgia Reports, 1851, p. 582.

for their own behoof did the Jews live, as Bracton puts it, nor merely for the king's, but also for that of his people. Philip Augustus in 1182 remitted to every man his debts to the Jews on payment of a fifth part into the royal treasury.[57] Saint Louis remitted a third part of all such debts for the salvation of his own soul and the souls of his ancestors; 'et quia pacem operatur justicia,' continues the chronicler, naïve in morals as in grammar, 'dedit Deus sibi pacem et regno tranquillitatem.'[58] And there is an edict of Henry III of England in the year 1266, recorded in the *Red Book of the Exchequer,* to annul the debts of Christians to Jews in toto, as well as many special orders, in the reign of John particularly, annulling the debts of individuals.[59] At the last, when the Jews were banished from England, they were deprived of all their landed property at a stroke; and as late as 1542 the great leader of the Reformation proposed to the princes and people of Germany, in his sorry pamphlet *Von den Juden und ihren Lügen,* that their synagogues and houses should be burned or destroyed, and they themselves deprived of all their wealth, their books and their prayer-books, and put to work with spade or spindle.[60] With such treatment of the race lingering in men's memories, small wonder that Jessica, as she runs away with her Christian, should, to the satisfaction of everybody on the stage or off it, carry some portion of her father's jewels and ducats with her; and that the Duke, in the simplicity of his soul, should think it a virtue and a mercy to spare the life of the outraged Jew at the cost of all his goods. 'Thou shalt see the difference of our spirits,' Shakespeare, in all good faith, makes him say.

[57] *Recueil des lois,* i, p. 170.
[58] Hallam, *Middle Ages* (N. Y., 1854), ii, p. 484. *Beati Ludovici Vita, Recueil des historiens des Gaules* (1876), t. 23, p. 164.
[59] *Red Book* (Rolls Series), p. 978: 'Ke totes les dettes a Gyus seent quites a Crestiens ke les deyvent et a lur eyres a tuz jurs!' Madox, *History of Exchequer,* p. 157 (Lacroix).
[60] *Werke* (Altenburg, 1662), Theil viii, p. 260.

8.

Enforced conversion, or rather conversion suborned, a feature as we have seen, not to be found in other pound of flesh stories, and to be attributed to Gosson's old play [61] or to the *Jew of Malta,* is another matter which shocks us. It need not do so: it is a better way than the ways of Whitgift, Bancroft, and Laud. Even so late as 1635 there is a case recorded as before the High Court of Commission, of one Mary Chester, a Jewess, prisoner in Bridewell, who was 'enlarged' upon acknowledgment and recantation of her errors in holding certain Judaical tenets touching the Sabbath and the distinction of meats, after putting in bond to appear.[62] Coercion of unbelievers was an immemorial practice, not in Shakespeare's day by any means discredited, and never condemned by Shakespeare himself. 'Personal religion', 'convictions', were terms not then current; and according to the rough-and-ready manners of the time, Antonio's mercenary stipulation—not much more so, by the way, than that with which nowadays a Catholic king offers his hand and crown to a Protestant princess—is of course to be reckoned (though in disguise) an exemplary kindness, or, as Portia calls it, a mercy rendered him. 'Provided that for this favour he presently become a Christian!' The idea is old-fashioned, like the Duke's notion of clemency to Jews, or Saint Louis' expedient for making his own and his ancestors' salvation sure; but nothing could be farther from Shakespeare's thought than Professor Jastrow's suggestion of satire or irony.[63]

[61] The lost play, representing 'the greediness of worldly chusers and bloody minds of Usurers,' mentioned by Gosson in his *School of Abuse* (1579). In the *Jew of Malta,* I, ii, the Jews are given the alternative of losing their property or becoming Christians.

[62] *Calendar of State Papers, Domestic,* 1636-6. For enforced baptism or conversion see Graetz, *passim,* and Lecky, *History of Rationalism* (1870), ii, pp. 278-82.

[63] Mr W. H. Hudson (*op. cit.*) takes notice, with just scorn, of an equally remarkable opinion to the effect that Shylock had been brought to realize that, in insisting upon his conversion to Christianity, Antonio was acting only for his good. For this, as for irony, there is no evidence.

Once Launcelot rallies Jessica on the subject of Jewish damnation, and Dr Brandes thinks it a proof that Shakespeare does not entertain that belief. But it is jesting pure and simple, without touch of satire; and although the like of it would hardly be expected of a Puritan, say, or of a Methodist, one who takes his own or others' religion much to heart, it might easily be expected of Shakespeare. Hell and damnation in general are a favourite subject of mirth with him—witness the Porter scene in *Macbeth*—as with the coarse and cheerful but orthodox world before and since; and he would hardly have pulled a long face when the joke touched the Jews. He was on the whole a gentler, though less refined, spirit than Molière; yet what Lemaître says of the latter may fairly be said of him: 'Il ignorait l'art, relativement récent, de s'attendrir sur les croyances qu'on n'a pas.' The damnation of the Jews was a doctrine of the Fathers, never doubted, daily, idiomatically reaffirmed;—the blood is on them and their children;—and it was warrant for endless insult and discrimination.

In the Middle Ages and after they were treated as things unclean. Their blood, it was thought, was black and putrid; the stench, a notion prevalent in England as late as the middle of the eighteenth century, came, not, as might have been expected, from the devil that possessed them, but as a curse from Christ.[64] They were forbidden to touch, at market, food which they did not buy, and to consort with Christians at the alehouse, the bath, or one another's houses;[65] and they were barred not only from the church but from the brothel—from commerce with Christian soul or flesh.[66] Intermarriage with them was an abomination, and in the reign of Saint Louis Christians who

<hr />

[64] Browne, *Pseudodoxia*, bk. iv, ch. 10; Tovey, *Anglia Judaica* (1738), p. 95. In the Saints' legends the devils have this attribute, as the angels, like the pagan gods, have the opposite one.

[65] Du Cange, *Judæi*, Lecky.

[66] By the Council of Oxford, 1222; Lecky, *History of Rationalism*, ii, p. 275.

kept Jewish concubines were burned. Because of their
unholy influences they were forbidden to hold Christian
slaves, and for the strangest of reasons, to hire Christian
nurses.[67] A special dwelling-place, cemetery, and daily
garb, were assigned to them, and, by decree not only of the
state but of œcumenical councils, the Jew-badge and the
high-crowned yellow hat, or *pileus cornutus*. Provoked and
invited by these distinctions there arose a world of insult
and savage jest. In Holy Week, at Toulouse, a Jew was
compelled to stand at the Cathedral door to receive buffets
from the worshippers as they came in and out. At Béziers
the populace stoned Jewish houses. The tariff of tolls at
bridges and turnpikes in France distinguished between
Christians and Jews, Jews and Jewesses, and Jewesses fat
and lean, and put all Jews on a level with cattle; and in the
same country, until the fourteenth century, when a Jew was
hanged it was head downwards between two dogs.[68] The
race between Jews and horses at the Roman Carnival was,
we may be sure, the sweetest jest offered the rabble during
the year; and at last the Jews paid the magistrates three
hundred scudi annually to be rid of it. In the atmosphere
of such abhorrence and inhuman contempt and ridicule it
was that Antonio learned to call Shylock devil, misbeliever,
and cutthroat dog, to kick him and spit upon his beard and
Jewish gabardine, with 'no sign', as Mr Woodberry
observes, 'that Shakespeare saw any wrong in all this.' In
1381, according to a letter in the royal archives, cited by

[67] Tovey, pp. 103-105, letter of Innocent III to the Archbishop of Sens
and proclamation of Henry III of England. The reason given is the impiety
of the Jews in forcing the nurses to milk themselves into a privy for three
clear days after taking the Sacrament. Here is the same materialism of
conception that is to be found in Synge's *Pegeen* (to the Widow Quin):
'Doesn't the world know you reared a black ram at your own breast, so
that the Lord Bishop of Connaught felt the elements of a Christian, and he
eating it after in a kidney stew?'

[68] Lecky, quoting Michelet, *Origines du Droit* (1837), p. 368. Lacroix,
Moyen Age, Juifs, fol. ix. Here and there I may be reproducing something
mythical; but what concerns us is not so much facts as sentiments—which
made the myths.

Du Cange, a certain Jehan La Barbe, 'having been spit upon in the face, was moved to wrath at the outrage, seeing that he was no Jew, in whose face it was proper to spit'.[69] Such a method, we have seen, Bishop Hall would recommend to the Pope for receiving the Jews when they came to him bearing the gift of the Bible; and certainly it had already something of hieratic sanction, for in the Eastern Church spitting at the devil was a picturesque, though not a pretty, part of the ritual of baptism.[70] Nor was the Jew, in medieval imagination at least, in those impetuous, intemperate days to be outdone, for according to Luther, who in his diatribe has all too much to say of the matter, whether metaphorical or literal, a triple expectoration accompanied the Jews' cursing of Christ.[71]

9.

Here we touch on one of the charges against the Jews which lie embedded in Shakespeare's other work, among the few casual references which he makes to them. 'Liver of *blaspheming* Jew' is cast into the cauldron by the witches in *Macbeth,* along with other unholy odds and ends:

> Nose of Turk and Tartar's lips,
> Finger of birth-strangled babe
> Ditch-deliver'd by a drab.

Blasphemy is a charge made from the time of the Fathers.[72] Three times daily the Jews were supposed to rail against Christ in their prayers, and that they should be restrained from such blasphemy was a special recommendation of the committee appointed by the Council in 1665 to consider

[69] Sub. voc. *Judæi*: 'a qui on deust cracher au visage.' As Professor Keller reminds us, the Queen herself, child of impulse, spat on a courtier's cloak that displeased her.

[70] Roskoff, *Geschichte des Teufels,* i, p. 291.

[71] *Op cit.,* p. 254.

[72] Justin, Origen, Epiphanius, Jerome. *V. Jewish Encyclopædia,* article *Church Fathers.*

the resettlement of the Jews in England.[73] Those were
the days when a man had to look out for his God as well
as for himself, and Luther took this matter of blasphemy
particularly to heart. Again and again in his tractate he
belabours the Jews for it; and he would have their synagogues and their houses, as the scenes of such impiety,
burned down and removed forever from the sight of man.
'Und solchs sol man thun unserm Herrn und der Christen-
heit zu Ehren, damit Gott sehe dass wir Christen seyn!'
In those days one must show one's colours. Hardness of
heart is another implied accusation, several times repeated.
'A Jew would have wept,' sobs Launce before his cruel-
hearted cur; 'to have seen our parting.' Shylock himself
is intended as a capital instance: the Duke, Antonio, Bassanio, and Gratiano all recognize in him the 'Jewish heart',
'uncapable of pity'—'than which what's harder?'—and this
it is that gave point, now lost, to Portia's praise of mercy.
People generally—Protestants like Luther and Prynne, for
instance—believed, as in some parts of Europe they believe
still, that the Jews, especially about the time of the Pass-
over, caught little Christians and crucified them, poisoned
the wells or the air, and dealt death and destruction about
them as freely as Barabas in the play.[74] Catholics thought
they mutilated the Host, till it bled again. After all this,
one other charge, no more than vaguely hinted at in Shakespeare but made explicit, as we have seen, in Marlowe—
that of atheism—need not surprise us. Absurd as it is, it
comes down from ancient times, and it is no more absurd
than Luther's charge of blasphemy and idolatry,[75] made not
many years before Marlowe wrote.

10.

Now this survey of the anti-Semitic prejudice does not,

[73] Hyamson, p. 205.
[74] See Graetz, *passim;* or any history of the Middle Ages.
[75] *Von den Juden und ihren Lügen.*

of course, prove that Shakespeare could not have presented his Jew as a serious and sympathetic figure had he cared to do so. A Jew had, for a purpose, been presented in a more favourable light by Wilson, we have seen, in the *Three Ladies of London;* and, long before, by Boccaccio, in the second and third tale of the *Decameron,* though this is a Jew converted. But it is clear that Shakespeare did not care to do so. Had he cared to make a serious and sympathetic figure of Shylock, he would not have made him after the similitude of those created by the prejudices and misconceptions awake or slumbering in his day—not one avaricious and miserly, crafty and treacherous, hard-hearted and pitiless, fiercely thirsting for the Christian's blood and hungering—pork excepted—for his goods,—not made him a cur and devil, in short, to be spurned and spit upon, despoiled and forcibly converted. And he would not then, by dint of all his artful preparations and contrivings, have exposed him to unrelenting laughter. Spedding, as Mr Woodberry well says, admits of no reply:

The best contribution which I can offer to this discussion is the expression of an old man's difficulty in accepting these new discoveries of profound moral and political designs underlying Shakespeare's choice and treatment of his subject. I believe he was a man of business,—that his principal business was to produce plays which would draw. . . . But if, instead of looking about for a story to 'please' the Globe audience, he had been in search of a subject under cover of which he might steal into their minds 'a more tolerant feeling toward the Hebrew race,' I cannot think he would have selected for his hero a rich Jewish merchant plotting the murder of a Christian rival by means of a fraudulent contract, which made death the penalty of non-payment at the day, and insisting on the exaction of it. In a modern Christian audience it seems to be possible for a skillful actor to work on the feelings of an audience so far as to make a man engaged in such a business an object of respectful sympathy. But can anybody believe that in times when this would have been much more difficult, Shakespeare would have chosen such a case as a favourable one to suggest toleration to a public prejudiced against Jews?

II.

We do not forget that Shylock was also a usurer. Dr
Honigmann, who is one of them that interpret the *Merchant
of Venice* as a plea for toleration, says that in Shakespeare's
day the word did not carry with it any stigma.[76] Never,
surely, was opinion more mistaken. By laws civil and
ecclesiastical, usury—that is, the exaction of interest of any
sort—was a crime. With expanding trade and manufac-
ture the practice was widening, but was by no one approved
in principle. By 37 Henry VIII, cap. ix, the old laws
against usury are, indeed, abolished, and a rate of ten per
cent is indirectly legalized by the fixing of severe penalties
for any rate higher; but the practice is condemned, and
classed with corrupt bargains, and the reason given for the
present enactment is that the old 'Actes bene of so little
force and effect that by reason thereof little or noe punysh-
ment hath ensued to the offenders of the same.' In 1552,
however, by 6 Edward VI, cap. xx, the act of Henry VIII
is annulled, though 'not ment or intended for mayntenance
and allowaunce of Usurie, as dyvers parsons[77] blynded with
inordinat love of themselves have and yet doo mistake the
same'; and severe penalties are enacted against any usury
whatever, 'forasmuch as Usurie is by the word of God
utterly prohibited, as a vyce most odyous and detestable,
as in dyvers places in the hollie Scriptures it is evident to
be seen, which thing by no godly teachings and perswations
can syncke in to the harte of dyvers gredie, uncharitable
and couvetous persons of this Realme, nor yet by anny terrible threatenings of Godd's wrathe and veangeaunce,' etc.
In 1570, by 13 Elizabeth, cap. viii, 6 Edward VI is annulled
and 37 Henry VIII re-enacted, but, 'foreasmuch as all
Usurie, being forbydden by the Law of God is synne and
detestable,' it ordains that even interest at ten per cent or

[76] *Jahrbuch,* xvii, p. 216.

[77] 'Persons,' as the context shows. In these passages I follow the *Statutes
of the Realm.*

under is forfeitable. In case of interest above ten per cent the penalty of 37 Henry VIII remains, that of thrice the principal. In both this act and the next following, 21 Jac. I, cap. xvii, which introduces further modifications, it is expressly provided that all offenders shall 'also be punished and corrected according to the ecclesiastical laws heretofore made against usury.'

What were these? By the canons of 1603, cap. cix, it is ordained that 'if any offend their Brethren, either by Adultery, Whoredom, Incest, or Drunkenness, or by Swearing, Ribbaldry, Usury, or any other Uncleanness and Wickedness of Life . . . they be punished by the severity of the Laws, according to their deserts; and such notorious Offenders shall not be admitted to the holy Communion, till they be reformed.'[78] And by 5 Eliz., cap. xxiii, usury is one of the crimes expressly specified in case of which, if duly charged in the writ *de excommunicato capiendo*, the writ shall have force. 'Incontinency, usury, simony, perjury in Ecclesiastical Court, and idolatry', is the list.[79]

12.

Such was the law of Church and State, and it was fully supported by popular sentiment. No doctrine of the Church was ever less disputed, or less obeyed: as usual, the prejudice of the public, which borrows rather than lends, prevailed. Supported by the teaching of the Fathers,[80] on the basis of the Old Testament prohibition of usury and a mistaken interpretation of a passage in the Vulgate New Testament, but really more by the general sentiment of the ancient world, as voiced, for instance, by Plato, Plutarch, Cicero, Seneca, and above all, Aristotle, the Catholic Church, in the decrees of twenty-eight councils and seventeen popes,[81] declared against it with almost uniformly increas-

---

[78] Gibson's *Codex Juris Ecclesiastici Anglicani* (1761), p. 964.
[79] *Ibid.*, p. 1058.
[80] See list in White's *Warfare of Science,* ii, p. 265-6.
[81] Lecky, *Rationalism,* ii, p. 255.

ing severity up to the promulgation of the bull of Benedict
XIV, *Vix pervenit*, in 1745, not abrogated at the present
day.[82]   Lactantius called it robbery; Ambrose, as bad as
murder; the theologians of the seventeenth century, a mortal sin.   Dante thrusts usurers down into the seventh circle
of hell, to sit, each with a pouch hanging from his neck,
under the falling flames, on the baking sand, scratching
like dogs bitten by fleas, or flies, or gad-flies.   The ecclesiastical penalties in the Middle Ages were exclusion from
Communion and the rights of testation and Christian
burial.[83]   In England (and generally on the Continent),
where by repeated enactments usury was forbidden from
the time of Alfred,[84] the property of the usurer escheated
at his death, as if deodand, to the king.   A will he could
no more make than a felon or a traitor.[85]   As with many
another popular prejudice and superstition, that against
the Jews for instance, the Church took it up from the
people and rendered it back again, doubly dear.   It was
the English people in Parliament assembled that enacted
the statute *De Judaismo,* forbidding usury to the Jews.
Likewise, in 1390 the City authorities forbade the putting
of gold or silver into the hands of any person to receive
gain thereby; and in the same year the Commons prayed
the King that the laws of London might have the force of

[82] H. C. Lea, *Yale Review,* 1894, *The Ecclesiastical Treatment of Usury.*
[83] Lea, *op. cit.,* pp. 359 ff.; St. Thomas Aquinas, *Summa,* iv, 496: 'Sunt
infames, admitti non possunt ad sacram communionem." The penalties were
imposed by the Œcumenical Council of Vienne, 1312.
[84] *Laws of Alfred,* Camb. MS., Intro. cap. 35—'ne niede thu hine swa swa
niedling, ne gehiene thu hine mid thy eacan.' Cf. the so-called *Leges
Edwardi Confessoris,* cap. 37, 'ne esset aliquis [*usurarius*] in regno suo.'
[85] Coke, *Third Institutes* (1680), cap. 70, where the Statute of Merton and
the jurists Glanvil and Bracton, etc., are cited; Stephen, *History of the
Criminal Law of England,* iii, 196 f.   Blackstone (1876), ii, 449, observing
that in his day the usurer was not deprived of the right of testation,
expresses a doubt whether he ever was deprived; but the preceding
authorities would seem to settle the matter.   'Manifestus usurarius est intes-
tabilis' (Fleta); 'usurarii omnes res, sive testatus, sive intestatus decesserit,
domini regis sunt' (Glanvil, lib. 7, 16; cited from Coke).   So it was, too,
under the Civil Law, on the Continent.

statutes throughout the realm. Burckhardt repeats a striking story of the people of Piacenza, who, in 1478, suffering from torrential rainfall, hit upon the cause of it in the recent burial of a usurer in consecrated earth, and, as the bishop was slow to act, dug it up, dragged it about the streets, and at last threw it into the Po.[86] According to the medieval principle, not yet outworn, your money-lender is a blood-sucking monster, and the man who has had the spending of his money, his unoffending prey.

It is before a public of like mind that Shylock gingerly avows his practices: 'my well-won thrift' (the right word seems to taste but ill) 'which he calls interest,'—'for use of that which is mine own.' 'Ein Wucherer,' said, in 1542, the greatest of reformers, 'ist ein Ertzdieb und Land-räuber, der billich am Galgen siebenmal höher denn andere Diebe hengen solt.[87] Bacon is often cited as the first Englishman to take the modern point of view on the subject; but there is much misapprehension current as to what he has said. In the essay on Seditions he expresses the opinion that 'money is not good unless spread, and that this is brought about chiefly by suppressing, or at least keeping a strait hand upon the devouring trades of usury, engrossing,' etc.[88] In the *History of Henry VII* he approves the laws made by Parliament against usury, which, strict Aristotelian for once, he declares to be 'the bastard use of money.'[89] And in his Essay on Riches he avers that though usury is 'the certainest means of gain it is one of the worst: as that whereby a man doth eat his bread *in sudore vultus alieni.*' Nowhere in the Essay on Usury does he sanction it, and he takes care that he should not be so understood. He looks upon it as 'concessum propter duritiem cordis', and as 'inevitable,' as 'idle to oppose.' Like Calvin, who is reckoned the first to hold that usury

---

[86] *Cultur der Renaissance* (Leipzig, 1878), ii. p. 291.
[87] Luther, *op. cit.*, p. 249.
[88] *Works* (Boston, 1860), xii, p. 128.
[89] *Works*, xi, p. 134.

was not forbidden by Scripture (yet thought an usurer not tolerable in a well established Commonwealth, but utterly to be rejected out of the company of men),[90] he has no conception of the modern theory of interest as a just share, due to the lender of the money, in the profits of the borrower. Chief-Justice Coke,[91] Doctor Roger Fenton, and Bishop Joseph Hall attained not even to this measure of enlightenment. Not before the day of Saumaise and Filmer, about the year 1640, was the modern doctrine of interest approached; and both by moralists and also by public opinion these were followed only from afar.

13.

Tenets and doctrines, again, matter little, except as the reflection of popular opinion, but in the theatre opinion on such a subject is still less advanced. The world is a borrower; and 'I question,' to repeat the words of Bentham, 'whether among all the instances in which a borrower and a lender of money may have been brought together upon the stage, from the days of Thespis to the present, there ever was one in which the former was not recommended to favour in some shape or other, either to admiration, or to love, or to pity, or to all three; and the other, the man of thrift, consigned to infamy.'[92] The Elizabethan stage is of course no exception; Professor Creizenach remarks with justice upon the prejudice of Elizabethan dramatists in general against the prudent citizens and in favour of the aristocrats, who idle away their time, fritter away their

[90] John Blaxton, *English Usurer* (1634), title-page, a book which reflects the ecclesiastical abhorrence of usury even after Shakespeare's death. Chapter 3 registers the condemnation of it by six bishops, from Sands to Babington; chapter 4, that of thirteen divines, from Willet to Fenton. Thomas Nelson (*Discourse Uppon Usurye, 1572*) ranks the sin as 'next to Idolatrie and the renouncing of god and hys magistrates upon earth' (Sig. C iii).

[91] *Third Part of the Institutes,* cap. V.

[92] *Defense of Usury* (1787), p. 107. Cf. chapter ii above, p. 51, where the passage also appears.

money, and fall into debt. And Shakespeare, however
prudent in private life, is no exception as a dramatist.[93]
(Even today the sympathy is not with Shylock at the theatre, save as he is misrepresented by cuts and sympathetic
acting.) I cannot, for that matter, remember in the Elizabethan drama or the whole drama of the seventeenth and
eighteenth centuries, a single money-lender treated favour-
ably. The time for sympathy or the study of social causes,
of George Eliot's Silas Marner and Balzac's Goriot and
Grandet, had not yet come. Even these characters are in
novels: the stage, which must find favour with five hundred
spectators at once, has not much changed. And in their
prose writings many of the Elizabethan dramatists speak
of usury bitterly in their own person, Lodge, Nash, Greene,
and Dekker, among them.

Even in a court of justice at the present time the same
sentiment prevails when a professional money-lender
appears; and juries will always find against him, according
to Sir James Fitzjames Stephen, if they have any sort of
excuse for doing so. 'I have known cases,' he says, 'where
in defiance of strong evidence, and in spite of adverse sum-
mings-up, persons have been acquitted of perjury, conspiracy, and the obtaining of money on false pretences,
because the prosecutor was a money-lender.'[94] Shylock
was both money-lender and Jew. In him are embodied two
of the deepest and most widely prevalent social antipathies
of two thousand years, prevalent still, but in Shakespeare's

[93] Cf. Creizenach iv, 161-4; and Mr Frank Harris (who, like Mr Woodberry, anticipated me in some of the essentials of my conception of Shylock,
without my knowledge), *Shakespeare* pp. 191-4. Professor C. M. Lewis
(*Hamlet*, pp. 131-2) seems to me quite mistaken in his interpretation of
Timon of Athens, III, 5. He finds the author's sympathy to be on the side
of the cowardly, usury-taking senators, not on that of Alcibiades, the gallant
soldier, pleading for his friend who had committed homicide in vengeance.
The author (Shakespeare or another) is clearly on the side of the men of
valour, as the audience would have been, not on that of those whom the
senators call 'truly valiant.' Dekker at times takes the point of view of the
citizen virtues, but not that of money-making pacifism.

[94] *History of the Criminal Law of England,* iii. p. 195.

day sanctioned by the teachings of religion besides. All that
was religious in them Shakespeare probably shared like any
other easy-going churchman; but all that was popular and
of the people was part and parcel of his breath and blood.⁹⁵

14.

It is impossible to undertake a minute and particular
refutation. To show that Shakespeare is entering a plea
Shylock has on the one hand been conceived as a good man,
much abused; and on the other hand as a bad man made bad.
The misconception in the first case is so gross—as Professor
Schelling has said, so preposterous—that we will not linger
upon it. It is the result of reading Shakespeare—and very
inattentively too—as if he wrote but yesterday. Shakespeare, as we have seen, takes pains with first impressions
and general effects, and is often careless of detail; if the
detail is important it is repeated or enlarged upon. Modern
authors,—Browning, Ibsen, and Mæterlinck, in the drama,
Dostoevsky in the novel,—frame characters and plots that
are studies and problems, in which detail is everything. We
are likely at first to sympathize with Helmer instead of
Nora, in the *Doll's House,* and with Guido instead of Prinz-
ivalle or the heroine, in *Monna Vanna.*⁹⁶ If we lose a word
or a look, we may lose the meaning of the whole. Turning

⁹⁵ I am at a loss to say why Professor Creizenach, who (*Geschichte* v, 21)
avows himself of my opinion concerning Shylock, should in the matter of
interest-taking in Elizabethan times follow Honigmann and Brandes, and
declare that the prejudice had disappeared. The fact is, I have here presented only a small part of the evidence. The important thing, however, is
the prejudice apparent in the play; and that Creizenach recognizes. That
Shakespeare himself should have taken interest would not matter here; though
for Creizenach's hint that he took it I know of no warrant in fact. In his
suit against John Addenbrooke, March 15, 1609, he was awarded the payment of the principal of the debt and *damages,* which was according to
the medieval practice. That is, no interest but *damnum emergens,* often
of huge dimensions, in case the debtor kept not his day.

⁹⁶ See below, chapter on Falstaff, section 2. The principle of emphasis,
taken up in section 16 of the present chapter is by the modern dramatist not
violated, though that of first impressions is (cf. above section 2, p. 264).
Compare also chap. vii, below, section 14, page 389 and note 33.

straight from these to Shakespeare, we are likely to lose the meaning of the whole in our eagerness to catch every fleeting word or look. Clues to the situation have been found in matters such as the bits of satire in which Shylock, like Barabas, lets fling at the ways of Christians, which one might as wisely take for one's leading-strings as the gibes of Mephistopheles in *Faust;*[97] or such as the Christians' willingness to feast with the Jew, Launcelot's scruples against running away from him, or the Jew's opinion of Launcelot as a lazy glutton. It is by this process of making the big little and the little big, as in the reflection of a convex mirror,—this process of reading into Shakespeare a lot of considerations of which he knew nothing, and reading out of him all his minor improbabilities and inconsistencies,[98] that Dr Honigmann[99] and Professor Jastrow[100] arrive at the conception of Shylock as advocate and avenger—injured by a daughter ill brought up (they say) by this Launcelot, actuated by a sense of justice, swearing his oath in a paroxysm of moral self-coercion like another William Tell, hating Antonio, not because he is a Christian, but because by lending money gratis he deprives Hebrews of the means of livelihood, and inveigling him into signing the bond that he may humble him and then—by an act of generosity heap coals of fire on his head! One wonders whether the language of Shakespeare is any longer capable of conveying thought or is become indeed a cryptogram. The Christians feast the Jew not from respect for him, but to give Lorenzo

[97] Shakespeare's intention is nowhere so evident as in Shylock's outcry:
O Father Abraham, what these Christians are
Whose own hard dealings teaches them suspect
The thoughts of others!
The satire is not bad; but the critics forget (what Shakespeare had seen to it that the audience should not forget) that this is unctuous piety, 'to hide a villain's mind.' See below, p. 323. It is such satire as that proceeding from the atrocious Barabas and Zariph and the devils in the mysteries.

[98] See quantities of these in the appendix to Professor Bradley's *Shakespearean Tragedy*.

[99] *Shakespeare-Jahrbuch*, xvii, p. 200 ff.

[100] *Penn Monthly* (1880), p. 725 f. (Schelling).

a chance to run away with Jessica; just as Lorenzo runs
away with Jessica and the ducats, not, as François Victor
Hugo thinks, to satisfy his own or the dramatist's enlightened convictions on the subject of intermarriage between
Jew and Gentile, but, so far as the purposes of the play are
concerned, to give point to Shylock's revenge. Both are
matters of story, of improbabilities, not in modern fashion,
smoothed away; or very likely, if Gosson's play were known,
to some extent a matter of sources. And as for Launcelot's
scruples, they are a joke, like his laziness and gluttony; or
like Shylock's sneer at 'these Christian husbands', Bassanio
and Gratiano, who, unconscious of the presence of their
newly wedded wives, vow, in the fervour of friendship, that
to save their friend they would sacrifice their wives and all.
'Censure of profane swaggering about the purest sentiments,' observes Professor Jastrow, as if Shylock were a
parson, or else the dramatist were.

Those who will have it that Shylock, though bad, was
made so, do violence to Shakespeare in two different ways.
In the first place, they have recourse to an all-pervading
irony. Antonio, gentlest and humblest of Shakespeare's
heroes, kicking and spitting at Jews and thrusting salvation
down their throats,—such, they say, is the spectacle of race-
hatred pointed at by the poet.[101] And those others who will
have it that Shylock is a noble spirit brought to shame,
carry the irony still further, into the characterization of
Antonio and his friends. He, not Shylock, is the caricature:[102] his virtues are but affectations and shams; his
friends are parasites, spendthrifts, and fribbles! They make
no effort to raise the three thousand ducats to save him,
they do not even provide him with a surgeon against his

---

[101] A. Brown; Sir Theodore Martin; J. W. Hales, *Eng. Hist. Rev.* ix,
p. 657; Frederick Hawkins, *Theatre* (1879), p. 194 (quoted by Furness):—
'In availing himself of the greatest popular madness of the time, he sought
to appease it.' I sympathize with Mr W. H. Hudson's impatience with the
theory—'perilously near to talking downright nonsense.'

[102] Jastrow, *op. cit.*, 737.

need.[103]   That is, nothing is what it seems; a comedy ending in moonlight blandishments and badinage is a tragedy, and the play written for the customers of the Globe flies over their honest heads to the peaks of nineteenth-century criticism.   Irony is surely unthinkable unless the author intends it, and here not the slightest trace of such an intention appears.   Moreover, a play of Shakespeare's is self-contained; the irony is within it, so to speak, not underneath it.   There is irony in the appearance of Banquo at the moment when Macbeth presumes hypocritically to wish for his presence at the feast; or, more obviously still, in the fulfilment of the Witches' riddling oracles; but there is no irony, as we have seen,[104] such as Mr Yeats discovers in the success of Henry V and the failure of Richard II.   There is irony in the situation of a king so powerful reduced to a state so pitiful, before he has 'shook off the regal thoughts wherewith he reigned'; but Shakespeare does not dream that to fail and be a Richard is better than to succeed and be a Henry—or an Antonio.   He knows not the way of thinking which lightly sets the judgment of the world aside, nor the ways of modern artistic expression, which almost withholds the purport of the higher judgment from the world.   No abysmal irony undermines his solid sense and straightforward meaning.   Shylock is indeed condemned; Sir Henry Irving took no counsel of the poet when he made his exit from the ducal palace in pathetic triumph.

Nor is Jessica treated with malice, in mockery or irony,[105] as, having forsaken him and robbed him and never since given him a regretful or pitying thought, she now revels in jest and sentiment, in moonlight and melody, at Belmont.

---

[103] These are only cases of neglect, which in Shakespeare abound. But as I have said elsewhere, only the positive counts, or else the negative made as prominent as the positive. On the stage—particularly the popular and Shakespearean stage—it is what a man does, not what he leaves undone, that makes the character; on the stage there are, so to speak, no sins of omission.

[104] See above, chapter iv, section 14.

[105] 'Malizia, quasi dello scherno,'—Croce, *Ariosto,* etc., p. 115.

What right has Signor Croce to call her ecstasy sensual?
Since her father had made home a hell to her and Launcelot,
and in robbing him she has acted with the approval of
everybody, as did the son who robbed Harpagon, has she
not a right, in the world where she now lives, to be really
happy? Signor Croce may be horrified at Jessica as was
Rousseau at the unfilial Cléante; but just as sympathy at the
theatre traditionally is for the debtor and against the
money-lender, so it is for the amorous son or eloping daughter and against the hard-hearted, stingy father. Thus it
had been on the stage since the days of Plautus; cheating
the old man was both sport for the slave and relief for the
son's necessities. Either consideration gave pleasure in the
comic theatre. It is not ideal justice—that is not the
business of comedy; but as Monsieur Donnay says of Harpagon's gold, 'nous sommes enchantés que cet or, mal acquis,
rentre dans la circulation. De tous les vices qui peuvent
s'emparer d'un homme, l'avarice est certainement le plus
détestable, et qui excite le moins notre pitié.'

And as for the Jew—' 'tis charity to undo a Jew,' both
thought and said the age. Indeed, is not Jessica what
might have been taken for a true daughter of her tribe, like
Rachel, who 'stole the images that were her father's' before
she fled; and like the daughters of Israel, who before they
went up out of the land of Egypt, 'borrowed' of their neighbours jewels of silver and jewels of gold? 'And they spoiled
the Egyptians,' adds naïvely and complacently the ancient
chronicler; and, having turned Christian, why should not
Jessica spoil the Jew? the Christians will be likely to ask.
But here, as in Antonio's notion of conversion, or the
Duke's notion of clemency to Jews, is the irony of history,
not of art. Shakespeare's thought is as simple and sincere
as is the old hagiographer's about the balancing of Jews'
ledgers by royal edict—*pacem operatur justicia*.

In the second place, they do violence to Shakespeare, as
Mr Hudson observes, in representing Shylock as the product

of his environment. The thoughts of men had hardly begun to run in such channels; the ancient rigours of retribution held fast; men still believed in heaven and hell, in villains and heroes. Though in Shakespeare there is little of George Eliot's moral austerity, as brought to bear on Tito Melema, for instance, Mr Yeats errs, I think, in the opinion that his plays are, like all great literature, 'written in the spirit of the Forgiveness of Sin.' Macbeth is not forgiven, nor is Othello. Richard III and Iago were damned even in the making. Though the shortcomings of Falstaff, Bardolph, Pistol, and Nym serve a while as food for mirth, Shakespeare is in full accord with Henry V as he casts his fellows out of his company and out of his mind, to meet their end, maybe, in the brothel or on the gallows. And he is in full accord with Portia and the Duke in the judgment scene. Except in comedy, he has not the spirit of forgiveness which, like Uncle Toby's towards the Devil, comes of mere kindness of heart; and neither in comedy nor in tragedy has he the forgiveness of our psychological and social drama and novel, where both villains and heroes are no more, which comes of fulness of knowledge. Thus he deals with poverty, the hard-hearted, greasy, foul-smelling, ignorant and ungrateful multitude, for which he so often utters his aversion; and thus he deals with the kindred subject of heredity. If a scoundrel is a bastard, or is mean of birth, the fact is not viewed as an extenuating circumstance, but is turned to a reproach. It may in a sense explain his depravity, but never explain it away. It sets the seal upon it. It confirms the prejudice that there is a difference between noble blood and that of low degree. So, though our hearts are softened by Shylock's recital of the indignities he has suffered, the hearts of the Elizabethans, by a simpler way of thinking, are hardened. It confirms the prejudice that there is a difference betwixt Christian and Jew. The Fathers, Protestant theologians like Luther, seventeenth-century lawyers like Coke and Prynne, review the

pitiful story of the Jews in Europe grimly, with at best a
momentary and furtive pathos.[106] It proves their notion of
the curse.   What else, in an age when it was the universal
belief that Jew and Gentile alike took upon their heads the
curse of Adam's sin on issuing from the mother's womb?
Even to-day a man who is abused in the street is supposed,
by bystanders, to deserve it: the world barks at rags and
poverty like the dogs: and everyone knows that there are
certain scars (as of branding) and certain diseases (though
people without them may be equally guilty) which a canny
man does not complain of or betray.   And how much more
in the days of literary and theological bludgeoning; when the
reformers were to the common enemy, and to one another,
dogs, hogs, and asses; when Shakespeare himself let one of
his noblest characters cast it up to another that he possessed
but one trunk of clothes; when Milton was reviled, in
scholarly Latin, for his blindness and (in defiance of fact)
for his guttering eyelids; and when Dryden never heard the
last of the beating he got at the instigation of a fellow poet
in a London street.   For everything there is some one to
blame, is the point of view, and who so much as he who
has the worst of it?

> And every loss the men of Jebus bore,
> They still were thought God's enemies the more!

Such is the logic of Luther as he puts to the Jews the
crushing question (naïvely exhorting Christians, if they must
speak to Jews at all, to do likewise, and 'not to quarrel with
them') : 'Hear'st thou, Jew, dost thou know that Jerusalem,
your temple, and your priesthood have been destroyed now
over fourteen hundred and sixty years?'[107]   Even at the
end of the seventeenth century Robert South, as he considers

[106] In his *Short Demurrer* Prynne tells at length the story of their sufferings, seldom with an epithet of commiseration, frequently in terms of
reproach. Coke, in his comment on the Statute *De Judaismo,* tells the tale
of the outrage committed in 1290 at the mouth of the Thames, not without
tokens of satisfaction at the 'divine ultion.'
[107] *Op. cit.,* p. 208.

the universal detestation in which, through the ages, Jews have been held, must conclude that there is 'some peculiar vileness essentially fixed in the genius of this people.'[108] That no one is to blame does not occur to him, or that the cause of the detestation lies in race-hatred, the incompatibility of temperament and customs. 'What's his reason?' cries Shylock. It is the reason which Antonio—that is Shakespeare—is not analytical enough to recognize or cynical enough to avow. Steadily the Jewishness of Shylock is kept before us; like Barabas, he loses his name in his nationality —'the Jew,' 'the dog Jew,' 'the villain Jew,' 'his Jewish heart';—and it is not merely according to the measure of his villainy that at the end and throughout the play he suffers. With Robert South Shakespeare himself might have said that the reason was his 'essential Jewish *vileness*'; but we, who, in the light of modern psychology and the history of society, are aware that no man and no age can render adequately the reason why they themselves do anything, recognize that the famous reason given by Shylock himself, in the heat of his *ex parte* pleading with which Shakespeare so little sympathizes, curiously enough hits the mark.[109]

15.

With this conventionality in mind we may approach the final question, whether villain and butt as Shylock is, he may not also be, as Professor Schelling thinks, a pathetic creation. As we have seen, he speaks of Shylock as 'semi-humorous,' a character in whom there is a grotesqueness bordering on laughter and a pathos bordering on tears. The union of butt and villain is common in Shakespeare's day, as old indeed as the stupid devils of the miracle-plays; and the union of villain and droll goes back to the cleverer devils,

---

[108] *Sermons* (London, 1865), ii, p. 228.

[109] Yet it is no case of poetic divination, or of writing for the comprehension of a later age. 'I am a negro!' a victim of race-hatred will say to-day, with as little comprehension of the psychology of race-hatred or of Professor Sumner's theory of the *mores*.

and the devils of Dante and medieval painting, and underlies
the characterization of most of the villains—Aaron and
Iago, for instance—in Shakespearean and Elizabethan
drama. But villain, butt, and pathetic figure, all in one, is
a thing difficult to conceive. Drollery (or ludicrousness)
and pathos coalesce, now as then, in Ibsen's Ulric Brendel
as in Shakespeare's Mercutio and his clowns; but derision
mingling with pathos would be like water poured into the
fire.[110] Before, then, we take up this question whether Shylock is also pathetic, we must consider some fundamental
principles, too much ignored: 1. That the interpretation of
literature—and of drama even more—is, as we have seen,
mainly a study in emphasis. 2. That much comedy skirts
the confines of tragedy, and what keeps it comedy is
emphasis, or a conventional 'isolation', as Monsieur Bergson
has called it. 3. That comedy follows without question
the manners and prejudices of the time. 4. That in the
Shylock scenes there is so large an element of formal
external comic technique that it is impossible to consider
Shylock only 'semi-humorous,' in part pathetic.

16.

The first principle, that the interpretation of literature is
mainly a study in emphasis, should be self-evident, and be
disputable only in its applications. By manipulation and
arrangement, unification and subordination, repetition or
contrast, not by explicit and prosaic comment or statement,
the purpose and fairly the whole purport of a piece of literature are revealed. What is important and what is unimportant, what is merely of the story and what is central
thought and animating mood or emotion,—these are the
main questions we should ask in criticism, and they are
answered by a study of emphasis almost alone. It is the
matter of light and shade, of balance and perspective, of

[110] See below, pp. 318-19; and 307, 309, 312-14, 315-16, for various
examples.

focussing, as in a picture. Some years ago the isochromatic photographic process was introduced as a great improvement, which made it possible to reproduce paintings exactly, what is lighter in the picture being now lighter in the photograph, and what is darker in the picture being darker in the photograph. Now some, recognizing that Shylock was by Shakespeare meant to be a comic villain, say that he was meant to be pathetic too; and others, that he was meant to be a 'supremely pathetic figure' for us at least to-day, the dramatist having knowingly or unknowingly put in little touches that warrant this different, later conception of ours. That is, the emphasis, chief means of expression at the command of the artist, is considered adjustable; what was dark turns light; what was less important becomes more important; the comedy becomes a tragedy; and Shylock forcibly, though legitimately, becomes what Mr Schelling indeed says he is and always was, the hero instead of the comic villain. How irrelevant then become both author and work! Thus the title of the quarto, 'The Comical Historie of the Merchant of Venice, with the extreme crueltie of Shylocke the Jewe towards the sayd Merchant in cutting a just pound of his flesh, and the obtayning of Portia by the choyse of three chests' becomes, in the mocking words of Mr Poel: 'The tragicall Historie of the Jewe of Venice, with the extreme injustice of Portia towards the sayd Jewe in denying him the right to cut a just pound of the Merchant's flesh, together with the obtayning of the rich heiress by the prodigal Bassanio.' With the same text, with the same characters, we have a different play, the important becoming unimportant, the unimportant, important, comedy a tragedy, the wrong a right, and the right a wrong.

As for the second principle—comedy skirts tragedy—it is surely obvious. Behind many a comedy there is, more or less apparent, a tragedy, just as something tragic or pathetic is behind almost every joke. And that somewhat (though not altogether) explains why it is that the transformation of comedy into tragedy is in criticism so frequent. For the *Merchant of Venice* is not the only comedy, and Shakespeare not the only comic poet—*L'Avare, Le Misanthrope,* and *Le Tartuffe* were changed in much the same way, at almost the same time. '*L'Avare*', says Goethe, 'where vice destroys all natural piety between father and son, is especially great and in a high sense 'tragic.'[111] Romantic seriousness and sympathy, at the end of the eighteenth century and the beginning of the nineteenth, made them so; and only in recent years have criticism and the actor's art forsaken their strange imaginations and returned to Molière. In England and America we are slower in recovering from our Romantic excesses and aberrations; and the sympathetic and altruistic Mr Masefield sadly and wonderingly shakes his head as he owns that 'some people find humour in the Simpcox and Cade scenes' in *Henry VI,* where he finds only 'sadness and horror of heart'; and Professor Matthews avers that *All's Well, Measure for Measure,* and *Troilus and Cressida,* certainly meant for comedies, 'are far from being comic in their intent or in their effect' and 'move us to sadness rather than to mirth.' Sir Walter Raleigh, with his learning and imagination, does not think so;[112] the humble audience to-day, with none of the one and little of the other, but in spirit not far removed from the Elizabethan, does not either. So with the comic novel as well; and it was Hugo, the great romanticist (he who in his Romantic exaltation transformed the most purely comic of dramatists since Aristophanes—Molière—into the 'moqueur pensif comme un apôtre') who, deploring in Cervantes the fact that he mocked at the ideal, yet in his eye found a tear. But Sainte-Beuve, seeing more clearly, insists that Don Quixote is a masterpiece of clarity, that Cervantes himself, in the

---

[111] May 12, 1825, Eckermann. Goethe then complains of the weakening of this effect in the German version, where the son becomes only a relative. Evidently at this time it was necessary, in order that the comedy might remain such on the stage.

[112] *Shakespeare* (London, 1909), p. 219.

midst of the direst misfortune, was a miracle of gaiety and good-humour, and that to remain true to him and his words we must content ourselves to dry the tear, or better still, keeping nothing back, confess freely that 'Cette larme lui sied mieux, selon nous, et c'est nous qui la lui mettons.'[113] In this opinion, he adds, he has the suffrage of Hallam, Ticknor, and Mérimée, before him.

The point is, that while, on the one hand, comedy skirts the confines of tragedy, on the other hand, it respects the boundary line and does not go philandering over the border. Behind a comedy is a tragedy, but that is not the comedy; behind a joke there is something tragic, but that is not the joke. Such tragedy is of our making, or our discovering, not the dramatist's. Comedy becomes tragedy when we stop and consider; but, kept under the comic spell, we do not stop—we judge, react, are swept and whirled away, not in grief but in laughter, not by our sympathetic passions but by our social prejudices or antipathies. 'A line higher,' as Sainte-Beuve says, 'and the comic effect ceases, and we then have a character purely generous, almost heroic and tragic,' [114] —or pathetic, one may add. This is true of the chief characters of Molière, unquestionably comic in effect when rightly played, whether in our time or in their own; but when read and thought about to-day, easily changed. Then George Dandin, Arnolphe, the Sganarelle of the *École des maris,* all of them cuckolds or deceived lovers, become pathetic; Alceste, the Misanthrope, becomes heroic; Tartuffe, the hypocrite, on the other hand, and Harpagon, the miser, become villainous. But once this change comes about, we have quite passed from under the spell of the author, out of the little magic circle of his comic art, into the vast world of fact and reality, of cause and effect.

There the joke dies within us, and laughter fails. It rings out only within doors, not when we look beyond or afar.

[113] *Nouveaux lundis* (1872), viii, pp. 39-40.
[114] *Portraits littéraires,* ii, 22. Cf. the note following, Sarcey.

The comic dramatist, as Monsieur Bergson says—the jester
—*isolates* his material, insulates it, indeed.   The comic
current runs through the scene, charges its every fibre and
filament, close to earth but never suffered to touch it and
escape.   From Eden down, no doubt, a man whose wife
deceives him has, to those in the comic mood, been an object
of derision,—so he is in Aristophanes as in the medieval
farces; and under the sway and tyranny of that sentiment
George Dandin, Arnolphe, and Sganarelle are made sport
of, and all their griefs and torments, their confidence sur-
mounting their suspicions, their devotion drowning their
resentment, and their cries of love thwarted and affection
hopelessly thrown away, are at no point permitted to touch
us too nearly but serve only to heighten the comic effect.
They are oil (with a little water) to that lambent flame.
Many of these speeches taken by themselves may touch us
as do some of Shylock's,—that is, when disconnected like
his, short-circuited, the electric current stopped.   They are
honest, kindly, affectionate souls—'les cocus sont les meil-
leurs gens du monde', says Mlle. de Molière. in the
Impromptu de Versailles—but what of it?   As Sarcey [115]
says, what of it if Arnolphe is honest, generous, and tender?
Or what of it if Monsieur de Pourceaugnac, of Limoges, has
done nothing at all to merit the tricks played upon him
during his brief visit to Paris?   Such sympathy comes
uncalled for, spoils the sport, falls like a wet blanket on the
joke, blights and kills the comedy.   Both Michelet and
Claretie took Pourceaugnac's part; but as Monsieur Donnay
has said, they might as well have been moved to compassion
for old father Guignol, a prey to the practical jokes of that
rogue of a Guignolet.   Their misplaced sentiment makes

---

[115] *Quarante .ans,* ii, 80-81, Sarcey rightly shows that Arnolphe's virtue
and age have nothing to do with the case.   To the same effect his whole
'Essai d'une Esthétique de théâtre' (i. 119 ff.), especially section v, p. 152 f.:
'Molière à cet égard est un modèle: il n'y a guère de pièces (sauf les
farces) où il n'ait eu l'occasion de glisser dans le pathétique: il s'est
toujours discrètement arrêté sur le bord.'

them strangers to mirth. And Arnolphe in trying to engross
and monopolize the young girl's affections, and to lock up
not merely her person but her mind and heart, was prodigiously absurd. Rustics, cuckolds, though not rarities, then
were, and in some circles still are, openly recognized as
social eccentricities; and in comedy, which is the image, not
of life but of society, society records its instant verdict and
claps on it the penalty of laughter. George Dandin and his
fellows are cuckolds; Alceste, a bear; Monsieur de Pourceaugnac, a provincial come to town; Harpagon, a harsh
father and miser; Shylock a harsh father, miser, usurer,
and Jew:—nothing is considered further or indeed with
equanimity may be. Save Harpagon, indeed, all of Molière's personages mentioned are more or less in the right, as
Shylock, save in his character of Jew, is not in the right at
all; but that is neither here nor there; where ideal justice is
to be done comedy fades away, laughter collapses. Justice
in comedy is swift, simple, and matter-of-fact as that of
Judge Lynch, though bloodless.

On the third principle we have been touching already—
comedy bows to the customs and prejudices of the time.
This Rousseau pointed out long ago,[116] and Monsieur
Bergson has made it still clearer. The comic character is
'insocial,' out of harmony with his social environment; and
the spectator is kept 'insensible,' unsympathetic,—there, as
Monsieur Bergson says, are two pre-requisites. A critic
of late has complained of that hard-hearted king and his
hard-hearted court who laughed gaily at unhappy George
Dandin; but comparative hardness of heart for the time
being—that is, for three solid hours—is indispensable to
comedy, at least the comedy of manners; and without it—
in defiance of the sympathy which is both the pet emotion
and the pet virtue of our age—we cannot enter into the
comic spirit. In such comedy, as in most of Molière's and
much of Shakespeare's, social prejudice, the social, or (per-

---

[116] *Œuvres* (1822), ii, 24, Lèttre à D'Alembert.

haps more accurately) the society, sense of what is comic
prevails. Ideal equity plays no part, for though the hero did
marry above his rank—'tu l'as voulu, George Dandin,'—he
did not deserve to be beaten and bamboozled while his clever
but wicked wife and her lover went free. Here and in
other comedies it is the popular spirit of ridicule for one
who is jilted or is a cuckold—an old man who has sought
the love of a girl, a bourgeois who has won the hand of a
lady, or a jealous and suspicious soul given something to be
jealous for. In seventeenth-century France, Italy, or England, their tears touched no one. 'His tears will make you
laugh,' says Cecchi of the old man in love with a girl in the
prologue to the *Incantesimi* (1550):—'pensomi che vi darà
benissimo materia da ridere, benchè a lui sarà da piagnere.'
And such are the tears of Dandin, Arnolphe, and Sganarelle
—social offenders all. In some of the comedies it is the
social prejudice merely;—against the climber like Monsieur
Jourdain; the honest provincial come to Paris on a visit,
like Monsieur de Pourceaugnac; or the gentleman who, like
Alceste, will not do as others do—flatter as on occasion a
gentleman should.

Now, in London there was no such refined society, or
highly unified, organized, and sensitive social consciousness,
as in Paris at the time of Molière, or in Athens at the time
of Aristophanes; and Shakespeare, by temperament, was
not a satirist; but nevertheless the comic spirit and method
of all three dramatists had something in common, and the
less refined the social consciousness, the more vindictive it
is if aroused. Shakespeare's comedies are of course romantic, sentimental, and fanciful; but this contrast of low life
with high life is one of his sources of comic effect as well;
and honest but humble folk in *A Midsummer Night's
Dream, Much Ado, As You Like It,* and *The Winter's Tale*
are made almost unbelievably stupid and ridiculous, while
those who in vanity aspire to rise above their appointed
place and station, like Justice Shallow and Malvolio, are

cheated or made the victims of a ruthless practical joke.
Sir Toby, Maria, and the Clown sport with Malvolio while
he howls in torment; and Autolycus, to the delight of himself and the audience, fleeces simple, trusting souls who have
no fault save their rusticity. Malvolio, in a measure
deserves it; but these last, who do not, are no more expected
to evoke our sympathy than are the honest souls whom
Don Juan takes in, or Maître Jacques, in *L'Avare,* devoted
to his master and his horses, when he stands in the way of
young Valère, a gentleman and a lover. By our standards
Shakespeare, in comic vein, is, for all his sweetness and gentleness, hard-hearted like Molière (or a 'malin,' as the latter is called by Lemaître), but also like Chapman, Jonson,
Dekker, Marston, Fletcher, Fielding and Smollett, Rabelais, Ariosto, Cecchi, and Aretino, and of course their audiences or reading public as well. How harsh and personal
the jokes and pranks were that cultivated people then not
only read but in real life permitted themselves or applauded,
appears clearly from courtesy books like *Il Cortegiano.*[117]
But the most remarkable prejudice brought to bear for a
comic effect in Shakespeare, is (as, from what has been said,
might have been expected) not one which arises out of the
beau monde at all but out of the people, society in the largest
sense. It is the prejudice against Jew, miser, usurer. In
each of these rôles singly Shylock could not but be a purely
repellant or comic figure on the stage because he was an
object of derision in the street, indeed by tradition was on
the stage as a comic figure already established; and in these

---

[117] See Castiglione's *Book of the Courtier* (Tudor Translations), 1900,
pp. 159 ff., 185 and (pp. 184-5) the joke specially delighted in and approved
of, the reply of Alonso, unfit for any drawing-room, or even a tap-room,
to-day. And with what gusto the practical jokes are anticipated and carried
through! 'I will not give my part of this sport,' says Fabian in *Twelfth
Night,* for a pension of thousands to be paid from the Sophy.' There are
many parallels in Elizabethan drama; and Ambrogio in Aretino's *Marescalco* declares that rather than miss the wedding, outrageously forced upon
the misogynist, he would forego preaching, mass, and vespers (evidently a
deprivation) for a year.

rôles combined and united, not in a tragedy, but in a comedy, how could he possibly be thought pathetic at all? To the comic effect of Jonson's *Silent Woman,* not only in Shakespeare's day but long after, there is abundant and authoritative testimony—to the comic effect of the 'heartless ragging of harmless old Morose,' whose only shortcomings were a 'tight purse and extreme tranquillity.' These may have offended the *beau monde* as smacking of the bourgeois, the Puritan.[118] But to laugh and jeer at Shylock would have been less cruel, more human, in its inhumanity.

17.

However that be, lest our own laughter should fail—we here approach the last principle—the situation has been hedged about with the most explicitly comic technique and apparatus. There is in Shakespeare's comedy comparatively little, as we have seen,[119] which squares with the rationale of it in Monsieur Bergson's book; little of that highly developed, formal comic technique, which somewhat reminds you of the structure of music, abounding in Molière; but an exception is to be found in the scenes where Shylock appears. Here, quite apart from the social and racial prejudices brought so directly to bear upon him, are the comic devices of repetition and inversion, as well as others less easily designated.

18.

By repetition I mean, as in chapter iv, not the repetition of words or phrases at happy junctures (often comically used by Elizabethans like Dekker, as well as by dramatists so different and remote from one another as Plautus, Molière, and Ibsen) but the repetition of a *motif,* as in the daughter-ducats dialogue with Tubal, and in this case it takes the form of alternation:

[118] See a criticism of the revival of *Epicœne, Saturday Review,* November 22, 1924.
[119] See chapter iv.

Tubal. One of them showed me a ring that he had of your daughter for a monkey.

Shylock. Out upon her. Thou torturest me, Tubal. It was my turquoise; I had it of Leah when I was a bachelor. I would not have given it for a wilderness of monkeys.

This, most critics assert, the great historian of the drama almost alone dissenting,[120] is pathos: it is not the ducats behind the turquoise ('a diamond gone, cost me two thousand ducats in Frankfort!') but the thought of Leah that wrings his heart. 'What a fine Hebraism is implied in this expression!' cries Hazlitt. 'He has so deep a veneration for his dead wife,' says Hawkins, with impenetrable gravity, 'that a wilderness of monkeys would not compensate for the loss of the ring she had given him in youth.' [121] More Elizabethan fun running to waste! We may not be used to laughing at a man as he mourns the flight of his daughter, the memory of his wife, or the theft of his ducats; but neither are we used, any more than Salanio or the boys of Venice, to the manner of his mourning.

> I never heard a passion so confus'd,
> So strange, outrageous, and so variable.

Shylock is a puppet, and Tubal pulls the strings. Now he shrieks in grief for his ducats or his daughter, now in glee at Antonio's ruin. In his rage at the trading of a turquoise for a monkey, he blurts out, true to his native instincts, 'not for a wilderness of monkeys!' and the Elizabethan audience, as well as some few readers to-day, have the heart—or the want of it—to think the valuation funny. The rest may find it hard to laugh at this, as in the opinion of Rousseau, Taine, Mantzius, and many another candid spirit, it is nowadays hard to laugh at the plight of George Dandin or Arnolphe, or, to come nearer home, as it is hard to laugh at the torments of Malvolio; but the invitation to

[120] Creizenach (1909), iv, pp. 279-80.
[121] Quoted by Furness, p. 433. Cf. Jastrow, *op. cit.*, p. 733, for a like interpretation.

hilarity is in all these instances plain and clear. The true
Molière has been pretty well restored not only to the stage
but also to his right status in criticism; but in lands where
people see (however more profoundly) less clearly, Shylock's love for Leah moves men to tears, and Mr Sothern
can elicit sympathy for Olivia's stately steward pleading in
a madman's chains to be set free. But Mr Granville Barker,
at the Savoy a few years ago, and Monsieur Copeau, at the
Vieux Colombier, produced the latter play surely as Shakespeare intended it to be, and forebore to spoil and thwart
this purely comic scene.

The mistake of the critics is in some measure that of
viewing the text piecemeal and not as a whole. Wrenched
from the context, there are phrases, even sentences, that
may, indeed, seem pathetic. But Shakespeare, as soon as
Tubal enters, lets Shylock strike up the tune of 'my daughter
—my ducats,' and, adhering to the method of comic alternation throughout the scene, plays the familiar dramatic
trick of taking the audience in for a moment and of then
clapping upon the seemingly pathetic sentiment a cynical,
selfish, or simply incongruous one :—

Two thousand ducats in that; and other precious, precious jewels.
I would my daughter were dead at my foot—and the jewels in her
ear! Would she were hears'd at my foot—and the ducats in her
coffin.

The dashes are my own, replacing commas in the quartos
and folios; they are necessary, according to modern usage,
to carry out what seems the manifest intention of the author.
Such quick afterthoughts and comical anticlimaxes as we
have here are to be found elsewhere in Shakespeare and in
comic dialogue to this day. In *Le Malade imaginaire* Béline,
his designing second wife, is bid by the dying Argan to take
the money out of the cupboard—

Non, non, je ne veux point de tout cela. Ah!—combien dites-
vous qu'il y a dans votre alcôve?

Falstaff, taking account of his slender stock of virtues, recalls that he had paid back money that he borrowed— 'three or four times';[122] Sir Peter Teazle, speaking of Charles, declares to Joseph that never in life had he denied him—'my advice'; Bob Acres, replying to Jack Absolute as he reassures Sir Lucius ('He generally kills a man a week— don't you, Bob?') cries, 'Aye—at home'; and old Eccles, in the presence of the young folk, vows that 'there is nothing like work—for the young.' So Shylock cannot wish that his daughter were dead at his foot (if that really be pathos) without, at the same time, wishing that the jewels were in her ear, the ducats in her coffin;[123] he cannot hear that there is no news of them without bewailing what has been 'spent in the search'; he cannot think of Launcelot's kindness, as he parts with him, without also thinking—'a huge feeder!' —of his appetite; and when he hears of his turquoise exchanged for a monkey, thoughts of Leah, his bachelor-hood, and a wilderness of monkeys come clattering through his brain. Here is pathos side by side with laughter, but not—according to Mr Schelling's thought—the grotesque-ness bordering on laughter, the pathos bordering on tears. The nuance, the harmony is lacking—in true Elizabethan style, there is glaring contrast instead. The pathos is a pretense, a moment's illusion; the laughter alone is real. Nor is it restrained—it is nothing less than a roar; the grotesque-ness passes over the border of laughter—perhaps of tears.

I have used above the figure of the puppet and the string;[124] and surely nowhere else in Shakespeare do we

[122] *Henry IV*, III, iii, 21. Here, and in the clause just preceding: 'went to a bawdy-house not above once in a quarter of an hour,' there are in quartos and Folio no stops whatever; but the Clarendon editors have rightly inserted them.

[123] Professor Jastrow and Dr Honigmann, like Heine (*mirabile dictu!*) before them, see no fun here. Racial sympathy hinders them. 'He would prefer *burying his child and his gold*,' says the former, 'to knowing them to be in the possession of the Christian fools.' If Shylock buried it he would not forget the spot.

[124] See chapter iii. I used it also in the article on Shylock before I had read Bergson; it is, therefore, not owing to a preconceived theory.

get so distinctly as here that effect of the human being
turned mechanical—automaton, or jack-in-the-box—which is
frequent in comedy, as Monsieur Bergson has shown. We
are familiar, as I have said, with such comically mechanical
effects in ordinary life, when, for instance (to employ the
vernacular) we 'take a rise out of' a person. We speak the
provocative word—pull the string or press the spring,—
and, behold, the effect expected! Shakespeare does that
through the comfortable Tubal's alternate method of imparting his news, though he only continues the alternation
set at work when first Shylock learned of his double loss:—
Tubal pulls the strings of a puppet already in motion. The
situation is thus instinct with comedy, pathos could not possibly live in its midst. The same situation indeed was
already established on the stage as comic, as 'pathétique
plaisant,' for the outcries of robbed misers had entertained
'hard-hearted' audiences since the days of Euclio.[125] Marlowe's Barabas had displayed even the same jumble of
emotions, as he gloated over his girl and his gold, and
probably there had been others too.[126] A little later Cyrano
de Bergerac, in the scene of *Le Pédant joué,* noticed above,
presents comically, like Molière and Shakespeare, the pangs
of paternal affection contending with avarice, but attains a
climax not to be found in either. Unlike Géronte, Granger
does not yet know the amount of the ransom demanded to
save his son from hanging; but when he hears that it is a
hundred pistoles, the scale then and there ceases to balance
and kicks the beam. 'Go, Corbineli, tell him to be hanged
and have done with it.' [127] Here is the same grotesque, and

[125] The best example, of course, is Harpagon, in his famous soliloquy,
which, practically a translation of Euclio's, contains the appeal to the
audience—and then the words: 'ils me regardent tous et se mettent à rire.'
Despite that, the part was played tragically in the romantic period, and
down to Coquelin's time. 'A contresens,' with a vengeance.

[126] In the *Faerie Queene,* III, x, 13-15, Malbecco oscillates in the same
comical fashion; so does Jaques in Jonson's *The Case is Altered* (1598),
Act V, i, and iv.

[127] See above, chapter iv, section 11.

(for the hard-hearted) comical, preference of the loss of a child to a worse thing that might befall him, that we find afterwards in *L'Avare,* when Harpagon declares that the fact that Cléante (charged with having stolen his casket of treasure) had saved his daughter's life, is nothing, and tells her 'it were much better to have let you drown than have done what he has done.' 'Would she were hears'd at my foot—and the ducats in her coffin!' Harpagon, we remember, used to be misinterpreted, as Shylock still is; but Coquelin *cadet* changed that, and now again, as when Molière played him—and as when to Robinet he wrote of the playing—'d'un bout à l'autre il fait rire.'

19.

Then there is inversion, the tables turned. 'L'histoire du persécuteur victime de sa persécution, du dupeur dupé, du voleur volé, fait le fond de bien des comédies.' The trial scene is an example. To most critics Shylock has here seemed to be more or less pathetic, despite the fact that, as I take it, Shakespeare has employed almost every possible means to produce a contrary, quite incompatible effect.

Professor Baker holds that Shakespeare evinces a sense of dramatic values in presenting Shylock's disappointment as tragic in his own eyes, amusing in Gratiano's. How is the tragic value presented? By the miser and usurer's prostrate prayer to the Duke to take his life if he would take his wealth, or by the plea that he is not well? The biter bitten, is the gibe cast at him at the end of *Il Pecorone;* [128] and that, exactly, is the spirit of the scene. It is the same spirit and almost the same situation as at the close of Sheridan's *Duenna,* where another Jew, not nearly so culpable as Shylock, having now been fast married to the dragon herself, not, as he thinks, to the maiden that she guards, is jeered

[128] Talchè chiunque v'era presente, di questo faceva grandissima allegrezza, e ciascuno si faceva beffe di questo Giudeo, dicendo, Tale si crede uccellare, ch'è uccellato.' Hazlitt's *Shakespeare's Library,* Pt. i, vol. i, p. 348.

at for it, while one of the characters gives the reason,—that 'there is not a fairer subject for contempt and ridicule than a knave become the dupe of his own art.' Shylock's disappointment is tragic to him, but good care is taken that it shall not be to us. Shakespeare is less intent on values than on the conduct and direction of our sympathies through the scene. This he manages both by the action and the comment. The scene is a rise and a fall, a triumph turned into a defeat, an apparent tragedy into a comedy; and the defeat is made to repeat the stages of the triumph so as to bring home to us the fact—the comic fact—of retribution. When fortune turns, almost all the steps of the ladder whereby Shylock with scales and knife had climbed to clutch the fruit of revenge he must now descend empty-handed and in bitterness; and what had been offered to him and refused by him, he is now, when he demands it again, refused. With the course of the action the comment is in perfect accord and unison, marking and signalizing the stages of Shylock's fall. The outcries against the Jew and his stony heart, of the Duke, Bassanio, and Gratiano—protested against by Antonio as futile—give place to the jeers of Gratiano and the irony of the fair judge. Gratiano is not the only one to crow. 'Thou shalt have justice, more than thou desir'st —Soft! The Jew shall have all justice—Why doth the Jew pause? Take thy forfeiture—Tarry, Jew; the law hath yet another hold on you—Art thou contented, Jew? What dost thou say?' Aimed at Shylock as he pleads and squirms, these words fall from lips which had a moment before extolled the heavenly qualities of mercy! But for more than the meagre mercy which Shylock is shown there is neither time nor place, the crowing fits the latter part of the action as perfectly as the indignant comment had fitted the earlier, and we must equally accept it or divest the scene of meaning and sense. The Jew's very words are echoed by Portia and Gratiano as they jeer, and at every turn that the course of justice takes (welcomed by Shylock, while it was in his favour, with hoarse cries of gloating and triumph) there are now peals and shouts of laughter, such laughter as arises when Tartuffe the hypocrite is caught by Orgon,—'un rire se lève de tous les coins de la salle, un rire de vengeance si vous voulez, un rire amer, un rire violent.' [129] The running fire assails him to the very moment—and beyond it—that Shylock says he is not well, and staggers out, amid Gratiano's jeers touching his baptism, to provoke in the audience the laughter of triumph and vengeance in his own day and bring tears to their eyes in ours. How can we here for a moment sympathize with Shylock unless at the same time we indignantly turn, not only against Gratiano, but against Portia, the Duke, and all Venice as well? But Shakespeare's scene it is—Shakespeare's comedy,—not ours or Hazlitt's. [130]

One reason why the critics have, despite all, even in this scene, found pathos in Shylock, is that they well know that comic effects may keep company with the pathetic, in Shakespeare as in Dostoevsky and Chekhov. They remember Mercutio's last words, Mrs Quickly's report of Falstaff's death, or the Fool's babblings in *King Lear*. Laughter may indeed blend with tears when the character is treated tenderly; but here and in the daughter-ducats scene it is, as I have said, only the laughter of derision. In the judgment scene, moreover, there is—very clearly marked—the spirit of retaliation; it is a harsh and vindictive laughter; and if

---

[129] Sarcey, *Quarante ans,* ii, 132. Sarcey is replying to a critic who declares that at Tartuffe the audience does not laugh: having seen the play a hundred times, he knows better.

[130] Actors when not prejudiced feel a part as no spectator or critic can, and by them nowadays Shylock's comic villainy is recognized. The kindliest of men, Mr Poel, has recently made him comic; Moskovitch, still more recently, threw the emphasis on the fierce usurious Jew. Irving himself in a letter to Miss Terry admitted Shylock's ferocity though he said he could not play it; and that fine spirit, Lady Martin, says that in the trial scene 'my desire to find extenuations for Shylock's race and for himself leaves me, I see his fiendish nature fully revealed, and I long to pour down on his head the justice he has clamoured for and will exact without pity.' Booth's opinion is quoted above, at the beginning of the chapter.

Shakespeare had here intended any minor and momentary
pathetic effects such as critics nowadays discover, he simply
overwhelms them.   Professor Matthews says that Shakespeare meant the spectators to hate Shylock and also to
laugh at him, and yet made him pathetic—supremely pathetic too.[131]   The combination seems to me impossible, at
least in a comedy, and Professor Matthews seems to me to
be talking metaphysics and forgetting the stage which he
knows so well.   If hateful, Shylock would provoke in the
audience the *rire de vengeance,* an echo of Gratiano's jeer;
if pathetic also, he would—and should—provoke no laughter (at least of such kind as is known to me) at all.   In
comedy, at any rate, things must be simple and clear-cut; a
character which is to provoke laughter cannot be kept, like
Buridan's ass, in equilibrium, exciting, at the same time,
both sympathy and hatred.   For then the audience will
keep its equilibrium too.

The crowing is not indispensable to the process of comic
inversion, or the turning of the tables.   Even without it,
Shylock could quite well have been made to swallow the
medicine, drop by drop, and be now refused what he had
earlier been offered.   Portia's words about justice, the forfeiture, and the bond, whereby she reverses the machinery
that had been set in motion, might have been enough.
Gratiano's crowing is, then, a bit of formal comic technique, added to make the effect unmistakable and secure.
What pains comic dramatists take, and yet, in a century,
they may be futile!   Gratiano—and Portia also when she
turns against Shylock—makes the audience in the court
laugh, that in the theatre they may be certain to laugh too.
The twitting and crowing when the tables are turned is to be
found serving this same purpose elsewhere in Shakespeare,
as in *Love's Labour's Lost, Much Ado, Twelfth Night,* and
Henry IV; indeed (where there is no inversion) the merry
report by Salanio and Salarino of Shylock's 'strange' and

[131] *Shakespeare as a Playwright* (1913), p. 149-150.

'variable' lamentations, and of the outcries of all the boys in Venice, is introduced for a similar end. Sarcey, as he discusses *Les Femmes savantes* and *Le Monde où l'on s'ennuie,* observes that in these alike there is one method because there is no other:

> Le public n'y sent le ridicule des mœurs qui sont traduites sur la scène, que par l'étonnement que provoquent ces mœurs chez un personnage en scène. Il s'en amuse en les entendant railler; il rit par contre-coup,—*Quarante ans,* vi, p. 312.

The comic effect in the theatre is the echo and reduplication of that on the stage—somewhat as the shudder of wonder at the supernatural spreads and is caught up by the spectators from Horatio, Brutus, or Macbeth.[132] Laughter, we all know, is contagious—in an instant the electric spark circles the house, explodes the magazine.

There are still other comic devices, such as the anticlimaxes and prompt miserly afterthoughts of Shylock, comical on the face of them, and the whetting of his knife. All together, there is in the Shylock scenes such an array of these as is nowhere else to be found in Shakespeare save in the *Comedy of Errors* or in the *Taming of the Shrew.* As Mr Woodberry says, and Booth had recognized, Shakespeare 'did not hesitate to let the exhibition of these low qualities [avarice, cunning, and revenge] approach the farcical.' In general the comedy in Shakespeare is more a comedy of character than of situation, and the situations, as I have said, are seldom worked out and developed to the full; but here we have repetition and inversion, crowing and anticlimaxes, as in Molière; and in a comic tune wrought out so elaborately and emphatically that one wonders how any pathetic note could possibly find a place in it, save for the moment, and then only to contribute to the prevailing effect.

20.

Some supposedly pathetic passages remain to be consid-

[132] See above, chapter v.

ered. Unlike Sir Sidney Lee (if he still holds to the view),
I cannot find pathos in the remark,

> The patch is kind enough,

which Shylock makes as he looks after Launcelot dancing
out of the door, any more than I can in that about the
turquoise. Our symathies—even our softer ones to-day—
are engrossed and forestalled by Launcelot and Jessica, and
we are not likely to concern ourselves, as Sir Sidney would
have us do, about Launcelot's present deceitfulness and scant
deservings. Any pathetic sentiment, moreover, that the
remark might have evoked would immediately have been
swallowed up—even as is the thought of Launcelot's kind-
liness in the miser's breast—by the words 'but a huge
feeder' which follow; by his remembering that Launcelot
is 'snail-slow in profit' and 'sleeps by day more than the wild-
cat'; and by his eagerness, after all, to forego the lad's
company that he may help waste Bassanio's borrowed purse.
A reader—a philosopher—who lingers over and ponders
the line, might well end by thinking it pathetic, but an audience that watches the swiftly moving scene could not. It
is almost exactly parallel (though more obviously comical)
with the situation of Sganarelle in the *École des maris*, pitying his young rival Valère as, after receiving the ambiguous
message from Isabelle, he goes off, apparently rejected and
heart-broken:

> Il me fait grande pitié,
> Ce pauvre malheureux trop rempli d'amitié.

In both cases the momentarily kindly one has already been
recognized as the chief comic figure; in both cases he is at
that moment tricked and deceived; in both cases he is
wasting his pity, not only on the young man but on the
audience. The whole context and situation, therefore, makes
it impossible that the audience should because of his pity
or tenderness warm up to the old fellow—they are kept
insensible by the tyranny and isolating power of the comic

sentiment, though, in the case of Sganarelle, without such grotesque mercenary afterthoughts as to bring that sentiment home. And in both cases the pity is swallowed up in a deluded personal satisfaction. Sganarelle will now have the young girl all to himself; Shylock will now save 'board and keep.' [133]

Another supposedly pathetic moment comes with Shylock's last speech:

> I pray you, give me leave to go from hence.
> I am not well. Send the deed after me,
> And I will sign it.

'Get thee gone,' says the Duke, 'but do it'; Gratiano is permitted to jeer at him upon his christening; and Shylock's being unwell is received as would be a similar plea from a bully at school, just worsted in a fight. 'It's getting too hot for him,' the other boys say with a grin, or, more safely, think it. Twice before he had said the like:—'Give me my principal and let me go—I'll stay no longer question.' It is as if he were wriggling and squirming while they held him, and now that the Duke says 'Get thee gone,' Gratiano gave him a parting kick or buffet. It is the *rire amer*, as we have seen, still familiar to us to-day, but which rang and resounded through the theatre of the Tudors and the Stuarts, and is awakened again and again by the pages of Fielding and Smollett, Dickens and Thackeray, as in that chapter where Major Pendennis 'neither yields his money nor his life.'

In the passages which we have examined the apparent pathos has been thwarted and stifled by comedy; in others,

---

[133] See above, p. 312.—There is also a quite similar situation in Machiavelli's *Mandragola*. Nicia, like Shylock and Sganarelle a dupe at that moment, pities the youth all unworthy; and by his compassion, certainly, the audience were not moved to tears or intended to be. See V, ii, near end. A situation in some respects still more similar to that in the *Merchant of Venice* is the one in *L'Avare* where Harpagon rejoices in the honesty of his secretary Valère at the moment that he is conspiring against the miser with his daughter. I doubt if it brought tears even to the eyes of Rousseau.

it is by villainy instead. In the first scene in which he appears Shylock complains:

> Still have I borne it with a patient shrug,
> For sufferance is the badge of all our tribe.

It is poetical, no doubt; and throughout the century it has touched our humanitarian sympathies—because we have managed to forget the situation! At this moment Shylock is plotting to have the heart of him if he forfeit; already he has confessed to us that he hates Antonio because he is a Christian, but more for lending money gratis and bringing down the rate in Venice; and already he has vowed, if he can catch him on the hip, to feed fat the ancient grudge he bears him. His repetitions as he pulls at his beard—three thousand ducats . . . for three months . . . and Antonio bound—bode no good. Shylock is not only murderously plotting but at the same time playing the hypocrite. He pretends not to see Antonio when he appears; mutters, meanwhile, villainy to himself; and, once he speaks up, declares he was but debating of his present store, and though he has not the three thousand ducats in ready money, will borrow it—then suddenly sees Antonio and greets him effusively as a friend. Just before the above 'pathetic' speech, has not Antonio himself remarked upon his hypocrisy to Bassanio aside?

> The devil can cite Scripture for his purpose.
> An evil soul producing holy witness
> Is like a villain with a smiling cheek,
> A goodly apple rotten at the heart.
> O, what a goodly outside falsehood hath!

That much even Antonio, his victim, discerns (though he knows much less than we) after Shylock has put up his specious defence of usury, shamelessly avowed his abominable practice of it, and taken refuge behind the shrewdness of a patriarch of his sacred tribe. And presently the Jew's hypocrisy turns, in his anxiety lest his plot should fail, to downright fawning:

> Why, look you how you storm!
> I would be friends with you and have your love.

Who in his mind's eye does not see the Oriental gesture? Then, when Bassanio will not hear of so barbarous a contract, he takes to the cover of an injured innocence.

> O father Abram, what these Christians are,
> Whose own hard dealings teaches them suspect
> The thoughts of others!

Surely no audience, if dramatic method or context counts with them for anything, can be touched by pathos here. Often Shylock's phrases are poetical—as are Iago's.

21.

But the speech that to-day moves us most is 'Hath not a Jew eyes?' etc., discussed above. This, again, is the speech not so much of a comic character as of a villain; and like other villains in Shakespeare, as we have seen, he is given his due—a full chance to speak up and to make a fair showing for himself—while he holds the floor. But it seems quite impossible to take it as pathetic, so hedged about is it with prejudice, beginning on a note of thwarted avarice and of revengefulness, and ending on one of rivalry in revenge, of beating the Christians at what, however justly, he chooses to think their own game. Certainly it is not the plea for toleration that it has generally been taken to be,—here in the third act, after all this cloud of prejudice has been raised up against him, and after his avowals of ignoble hatred, on which he is harping still:

> He was wont to lend money for a Christian courtesy; let him look to his bond. . . . He hath disgraced me and hindered me half a million, laughed at my losses, mocked at my gains, etc.

As Dr Furness and others have observed, Shakespeare managed in this play very strangely if he meant to stand up for the Jews;[134] but even the human appeal is deliberately thwarted.

We are alienated, not by Shylock's avarice and revengefulness alone—he seems just before his defence fairly to be hungering for the pound of flesh that shall 'feed' his revenge,[135] to him more profitable (for all that he says that it is not) than the flesh of muttons, beefs, or goats,—but also by the comic circumstances. Here is a remarkable case of comic preparations and precautions, of 'isolation.' This is the 'daughter-ducats' scene, in which Shylock first appears after the ludicrous report given, in Act II, scene viii, by Salanio to Salarino, of his strange and variable lamentations; and to whom is he talking but to these two merry gentlemen at this moment? If in the theatre it is to be pathos, he should be speaking to some one more responsive on the stage; at every word he is expected to burst out in his 'daughter-ducats' vein once more; and presently so he does. Though we do not laugh at Shylock when he asks, 'Hath not a Jew senses, affections, passions?' good care has been taken that we shall not weep.

Indeed, I cannot but think that even this speech has for generations been misread, simply taken, like the other supposedly pathetic passages, out of its context, and a meaning superimposed. Not only does every one forget how it begins and how it ends, but every one fails to see the thread running through it, the idea, not that Jews have been inhu-

[134] The same considerations that are urged by Professor Brandl against Professor Schröer's notion that in *Titus Andronicus* is expressed the idea of tolerance towards an alien race, may be urged here—Aaron's plea is tardy and belated, and by his conduct no favourable light is shed upon it. *Gött. Gelehrt. Anz.* (1891), p. 716.

[135] It must be remembered that Shakespeare is skirting the fringes of a horrible superstitious prejudice—the notion that the Jews, not only crucified Christian children, but, when they had a chance, ate of a Christian's flesh. In John Day's *Travels of Three English Brothers* (1607), the Jew Zariph says:

Now by my soule 'twould my sprits much refresh
To tast a banket all of Christian's flesh.—p. 54.
Sweet gold, sweete Iewell! but the sweetest part
Of a Iewes feast is a Christian's heart.—p. 60.

manly treated but that from a Jew mistreated you may expect the same as from a Christian—revenge, but in a richer measure. 'And what's his reason?' he begins, 'I am a Jew.' And then and there, we, with our humanitarian impulses, jump the track—at once we are, one and all, over on Shylock's side. But Shylock's answer is not meant to have such a disconcerting effect; we must remember the cry of the London mob when Lopez paid the penalty, and Antonio's words, 'I am like to call thee so again'; we must remember Luther, Coke, Bishop Hall, James Howell, Jeremy Taylor, Robert Smith, William Prynne, the Elizabethan dramatists, Shakespeare himself throughout his play.

> A perfect Judge will read each work of Wit
> With the same spirit that its author writ.

For *Jew,* read *German,* time, 1914-18, place, Belgium or France, England or America, and we have, with greater provocation, that spirit approximately. Shakespeare does not jump the track himself. Hath not a Jew eyes? Hath not a Jew hands? and he proceeds to show that a Jew, having the wit to perceive an injury, the hand to avenge it, quite the same organs, senses, and passions, in fact, that a Christian has, he will when hurt do all that a Christian will do, and a good bit besides. 'Let him look to his bond.' There is no suggestion that Christians should no longer do any hurt to the Jews, and we make Shylock overstate his case. He is only defending himself in what he intends to do; we make him defend his race against all that has been done to it. He is putting in a plea for the right of revenge; we turn it into a plea for equal treatment at the outset.

Of itself, to be sure, provided we can forget both beginning and end and the far from mitigating circumstances, this celebrated defence might touch us. In this regard it is, as we have seen, like other speeches of Shylock's, that about Leah and the turquoise, that about Launcelot's 'kindness,'

and the last speech of all, at the trial—they too would touch
us were it not for the context and situation. That is,
Shakespeare's method is not the ordinary method of caricature. He does not distort or grossly exaggerate the Jew's
features, but flings a villainous or comic light upon them,—
does not turn him into a gargoyle or hobgoblin like Barabas,
but gives him, to an extraordinary degree, the proportions
and lineaments of humanity and of his race, scoundrel
though he be. Shylock's Hebrew pride supports him, even
when he crouches and cringes. Living in humiliation, he
has within him a great bitter well of scorn and sarcasm—
for bankrupts and prodigals, for the lazy and frivolous, for
the light and weak of wit, and the frailties and inconsistencies of Christians. He takes a Puritanic, or Pharisaic,
pride in his sober house. He has a regard for law and the
letter of it, is stiff-necked and tenacious in insisting on his
rights, and keen and dexterous, though specious and cynical,
in his defence of them. And like all Jews, he fights, in
argument or lawsuit at least, to the last ditch. By force
of circumstances it is he, not Launcelot, that is of Hagar's
offspring, and his hand is against every man save his
daughter and those of his tribe; but for them and for the
memory of Leah he has traces of a racial, a patriarchal
affection,—they are his flesh, his blood. He remembers the
past—having no particular reason to remember the present
—the great but remote names of Scripture; and there is
something of the dignity of such memories clinging to him,
both in his bearing and his speech. And there is to his
speech that indefinable individuality and identity of tone—
in general, Shakespeare's greatest achievement in characterization—perceptible in the cast of phrase, the sound and
rhythm of it, his repetitions, exclamations, and rhetorical
questions—a tone hard and grating, sly and dogged, and
yet not without stateliness. Heine has best described it,
contrasting Shylock with Portia:

Wie trübe, kneifend, und hässlich sind dagegen die Gedanken und Reden des Shylock. Sein Witz is kramphaft und ätzend, seine Metaphern sucht er unter den widerwärtigsten Gegenständen, und sogar seine Worte sind zusammengequetschte Misslaute, schrill, zischend, und quirrend.

Harsh and repellant, he is real and individual; and there is poetry in him, as there is in almost all of the characters of Shakespeare, even the villains and the grotesques, and more than there is in many of these.

Now, though, as I conceive it, there is nothing in the figure rightly to be taken as pathetic, one can see how easily, in forgetfulness of the context, it may be so taken by the modern sympathetic mind. The very dignity and isolation —the picturesque aspect—of the figure makes it pathetic for us, such sentimentalists are we! But in so doing we ignore the rest of Shylock, the traits not noble or appealing at all. Though not an ogre or scarecrow like Barabas, he is villainous enough and comic enough, as it were, in his own right. He is, as we have seen, a trickster, a whining and fawning hypocrite, and he sweareth to another's hurt and changeth to avoid his own. His oath and his horror of perjury are belied, not only by his clutching afterwards at thrice the principal although he had refused it—or if not that, at least the principal alone—but also in his prompt abandonment of his suit the moment he hears that a drop of blood means the confiscation of his goods. To keep them in his grasp is to him of more moment than to lay perjury on his soul; though that he had said he would not do, no, not for Venice. He could have commanded our respect if he had reverenced his oath, or if without swearing at all he had followed his losing suit (of which he is so proud) to the bitter end; but he is not a hero, even in racial revenge and hatred. His sacred nation he has forgotten long since; the curse upon it he had never felt until he lost his ducats; and in his suit, once fortune has turned against him, Shylock, in all his pretenses, shrivels up. He stands on his oath no longer; of law he has for once had enough; and if nothing else showed that his last words were meant to be comic—'I pray you give me leave to go from hence, I am not well'—It is his whimpering before that—'Give me my principal and let me go', 'Shall I not have barely my principal?'—his tearing the bond with a curse rather than take the forfeiture and declaring he will stay no longer question,[136] and his abject miserly cry to the Christians to take his life if they will take the means whereby he lives. A losing bargain or suit, after all, is not in his line; his dignity is external, and vanishes once his fraud is revealed. And for this upshot there has been ample preparation. His hypocrisy and trickery glitter through his ruminations and repetitions when first he appears before us, and are fully revealed in his brief soliloquy. But drolly it has been idealized. Jacob and Rebecca he remembers reverently,— Jacob because of his crafty dealing with Laban, and Rebecca because, in palming him off upon Isaac, as a 'wise mother she wrought in his behalf.' Sharp practise he respects, and he dwells fondly upon it in Scripture.

22.

There is much besides that is comical in him, details of his miserliness and his 'Jewishness' which should tickle the risible senses of any ordinary audience, Elizabethan or modern: a touch more rare is in the strait and rigid way that his mind and heart are cooped up within the confines of the law and the letter of it. 'Then must the Jew be merciful,' says Balthazar. 'On what compulsion must I?' It is Greek to him, not Hebrew, these words and the following ones:—'Have by some surgeon, Shylock.'—(Is it so nominated in the bond?)—'It is not so express'd; but what of that? 'Twere good you do so much for charity.'—But

---

[136] Certainly Mr Poel is right in saying that at line 345 Shylock should tear the bond, as he does in *Il Pecorone*. Cf. l. 234: 'Be merciful; take thrice thy money; bid me tear the bond.' Now, to get away, he does it himself.

only half does he hear what she is saying; and he pores over the writing—'I cannot find it; 'tis not in the bond.' Surely he is not feigning; and though some may rather think it tragic, this spiritual blindness—and indeed the tragic crisis is not yet past;—the contrast contrived and the repetition employed seem calculated deliberately to bring home to us that rigidity, or 'raideur,' of the human spirit which Monsieur Bergson finds essential to comedy. The mercy must be down in black and white, signed and sealed. He is after all pretty much of a piece, a thorough grotesque; and in his quaint antique fashion business is business to him, a contract is a contract, a bargain a bargain. Everything is a bargain to him, good or bad, and it is often with a subtle and unobtrusive hand that Shakespeare makes this apparent. We have noticed his rage over the exchange of a turquoise for a monkey; but it is droller still to see how the contract for the pound of flesh is to him a good bargain even while with gruesome jesting he makes it out a bad one.

> . . . what should I gain
> By the exaction of the forfeiture?
> A pound of man's flesh taken from a man
> Is not so estimable, profitable neither,
> As flesh of muttons, beefs, or goats.

Literal-minded still! He might have said to Bassanio, 'Only a formality; a contract is not a contract without interest or forfeit?' But he cannot shake off his inveterate materialism, or the language of the market; and must needs look upon the forfeit as a precious commodity, flesh like other flesh (though in his chaffering, higgling way he vows that it is not), of which the price is high. ' 'Tis a good round sum.'

And what of Shylock at the very end, in the last act, where no one speaks or thinks of him, and the spirit of romance is once more regnant? Professor Baker asks why, 'if Shakespeare wished to create laughter by Shylock, he kept him out of the fifth act, thus losing the many opportunities

which his forlorn, defeated condition would have given to
delight the Jew-baiters.' But that would have been to make
a point of the matter, and to raise the Jewish question in a
play where the Jew's story is, and is meant to be, but an
episode. That question, or the slavery question, which Professor Jastrow [137] —not Shylock—raises, or the sex question, or any other, as has been seen,[138] had for Shakespeare,
or his brother playwrights, no existence. To him things were
solid and settled; and in his plays he held no brief, followed
no program. The Jews he made comical not because he
himself had a grudge against them, but, as he made London
citizens, Puritans, Frenchmen, and Welshmen comical,
because, as he might have said, they were so. He took the
world as he found it, and in no respect more than in the
matters of mirth. He was no Rabelais, Montaigne, Swift,
or Voltaire, Bernard Shaw, or Anatole France, who have
found out precious new things to laugh at.

23.

I have been at pains to ascertain and define the attitude
of the author and his public, and so interpret the play.
I have found in Shylock the comic villain, and though finely
and delicately done, nothing really and sincerely pathetic
in him at all. Pains wasted, some present-day writers of
the eminence of Professor Matthews will say; though the
number of them is relatively fewer than it used to be.
What Shakespeare intended does not much matter—what
matters is what he did—and we have as good a right as
Shakespeare to our opinion of Shylock, though 'the comic
aspects of Shylock have disappeared from our modern
vision and the pathetic interest of the desolate figure is now

---

[137] p. 737:—'The Jew reproaches the Christian with his sinful traffic in
human flesh.' Surely not; that would have spoiled Shylock's argument from
analogy; and here we have a neat example of reading with modern spectacles, and by sentences rather than by speeches, by speeches rather than
by scenes.
[138] See chapter i, pp. 12-13.

most obvious.''[139] Art then [140] ceases to be a means of communication from soul to soul, the author and his meaning
are a matter of indifference, and there is really no work of
interpretation, but only of expatiation, to do. Apart
from Shakespeare's opinion, what Shylock is there? one
wonders, bewildered. There is, we are assured, an
Elizabethan Shylock and—'even though Shakespeare might
himself protest'—a modern one, equally legitimate, though
for us the modern is the real. And Shylock then is ambiguous, Janus-faced. Professor Matthews well knows what
it is for an actor to misinterpret his part, to play it *à contresens;* but it is permissible in actor and critic too, it seems,
when the play is three hundred years old. It is impossible,
rather, for in that space of time a new meaning—mysteriously, but legitimately—develops, somewhat as a beard can
grow in the grave, or as razors sharpen in the drawer.

Such a prodigious ambiguity—ranging between the satiric
and the pathetic—would, I think, be a serious defect in a
character; but I do not believe it is there. The mistake,
as I conceive it, of Professor Matthews and other modernizing critics is that they either ignore the intention of the
author or establish such an antinomy between what the
author intended and what he did. There are cases, no
doubt, where an author fails in his intention, but there is
no opposition or discrepancy between intention and achievement here; for his intention we gather from what he
did, and by that we mean the emphasis, the arrangement,
the preparations and fulfilment, the comment, the villain's
attempt and the turning of the tables upon him,—all that
larger meaning which is to be found not so much in the
letter of the text as in the spirit of it and in the structure
of the whole. To this the modernizing critics do not rightly
attend; they read the text but they read it to suit them-

---

[139] *Shakespeare as a Playwright,* p. 151. Cf. also an essay by Mr Matthews
in *Columbia Shakespeare Studies* (1917).
[140] See section 1 of this chapter.

selves,—they read the lines or pages, not the play. Yet the
intention—all this pervading spirit and purpose—is as
important as the wording itself;—the intonation and accent
and gesture of a spoken sentence convey as much of the
meaning as the mere words do;—and to attend to these last
alone is to do violence to the author and his work. What
this means Professor Matthews also knows—for Macready
and Barrett to cut the piece down to a Shylock play in three
acts, ending with the trial, he says, is 'plainly a betrayal of
Shakespeare's intent.' [141] Is it less a betrayal to keep the
text intact, indeed, but read into the half of it what to his
intent is directly opposed?

In insisting on the historical aspect of the question—that
is, to the effect of asserting our right to be modern, to be
what we are—Professor Matthews and the others are really
confusing the issue. The considerations of historical character which we have been urging are secondary: the primary
consideration is the technical—that of the emphasis, the
arrangement, the comment, and the like, just mentioned
above, which convey the author's meaning—and the historical considerations serve but to make that meaning more
clear. That done, the figure stands before us, not a 'scientific curiosity,' or a bit of hopelessly old-fashioned Elizabethan stage-furniture, but (though handled roughly) a
human being; and it has the considerable advantage of being
real, whereas the modern is a chimæra, a myth. It is not
resident in the faraway Elizabethan age any more than in
ours, but in the mind of Shakespeare. The history, if it
troubles us, can be quite forgotten. Treat Shakespeare as
if a modern, and yet our reasoning applies. Read 'Ibsen'
for 'Shakespeare' in the opinion rendered: 'What *Ibsen*
intended does not much matter—and we have as good a
right as *Ibsen* to our opinion of Rebecca West.' To that,
I know, Professor Matthews and some of the others would
demur. But by this same method of ignoring the author's

---

[141] *Shakespeare as a Playwright*, p. 145.

intention or misreading his text, Mr Huneker makes of that unscrupulous but unmalignant woman (who lures indeed Beata to her death but only in order to enable Beata's husband to attain to his high destiny) a monster, a Medusa. She is a Real-politiker, is *jenseits von Gut und Böse,* is (though terribly) enlightened. But Mr Huneker has a right to his Rebecca if Professor Matthews has a right to his Jew. And Ibsen? He has nothing to say!

It is only a question of clear thinking, of knowing what we are doing (or not doing) and freely and honestly admitting it. On the popular stage, to be sure, Shylock must be played pretty much as Irving played him (though, like Irving himself, we should at the same time remember that this is not Shakespeare's Shylock at all) ; but criticism, unlike acting, has to do with the truth alone. If in reading the play we find a tear in Shakespeare's eye shall we not like Sainte-Beuve catch ourselves, and if we cannot find it in our hearts to dry the tear, at least candidly acknowledge that it is we ourselves who put it there? It is the French who see straight. As I have had occasion repeatedly to notice they have brushed away the Romantic cobwebs and moonshine from Molière, and on the stage and in criticism he is himself again; whereas Professor Matthews does to Molière much as he does to Shakespeare, finds George Dandin and Arnolphe, too, pathetic, is inclined to find *L'Avare* and *Le Tartuffe* tragic, and blurs the fine sharp outlines of the master's comedy. But Sarcey and Lemaître, one the most sensible, the other also the most sensitive of men, do nothing of the sort. Lemaître rises to heights even above those of Sainte-Beuve, for he not only retracts his opinions but—utmost flight of the candid mind—pokes fun at his own verses:—

Oui, je sais, *George Dandin,* entre toutes les comédies de Molière, a une réputation particulière d'amertume.[142] C'est incroyable ce que les vers de Musset sur cette mâle gaieté de Molière—

[142] That is, of pathos in the character, of bitterness in the author.

si triste et si profonde
Qu'après qu'on vient d'en rire on devrait en pleurer—

ont fait dire de sottises aux snobs que nous sommes tous.

Then Lemaître quotes himself :—

On ne rit pas toujours, maître, à ta comédie;

. . . .

Ce niais est navrant encor qu'il soit grotesque.
Pour peu que l'on y songe, on entrevoit soudain
Un drame sous la farce, un martyr chez Dandin.

Oh! là, là, que d'affaires! Je relis *George Dandin* et je n'y
retrouve rien de tout cela. C'est une farce . . . amère? Oh! Dieu,
non.—*Impressions* (1895), viii, 53.

There we have what may be called the critical spirit, that
spirit so rare and precious,—the earnest effort to read the
words by the light in which the poet wrote them, the search
for a meaning, not the imparting of one, the suspicion of
error, the unreserved surrender to the truth. On its altar
all the critic's sentimental finery and vagaries are laid un-
flinchingly, gaily! And by coincidence the very words
Lemaître applies to Molière in dealing with George Dandin
are not out of place for Shakespeare in dealing with Shylock.
'Mâle gaieté,' and (not quoted above) 'une férocité toute
joviale et sans nul fiel'—that is, in this case, with no bitterness or indignant irony directed against either Jews or the
haters of Jews.

Not only is the modern meaning foreign to Shakespeare
but it is, as we have suggested, superfluous. Critics speak
as if it were impossible for Shylock to mean anything to us
unless thus sentimentalized and tragicalized. Indeed, as we
moderns have done with many another rough customer in
history, literature, or holy writ, we have tamed and domesticated the 'dog Jew', and drawn his 'fangs.' 'He will
speak soft words unto us,' he no longer grins and he cannot
bite. But Shakespeare and the Elizabethans, as we have
seen, shuddered at him and laughed at him; and except at

popular performances, where racial antipathy is rather to
be allayed than fomented, so should we, as much as in us lies,
do to-day.   Thus we shall come into sympathy with the
manifest intention of the poet, with the acting of the part
on the Elizabethan stage, with the conception of the money-
lending Jew in the contemporary drama, character-writing,
and ballad, and with the lively prejudice of the time.   A
villain and a butt, 'une simple figure à gifles,' as Francisque
Sarcey shrewdly observes, 'un monstrueux grotesque, sur le
nez de qui tombent à l'envi d'effroyables nasardes,'[143]
(only, as we have seen, he is not a monster, not a caricature) ;—such, save for the happily human elements and
lineaments of his make-up, and for the splendour of poetry,
shed, like the rain and the light of heaven, on the just and
the unjust, is the impression which Shylock makes after he
has been duly restored to the sixteenth century, an impression in which pathos has no place, and with which our
notions of justice and social responsibility, on the one hand,
or of ironical art, on the other, have, so far as they are
merely modern, nothing to do.   So he is not lost to us.
That Hebraic and picturesque figure will be remembered
long after he has retreated from the warm circle of our sentiments, and be visited again and again, by an exhilarating
sally of the imagination, in the midst of the harsh and
sturdy life to which he belongs.[144]

1911

[143] *Quarante ans de théâtre: Shylock.*
[144] The pathetic conception of Shylock I have above charged to the
account of the Romantic Age, though I have taken notice of a similar
tendency in French criticism, regarding Molière, as early as in Rousseau.
But the ferment of sentimentality and humanitarianism had long been at
work, overwhelming the comic spirit and blinding readers to it even in the
writings of the ancients. See Mr Ernest Bernbaum's *Drama of Sensibility*
(1915), chap. ii, for an interesting presentation of the misinterpretation
(which lingers on almost to the present day) by Steele and Lessing, Diderot
and Destouches, of Plautus and Terence, as if these comedies were sentimental and pathetic like their own; and, see pp. 61-2, for further light on
the eighteenth-century sentimentalizing of Molière, particularly the *Misanthrope.*

CHAPTER VII

THE CRIMINALS

LITERARY characters become extinct like races of men and beasts. The Vice with his lath and the Fool with his bells and bauble have vanished like the Mound-Builder or the aurochs, and their fossil remains are buried in old plays and prints. They dropped from the stage as the form of life (or the conception of it) which they represented dropped out of the world. Out of the one and off the other passed Fool and Devil long ago, and after them, in the last century, the villain. He could not bear the light or breathe the air of our day.

Black and piratical of hair and of look, as we remember him, he was at the beginning an outcast, but before the end cock of the walk, and the tragedy was pretty much of his making. The world had dealt hardly with him, and he dealt still more hardly with the world. He scoffed at respectability and jeered at the cowardice and stupidity of everybody about him, yet he himself, much given to free thinking, was plunged into melancholy. He was the villain and he knew it, until the end. Then his heart was touched, once he had been given the death-blow or had given it.

Such, with boasting and gloating, blasphemy and atheism added to him, and all excuse utterly taken away, was the villain of the Elizabethans. In him was more poetry, less humanity, or no humanity worthy of the word. There, in three centuries, was change enough you would think; and why is his like now no longer to be found in higher drama and fiction, but cast into the outer darkness of penny dreadfuls and melodrama? One reason lies without us, in

337

our present knowledge of criminal character; the other, the deeper, in the spirit and temper of our age. And it is the purpose of the present study to show this; and to endeavour to make it clear that the criminal characters in Shakespeare, however remarkable as creatures of the imagination, are not depicted from our point of view—or indeed wholly from their own—and cannot be proved real, as critics and criminologists continually endeavour to prove them real, by reference to life and fact. In part this is owing to technique, the limitations of Elizabethan or other drama; in part it is owing to the Elizabethan conception of character.

I.

The instinctive or incorrigible offender against the person, as we now know him, is no such compact and single soul as Richard III or Iago. He may be a survival of savagery or the fag-end of degeneration, and is likely to be the most rudimentary and inconsistent of men. Remorse he has none, of moral sensibility he has little, and yet seldom is he by instinct wholly cruel or base. It is the common notion, and also the Elizabethan, that if there be any good in a criminal, it will take the form of repentance for his crime: the fact is that much oftener it has nothing to do with his crime. A murderer like Lacenaire or Dostoevsky's Raskolnikoff will risk his own life to save a cat's or a canary's, or will tenderly cherish the life of a comrade or of his aged parents, though with a heart of flint for his victim. Nor does he love evil for its own sake. If he boasts, it is simply of the achievements of his genius; if he gloats, it is over his inferior adversary; and it is an impossibility, as Tolstoi avers, for him to think ill of himself. Instead of being atheistical or irreligious he is particularly inclined, primitive being that he is, to be superstitiously devout in the performance of religious duties; and at most he shows at times that disposition to jest and flout at what is sacred which, in the lower classes, and in the simpler peoples such as the medieval Christians and the Greeks, is not incompatible with entire and implicit faith. All in all he is a man, the devoted victim of his brutal instincts, not a devil. He is not the antithesis, least of all consciously the antithesis, of what is human.

These things men know as the fruit of wide observation and of scientific study in the nineteenth and twentieth centuries. *A-priori* thinking has proved of as little avail in psychology as in chemistry and medicine. What turned men away from it to the study of the object itself was, however, the new spirit, the more humane, revolutionary sentiment of the century before. Romantic sympathy and the philosophy of the return to nature began to do away with the villain even before men had studied the criminal. 'Damns had had their day,' and poets petulantly made him the hero. It was the age of the noble bandit and the 'magnanimous highwayman' (though of course the ignoble ones lingered on), of Goetz with the iron hand, Karl Moor, Rob Roy, and the 'villain-heroes' of the Terrific School and Byron. All these were variously incompatible, sentimental mixtures of utter good and utter evil that grew more piquant but hardly less preposterous down to the days of Bulwer and Victor Hugo. No such beings as Bulwer's Eugene Aram, or Hugo's Dona Lucrezia, Claude Frollo, and Jean Valjean ever blessed or cursed the earth. 'Embodied antitheses, premeditated paradoxes,' as Hugo's characters have been called, they are attempts at representing the complexity of life which are themselves, as has been said, quite simple. No convict who, after eighteen years in the galleys, had risked everything to escape from them and everything to keep from returning, would, with death in the shape of Thénardier and his jackals staring him in the eye, have burnt his own arm instead of theirs and tossed the poker out of the window. This is the very coxcombry of charity, the frenzy of chivalry, not human nature if we know it. No bandit like Schweizer, for such cause, ever blew out his own brains; no bloodhound like Javert ever threw himself into the river. And no robbers or murderers like Clifford or Aram ever spoke, from their hearts, with the tongues not of men but of angels. The mystery of the inconsistency and complexity of human character, criminal or normal, cannot be comprehended in a formula or penetrated by a flight of imagination; and it was reserved for such as Mérimée and Dostoevsky, Zola, Ibsen, and Mr Hardy, to give the mystery form and life by a surer but more devious method. Dostoevsky and Zola followed and shadowed the criminal mind as the detective shadows the criminal; Mérimée and Mr Hardy explored the illogical and pragmatic morality of the lower classes or simpler races; and one and all they endeavoured to leave the impedimenta of their own morality behind. Hugo and Bulwer think they are holding up the mirror to nature when they make their Ishmaelitish heroes both good and wicked, but these—and Dostoevsky, Balzac, and Zola admit as much—make them neither. 'Men are neither good nor evil,' says Balzac, 'but are born with instincts and inclinations.' 'My characters are not wicked,' says Zola in the preface to *L'Assommoir;* 'they are only ignorant, and are stunted by the harsh toil and misery of their lives.' *Jenseits von Gut and Böse,* in short, is the word, and this monistic, or indeed biological, attitude has made it possible in some fashion to comprehend and harmonize traits which otherwise remained irreconcilable. In Nature the good and the bad, the healthy and the degenerate, are inextricably interwoven, are one.

It was quite another atmosphere that Shakespeare breathed, an atmosphere charged with the dualism of the Middle Ages and earlier times. Good and evil then were as the poles asunder: God was in his heaven, no doubt, but the Devil was in the world. The exuberant pantheistic philosophy of Giordano Bruno, friend of Sidney and Greville, had left no impress upon English thought. To the four elements still were attributed four qualities—hot, cold, moist, and dry—not, as our monistic science would demand, merely two. The world was divided between light and darkness, and the darkness was as real as the light. There were devils of fire and water, the earth and the underworld; and every man had one of his own, to whom, if like Brabantio he 'cursed his better angel from his side,' he fell a prey. Atheism then meant not scepticism but enmity with God. A man had to take sides, just as then— and nominally in some countries of Europe to-day—a man must be either Protestant or Catholic. It was still an age of violence and suspicion, when a man's hand was against every other man, and the *entente cordiale* between nation and nation and stranger and stranger was unknown. 'An enemy hath done this' was the first thought of Benvenuto Cellini when his luck turned, as it was of the man in the parable; and again and again, with cause or without cause, it is the thought of people in a like plight in Shakespeare. In all cases the enemy was a man, or Fortune, or the stars. Such a spirit is a motive force in the drama. In the mysteries God and the angels were enthroned at one end of the stage and Hell-Mouth yawned at the other. To do the mischief devils were ever at hand: in the Elizabethan plays there were villains. At this point the art of the playwright was in sympathy with the popular literature, with the legend or novella (essentially a literature of intrigue) from which he drew his plot, and with the drama of the ancients. But the villains took on larger and demonic proportions as the fate and the gods of the ancients receded from view. In Elizabethan drama 'fate' is mainly a commonplace of Senecan rhetoric; whatever the heroes may say when the world is against them, their wills are free; and the 'fate' of Othello is Iago. As Mr Bradley has shown, it is nearly always evil that in Shakespeare brings about the convulsion in the order of things; and in that day when men still believed in diabolical possession and total depravity it was natural that often the evil should be embodied in a particular person. In Desdemona's case the cause might have been neither personal nor evil; it might have been her disregard of her father's wishes and the proprieties of Venetian society, or, again to quote Mr Bradley, a misunderstanding between herself and the Moor 'due to racial differences in physiognomic expression'; but it is—much more picturesquely and expeditiously for the stage—the tempter, 'his Moorship's ancient.' In Lear's case or in Gloster's it is not mainly their own folly but the ferocity of their children. In no case does Shakespeare represent men as overwhelmed by anything so vague and neutral as social forces, or as devoured by their own passions alone. It is by other men's passions, other men's deeds; and life is a temptation, a hand-to-hand struggle. Ibsen's Hedda Gabler and Pinero's Second Mrs Tanqueray, on the other hand, go to rack and ruin of themselves. Out of their hearts—out of the bosom of an indifferent world—are the issues of their lives; and a bustling villain would but be in the way.

2.

It is not, however, mainly a matter of dualistic philosophy and a belief in human malignity that prompts the dramatist in tragedy or in comedy to call in the villain. It is mainly his conception of a play as a story on the stage. Like all dramatists before him—like all audiences before his own—he and they looked upon it not merely as the unfolding of a character but as a 'plot' or 'intrigue.' 'Conspiracy' the word at bottom means in the chief modern languages to this day, and a mere word can tell a tale. Dramatist and audience alike craved action, external action and struggle: in the Greek drama it had been provided by fate and nemesis, in the Senecan by fate and a villain too, and in the drama of the Renaissance it had to be a villain merely. Almost all the stories of the time—tragic or comic, and on the stage or off it—are provided with one of some sort or other; and it is only recently—witness the novels of Dickens and even of Mr Hardy—that those of our time have got rid of him. For long, no doubt, it has been thought that

> In tragic life, God wot,
> No villain need be! Passions spin the plot:
> We are betrayed by what is false within.

But the making on such lines of a novel—and of drama all the more—is quite another matter. *Votre philosophie dirigera votre art*—eventually. And such a philosophy was not that of Shakespeare or his age. Even 'the dramatization of history to him and his age,' as Mr Alden says, 'was the dramatization of its great personages, and their passions, vices, and ambitions.' It was Chatham who said that he had learned his English history from Shakespeare; but he could not do it now.

3.

As a result of their concrete and dualistic way of thinking and of their relish for action and intrigue, the Elizabethan playwrights paint their villains many a shade blacker than they find them. The wickedness of Aaron and Iago, of Webster's Flamineo and Bosola, is quite above and beyond the mark, and overtops that in the chronicles and novels whence they came. The public hankers after sound and fury, the dramatist requires a propeller for his play, and both crave contrasts total and acute. Nowhere does this tendency appear so unmistakably as in the handling of what was in the beginning popular and non-dramatic material, the misconception of Machiavelli. The Elizabethan Machiavel is a diabolical figure such as that sketched of the Elizabethan villain above, and, besides, one who has at his beck and call the qualities of the lion and the fox (or violence and craft), who loves himself alone and uses other men 'as nails to drive out one another,' hates God, jeers at his conscience, and revels and riots in lust, dissimulation, blasphemy, and murder. Thus the Florentine statesman became a mythical figure, a devil-let-loose like Judas, and, like him, was fabled to have perished, despairing and blaspheming, by his own hand. On the stage he was a standing type of the villain, as the Clown, the Fool, or the Braggart Soldier was of the humorous person: now he appears as Marlowe's Barabas and Shakespeare's Aaron, quoting, in more or less garbled form, maxims from the *Principe;* and now as Iago, not in explicit terms a Machiavel at all. Indeed, like these other types, he is but old wine in a new bottle; for out of Seneca, along with much else, came into Elizabethan tragedy a character such as Atreus, who likewise practices villainy wholesale, lies and dissembles, gloats, blasphemes, and pays homage to the powers infernal.

Such, even among literary men in Shakespeare's day, is the current notion of the character of the most enlightened political thinker of the age; and of the instinctive dualism of the age no more signal proof could be required. Mistaking him for a deliberate enemy of society, they turn him into a ravening beast of prey. And monster of iniquity that he is, he knows it. He puts himself in the wrong. He canvasses the situation from top to bottom, and, complacently or defiantly, stands a villain self-confessed and self-confuted. It is a paradox imbedded in Christian and other religious belief that your devil and your sinner well know what they are. Machiavelli, if a sinner, did not know. He and Aretino, who—far more justly—shared his infamy, were deaf to the claims of conscience, but they did not flout them or brush them aside; they were far from being atheists; they and their contemporaries such as Cellini and the Borgias kept the innocence and buoyancy of their spirits to the end, and they surprise you in their portraits, as Vernon Lee has remarked, with the nobility of their countenances. There, side by side, are truth and Elizabethan fiction; and, as in the adage, truth is stranger. 'Shakespeare,' says Mr Shaw, 'was a devout believer in the existence of the true villain—the man whose terrible secret is that his fundamental moral impulses are by some freak of nature inverted, so that not only are love, pity, and honour loathsome to him, and the affectation which society imposes on him a constant source of disgust, but cruelty, destruction, and perfidy are his most luxurious passions.' But for him and the audience the secret was an open one.

Of Machiavels there are many on the Elizabethan stage, from Marlowe's Jew of Malta on. Shakespeare has three —Aaron, Richard the Third, and Iago. At the hellhound Aaron, though some there are that disdain to account him Shakespeare's, we will take a look because he embodies and illustrates something of the spirit of Shakespeare and his age. With his Moor the poet out-Marlowes Marlowe with his Jew. He is of a burlier strain of villainy, and in bluster and jocular ferocity he makes up whatever he lacks in fawning and fraud. His atheism is more emphatic and mutinous than that of Barabas. Like him he is repeatedly called a devil; but because of his colour, not his race, for it was an old superstition, not then extinct, that the Devil when he appeared took the form of a Moor, while the Jews (ye are of your father, the Devil!) were held to be devils born. But by suffering his unholy light to shine Aaron earns the title for himself, and he carries it with obstreperous complacence. He ha-ha's when he stabs a man, and roars and curses when he is foiled; he brags of the 'evils he has done,' wishes at the end that he might do ten thousand more, and if one good deed in all his life he did he does repent it from his very soul. Fee, faw, fum! A completer product there could not be of that dualistic way of thinking which conceived (as we, for that matter, instinctively do still) of cold and darkness, not as negative, but as opposed and antagonistic to heat and light, told the tale of the mortal combat between the gods of summer and of winter, and gave birth to such conceptions as hell and heaven, Antichrist and devil, devil's mass and devil's litany. Morally, this is man turned upside down, or wrong side out, and thrust beyond the pale of the species.

But the criminal is human, and in the biological scale nearer man than beast. The more we know of him, the less unlike him we are, we shudder to discover. We are but tamed, domesticated.

4.

Richard Crookback, who is Shakespeare's beyond cavil, is cast in Aaron's mould. He is one, as Richmond says to his soldiers, who hath ever been God's enemy. Fitted out with teeth at his birth like the offspring of the incubus (or devil) known to folklore, hunchbacked, lame, unutterably hideous, he resolves, quite summarily, after a fashion not warranted even by the exigencies of 'exposition,' that since he cannot be a lover he will be a villain—

> I am determined to prove a villain
> And hate the idle pleasures of these days.

Or as he puts it, more roundly, in *III Henry VI,*

> since the heavens have shaped my body so,
> Let hell make crook'd my mind to answer it.

'I, that have neither pity, love, nor fear,' he in this passage exclaims again, to the same effect as in the later play—

> And if King Edward be as true and just
> As I am subtle, false, and treacherous—

and in neither passage is there an inkling of irony. A queer creature, this, to have the gift of seeing himself as others see him, both body and soul, as hardly any one of us can do. As a matter of fact, just as the criminal fails to realize his depravity, so the cripple, as Dr Brandes remarks, often fails to realize his deformity. But Schiller's Franz Moor, modelled upon him, 'sees all his own ugliness and insults it.' 'Ce qui est humain,' says the French critic, Monsieur Kontz, 'c'est la parole du berger noir de Virgile: Nec sum adeo informis.'

At either point—his looks or his inner nature—Richard is

but the voice of poet and people concerning him. In accord with their sentiments he looks upon his deformity as putting him beyond the verge of all that is human, as setting the seal on his depravity instead of explaining and extenuating it. Such was the temper of Shakespeare's time. No psychology enters into the question: Richard, in his avowals above, cheerfully takes the responsibility on himself. Let hell complete the work of heaven! And it does. He is charged to the muzzle with Machiavellian principles of egoism, promptitude and resolution, violence and fraud.[1] Like other Machiavels he boasts and gloats, fawns upon and fondles the minions of his villainy, and he plays the hypocrite as egregiously as Barabas. When Buckingham brings to him the Mayor and Aldermen with the offer of the crown, the ruffian buffoon appears to them in a gallery, prayer-book in hand, between two bishops, and 'plays the maid's part, still answers nay and takes it.' A character of such finesse, he was recently taken by a great student of criminology to be the highest example of the criminal player of a *coup d'état!* A character of such unmitigated ferocity, overriding, espousing, butchering whom he will, he was recently taken by two criminologists and the Head of the Danish Police to be the type of a kingly cripple struggling with a harsh and pitiless environment. If anything, the environment struggles with him.

On the eve of battle, however, Richard is no longer himself, the brisk Machiavel of old. Though it is crudely and ambiguously represented, he experiences something like remorse. The Machiavel, monstrous and grotesque as he was, had the grace, in the person of Aaron, for instance, to disdain the sentimentality of a deathbed repentance. In him, of course, this is the bravado or 'reprobate mind' of the enemy of God: in the criminal the unrepentant state is simply the unobtrusive, unconscious symptom of 'moral

---

[1] As above; and cf. Professor E. S. Meyer, *Machiavelli and the Elizabethan Drama.*

atrophy,' or defective intelligence. Richard dreams that the souls of all those whom he had murdered come to his tent, and 'every one did threat to-morrow's vengeance on the head of Richard.' Once Queen Anne complains that as she lay by his side, with his timorous dreams she still was waked. 'Their sleep is disturbed by no uneasy dreams,' says Dr Wey, of Elmira, concerning the criminals he has observed; and investigators from Gall to Lombroso agree with him that in criminals signs of repentance, remorse, or despair are seldom to be detected. Among four hundred murderers Bruce Thompson found signs of remorse in but three, and of seven hundred criminals Ferri found only 3.4 per cent that showed signs of repentance or appeared at all moved in recounting their misdeeds. If criminals have regrets, it is, as with Aaron (though by no means to the tune of his devil's litany), because they have not committed more crimes or because they have let themselves be caught. Very simply, they are sorry not for the good they may have done but for the pleasure and profit they have missed. Only those betray acute sorrow and real remorse, says Despine, who have committed the criminal act under the influence of a violent passion or by accident; quite naturally, only those repent who are endowed with the moral capacity; and in neither class is Richard. 'One may disavow and disclaime vices,' says Montaigne, in whose book Shakespeare had read, 'that surprise us, and whereto our passions transport us: but those which by long habite are rooted in a strong and ankred in a powerfull will, are not subject to contradiction.' These ghosts, indeed, that visit Richard are no mere voices of conscience but the fierce old-fashioned sort; when they rise the lights burn blue, and—primitively and superstitiously—they appear at the same time to another, Richmond, the victor of the morrow. Yet, from an historical point of view, the superstition of the appearance of the ghost of the murdered to the murderer is the beginning and basis of the spiritual phenomenon we call remorse; even in Shakespeare's day it meant not supernatural punishment and nemesis alone; and quite out of keeping with his Machiavellian scoffings at conscience before and after, Richard takes the ghostly words to heart.

5.

What prompted the poet here was his morality. After a crime or in the clutches of death many of his criminals have qualms of some sort or other. In part, it is a story-telling device, old but ever new; like that whereby the slayer —be he villain or hero—furnishes a good situation lamenting his fallen foe, as does the Percy in the old ballad, or Æneas when he bewails Lausus, hard as he had tried to kill him. But the pith of the matter is that Shakespeare cleaves to the conscience of the Elizabethan age. From of old, among Christians as among pagans, in the Hebrew prophets as in the Vedas, there has prevailed the notion that, as Westermarck puts it, in sin itself there is a power which must destroy the sinner; and when so late as the nineteenth century the Calvinist Chalmers speaks of 'the inherent misery of the evil affections,' the notion merely survives in philosophic form. Hence the innumerable tales of bad men making a bad end; hence the Furies or Erinnyes; hence, in the long run, Dante's hell, where each crime is its own punishment and the homicides stand boiling up to the brows in blood. In all this is involved nothing like sorrow for the sin itself, compunction, or repentance. Cardinal Beaufort, in the *Second Part of Henry VI*, dies an unrelenting murderer; yet he has 'the horrors,' as we say; and so bad a death, Warwick moralizes, argues a monstrous life. And the Queen in Cymbeline, foiled and baffled,

> Grew shameless-desperate; open'd, in despite
> Of heaven and men, her purposes; repented
> The evils she hatch'd were not effected; so
> Despairing died.

The devils themselves believe and tremble! This is the

end of the reprobate, in a certain fearful looking forward
unto judgment (which was a case of conscience as men then
thought) whether it be in defiance or in mere despair. Even
Milton and Bunyan so consider it; even to them and the
Evangelicals conscience is thus in a certain sense external,
the voice of God—rather than of the better self within,—
the worm that never dies. So at times Milton represents
Satan himself. 'Oh! how the thoughts of Death, of Hell-
fire, and of eternal Judgment did then wrack his conscience,'
says Bunyan of Mr Badman. 'God gave him up now to a
reprobate mind,' he observes; and like Cymbeline's Queen,
Badman dies despairing and blaspheming. Despair, used
thus theologically of one at death's door, had then a very
definite meaning, in Shakespeare and the other dramatists
frequently apparent. It is the condition of the man in the
Iron Cage at the Interpreter's House, whom 'God hath
denied repentance'; and Robert Burton in his *Anatomy* [2]
dwells upon the symptoms clinically, at length: a burning
fever of the soul, troubled, sleeping or waking, by ghosts and
the Devil and fears of judgment,—the state, at the end,
of Cain, Saul, Achitophel, Judas, Nero, and Richard III,
leading often to blasphemy and suicide. 'Whom God for-
sakes,' says Burton (and there is dualism indeed), 'the
devil by his permission lays hold on. Sometimes he perse-
cutes them with that worm of conscience, as he did Judas,'
etc. So at the beginning of the play Queen Margaret curses
Richard—'the worm of conscience still begnaw thy soul';
and like all other curses in the tragedy, this must be fulfilled, and Richard has no remorse after all. In the same
breath she calls him son of hell; and a conscience, according to our notions, he then cannot have. He speaks of it,
indeed, but as Bunyan and Burton speak of it in this connection, as something visited upon him. 'Despair and die!'

---

[2] *Mr Badman* (Cambridge Classics) pp. 90, 143, 159, 169-70; *Anatomy*,
3:4:2:3. The first books of *Paradise Lost* present Satan best, in his 'injured
merit.'

had cried each of the eleven apparitions. 'I shall despair,'
he says for the moment himself. But he dies in battle.
Truer at this point to the popular dramatic type, Aaron
and Marlowe's Barabas end cursing and blaspheming; and
Lady Macbeth, having been troubled both awake and
asleep, dies in despair—dies of it, and possibly by her own
hand.

6.

Of unrepentant horror there is more in Shakespeare's
characters than has ordinarily been observed, even in those
who are not unmitigated villains or Machiavels. *Macbeth*
is commonly spoken of as a tragedy of remorse, and in
hero and heroine as criminals *par passion* or *par occasion*
(which, we need not determine) remorse would not have
been out of place. But remorse really they have none.
Professor Bradley, following Campbell, grants as much in
the case of Lady Macbeth; [3] yet although he recognizes
that at its face value the language of Macbeth does not
bear him out in this opinion, he holds that the inner being
of the thane and king is convulsed by conscience. Professor
Sharp, on the other hand, contends that in both hero and
heroine there is no remorse, but fear, 'not sorrow for sin,
but fear of the dagger and the poisoned cup.' Such feelings
and considerations play in both characters, no doubt, a
large part; but, as Mr Bradley makes plain, surely neither
is delivered up to the fear of detection and punishment
alone. Macbeth and Lady Macbeth have a horror of

[3] Of this opinion are the best critics nowadays, as in the eighteenth century; but during the nineteenth she was, like Iago, much sentimentalized,
and thought to be wifely and even motherly in spirit. This was in reaction,
no doubt, against the statuesque terrors of Mrs Siddons. Mrs Montagu and
Rümelin, (*v. infra*) whom I came to know only after writing the article
in 1912, anticipate me somewhat in the conception of her merely external
conscience. Mr Arthur Symons (*Studies in Elizabethan Drama*, p. 34),
recognizing that in Lady Macbeth there is no repentance or regret, says that
she dies 'not of remorse at her guilt but because she has miscalculated her
power of resistance to the scourge of an over-acute imagination.' That
is a psychological version of what for Shakespeare was rather moral and
religious. 'Mean souls alone repent in misery'—which here is nemesis.

murder and of blood, and, enfolded in that flame like Dantesque spirits, they live and perish. Even in horror of the crime they perpetrate it. When the thought first comes to Macbeth it is a 'horrid image,' which sets his hair on end and blinds him to the world about him; it seems a 'horrid deed' as he ponders it; and as to his victim he stealthily takes his way, 'withered Murder towards his design moves like a ghost.' Immediately afterwards, his hands are a sorry sight, and he is afraid to think what he has done—look on it he dare not. And all that follows is but nemesis—the blood that will not wash out of his own or his Lady's memory, the Amen which sticks in his throat, the voices that bid him sleep no more, the visitation of the ghost, the sleep-walking and 'the terrible dreams that shake us nightly,' the 'scorpions' in his mind, the 'torment' and 'restless ecstasy.' No sheer dread of detection or punishment is this, neither is it anything recognizable as remorse or repentance, but a bodying-forth of unearthly fears and more than mortal misery. It is in the form of fear, say Lippert and Westermarck, that conscience appears among the simpler peoples. Orestes and other impious ones, hated by the gods, and hounded by the Eumenides, do not humble themselves but go mad. Perhaps Shakespeare was endeavouring to present something equivalent to the ravings of the ancient blood-stained hero or the wailings of the chorus. Certainly, as we shall see, he was following the tradition not only of Senecan but of Elizabethan drama in making the hero and his lady see all the tragic horror of their deed, both before and after its commission. And not only dramatically but psychologically he was for the age correct. The poet wished to present the fall of a not ignoble soul, thrust on by his wife and by what he takes for the sanction of fate. To have made him feel a real pity or repulsion before the deed and a repentance unto life immediately after it (if really we can conceive the like) would have made him seem more of a hypocrite than to some he appears already.[*]

Ne pentere e volere insieme puossi.

A distinction is no doubt to be made between Macbeth and Lady Macbeth. Hers is the clearer case of theological 'despair,' or 'the horrors,' ending, as Burton describes it, in suicide; she, if any one, has 'cursed her better angel from her side and fallen to reprobation.' Macbeth is cut off before he has got so far. He is not much troubled, indeed, by thoughts of hell or judgment, but by the miseries of a murderer in this world—'but here, upon this bank and shoal of time.' 'The pricke of conscience,' says Holinshed, '(as it chanceth ever in tyrants, and such as atteine to anie estate by unrighteous means) caused him ever to feare least he should be served of the same cup, as he had ministered to his predecessor.' But the voices that he hears and the torments that he suffers prove that his fears stick deeper than that. Tom Davies was nearer than we to the stage tradition; and it is so that he understands the case as he speaks of Macbeth's 'remorse and agonies, and the torments he suffers in the midst of successful villainy,' though he of course failed to notice that such a conscience was psychologically inappropriate. In Shakespeare and the Elizabethan drama in general conscience is often presented thus pragmatically and concretely. It concerns itself with punishment, and expresses itself rather in terms of punishment than of sorrow for the sin. As we have seen, the wicked suffer remorse for the most part just before death. Leontes, as Wetz remarks, sees no fault in himself until overtaken by misfortune, which he considers a judgment; and so both Gloster and his two sons look upon his blindness. In character after character in *Richard III* conscience awakes only

[*] See the discussion of Macbeth's character and these phenomena of conscience in chapter iii, section 1, *et seq.*, to which this is supplementary.

when they suffer, or when they are troubled by supernatural voices or visitations, as in Cardinal Beaufort, Macbeth, and Alonso in the *Tempest*. Indeed, they that have done ill, the good and the bad alike—Claudio in *Much Ado,* Othello, Leontes, Borachio, Posthumus, Iachimo—sometimes long for punishment, and to have felt punishment relieves them. That Borachio or Iachimo should have such feelings is about as plausible as any real remorse in Richard or in Massinger's Domitian—this last case, indeed, and Richard's and Macbeth's are similar, all three undergoing spiritual sufferings without penitence or pity and visited by their victims' ghosts.

The Machiavels, on the other hand, are cheerful, untroubled almost to the end; and, despite the defiant and diabolical quality in their merriment, they are therefore far nearer to the criminal nature as we now know it and represent it in art. But the less deeply dyed in evil of Shakespeare's time, and also before his time and after, are gloomy, and suffer in this rather external spiritual way. It is nemesis, and certainly the example of the Greek Orestes and the Senecan Hercules affects the poet, as well as his own moral and theological psychology. A similar torment of mind, from without rather than from within, is to be found not only in Shakespeare's earlier plays but in many others of the time, such as *Arden of Feversham,* the *Warning for Fair Women,* and the anonymous *True Tragedie of Richard III;* the hero of which last is troubled after his coronation by raging fiends, and later, sleeping or waking, by ghosts gaping for revenge. Regan, in the old play of *King Leir* (1594), declares, in soliloquy, without the slightest warrant, that she feels 'a hell of conscience in my breast.' The Duke in Webster's *Duchess of Malfi* reels and staggers when he sees the face of his sister, whose cruel death he had caused and with his whole heart desired, and almost immediately goes mad. In his subsequent incoherent utterances he dwells in memory on the scene and

circumstances of his crime, as does Lady Macbeth in her
sleep-walking, but is not so much penitent as, in Bosola's
words, bowed down under a fatal judgment. As Rümelin
says of hers, his conscience is given a demonic, not a psychologically conceivable character. And without the madness,
there is the same unpsychological conscience even in more
modern work. Racine's Phèdre has seemed to Chateau-
briand 'la chrétienne reprouvée, c'est la pécheresse tombée
vivante dans les mains de Dieu'; and generally her spiritual
state has been interpreted in the terms of Jansenism. But
it is sufficiently explained by the influence of Euripides and
Seneca, as in these words:

> Quid poena præsens conscius mentis pavor
> Animusque culpa plenus et semet timens?
> Scelus aliqua tutum, nulla securum tulit.
>
> (*Phædra,* 163)

So Gozzi, in *Il Moro di corpo bianco,* gives Don Enrico,
the villain, who knows no sorrow or regret for what he has
done, most unquiet dreams, invaded by furies and horrible
spectres.[5] And Schiller and Coleridge, perhaps reinforced
by their Kantian philosophy, have put before us, in Franz
Moor and Osorio, examples of what, in the latter case,
Professor Sharp has called a 'monstrosity, sorrow for a
misspent life, horror of crime and self-loathing, made to
arise in a nature that possesses neither sympathy nor honour
nor antipathy to treachery.' The President in *Kabale und
Liebe* is even more remarkable. Almost as deficient in
moral sense as mortal could be, he complains of the pangs
of conscience, his sleepless nights, his restless pains, even
while he mocks at honour and virtue and follows the paths
of wickedness.

7.

To-day we think differently. Carlyle, in the infancy of
the science, took even the psychologists to task:—

[5] III, i.

Psychologists commit one sore mistake; that of searching, in every character named human, for something like a conscience. Being mere contemplative recluses, for most part, and feeling that Morality is the heart of Life, they judge that with all the world it is so. Nevertheless, as practical men are aware, Life can go on in excellent vigour without crochet of that kind. . . . He who looks neither before nor after, any farther than the Larder and Stateroom, which latter is properly the finest compartment of the Larder, will need no World-theory, creed as it is called, or Scheme of Duties: lightly leaving the world to wag as it likes, with any theory or none, his grand object is a theory and practice of ways and means. Not goodness or badness is the type of him: only shiftiness or shiftlessness.[6]

Or, putting it somewhat differently but really to the same effect, this great man, himself none too sympathetic, again declares:

Were he [our enemy] the wretch of our imaginings, his life would be a burden to himself; for it is not by bread alone that the basest mortal lives; a certain approval of conscience is equally essential even to physical existence; is the fine all-pervading cement by which that wondrous union, a self, is held together.[7]

And such is the spirit in which villains are to-day presented. Even so recently as in 1893 James Runciman declared that the only ones correctly drawn were Barry Lyndon and Little Stubbs, who are untroubled in their self-esteem,—and have a correspondingly poor opinion, I may add, of their enemies and the virtuous. But the pangs of conscience do not much trouble Ibsen's characters either —though of villains he has none—not Gina, who has had too much to do getting through the day's work, nor Rebecca West, who had lured Beata to her death, nor Hedda who lured Lövborg, nor Borkman, nor the pious serpent the Princess Helena. Chekhov's Uncle Vanya, otherwise not at all a bad fellow, tries several times in succession to kill a man for the mere fault of a selfishness which had marred the happiness of the family, and regrets not the attempt but its failure. Mr Granville Barker's Voysey lives on the

[6] *The Diamond Necklace.*
[7] Essay on *Voltaire.*

difference between the four per cent he pays his clients and the fruits of his speculation without a qualm, hoping to pay them back their principal if he can. Even fine and serious men and women do not regret their sexual transgressions as (when the men are not joking about them) they do in Shakespeare, if we are to judge by Hauptmann's Rose Bernd, Sudermann's Marikki, or Jones's Michael. And in the novel—if we pass by the comic characters, for these, as we shall see, were, even in early times, treated more realistically than the serious ones—there are the characters, not wholly good or bad, of Stendhal, Zola, Balzac and the great Russians, who if they do wrong do not so promptly and perfunctorily suffer for it. Hardy's Tess has no remorse after she has killed the man; Stendhal's fine and exquisite Duchess of Sanseverina has none either; and Emily Brontë's Heathcliff, near his end, declares, 'I have done no injustice, and repent of nothing.' Even Sophia, the worthy dame in Bennett's *Old Wives' Tale*, does not trouble herself much about the money she took from her aunt when she eloped, and not at all about the £200 she took from her unworthy husband before she left him. And the hero of Wells' *Tono Bungay*, treated very sympathetically, shares in a commercial swindle, is unfaithful to his wife, kills a man in Africa, and never suffers from remorse at all.

8.

And the facts are for us. Gloom, in remorse or spiritual torment immediately after (if not before) the deed, and a troubled sleep—these are the striking characteristics of the murderer in earlier drama. We all, I surmise, have at least some vague, unaccountable notion of hardened and impenitent criminals as miserable and glum. 'In that gloomy brow,' whispers the heroine in melodrama, 'is written a volume of villainy.' And they that are good shall be happy, forsooth! The truth is that oftener it is the wicked, who are for the most part contented, cheerful bodies. After the crime they go on a lark or a debauch, buy new clothes and have their photographs taken, or, like Loeb and Leopold, play a demure game of cards with their own unsuspecting families. As they take it, they are not actors in a tragedy but in a comedy, or else that sort of tragedy (a taste for which is attributed by Hazlitt to Iago) in which they are not so much villains as producers and stage-managers. Here is a point at which Iago makes one of his nearest approaches to reality, as, with slight material motives, like Loeb and Leopold, he takes an esthetic or sensational—in any case egotistic—delight in crime.[8] But these are the intellectuals; and for the most part, as Mr Cabell says, men go wrong (consciously or unconsciously) without dignity, and, as it were, sin from hand to mouth. Indeed, as in early tragedy they do not, they oftener sin and commit crimes without planning or contriving, on the spur of the moment, like Diana of the Crossways (though her fault was not so serious) in 'a swoon of the mind' and through an impulse, or, like the hero of Rossetti's *Last Confession* and Masefield's *Nan*, in a fit of jealous indignation. Yet in such cases the reader or audience expected it if the doer did not, and the deed was a natural outburst of passion, not a freak or whim. And instead of hearing, like the Scottish thane and the English king, ominous voices, they are likely, after a murder, to fall asleep on the spot, like Pozdnyshef in the *Kreutzer Sonata;* or at least, like Benvenuto Cellini, Raskolnikoff in *Crime and Punishment,* and Julien Sorel in *Rouge et Noir,* to sleep the better after-

---

[8] In Loeb and Leopold, of Chicago, this is very obvious. According to reports they were seeking the 'perfect crime,' to satisfy their delight in intrigue and mystification, in notoriety, and in emotions for their own sake. Loeb discussed the murder, the day it appeared in the papers, with his mother, who was properly, delightfully horrified, and as he said afterwards, 'he got quite a kick out of it.' In Iago, however, this esthetic aspect is much overshadowed and obscured by his sheer love of evil. In Loeb and Leopold there is nothing hellish—in them human sympathy and moral sense are reduced to zero, so to speak, not below it.

wards.⁹ They have done their work, they have had their way.

9.

Much of this effect of 'the horrors' is produced by what is purely technical: like most Elizabethan and many Shakespearean characters, Macbeth often comments on his feelings instead of uttering them. He dwells on the misery and hideousness of his situation rather than on his own purposes and the end in view. As he approaches the royal chamber, it is a dagger that he sees before him, not the crown. And he dwells on the circumstances and consequences of the crime—punishment, public indignation, the deep damnation of violating the laws of hospitality and of killing a king so virtuous and meek. He is preoccupied with all the scruples of pit and poet. Likewise he has a curious eye, as critics have remarked, for what poetically befits the occasion, and cries to the earth not to hear his steps for fear the very stones prate of his whereabouts—and so betray him?—and so 'take the present horror from the time which now suits with it.' Thus King John, in the midst of his bloody instructions to Hubert, expresses a wish, as Professor Raleigh observes, for the fitting stage effects— darkness, the churchyard, and the sound of the passing-bell. Lady Macbeth is more business-like while she is strengthening her husband's feeble knees, but even she appeals to his pride, as Professor Firkins says, rather than to his ambition, and in her solitary meditations she flies wide of the mark. Mr Sharp sees in her invocation 'come you spirits that tend on mortal thoughts' signs that she had taken to her husband's sentimentalizing ways. Instead of praying to be unsexed and filled from crown to toe top-full

⁹ 'Tully,' says Burton, 'makes it an argument of Roscius Amerinus' innocency, that he killed not his father, because he so securely slept.' But compare the criminologists; and such cases as that in the *Times* (London), Oct. 1, 1922, of the farm lad near Nantes, who, in a fit of rage, killed seven in his master's family, and then went home and slept.

of direst cruelty, she might more appropriately be longing
and scheming for the 'golden round' of Scotland, 'burning,'
as Holinshed says, 'with unquenchable desire to bear the
name of queen.'

But by her sentimentality, if for the moment we must call
it that, Lady Macbeth came honestly enough. The kings
and queens (good or bad) in the early histories such as *King
John, Richard II,* and *Richard III,* measure and analyse
their woes or vie with each other endlessly in their lamentations, declare their passions to be greater than all
other men's or wish that they themselves were equal to
them, though some necessary question of the play be then
to be considered. And in so late a play as *Antony and
Cleopatra* the hero, when his star is setting, cries, dropping
into a Hebraism which a commentator has naïvely suspected
him to have caught from the lips of King Herod or picked
up in the streets of Jerusalem,

> O, that I were
> Upon the hill of Basan, to outroar
> The horned herd!

Teach me, he beseeches, and such a lesson Elizabethan
heroes are ever and again beseeching to be taught, though
they know it but too well already:

> Teach me,
> Alcides, thou mine ancestor, thy rage.
> Let me lodge Lichas on the horns o' the moon.

He has in mind the Hercules of Seneca, and it is from
Seneca, in large measure, though not directly, that this vein
of self-conscious comment and declamation is derived. With
her husband's ways Lady Macbeth's invocation has nothing
whatever to do. There is many another like it—Othello's
invocation to black vengeance in the hollow hell, Iago's
climactic outcry to hell and night, and those speeches which
are the source of all these, the fire-eyed invocations and
apostrophes to the infernal powers of Seneca's Medea and

Atreus. The psychology for the moment is of the simplest: your hero prays to God, and your villain prays, with the Jews and the heathens, to the Devil!

> Noctis æternæ chaos,
> Aversa superis regna manesque impios
> Dominumque regni tristis et dominam fide
> Meliore raptam, voce non fausta precor.
> Nunc, nunc adeste, sceleris ultrices deæ—(ll. 9-12)

cries Medea, and Dolce's Marianna after her; or as Guinevere has it in the *Misfortunes of Arthur* (1587):

> Come, spiteful fiends, come heapes of furies fell,
> Not one by one, but all at once! My breast
> Raues not inough . . . I, ii.

Though she is rather echoing Atreus:

> non satis magno meum
> ardet furore pectus, impleri iuvat
> maiore monstro—(*Thyestes* 252-3)

Or as Browne has it in the *Warning for Faire Women* (1599) [10]

> O sable night, sit on the eye of heaven,
> That it discern not this black deed of darkness!
> My guilty soul, burnt with lust's hateful fire,
> Must wade through blood to obtain my vile desire.
> Be then my coverture, thick ugly night.

And as for Macbeth's preoccupation with the horror of the deed, not only after but before it, that is like the conduct of other murderers and evil-doers in Elizabethan drama (besides those just mentioned), both the nobler and the less noble than himself. The most remarkable case of horror before the deed in Elizabethan drama is that of Mrs Frankford and Wendoll, her paramour, in Heywood's *Woman killed with Kindness,* written about the same time as *Macbeth.* As the Scottish thane thinks not of the glory of the crown, so they think and speak not of their love

---

[10] The parallels to Lady Macbeth's invocation in this and the other Elizabethan plays were noted long ago, in the old *Variorum.*

and the joy of being in each other's arms, but only of the wickedness of it, even to each other. Who sins thus, against the grain?

This apparent self-consciousness, then, is another instance of the self-descriptive method, considered above,[11] a dramatic technique not as yet entirely differentiated from the epical and the lyrical. But it is also a matter of morals and of tragic terror—the way of the transgressor is hard. Macbeth does the deed forgetful of his purpose, mindful only—as are Heywood's adulterous lovers—of the sin. He kills the king in horror; you wonder, and a few candid critics have wondered, how he manages to kill him at all. He pays tribute to Duncan's virtues before he kills him, and is without excuse. Every man, in order to be able to do a thing, says Tolstoi, whose sense of sin seldom overrides his sense of fact, has to consider it important and good. Or, as Croce says, we consider it good because we intend to do it:

Per risolversi a un'azione (dicono), è necessario aver giudicato: 'quest'azione è utile, quest'azione è buona.' Noi non vogliamo le cose, perchè le conosciamo utili o buone; ma le conosciamo utili e buone, perchè le vogliamo.

As in the days when there was no king in Israel, every man does, and always will do, that which is right in his own eyes. And the sinner sins nothing loath. 'In the joy of the actors lies the sense of any action. *That* is the explanation, that the excuse.' How shallow and obsequious of us to bow to Shakespeare and almost all the choice and master spirits in drama and fiction up to the present age, in their opinion that though there is joy in our hearts when we engage in works of justice and mercy there is no joy in the heart of the miser as he hoards or in the heart of the murderer as he kills! Do we do good because, despite all, we love it, but they evil because they hate it? We ourselves know better.

[11] See chapter iii, section 4.

Yet, even Tolstoi, his sense of fact for the moment quite overriden by this superstitious notion of sin, lets Nikita, in *The Power of Darkness,* abhor the hideousness of his crimes, whilst he commits them, as deeply as does Macbeth. 'But before Nikita was led into so dire a situation,' says Stevenson, 'he must have been tempted, and temptations are beautiful.' Beautiful they are, in Tolstoi's earlier days, to his Anna and Wronsky. 'You sinned with me a pleasant sin,' writes in her *Convent Threshold* Christina Rossetti, the passionate saint. 'Y-a-t-il rien de plus agréable?' cries Don Juan, defiantly. 'Il est vrai,' Sganarelle must needs confess; 'je conçois que cela est fort agréable et fort divertissant.' Ben Jonson, in his *Discoveries,* tells of the thief who had a longing at the gallows to commit one robbery more before he was hanged; and Jonathan Wild, in the same predicament, found even there a way to satisfaction by applying his hands to the chaplain's pocket and emptying it of a bottle-screw, which he carried out of this world in his hand. But in one of the thirteenth-century windows at Chartres Jesus is tempted in the wilderness by the Devil undisguised, hideous with leer and horn and tail. When, in popular lore, was the tempter ever beautiful, ever tempting? Only in recent times has, in painting, the carnal temptation of St Anthony been made plausible. Imogen, tempted by Iachimo, with overtures so repulsive that no lady could entertain them, is not really tempted at all.

10.

It is not, however, merely a matter of villains or evil-doers, of conscience and temptation. A frank way generally have not only wicked folk but good folk in Shakespeare and the later dramatists of talking or thinking about themselves and their doings and feelings. Lady Macbeth prays to be filled with cruelty and have her milk turned to gall; Macbeth calls his deed treason and murder and bewails his hangman's hands; and all the evil-doers, from Aaron to

Iachimo, and Proteus to Parolles, plead guilty, before the deed as well as after, as evil-doers seldom do.   But Proteus, in a comedy, where less rigour is exercised, might, you would think, have slipped into treason to his friend and his sweetheart, as in life he would have done, without knowing it.   And the good and virtuous, as we have seen, like Othello and Brutus, and the innocent, like Imogen and Miranda, are of their qualities well aware.   In part all this is owing to the natural and inevitable limitations of dramatic form, within which the dramatist has not the liberty of the novelist to comment in his own right and person.   Yet of substitutes for that, to preserve the integrity of the character, he does not (as we shall see below) avail himself as much as he might; and in part this self-descriptive method is owing to the fact that dramatic form was not yet completely evolved, but probably in equal measure to the fact that such development was not demanded by the public, at least, perhaps not by the poet.   No Elizabethan dramatist—no dramatist after all before the middle of the nineteenth century—quite realized, or showed that he realized, that a character is not one who tells his story but acts it, and speaks, not for audience or dramatist, but only for himself. In their dramaturgy, as in their stage-management, they used signs and placards.   Don John and Borachio call themselves villain, and the puritanical Angelo calls his passion for Isabella lust, just as in earlier times the devils in the miracle-plays bawl out to their simple-minded audience in the market-place or on the green that they are 'full of gret envy, of wrathe, and wycked hate'; or, for the matter of that, as did Seneca's truculent heroes and heroines more than a thousand years before.   In all times, and even long after the days of Steele and Sheridan, the purposes of satire have been accommodated by an unreasonable readiness in quack and pettifogger, rakehell and Delilah, through soliloquy or confidential conversation, to expose themselves; and all that keeps the good characters—not altogether effectually—from making their exhibit in turn, is, as they themselves immodestly remark, their modesty. So says that great marvel of Elizabethan art, Othello, as well as the eighteenth-century prigs and prudes; and many an Elizabethan hero like Shakespeare's Brutus and many a heroine like Imogen are somewhat spoiled for us by their complacence. For the same reason one can hardly help preferring to Antigone the less lofty soul Ismene, in Sophocles.

Artistic reticence such as ours, moreover, is, as I have remarked elsewhere,[12] out of harmony with the system of dramaturgy prevalent in Shakespeare's time, founded on the culture of the time. Whom to hate and whom to admire the Elizabethan audience was commonly told and taught, for the sake of explicitness, at the beginning; and in that day the dramatist, if so disposed, would not have dared to risk the puzzling of men's wits as only an Ibsen dared—and puzzled them—at the close of the century just gone by, by practicing on them any notions of relativity. The farther back we go, of course, the more plain-speaking there is. In Shakespeare's early tragedies and in Marlowe's there is more than in Shakespeare's masterpieces. Barabas and Aaron stalk down to the front of the stage and, in set speeches, tell the long beadroll of their high crimes and misdemeanours. Marlowe's Baldock is not a Machiavel, and is not soliloquizing either, and yet speaks as no man could and live:

> Spencer, thou know'st I hate such formal toys,
> And use them but of mere hypocrisy,
>
> .   .   .   .
>
> Which made me curate-like in mine attire,
> Though inwardly licentious enough
> And apt for any kind of villainy.—*Edward II,* II, i.

That is almost in the unabashed and whole-hearted vein of the mysteries; but this frankness lingers on in later popular

[12] Cf. 'Anachronism in Shakespeare Criticism' (*Mod. Phil.,* 1910), pp. 561-62, 567-68, and the chapter on Shylock, above.

plays such as Heywood's *Iron Age,* where Sinon and Thersites touch freely upon their ugliness, cowardice, and villainy. The Phædra of Euripides and Seneca recognizes beforehand the criminal character of her passion and intrigue, as does Macbeth that of his, without the psychological warrant and justification given her by Racine, who makes her debate and resist it. Even in the more refined art of Sophocles, as in the *Œdipus* and the *Ajax,* the great men and the pure women reveal their greatness or purity more clearly and directly than in life or in drama they would to-day. Thus do loose or scabrous people lay bare their own vices in Plautus.[13] And if Shakespeare's Julius Cæsar seem to us to boast and swagger unduly, the self-descriptive manner, as has been shown, comes down from the heroes and tyrants of Senecan and Renaissance tragedy, and from the mysteries too. And the same dramatic method appears in the French, German, and Spanish drama; Lope and Calderón, for instance, betraying a greater degree of directness and plain-speaking in early stages of their development and a less in the later. In English drama it abounds until after the day of Ibsen.

II.

The technique of the time, then, and of earlier times, is in this directness and plainspeaking of Shakespeare's evil-doers apparent; and it is this that I am concerned to show, (and that in such regards they are not, as the critics say, the images of Nature) rather than to answer that other question (which we immediately approach) whether Shakespeare himself conceived them differently. The truth is, apparently, that the standard of morality is a rather rigid one, and Shakespeare makes his criminals conform to it even in their non-conformity. Macbeth and Lady Macbeth themselves call it a murder because it is a murder, because public and poet could see it in no other light—not in *their* light, to

[13] See the *Mostellaria,* I, ii, the soliloquy of Philolaches.

be sure. Or rather, the poet did not see it consistently. 'This night's great business'—'our great quell'—she once calls the murder—quite truly, in her exaltation. There is much in Shakespeare which shows that he himself had observed (though he does not always write accordingly) the truth registered by the great Lord Chancellor—that 'there is no man but speaketh more honestly than he can do or think.' Everybody, for that matter, knows that everybody else is not quite what he thinks he is; and if a man troubles to tell us his word is as good as his bond, and a woman that she abhors gossip, we are the less likely to entrust money to the one or a secret to the other. And a wickeder man or woman is not likely to be franker with others or himself. Often your thief still protests after the booty has been found upon him; the wench protests to landlady and doctor even in the hour that her child is born; and the murderer calls God witness to his innocence at the moment when, as he believes, he is to appear in judgment before him. But it was mostly in a comic light that poet or public then looked on a criminal's fair-speaking, as in those very explicit instances where the words 'convey' and 'purchase' are used for 'steal,' where Shakespeare's and Dekker's whores and bawds indignantly disdain to answer to such names, and where Falstaff calls himself and his fellows 'gentlemen of the shade, minions of the moon.' It was so in France as well. 'En France c'est en général du côté du sarcasme qu'ont glissé nos réalistes,' says M. Faguet; 'le réalisme aux siècles classiques n'est d'ordinaire considéré que comme matière d'œuvre comique.' Much the same may be said of Italy in the same period and before. Thus before the nineteenth century only the slighter forms of criminality got treated with any measure of realism and truth. The giddy comic muse ventured far nearer to fact than the tragic, but she shied away from murder.

And another truth is, that the poet, like others of his day and after, does not seem to realize the spontaneousness, the unconsciousness of sin. Lying and hypocrisy come to a man naturally, but in Shakespeare or in Molière, in Corneille, Steele, or Sheridan, no man, however hardened, ever slips into either. The Lying Lover is virginally aware that he is a liar; Tartuffe both is, and intends to be, a fraud. La Bruyère and Marivaux, in a later age, glanced satirically at hypocrisy made thus deliberate and obvious, though in even their own hands it is still conscious enough, and does not become otherwise till the days of Browning and Meredith, Ibsen and Becque.[14] So Richard and Macbeth are the murderers they intend or hesitate to be. Men of principle, these, not of impulse.

And here, no doubt, is a reason why the merry rogues of Shakespeare and his times leave us to-day somewhat cold. They are conscious and therefore malicious—Falstaff, Autolycus, Panurge. Falstaff himself is not a pretty sight fleecing his landlady, the helpless conscripts, or even Justice Shallow, however rich his humour and quick his jests. Monsieur Bergson insists that it is the unconscious self-betrayal or inconsistency that is comical; so for the most part it is in Molière, with whose practice, especially, he squares his theory; and though this is not the whole truth it is that part of it which is more in keeping with our taste to-day. Consciousness in the rogue—unconsciousness in the victim—that was the method of Plautus and of Shakespeare, and of Molière too sometimes; but in the rogue we prefer unconsciousness. Frau Wolff in the *Biberpelz,* intent, both for herself and her family, on getting ahead, is an example. She is a liar and a thief, but a fond mother and hard worker, and both bears a good reputation and, in a fashion, deserves it. 'You steal too much for an official of your rank,' says his chief to a subordinate in Gogol's story.[15] Or really to cut a slice from life, a burglar sentenced lately by the British Military Court at Cologne for illegal pos-

[14] See above, chapter iii, section 13.
[15] Quoted by Bergson.

session of a revolver, complained, to the German court, of
injustice, saying: 'Surely any one can see that I could not
carry on my work in this profession without a revolver.'
And a burglar in prison at Stillwater, Minnesota, recently
wrote to the department of chemistry at the State University making inquiry concerning certain new and powerful
explosives which, he thought, might prove useful to him
'in his profession.' (In American prisons offenders are
treated so considerately nowadays that they keep their
naïveté unimpaired.) Or, to return to fiction, 'Fielding's
Jonathan Wild,' says Meredith, 'remarks upon the unfair-
ness of a trial in which the condemnation has been brought
about by twelve men of the opposite party . . . it is
immensely comic to hear a guilty villain protesting that his
own party should have a voice in the law.' But when a
rogue in Shakespeare speaks more honestly than he acts or
thinks, it is generally a joke of which he is aware.

12.

That to Shakespeare himself his criminals' frankness
and self-consciousness are not altogether a matter of technique and the needs of the audience, is fairly evident, not
only from these but from other considerations. In the
first place, there is much plain-speaking that is unnecessary.
Comment by others, together with his own conduct and the
irony of the fate that befalls him (with appropriate comment again), would sufficiently reveal the wickedness and
duplicity of an Iago; the like does sufficiently reveal the
wickedness and duplicity of Tartuffe. It is as with the mad-
men—in life they do not know it when they are going mad,
still less when they are mad; but in Shakespeare they do,
though (if this be necessary) the audience could depend
for information upon others.

In the second place, however ill the villain speaks of himself he need not speak so truly and justly of the good.
Such words are not needed for dramatic purposes; and for

Iago to see the good in Othello and Desdemona (as Richard does in King Edward, Oliver in Orlando, or Edmund
in Edgar) whom he hates and tries to injure, confuses the
outlines of his character, makes him either a demon or a
fallen angel, who sees more than mortal can—sees not
only himself but others, as still others see him and them.
His true vein is when he speaks of them as dolts and asses,
of Cassio as 'a pestilent complete knave,' and of cunning
time-servers as fellows who 'have some soul'; and so the
dramatist does not adhere to Iago's point of view as well
as he can and when he well might. And Lady Macbeth,
even when she is not speaking of herself, subdues language
to her thought no more than when she is, and draws up an
abstract of her dear husband's character as roundly as if
it were a bill of indictment:

> Thou wouldst be great,
> Art not without ambition, but without
> The illness should attend it. What thou wouldst highly,
> That wouldst thou holily; wouldst not play false
> And yet wouldst wrongly win.

Save one, the words might have been spoken by Saint Peter
at the gate.

In the third place, that it is not merely a matter of technique (or else of a highly inflexible one) appears also from
the fact that the moral point of view is not more adjusted
to characters of mingled nature than to the wicked. Shakespeare may have believed in the true villain, who said, 'Evil,
be thou my good'; or his proper use of the conventional
words for the virtues may have been a mere concession to
his audience. But no such reason could apply here, before
the deed, where there is indecision whether to turn to the
right hand or to the left. 'Pitiful,' cries the atrocious
Tamora, like Richard and Dionyza,[16] 'I know not what it
means'; but so says Cassius, too, in soliloquy.

---

[16] *Pericles*, IV, i, 9.

Well, Brutus, thou art *noble;* yet, I see,
Thy *honourable* metal may be wrought
From that it is dispos'd;

and proceeds to show that he is the one to do it. What is strangest of all is that he adds:

therefore it is meet
That noble minds keep ever with their likes;
For who so firm that cannot be seduc'd?

Cassius is not of the finer fibre of Brutus, yet he thinks himself an honourable man, and it would not be like him here to be joking. Iago, moreover, calls his love for Desdemona lust; but the same word is used by the Puritan Angelo in speaking of his love for the saintly Isabella, as by that fairly decent character Valerio, in Beaumont and Fletcher's *Coxcomb,* when speaking of his love for the pure-minded and beautiful Viola. In retrospect and remorse such a word might be in place, but thus in the tide of passion, never. Temptations are not hideous but beautiful, and no man, good or bad, can find it in his heart deliberately to besmirch his dearest desires. Men act from inclination, and they do not headlong incline to what they hate.[17]

Parolles is another case in point. Like Falstaff, Bessus, in *A King and No King,* and Roughman, in Heywood's

[17] It is not for us to limit the range of human nature, and no doubt there are, rarely, those who can for a time take a delight in what they think to be wickedness, for its own sake. But this is in the spirit of bravado or rebellion, or of pride in intellectual enlightenment, like Loeb and Leopold's, when they sought 'the perfect crime'; and really they do not think it so wicked as they say. Only extraordinary environment or egotistic development leads to such an attitude; and these must needs be presented to explain it. Proust is an artist and psychologist whom I admire; but as it seems to me there is little justification for the hellish light that he casts over the scene (in *Du Côté de Chez Swann*) of Mlle Vinteuil's sensual indulgence. Such natures as hers and her friend's would have come to it quite naturally; they would not have been checked, as they would in the case of robbery or murder, by any definite consciousness of crime; they would not have felt the reproach of her father's picture, still less have been moved to spit upon it. The pervert takes to his form of indulgence as simply as the natural person to his.

Fair Maid of the West, he confesses to his cowardice at the end, when he can no longer be serving the needs of the audience for information, the cat being already out of the bag:

> Yet I am thankful; if my heart were great,
> 'Twould burst at this. Captain I'll be no more;
> But I will eat and drink, and sleep as soft
> As captain shall. Simply the thing I am
> Shall make me live.

'Shakespeare,' remarks Sir Walter Raleigh in this connection, 'dared to follow his characters into those dim recesses of personality where the hunted soul stands at bay, and proclaims itself, naked as it is, for a greater thing than law and opinion.' But what Shakespeare means to intimate is that the coward expects shrewdly to turn his cowardice to account—'safest in shame,' not above but beneath it, not within but without it, naked as no soul can be and endure. 'Is it possible he should know what he is and be that he is?' the First Lord had indeed asked in an earlier scene, after overhearing him; but that means only, 'can he know the evil of his way and yet follow it?' And Cressida is such another, with her soliloquy of remorse (V, ii, 106-112), just after giving away Troilus' token to Diomed. Troilus' observations are enough for the audience—and one so light o' love would not (so soon at least) have sincerely moralized. But Shakespeare himself seems to have had a moral bias. Even the wicked folk in his theatre, as we have seen, suffer the pangs of conscience, and no good or fine natures who have done wrong escape them. If he had not been with the Elizabethan formula of moral retribution and self-description fairly well content, he would surely have broken through it here or there, and have created for once a Tess or a Duchess of Sanseverina.

And, last of all, that it is not merely a matter of technique appears from the fact that the same technique is employed in a way that involves especial and peculiar indifference, as it seems, to the unpleasant effect of mere self-consciousness. I mean such matters as the boasting and swaggering of the great, or the absorption of the sorrowful in their sorrows (though forgetful of the cause), or the reference of the innocent to their innocence, or the elaborate parade of virtue by Calantha in Ford's *Broken Heart,* when, after each bit of terrible news, she keeps on dancing, and of Shakespeare's Brutus when he hears of Portia's death. Here no vice is in question. In all cases but the last, there is no moral purpose thereby served, and no moral conception or prejudice obeyed, and yet, in all, the same self-descriptive method. This may seem to prove the contrary—a technique which the dramatist in his day could hardly avoid; but if so, it counted with him for more than his knowledge of psychology, in cases where it was particularly in danger of leading an audience (if concerned with such matters) astray.

An examination of the *loci* shows it. Swaggering and boasting such as we find in most Elizabethan royal or heroic personages, including Julius Cæsar and Henry V, was no doubt acceptable to Elizabethan audiences not only because of the ancient [18] and still living stage tradition of *decorum,* but because of their rooted regard for a king as almost more than mortal. If swagger he would, had he not a right to do so? But I see no reason at all for their accepting the self-conscious sorrows of the sorrowful, or the self-conscious innocence of the innocent, as if genuine, save in tradition alone. And such acceptance shows an indifference on the part of them and the author to distinctions in art between what is conscious and what is self-conscious, though they were familiar with them as a matter of course in life. The Queens in *Richard II* and *Richard III,* Constance in *King John,* Mariana in *Measure for Measure,* and many

[18] It is found not only in Seneca and Renaissance tragedy but also in the ancient epic. Æneas consoles Lausus with the thought that he dies by the hand of the great Æneas (x, 830.)

another character, female or male, speak of their sorrow rather than of the loss that caused it; and clutch it to their bosoms as if of it enamoured, and from comfort estranged, somewhat as women had done in ancient drama, though with no such religious duty of lamentation to warrant them.[19] Woe-begone Mariana is embarrassed at being found not without the solace of a song, until the fatherly Duke reassures her.[20] In general the words of Elizabethan grief-stricken women show a regard for the situation, as in the unbinding of their hair, the garbing of themselves in black, sitting on the ground, or like Beaumont and Fletcher's Aspatia and Lillia literally wearing the willow. But the method pervades the Renaissance drama, and is to be found in Calderón, for instance, and notably in that drama of jealousy which independently shows a striking resemblance to *Othello, El mayor monstruo los zelos.* Mariamne, in *her* willow scene, shows a self-consciousness of which Desdemona in hers shows little trace, and when asked by her attendant whether she shall sing to her, assents, if her grief be not diminished,—

> Pués empieza,
> con calidad que el dolor
> hagas mayor;

and Herod himself, before this, is in his woe almost as conscious.[21] So too, ladies so far apart in spirit and experience as Cleopatra and Imogen bethink them at terrible or critical moments of their pale cheeks, and Miranda calls to witness her 'modesty' and 'innocence,' though Cleopatra's paleness, at least, could have been remarked upon by her hand-maidens, and Miranda's modesty and innocence sufficiently appears from her father's words and her own demeanour.

[19] So Sophocles' Electra clings to her grief, out of regard for her father's memory, ll. 108, 142, 223, 240, 832, 853.
[20] *Measure for Measure,* IV, i, 7-14. For other outward signs of emotion displayed, cf. chapter viii, sections 10, 11, and note 61.
[21] Scene i.

But all these are as nothing to Calantha and Brutus, who
have been exposed to misapprehension on the part of candid
readers to-day, and would have been, one would think, in
their own times as well. It is not merely what they say but
what they do, and—the one a Spartan, the other a Stoic—
both make exhibitions of their fortitude. Brutus had
heard of his wife's death before, and had just told Cassius, when, Messala having entered with news from
Rome, he in answer to a question denies having had
news of her, draws Messala out, bids him tell him
true and, on hearing the news again, says, as if he hadn't
heard it already, winning praises for his fortitude,

> Why, farewell, Portia. We must die, Messala.

Lamb, as he contemplates Calantha, is led straightway to
think of Calvary; but Hazlitt and Mr Archer in calling
her conduct a bit of 'funereal affectation,' and Mr Brander
Matthews in complaining of Brutus' complacence, are,
though true to the facts of the presentation, false to the
dramatists' intention and the spirit of their audience.[22] In
both scenes in question there are beautiful touches and
strokes of nature, if we can forget the situation.[23] Character is treated poetically, so to say, instead of dramatically
and with due regard to motive and point of view.

In all these respects, then, Shakespeare imparted to his
characters, both evil and virtuous, a trait of self-consciousness more pronounced than that required by the limitations
of dramatic form or the needs of an audience, contemporary or modern. But is it not idle to separate form from
content in the work of a great popular artist? He must,
in a measure, speak the vulgar language of his audience,
but in the end he contrives to say what he has to say. No

[22] See my article on 'Drama Old and New,' *Modern Language Review*
(1925), from which some sentences are borrowed; and above, chapter iii,
section 4.—Some critics, to find a way out, doubt the text of the scene in
Julius Cæsar.

[23] Calantha's explanation, in the following scene, when on the point of
death herself, is so poignantly lovely that it blinded Lamb to its inadequacy.

doubt Shakespeare could take a character's point of view, and shift his speech accordingly, if ever dramatist could; but he was not careful to keep it when morals and conscience were at stake or the villain was on parade—did not bear in mind the psychological necessity or esthetic propriety of keeping it. Iago invoking hell and night is a different being from Iago telling Roderigo that ' 'ere I would drown myself for the love of a guinea-hen, I would change my humanity with a baboon.' And vividly as Shakespeare realized a character he was apparently not aware how the impression it made would suffer from a self-descriptive and self-conscious manner. He was not fully aware that it was now he who was talking, not the character, not Punch but only the showman behind the curtain. There is a parallel in the arts of acting and painting, when applied, as Shakespeare's art often is, to the very bad or good or great. The gesture then is often the artist's. Upon the entering of Pyrrhus on the stage Sir Roger told the Spectator that he did not believe the king of France himself had a better strut; and a strut at times, not to say a swagger, befits most of Shakespeare's kings and his Cæsar. And in early painting the humility and sanctity of saints and martyrs is often beyond all measure, as they roll their eyes, bow their heads, point to their wounds, or hold up their pincers and gridirons. They often give us the same wrong impression of complacence or self-consciousness as do the virtuous people in Elizabethan drama.

In short, the doctrine of the point of view simply had not arrived. There was as yet no Ibsen in the drama, no Henry James in the novel, no *Ring and the Book*. No doubt it took longer to introduce and establish the point of view on the stage: an audience can give up finger-posts and leading-strings less readily than can a reader. Of the new plays thirty years ago at the Théâtre Libre, Lemaître remarked, as of a novelty:

La vilenie des âmes s'y trahit sans se connaître elle-même,
l'égoisme le plus affreux y parle naïvement le langage du devoir,
et le vice même y garde les dehors et la sécurité de la vertu et y est
dupe de sa propre décence—*Impressions,* viii, p. 55.

This is no such novelty now; even earlier, in Ibsen, Lemaître might have observed something the same in what
might be called the biological treatment of characters such
as Hedda Gabler and Rebecca West, who do not seem
wicked to themselves (being intent instead upon their purposes), and are not thought so even by others. But for the
Elizabethans that is the explanation—drama not yet fully
evolved, drama, not the stage. It has been suggested, and
of late years it has well-nigh become a commonplace of
criticism, that the platform stage, with the resultant 'prox-
imity of the audience, explains, even if it may not altogether justify, the confidential communications which the
characters of the Tudor drama are in the habit of making
to the spectators before them and around them . . . without the self-flattering subterfuges and self-deceiving disguises which generally prevent even the worst of men from
perceiving themselves as they appear to others.' But the
same phenomena appear in Greek drama, in the Latin,
Spanish, French, and German,—in all early drama as distinguished from the modern, and often before larger audiences, and with the actors still farther away. By a similar
process of reasoning the quiet endings of Elizabethan scenes
have been ascribed to the lack of a front curtain. But these
materialistic, mechanistic theories really do not carry us
far.[24] Great artists, in the long run, are irresistible, and
dramatists are not at the mercy of the carpenter; it is
rather the actors and their art that they have to consider.
Drama, acting, and the stage are no doubt inter-dependent,
but it is the drama ordinarily that leads the way. If the

[24] Cf. a review of Professor Matthews and Mr Clayton Hamilton by
Professor Firkins in the N. Y. *Post* a dozen years ago.

Elizabethans or the ancient Greeks had needed the front curtain, or the modern picture stage, they would have soon got it. And if, as Mr Archer says, 'the realistic portrayal of life demands a realistic environment or background, which we know that the platform stage of the Elizabethans did not supply,' the platform stage certainly does not demand the unrealistic. It does not require that the character should impart confidences—though it may more readily permit him to do so—any more than the curtain, now that we have it, makes our scenes end with a snap and a flourish as they did twenty years ago. We now have Shakespearean endings despite the curtain and all our facilities, simply because they seem to us finer art.

13.

In life it is in quite another vein that your criminal talks of himself or others. He has no mind to remorse, we have seen, and he has none to plain-speaking as well. He has what Shakespeare has not always granted him, his own natural point of view, and is not consciously the antipode of all morality. *Fingersmith* is his word for thief, *apaier* for *assassinate*. 'Convey the wise call it,' says Pistol to Nym; 'Steal! foh! a fico for the phrase.' 'Nay, dear,' says Borrow's old apple-woman; 'we never calls them thieves here, but prigs and fakers.' It is the universal instinct not to admit a defect, whether moral or physical; of a beauty at the court of Charles II it was said that though her hair was red, she did not call it so, and she thus had all the advantages of red hair without the inconveniences. More than two thousand years ago Aristotle remarked that 'pirates nowadays style themselves purveyors'; likewise in the eighteenth century they called themselves 'gentlemen of fortune,' 'brethren of the coast;' and in Dekker's and Shakespeare's day thieves and other criminals had as elaborate a canting vocabulary, or *argot,* as they have on the continent of Europe at present. 'All vices,' says Dekker in

the *Belman of London,* 'maske themselves with the vizards
of Virtue.' And Fielding, speaking of thieves, in *Jonathan
Wild,* declares that 'they have the words honesty, honour,
and friendship as often in their mouths as any other men.'
'A plague upon it when thieves cannot be true one to another,' is a joke, but all the better because an unconscious
one. 'Mais je suis homme d'honneur,' says Mérimée's Corsican bandit Brandolaccio, as he explains why, in his necessity, he does not levy on the population. Rouet, stepping
on the scaffold where he was to suffer for robbery and
murder, muttered, 'Cause a man to suffer death for such
a trifle!' And Dombey, writing after his first murder,
said that he hoped he should be pardoned this bit of child-
ishness. Often, indeed, criminals go so far as to express
satisfaction with their conduct, like Lemaire, who avowed
that he did not repent of anything except that he had not
killed them all (both father and son). Avinian, another
murderer, begged as a favour that he might be buried with
Lemaire, 'who spoke so well'; and he himself, in emulation,
declared on the scaffold, like a martyr, that it was 'the
truth' that had brought him to it. 'Ivan the Terrible
thought himself the deputy of the Most High.' When
asked by Lombroso whether he had ever killed anyone, a
certain Number 377 retorted 'I am not a butcher'; but when
he was reminded of the fact that he had got away with
plenty of pocket-books, he exclaimed, 'Ah yes! but what a
fine thing to do!' 'Glad of it'—'I'd do it again'—cries
the daily homicide in the newspaper to the bystanders or
the police, and (unless this be bravado) if he change his
mind afterward it will be only after he has been wrought
upon in prison by public opinion and the fear of death.
Instead of putting themselves in the wrong they put others
there. 'Je meurs en femme honnête,' wrote the Marquise
de Brinvilliers, the parricide and fratricide, 'et je le dois à
mes ennemis.' Even on the scaffold, as we have seen, about
to go as they believe to everlasting reward or punishment,

most murderers protest their innocence to the end. And when this lady's confessor, says Lombroso, begged her to change her words, she felt so incapable of thinking otherwise that she requested him to do it for her. So the loose-living Josephine in *La Veine* of Capus, instead of admitting inferiority, turns upon those who detect it. 'Tenez, vous et Clémence, vous avez l'esprit gâté par la lecture des journaux. Vous êtes socialistes.' Far from evincing Shakespearean remorse, the murderer is inclined, according to the criminologists, to scorn his victim like a savage with the dripping scalp at his belt; and rightly Browning lets Ottima, and Dostoevsky lets Raskolnikoff, hate their victims after the crime more than before it.

'Pour moi tous ces héros de tragédie,' says the Sea-Captain in the preface to Mérimée's *Famille de Carvajal;* 'ne sont que des philosophes flegmatiques, sans passions, qui n'ont que du jus de navet au lieu de sang dans les veines, de ces gens enfin à qui la tête tournerait en serrant un hunier. Si quelquefois un des ces messieurs tue son rival en duel ou autrement, les remords l'étouffent aussitôt, et le voilà devenu plus mou qu'une baderne. J'ai vingt-sept ans de service, j'ai tué quarante et un Espagnols, et jamais je n'ai senti rien de pareil.'

Such is the nature of those souls who, according to ancient and modern doctrine, 'have the law written in their hearts, their conscience also bearing witness and their thoughts the meanwhile accusing or else excusing one another'; or who, according to a philosophy which takes no counsel of psychology and the ways of the world, are not blind, even the most consummate villain of them, to the transcendental significance of the moral law.[25]

Like other people, indeed, criminals, even the worst of them, have their pet weaknesses and their pet virtues too. Their weaknesses are their crimes, having become such

[25] He knew himself a villain, and he deemed
The rest no better than the thing he seemed.
James Runciman, provoked by Byron's couplet, wrote, not many years ago, an essay on Scoundrels to show that all whom he knew of considered themselves estimable men.

under the pressure of public opinion; their virtues are like the virtues of others, and much they make of them. Their more estimable qualities are those of which they may be unaware; in the case of murderers, for instance, a tenderness for children, animals, and even for relatives as such. But some virtue or other they are almost certain to have to comfort them, in the face of others at least. The murderous inquisitor or fanatic has his piety and the approval of his God. The erotic and polygamous Mohammedans and Mormons deny themselves wine or other strong drink, and the Mormons even tobacco. 'An ancient thief-taker' once told George Borrow that all first-rate thieves were sober and of well-regulated morals, their bodily passions being kept in abeyance by their love of gain.[26] The jockey, in *The Romany Rye,* relates of his grandfather, the counterfeiter, that he would not betray his comrades, but 'told the bigwigs, who wanted him to do so, that he would see them further first; and died at Tyburn, amidst the cheers of the populace, leaving my grandmother and father, to whom he had always been a kind husband and parent,—for setting aside the crime for which he suffered, he was a moral man; leaving them, I say, to bewail his irreparable loss.'[27] The gipsies teach their female children chastity but also stealing and double-dealing. 'I don't much care being called a thief and a liar,' says Ursula in the same vivid narrative; 'but I tell you what, brother, if you ever sinivate again that I could be the third thing, so help me duvel! I'll do you a mischief.' 'Nous avons, il est vrai,' remarks the Corsican Della Rebbia in Mérimée's *Colomba,* 'beaucoup de meurtriers mais pas un voleur.' 'Pas d'argent entre nous, lieutenant,' protests the helpful Brandolaccio at the end of the story. The eighteenth-century pirates also, British or American, had their niceties and points of honour, and often were very particular about the keeping of Sunday.

[26] *The Romany Rye,* ch. xii.
[27] *Ibid.,* ch. xli.

Bartholomew Sharp 'was deposed from command, among
other reasons, because he was not particular, and had
fought battles and taken prizes on Sunday'—reasons, I
daresay, never given in any navy. Another pirate captain,
Bartholomew Roberts, and his fellows drew up 'articles' for
their better government, which forbade gaming at cards
or dice for money, and the seducing of a woman or carrying
her to sea on pain of death.[28] Many of the blood-thirsty
Jacobins were Puritans, severe against carnal sin. But
where are the virtues, such as others could acknowledge or
cultivate, in Richard, Edmund, or Iago? Milton's Satan
has more.

14.

Of Elizabethan Machiavels and villains the greatest is
Iago, the culmination of the development through Aaron
and Richard III.[29] He professes those tenets common to
the Elizabethan Machiavel and Machiavelli himself; as
egoism, the simulation of the virtues because of their use-
fulness, and the glorification of the 'will,' or *virtù*. Besides,
he has all the ways of the Elizabethan Machiavel on the
stage: his frank delight in intrigue and avowal of evil—of
dissimulation, lust and murder—the league with hell, the

[28] See A. H. Verrill, *The Real Story of the Pirates*, 1923.
[29] I am aware that both Professor Bradley and Professor E. S. Meyer
do not consider Iago to be a Machiavel: Mr Bradley, on account of his not
avowing atheism; Mr Meyer, on account of his betraying no direct knowledge of the *Principe*. I cannot here undertake to dispute the point; but
below (note) I show reason for holding Iago to be atheistical in spirit,
and I might insist not only on the tenets mentioned in the paragraph above
but on a Machiavellian maxim of Iago's such as that, questioned by Mr
Meyer, in the last line of Act II. In all my writing on Elizabethan subjects,
moreover (cf. my *John Webster*, pp. 98, 200-201), I have deliberately and
uniformly used the word Machiavel in a sense larger than that which
signifies merely an explicit connection with the name, personality, or precepts (genuine or garbled) of the great Italian; being concerned rather
with the type of character which springs into being with Marlowe's Barabas
and Guise, in whom the connection with Machiavelli, or Elizabethan
notions of him, is explicit, and culminates in Iago, in whom such a connection is at least not obscured. That development and culmination is unmistakable: Iago is a Machiavel whether labeled as such or not.

manipulation of the catspaw Roderigo (like Richard's Buckingham or Barabas' Ithamore) for the rough and risky work, honest and merry manners with the world, but threats and blood-curdling malice in his speeches to the catspaw and in soliloquy and aside. The essential difference between him and the earlier representatives of the type lies in the subtlety of the outlines. The violence of Richard and Aaron is here dissembled: to look at him this Machiavel is no lion at all, but wholly fox. Here is none of Aaron's bluster, and yet none of Richard's slime. Iago fumbles no prayer-book, keeps no company with bishops, admits indeed that he is but a man among men, and, speaking of Roderigo, confesses, as if he were no better than he should be, that

> with the little godliness I have
> I did full hard forbear him.

And between him and his underling there are not the fulsome exchanges of hypocritical affection that there are between Barabas and Ithamore, Richard and Buckingham, crocodiles caressing and caressed. It is the franker manner of Richard, his bluffness and soldierly cynicism, that Iago more especially affects, modified and seasoned with bonhommie. There is almost as much human nature in him as stage villainy, and a highly individual tone as well.

Iago is the great devil of the seventeenth century, as Goethe's Mephistopheles is of the nineteenth. The latter, old legendary matter put aside, is after all not a fiend, not the antipode of morality or the enemy of the soul of man, but his indispensable companion through the world; and he reflects an age when the steep barriers between the 'spiritual' and the 'carnal,' 'good' and 'evil,' faith and unbelief, were breaking down, and the soul of goodness in things evil was being laid bare. 'Votre philosophie dirigera votre art.'

Taine's words are not truer of art than of criticism. The spirit of the times is reflected in the criticism of Iago as much as in that of Shylock, Falstaff, and Hamlet. As in the case of Shylock and Falstaff, the critics have dissolved away his malice or baseness; as in the case of Hamlet, they have furnished him with an apparatus of self-deception, and founded his character on the unsounded deeps of the sub-conscious. The cause of this, apart from the general tendency of criticism to read contemporary ideas into works of art, new or old, has been the monistic philosophy of the time and the naturalistic and experimental psychology; the occasion is Iago's directness in moral matters, his 'motive-hunting,' his failure to live up to the motives he finds, and that peculiar Elizabethan or Renaissance dramatic trait of playing a part (an honest man in Iago's case—the mad-man in Hamlet's) 'for all it is worth,' so that at times it is not easy to distinguish the natural from the artificial and assumed. It is this, the humanity and bonhommie, that the modern critics insist upon, and the rampant devil of his soliloquies and asides has been pretty well exorcised or smothered. Hazlitt, who nevertheless recognizes Iago's malignity, long ago discerned his love of power, his craving for action, to 'prevent ennui,' and his artistic delight in getting up his plot, not on the stage, but at home, casting the principal parts among his nearest friends and connec-tions. All this is egoistic, yet as we have seen above,[30] though inhuman, not unhuman; but in various ways these suggestions, to the neglect of what is unhuman and diaboli-cal in him, have been developed since.

This has been done most fully and finely by Professor Bradley; and he thinks that the superabundant motives which Iago alleges are pretexts, conjured up to overcome an 'inner resistance,' and that the real motives—craving for action, delight in a sense of superiority and in the pain of his victim as proof of his power—are subconscious. Iago, then, is like Hamlet, only his pretexts are for action not for inaction; and even a safety-valve has been provided for

[30] See p. 358 and note.

him—grossness and indecency of expression, as for Hamlet's pent-up-feelings it was feigned madness—to relieve him from the discomfort of his hypocrisy. But the Kantian 'resistance' of the moral law in every man's bosom (therefore in Iago's), and so monistic a motive as the 'sense of power,' are ill in keeping with the dualistic Machiavel, who scoffs at conscience, and revels in his villainy and the help he has from 'all the tribe of hell.' Far from being a discomfort, hypocrisy is part of Iago's program and profession, sweeter to him than honey and the honeycomb. The conscience darkly working within him is no more than that familiarity with the true moral values of which we have already taken notice. He puts himself in the wrong by virtue of his own self-consciousness—by virtue of his maker's naïveté,—as to himself and to others he applies the ideally appropriate epithets with all the rigour of the Recording Angel. And his irritation at the goodness of others and the motive-hunting in his earlier soliloquies are no signs of 'uneasiness' or 'aversion.' The very accumulation of his motives and the uncertainty and flimsiness of his suspicions but show the hellishness of his purpose. Instead of denying the devil a conscience or moral sense, as we should do, for good and all, it is according to Shakespeare's lights to give him one, but perverted, turned upside down. Iago thinks as we do, but is as we are not. Planted at the very pole of our moral world, he is nevertheless delineated, so to speak, without regard to latitude, as on Mercator's projection. The meridians of his thought run straight and undeflected—are identical with our own.

Certainly Iago, like Aaron and Richard, is meant to be a malignant being; and whether Shakespeare would have us conceive of him or not as that 'inconceivability' (so Mr Bradley rightly calls it), one who loves and does evil for its own sake, his candour in soliloquy and aside lends colour to that interpretation. So far from really deceiving himself he mocks at himself if for the moment he does it:

And what's he then that says I play the villain?

．．．．．．．．．．

. . . . How am I then a villain
To counsel Cassio to this parallel course,
Directly to his good? Divinity of hell!
When devils will the blackest sins put on,
They do suggest at first with heavenly shows,
As I do now . . .

'He is not, you see,' says Coleridge, 'an absolute fiend; or
at least he wishes to think himself not so.' But Iago gloats
over the fair veil of honesty his villainy is wearing, and in
the words, 'Divinity of Hell! when Devils will the blackest
sins put on they do suggest with heavenly shows,' he tosses
it aside with a jeer. Possibly the difference between us is
merely a matter of emphasis; certainly by his phrase 'the
motive-hunting of a motiveless malignity' Coleridge means
something stronger than Mr Bradley would make of it.
Yet Mr Bradley keeps the balance evener than critics such
as Maginn and Richard Grant White, who think that Iago
has hardly any malice in him at all, and in his desire to get
on is, as it were, wrenched from his moral moorings and
swept out to sea. White for this reason objects to Edwin
Booth's acting of the part; but Mr George Woodberry
rightly says that a great actor is likely to be nearer to the
spirit of Shakespeare than the critics, and notes with
approval that 'while Booth would have Iago outwardly
amiable, he has not the least idea of reducing the dye of
villainy in which the character has been steeped by those
of old time. Inside, Booth has no doubt, Iago was a
spirit of hate. . . . What (in soliloquy) was the first
thought on his lips? "I hate the Moor." And perhaps in
that most difficult moment of the rôle, the climax of Iago's
fate, the elder Booth was right in making the expression
of this intense enmity dominant in the Parthian look which
Iago, as he was borne off, wounded and in bonds, gave

Othello,—a Gorgon stare, in which hate seemed both petri- ⚡
fied and petrifying.'

To be sure, Iago's motives are, as we have suggested
above and as everyone has noticed, inadequate. Most of
his motives he touches on but once; and he demeans himself as Professor Bradley says, not at all like one stung
with resentment, fired by ambition, or consumed with hatred,
the poisonous mineral of sexual jealousy, or lust. He
takes no particular pleasure in Cassio's place once he has
got it, and his glee at the success of his intrigue is not that
of an injured husband or a libertine getting even, a wife
for a wife. Having motives, then, he acts as if he had
them not. Shall we therefore discard them, and, like the
critics, get him new ones of our own? In so doing we discard Shakespeare and his words. Rather let Iago run his
course regardless of motive; like Aaron, Richard III, or
Marlowe's Barabas, the badge of whose lineage he bears,
being a Machiavel, or stage villain, who is utterly given
over to evil and shrinks at none. As such he has a charter
to do evil, liberal as the wind. And roundly he goes to
work intriguing and destroying, fired by no particular passion, but flaring up again and again with the central flame
of hell:

> So will I turn her virtue into pitch,
> And out of her own goodness make the net
> That shall enmesh them all.

>   Work on,
> My medicine, work! Thus credulous fools are caught;
> And many worthy and chaste dames even thus,
> All guiltless, meet reproach.

So the case becomes, I think, fairly clear. There is no
reason at all for positing self-deception, or the subconscious,
but there are reasons against it. In the first place, the sub-

conscious is too intangible a thing for almost any dramatic art; and as I have shown above [31] and elsewhere, it is certainly out of keeping with the Shakespearean. When a character deceives himself it is he himself in aside or soliloquy,—as Hamlet, when he falls a-cursing like a very drab, or Iago when for the moment he dallies with the notion that he is not playing the villain, or Desdemona when, anxious for the arrival of her lord on the quay, she beguiles the thing she is by seeming otherwise,—that detects it. Shakespeare here is by no means alone, and all the hypocrites (save the quite modern ones) that I can remember, whether in the drama or out of it, Aretino's, Molière's, Joseph Hall's, or La Bruyère's, are conscious and deliberate through and through. Fielding, Dickens, and Thackeray had keener interest than the far greater Elizabethan genius in motives and psychological processes, and in the novel had ampler opportunity to exhibit them; but as Sir Walter Raleigh says of the hypocrites of the first named, 'they do not trouble to deceive themselves as long as they can deceive others.'

In the second place, the soliloquy, as I have elsewhere shown, or the confidence imparted to an accomplice, is the clue given to the audience, and must be the truth itself. There must even the liar speak true, and it is to knock the props from under Shakespeare's dramatic framework to hold that Iago's soliloquies are lies—that he lies to the audience, to himself. And here is no real exception. Iago alleges motives which—save in the one case, 'I hate the Moor,' at the beginning of the play several times repeated [32]—are not his motives, and by the audience are plainly understood not to be. Pretexts, they are but conscious pretexts, and as such are labeled in his first soliloquy:

---

[31] See chapter iii, p. 126. I have here repeated a sentence.

[32] 'Though I do hate him as I do hell-pains' I, i, 155; 'I hate the Moor' iii, 373; 'I hate the Moor,' iii, 392.

> I hate the Moor;
> And *it is thought* abroad that 'twixt my sheets
> He has done my office. *I know not if 't be true*
> But I, *for mere suspicion* in that kind
> Will do *as if for surety*. He holds me well;
> *The better shall my purpose work* on him.
> Cassio's a proper man: let me see now:
> To get his place and to *plume up my will*
> *In double knavery*—I, iii, 391.

The whole process of his thinking is clearly that of a human
devil, if such there be. I hate the Moor—and let me find
some reasons for it. 'C'est certain, dit Panther, il ne reste
qu'à le prouver.' He is whipping himself on, or betraying 'his vile suspiciousness;' or else he is merely deceiving
himself—as Elizabethan characters do—barefacedly, in
the open. Later he conjures up a lust for Desdemona,
which he avows is partly to 'diet his revenge.' From all
this an audience would not find it difficult to take the hint
—their cue,—and the fact that these human and intelligible motives do not later shine through word or deed
only makes it clearer. What else was to be expected?
Have they not from the outset been told that

> Hell and night
> Must bring this dreadful birth to the world's light?

And the first words are of course the telling ones—those
which, as Mr Woodberry thinks, any dramatist, actor, or
audience would not discount—though Mr Bradley thinks
they would or should.[33] The case is, though not so clear
and obvious, just as certain as that of Barabas, Aaron,
and Richard III, or of Medea and Atreus. With her, as
Professor Vaughan well says, it is crime for crime's sake.
'She does not commit crimes for her designs, she forms
designs that she may commit crimes.'[34]

[33] *Shakespearean Tragedy*, p. 224. See below, chapter viii, section 2, and
note 9.
[34] *Types of Tragic Drama*, p. 91; and cf. *Medea*, ll. 45-50, 900-905. The
above interpretation of Iago's motivation is essentially that which I
offered in my article in the Kittredge Anniversary Papers (1912). Professor

15.

As for Iago out in the world—and out of the lime-light, as it were, of the Judgment Day—he is a different creature, extraordinarily vivid and human. To him apply some of Hazlitt's and his followers' analyses quite admirably,— love of action, sense of superiority, and the artistic instinct. But these motives are not subconscious, are not the motives that started him on his course, for on that he was already embarked in his all-too conscious diabolical soliloquies, and in his conversations with Roderigo, which save in what really concerns this silly gentleman are almost as frank. But what is genuine, what feigned, we cannot tell. Nothing in the drama of Shakespeare and of the Renaissance in general indicates so clearly the indifference of the dramatist to what we call psychology as this—characters feigning virtue, madness, melancholy, love, even villainy, almost throughout the play. It, together with the disguises, deliberate deceptions or involuntary delusions, slanders, misunderstandings, and mistaken identities, pervades all the drama of the Renaissance, tragedy and comedy alike; and this it is, no doubt, that has led the great director of the Burg-Theater in Vienna, Alfred Berger, to the opinion, referred to above, that life was to Shakespeare all a monstrous bit of play-acting, and justified passion as a cause of tragic conflict a thing to him wholly unknown. But it is not reasonable to infer from the plot or fable of a play or of many plays together, the poet's conception of

Schücking (1919) pp. 208 ff., offers an interpretation which at first seems different, but which, if consistent, is not so. He quotes with approval (as from the above the reader may infer that I would) Dr Wolff's opinion that the show of motives but proves Iago's 'vile suspiciousness.' But in his anxiety to keep intact the principle (which I propound above, as in my article on Anachronism in Shakespeare Criticism, 1910) that the information imparted in soliloquy is to be relied upon, he declares some of his motives to be bona fide, others bona fide for the moment, still others to be intentionally contradicted by the context and his conduct. To the audience, I think, most of these considerations and distinctions would not, and could not, be expected to occur; and are therefore beyond our purview.

life, particularly from the plays of the Renaissance, in
which the situations are violent and extreme and the result
of direct contriving. In the case of a person of the drama,
likewise, particularly the chief contriver or intriguer, it is
not reasonable at every point to infer something certain
concerning his character as a human soul. Richard Grant
White, to be sure, thinks Iago's honest and friendly manner
natural to him, calls him a prince of good fellows, the
most popular young man in Venice; and holds that the
word 'honest,' a score of times repeated, was to keep us
from representing him as a hypocrite and fraud, not, as I
think it must have been, to keep us from forgetting—and
the other characters on the stage from suspecting—that he
is one. And he thinks too that Iago, like Cowper, would
not have trod upon a worm, had it kept out of his way
and been no barrier to his success in life, and would rather
have done a service than an injury. Really what we should
do in the case of Iago and of Hamlet too is frankly to
say as Christopher North said of Iago—that the character
'is a riddle.' 'Now all human nature,' he continues, 'is
full of riddles; but it is the business of dramatic poets
to solve them—having proposed it he was bound either
to have solved it, or to have set such a riddle as the wit
of man could have solved in two centuries'—we may now
say three. It is not, however, the motives, the internal
make-up or mechanism of either character, that makes him
alive and immortal, but (as I am continually repeating) the
individual tone and manner, the expression, the life-giving
touch. And these characters are riddles only as we consider
them more curiously than we were intended to do.

16.

One of the vagaries of the criminologists is the finding
in Shakespeare's treatment of criminals traces of scientific
determinism. The incorrigible criminal, it is commonly
believed, is born such, is called indeed the *delinquente nato;*

and even those criminologists who do not adhere to such opinions regard the criminal as irresponsible, or almost wholly so, being the product of disease and degeneration, heredity and environment. Above we have considered how little this point of view applies to Richard, and in relation to Shylock [35] I have shown how utterly foreign it is to Shakespearean and Elizabethan ways of thinking. The bad blood in a man's veins and the bad company he had kept were then no extenuating circumstances. Jewish blood, Moorish blood, bastardy, ugliness, and poverty are the heritage of Elizabethan and Shakespearean villains, and they are but badges of infamy and shame. For the villains, moreover, there is no such refuge as that provided for the erring hero, the decree of Fate or Fortune. Aaron, Richard, and Iago, unlike Romeo or Othello, acknowledge none such, and their sins are on their own heads. They detect their own motives, acknowledge them to be evil, and follow them—uncoerced, unhindered—none the less. All that hinders them is without them, and in their hands they 'hold the twists of life.' How differently move the creatures of Balzac, who, like Hulot, stagger and even cry out under the tyrannous weight of their passions; or of Zola or Dostoevsky, who are seized by blind impulses like those of beasts of prey; or if it be objected that these are in the novel, those of Ibsen, Hervieu, or the modern Russians, who breathe the heavy air about them, creep through the tangle, and are caught in it they know not how or why. For this is another world than that revealed by earlier, explicit art, where the will is free and vision unclouded, and where, openly as on the plains of Troy, the game of life and death is played by man and man, God, Fate or Fortune, and the Devil. There all are free—all are at war.

But critics and criminologists will not have it so. Applied to criticism at any rate, Coleridge's words contain a truth, however it be with the contemplation of nature:—

[35] See chapter vi, section 14.

O Lady, we receive but what we give.

Two notions to-day possess us—that man, though often perverted, is not evil or in love with evil, and that he is the creature of heredity and environment. Neither idea plays any part, philosophically or practically, in Shakespeare, and yet people freely find it there. Richard struggling with a pitiless environment, Shylock more sinned against than sinning, Iago by misfortune 'warped out of humanity,' or as Mr Masefield would have it, 'by the world's injustice'—here the whole intention and purport of Shakespeare's writing is turned awry. Everything must be explained, and related to causes, regardless or even in defiance of the writer; and if Lear's daughters are wicked in the extreme, we are not content to impute it to the stars, as Kent wonderingly does, but must blame it—on their father. 'He has lived wholly in himself,' says Mr Stopford Brooke, . . . 'compact of vanity. Just imagine what those two haughty, high-tempered, hard-hearted, icy-minded, very intelligent women, who were now about forty years of age, had suffered from their over-bearing, hot-tempered father.' 'Poor man, he had a fool for a wife,' is an interpretation I have twice heard given for Browning's *My Last Duchess*. Had the critics scope, they would explain away the villainy and perfidy of Judas. How could he have been better, labouring under constant suspicion, and plainly told beforehand, as he is given the sop, that he is to be the traitor? The best, we know, not the worst, should be expected of pupils or disciples; and only by an humble faith can the gospel narrative be approved—only by an humble regard for the author's intention can it be understood.

17.

Concerning the religion of his villains Shakespeare is comparatively silent. Prudence and practical sense as an actor-sharer may have been the reason, or simply his

English inclination to let sleeping dogs lie. Desperate or villainous fanatics in his time abounded, but he let them be, and his clergymen are such hardly more than in name. Of his Machiavels, Aaron the 'misbelieving Moor,' evidently an atheist, is less blatantly such than Eleazar in *Lust's Dominion;* Richard III scoffs at prayer and holy thoughts, but after his dream prays on the spur of the moment to God and Jesus; Iago has not a word to say on the subject, though he repeatedly identifies himself with the devils and their cause, declares the will alone supreme, and in life and in the teeth of death keeps the haughty, contumacious tone of the enemy of God.[36] And the illegitimate Edmund, like Eleazar and the hero of Tourneur's *Atheist's Tragedy,* appeals to nature as his goddess. With this bias are conceived Shakespeare's villains generally. If they approach God they do it like the King in *Hamlet,* in hypocrisy or remorse. For them is reserved the stigma of scepticism: it is Edmund and Iago who pooh-pooh Providence and the stars. Quite so Don Juan, according to Sganarelle, does not believe in God, not even in the *loupgarou.* This conception of the criminal as an atheist, that is, God's enemy, or as a skeptic, lingers on popularly, of course, to-day, and in literature has died a hard death. Even Schiller made a sceptic of Franz Moor; and only of late have writers, like Stevenson in his portraits of cutthroat Calvinistic uncles, seen the expediency of making their criminals the contrary. That Browning's villains should be believers appeals to Mr Chesterton because it is wholesome doctrine (which would have startled the Elizabethans not a little), but it appealed to Browning himself no doubt because it is psychological

[36] The type of the Machiavel, enemy of God, is preserved, in nobler form, even at the end. Ordinarily Machiavels die cursing and blaspheming. Iago says, 'From this time forth I never will speak word.' 'What,' rejoins Lodovico, 'not to pray?' and that is the point intended. Generally the bad men in Shakespeare who are not Machiavels, as Edmund, have at the end a change of heart.

truth. Among two hundred assassins Ferri found not one avowed free-thinker. Of five hundred criminals, according to Lombroso, 71 per cent attend church, as compared with 70 per cent of ordinary people. Among 28,531 admissions to three metropolitan prisons, observes the Rev. J. W. Horsley, only fifty-seven described themselves as atheists, some of these being Mohammedans and Chinese. Thieves have masses said for luck; *chaque voleur a sa dévotion,* runs the proverb.

The thief invokes God, says the Talmud, while he breaks into the house. 'The theefe, the pirate, the murtherer, yea and the traitor,' says Montaigne, 'all call upon him, all implore his aid, and all solicite him, to give them courage in their attempts, constancie in their resolutions, to remove all lets and difficulties, that in any sort may withstand their wicked executions, and impious actions; or give him thanks if they have good successe.' And he proceeds to repeat a story of Queen Margaret of Navarre's about a Prince, then well-known, who on his way to and from an amorous assignation always stopped at a certain church to pray. 'Casanova,' says Lombroso, 'declares that all who live by an illicit trade have an exaggerated confidence in the aid of God.' Pope Alexander VI, as is well known, was one of the wickedest of men. Benvenuto Cellini had heavenly visions in prison, wore an aureole (rarely discernible, he says, by others) about his head ever after, and through life felt that God was at his right hand to guard and to bless. He composed psalms and read the Bible devoutly, certain of salvation, 'sanctified' as certain Methodists used to claim to be. The Marquise de Brinvilliers, one of the wickedest, as we have seen, of women, was, if wanting in remorse, far from wanting in piety; and it was from a convent, where that very day she had scrupled to avail herself of a dispensation from the duty of keeping the fast, that she was haled to prison and death. We all know that it is not well to trust too far deacons or elders,

Sunday-school teachers or superintendents, even though they may not be hypocrites; and Blunt and Wallin among the Mohammedans, found, according to Westermarck, those most assiduous at prayer the greatest scoundrels. When Lavengro offers to buy a bible for the old apple-woman of London Bridge, 'No, dear, no,' she replies, 'you are poor, and may soon want the money; but if you can take one conveniently on the sly, you know——.' Marc——, a young Neapolitan, who had killed his father, avowed to Lombroso that he had prayed to Our Lady of the Chain for the strength necessary for the undertaking. 'Oh, if God would have pity on us,' wrote to her accomplice, according to Mr Havelock Ellis, a woman who was poisoning her husband; 'how I would bless him! When he complains, I thank God in my heart.' And the accomplice answers, 'I will pray to heaven to aid us.' It is almost in the same terms that the paramours at Agra wrote, in 1912, as they were putting the woman's husband out of the way. On what intimate terms with God is the Princess Helena, in the *Emperor and Galilean,* cruel and faithless and lustful as she is! The women Anisya and Matrena, in Tolstoi's *Power of Darkness,* make it a point of conscience to baptize the infant before killing it. And of God they speak familiarly, not hypocritically; like Stevenson's Markheim, also, who kills in cold blood. Twice Dostoevsky's Fedka, a robber and a murderer, reproaches Pyotr Stepanovitch for not believing in God himself, the true Creator.[37] 'God has sent him,' whispers Kipling's Pambé Serang as he hears the voice of his victim; 'now I can die,' he murmurs with a sigh of relief as he sinks to his pillow after having driven the knife home. Of all these the attitude is not that of Lady Macbeth or Iago invoking the powers of darkness; but more nearly that of the simpler people with whom criminals are anthropologically akin, Christians and heathens early and modern, for example,

[37] *The Possessed,* chapters ii and iv (Mrs Garnett).

who pray and vow to their God before the fight and praise and pay him afterwards.

18.

The difficulty with Shakespeare's tragic evil-doers, then, is that they are too conscious and consistent, both in thought and in deed; (though it is a difficulty only as by a misguided criticism they are taken to be 'the real thing'). Knowing that they are wicked, as they are, they cannot think, as they should, that they are on the side of the angels or are the children of God. So far as the instinctive religiosity of the evil-doer is concerned, Shakespeare in one of his earliest poems, strange to say, is nearer to reality than in any of his tragedies. As Tarquin approaches Lucrece' chamber-door 'to pray he doth begin.' But in the midst of his prayer, with an unnatural but spiritual discernment, he realizes the impropriety; and that impropriety Shakespeare seems ever after to remember. And this despite the fact that he had the example of the chivalric literature before him, and the story of Arthur and the *Decameron,* where piety, like courtesy, is not incompatible with adultery: and of Marston and Chapman, in whom, under continental influence, this spirit, infelicitously, reappears. But that was not in the *mores* of the English people, and of Shakespeare who was of them. To him the piety of Chapman's Bussy and Tamyra must have seemed, as indeed it should seem, sheer hypocrisy and blasphemy. He never presents adultery with any sympathy at all; but the spirit of sympathy for it and approval of it in Chapman and Marston, in the Arthurian story and in the *Decameron*—sympathy and approval on the part of excellent and charming people for lovers faithful to each other but faithless to husbands to whom faith was plighted before God—might have opened his eyes to the relative point of view, not in one person, to be sure, but in an age.

It is an *a-priori* psychology, as we said, scooped out of

the imagination, but descending from the days of Seneca, almost to our own. Yet in this regard, of course, evil human nature was then as it is now. The candour in wickedness of Shakespeare's villains Dr Wolff would explain as owing to the frankness of the Renaissance, which laboured under no such weight of public opinion as does ours. That, according to Professor Schücking, is as much as to say the Babylonian five-legged lions were owing to the fact that in those days there were lions with five legs. A softer but not so apt an answer would be that such is not the effect of public opinion upon the criminal—it does not stifle his consciousness of his own wickedness but (if it have any effect) instills it into him.

What we know from the chronicles and biographies of the Renaissance does not harmonize with Elizabethan dramatic portraiture. In life it is clear that Macbeth and Richard III were fairly good kings, though not good men; and Lady Macbeth bestowed pious gifts upon the church. Iago had the human motive of revenge for scorned love, which plays no part in the play. And how different are the cardinals of Webster from those of Browning and of Italian history,—cruel and corrupt as they, but atheistical, not orthodox, not pious. Webster's Vittoria is a proud, conscious, dazzling, and defiant woman of sin, in life as in death; whereas in reality the paramour of Bracciano was naïve and innocent in manner and ended her days in the odour of sanctity. 'And indeed,' says Vernon Lee quite justly, 'the great villains of the Renaissance never take up the attitude of fiends. . . . There was no barrier between them and evil; they slipped into it, remained in it, became accustomed to it; but a vicious determination to be wicked, a feeling of the fiend within one, like that of Shakespeare's Richard, or a gradual, conscious irresistible absorption into recognized iniquity like Macbeth's, there was not.' In manner and looks they seem to have been like their portraits; and though the Borgias were the patrons of art (and in part, to be sure, that fact explains their attractiveness on canvas) the artists were— Raphael, Pinturicchio, Michelangelo. Though more vigorous, these art-loving criminals were not unlike Thomas Wainewright—friend of Lamb, Hazlitt, Hood, De Quincey, Allan Cunningham, Maginn, Talfourd, and John Clare; a writer, a painter, one of our earliest art critics,— who forged a check, poisoned uncle, mother-in-law, and sister-in-law, and tried his hand less successfully on those less near and dear. 'Kind, light-hearted Wainewright', Lamb called him, not knowing him wholly; his conversation and manner, both then and long afterwards in Van Diemen's Land, were winning in the extreme. A lover of nature, he was peculiarly susceptible to the spiritual influence of Wordsworth's poems. In his youth, he says, 'I wept over them tears of happiness and gratitude.' His prose was capital, declared Lamb and Hazlitt; and he was generous in his appreciation of his fellows and rivals such as Hazlitt, Hunt, and Barry Cornwall, 'without anything' —a false note there perhaps—'of the malice of a friend.' He was abnormal, inconsistent, dangerous, but not devilish.

The ways and manners of criminals, as we have seen, particularly of criminal men of genius such as Wainewright, Villon, Verlaine, or O. Henry, seem, until prison and harsh 'environment' made them self-conscious, to have been simple enough. After the crime they go on a lark, play cards with the family, or take a nap. Runciman, in the essay referred to, tells of the arch-rascal among English thieves living quietly in a London suburb, solacing himself with high-class music and poetry—a cheery little man with decent frock coat and a clean respectable air. Féron, after killing a man, went, like Browning's Ivan after killing the woman, and played with children. Troppmann, after he had massacred a whole family, wept on hearing his mother's name mentioned. Eugene Aram, the school-master murderer, was observed by a neighbour to

tread warily in the garden, like Cowper and the Iago of
the critics, so as to spare snails or worms. They all act
simply and naturally (or else with a sentimental and unnatural goodness, in revulsion or compensation) as, on ordinary occasions, do those fairly respectable people in
America who gather in crowds to burn negroes or 'scabs'
alive. But this last is bourgeois, irregular and unexpected,
not in the tragic vein. On the stage from the days of
Æschylus and Seneca criminals have gloried in their wickedness and defied man and fate and the gods; and since
the days of Seneca, as we have seen, they have invoked
the powers of evil, and wished that they might be wickeder
still. 'Teach me thy rage'—'my heart raves not enough!'
'Sommes-nous assez canailles? Le sommes-nous?' And in
Seneca, Shakespeare, and the Elizabethan drama, when a
murder is in hand the sky darkens, lightning flashes, and
heaven and earth are in a tumult. I need but mention the
eclipses and tempests in *Macbeth* and *King Lear,* the tempest dropping fire and celestial armies drizzling blood in
Julius Cæsar, or Duncan's horses which ate each other.
And if these or the like are not forthcoming, Macbeth or
King John, Tamburlaine or Othello, is there to cry out for
them.

> Stars, hide your fires!
>
> Methinks it should be now a huge eclipse
> Of sun and moon, and that the affrighted globe
> Did yawn at alteration.

Here, as not in King John's wish for the fitting stage-effects
mentioned above, there is not only emotional justification
but much poetry; and there is much in the various invocations of evil, and a little in the unmitigated villain's
grotesque gloatings, curses, and threats, though oftener
there is bombast and melodrama. Through it all runs
the notion that the moment of sin and the manner of the
sinner are something prodigious and beyond the bounds
of nature, as indeed they appear to be in the person of

many a famous actor who saws the air in old paintings and prints. Even later poetry and fiction have been slower to return to nature than one would think, and as in the eighteenth and nineteenth centuries villains become less villainous, their manners become perhaps more sublime. So it is with Byron's and Bulwer's. Hugo makes Javert give a roar as he pounces on poor Valjean; and even Balzac makes Vautrin, when taken by the police, undergo a sort of infernal transfiguration. How differently evil is done in Ibsen or Pinero! By making use of the checkbook Iris entangles herself before she knows it; and Mrs Thaddeus Mortimore destroys her brother-in-law's will 'as if it were the most natural thing in the world.' How differently—and naturally—it is done in real life I need not undertake to tell.

19.

'Shakespeare is nature,' cry the critics still. There, in our every chapter, lies the whole difficulty with which we have to cope. Though he was widely different, I cannot see that as an artist he was greater, or was truer to nature, than Michelangelo. In all that pertains to the representation of the human form why not let Michelangelo be nature too? Certainly he knew the human body as well as Shakespeare knew the human soul. We marvel at the bold and subtle drawing of hands, limbs, and articulations. But not long ago a great artist pointed out the fact that in the ceiling of the Sistine Chapel some of the grand and imposing attitudes are physically impossible. The man is standing, but by the laws of nature he should fall. Such a thing a Whistler or a Sargent, without being so great a painter, is not so likely to be caught doing to-day. In art he who in standing must take heed lest he fall, is now ridiculous: we assent and conform to fact. Our painters and poets, whose lesser genius is not identified with nature, have studied her, have discovered the fact, and with such result that to them or to us an attitude, word, or accent can no longer be completely satisfying unless it be in accord with this larger measure of truth. The sixteenth-century painter, who had discovered a lesser measure of truth, was freer to treat the human form as a design or pattern, and to flare out upon wall or canvas his sublimest impressions and imaginings, imbued with the religious and social prejudices and ideals of his time. The sixteenth-century playwright was free to weave a fantastic plot, pen speeches that are rather a song, a story, or a comment, and body forth impressions and imaginations as sublime and as deeply imbued. Both the painter and the playwright followed convention, held up the mirror to man as they knew him, and painted—saints and satyrs, devils and demigods. Neither of them—no genius in fact, however great—can be identified with Nature's self; either of them is a soul teeming with audacious shapes and attitudes which nature never knew; and in the case of the playwright it is as true as in the case of the painter that such attitudes, particularly some of those struck by his criminal characters, are impossible, poetically imposing though they be.

1912

CHAPTER VIII

FALSTAFF

In Shakespeare criticism, as in most things Anglo-Saxon save sport, there has been little professionalism. The best as well as the worst of our scientists and artists have done their work without painfully learning how to do it, and our critics, like our soldiers, have won their Waterloos on cricket fields. For two hundred and fifty years Englishmen and Americans have been writing about the character of Falstaff, and hardly three or four of these have been students of the stage. Since 1777 they have followed mainly in the steps of Maurice Morgann,[1] a country gentleman of philosophic bent and literary taste, who seems to have known little of the stage and to have loved it less. In reading Shakespeare he is not reminded of Plautus or Terence, of Fletcher or Molière, of Wycherley or Farquhar. We all know what sort of opinions, in ignorance of technique and historical development, were entertained in Morgann's time and after by men so delicate in sensibility as Walpole and Shelley, concerning Greek sculpture, Italian painting, and Gothic architecture; and is it likely that his opinion concerning Falstaff, though in England and America it has stood now for much more than a century, should be less fallible? Time establishes sentiments, customs and institutions, not truth. But though still we may hear that pointed construction was the immediate expression of the gloom and aspiration of the Middle

---

[1] *An Essay on the Dramatic Character of Sir John Falstaff,* often since reprinted, and twice within the last ten years.

Ages, and that groined vaulting and pillared aisles were devised in imitation of God's first temple, the over-arching forest, Anglo-Saxons have had their eyes opened to the technique of art as not to the technique of the play. What might be called the external history of the drama has been explored, but the history of technique and convention has been neglected, and still anybody ventures to write on Shakespeare who has taste and a style—and many without them. Few among these would appreciate the remark of Stevenson that to read a play is as difficult as to read musical score. And to read an old play is as difficult as to read old score.

I.

Morgann, in his fine and subtle essay, shows that he has read it like a true Romantic; and discovers in the effect of Falstaff upon us in the two Parts of *Henry IV* an opposition between feeling and understanding. 'Shakespeare has contrived to make secret impressions upon us of courage in favour of a character which was to be held up for sport and laughter on account of actions of apparent cowardice and dishonour.' Falstaff's conduct is cowardly; his character, that subtler essence, is courageous.[2] Contrary, however, to what might be expected, the cowardice and dishonour, which are perceived by the understanding, are the obvious traits, those 'thrust forward and pressed upon our notice'; and the favourable mental impressions are reached on the part of Morgann himself, not by the mystical faculty alleged, but through deliberate conjecture and devious ratiocination, that is, by the understanding, too. Whatever the process, the direct effect, he thinks, of the incidents of Gadshill and Shrewsbury, of Falstaff's own confessions, and of the downright ridicule of him by the Prince, Lancaster, and Poins, is counteracted by inferences from

---

[2] Cf., among many, Professor Bradley, *Oxford Lectures,* p. 266: 'sometimes behaves in a cowardly way, but that does not show that he was a coward.'

the casual remarks of characters such as Doll Tearsheet,
Shallow, Lord Bardolph, and the Chief-Justice, and by
such circumstances as his earlier 'familiarity' with John of
Gaunt, a 'dozen captains' calling him to court, and his
appearance once on the eve of battle in the presence of
the King. At times the critic goes farther, and, in the
faith that Shakespeare's characters are 'essentially different
from those of other writers,' considers Falstaff as if he
were an 'historic rather than dramatic being,' and the text
as if it were a report, not wholly exact or sufficient, instead
of being Falstaff's whole story, quite all there was to tell
or can now be told; and adventurously inquires into his
hopeful youth, the company that he had kept, his family
and his station, inferring from these that he must have
had the constitutional instincts of courage although he had
lost the principles which ordinarily accompany them. So
firmly has this notion of Falstaff as a real person [3] taken
hold of him that now and then he breaks out into exclamations against the 'malice' from which Falstaff's reputation
suffers, appeals to the reader's good nature to right him,
and, when confronted with the more unequivocal acts and
utterances of his favourite, can but call them 'unfortunate,'
and, as if he were a friend in trouble, deplore his loquacity
in soliloquy and 'imprudence' in deed. He pleads Falstaff's
case, thinks that on Gadshill 'he did not roar,' and begs us
to remember in extenuation of his short-comings his old
age and corpulence. In this spirit of unesthetic tenderness
and in accordance with his principle of preferring to the
prominent and obvious what is latent and obscure, he dis-
credits the testimony of Lancaster and Poins as prompted
by envy and ill-will, and the Prince's as given in raillery,
makes much of the compliment implied in the surrender
of that 'famous knight and and most valorous enemy' Col-

[3] There is excellent comment on this trick of Morgann's and its effect on
Shakespeare criticism since, in Mr A. B. Walkley's *Drama and Life*. I
cannot help thinking, however, that the fallacy would have prevailed even
had Morgann never perpetrated it. See above, chapter ii, and iii, section 9.

ville of the Dale, and is of the opinion that a man who takes captives, and jests and dallies on a battlefield, has not got so frightened as to lose his presence of mind. Love of humour is the mainspring of his character: he falls flat at Shrewsbury for a jest and none of his lies and braggadocios is intended to deceive. The escapade of Gadshill, which Shakespeare in the story places first, Morgann, who regards it as the 'source of much unreasonable prejudice,' considers last, and even if it must be thought an exhibition of cowardice holds it to be a single exception. And the virtue of the jest afterwards in Eastcheap is in the 'reproof of the lies,' which are but humour, and not in the exposure of the cowardice, which is a 'venial and momentary aberration.'

In sum and substance and often in minute detail these views have been reproduced or developed since by English critics [4]—by Coleridge and Swinburne; by Hazlitt, Lloyd, and Maginn, who take for a jest even the headlong flight from Gadshill; and most elaborately, though most subtly of all, by Professor A. C. Bradley. His main achievement is the development, after Rötscher and others, of Morgann's notion of Falstaff as a 'military free-thinker' into that of one who by his humour dissolves away into words and airy nothings not only honour but those other obstacles and 'nuisances'—truth, duty, devotion to one's country, the terrors of death and religion, everything in short that makes life real and earnest, thereby 'lifting us into an

---

[4] This is my only justification for paying so much attention to the ingenious but unplausible arguments of a critic so far removed in time; this, and the stamp of approval laid upon them by Swinburne, Professor Bradley, and (perhaps most remarkable of all) the student of roguery, Professor F. W. Chandler, in his introduction to *Henry IV* in the Tudor edition. Even the Germans, as I suggest below, owe more to Morgann than they may be aware. Among English critics two conspicuous exceptions are Mr Courthope (*History of English Poetry*) and Mr E. K. Chambers (*Red Letter Shakespeare*, introduction to *Henry IV* Part II); but they give no reasons and permit themselves no more than an oracular sentence.

atmosphere of perfect freedom.'[5] Among the Germans Falstaff the philosopher has of course passed unchallenged, but among these students of the technique and history of the drama he has generally had to bear the badge of a coward too.

Johnson scoffed at his friend Morgann's innovation,— 'Why, Sir, we shall have the man come forth again; and as he has proved Falstaff to be no coward, he may prove Iago to be a very good character,'—and critics since have been disposed to repay him in his own coin. But they would hardly have been so quick to do it to Dryden, though twice explicitly and without qualification he calls Falstaff liar, coward, glutton, and buffoon.[6] And Thomas Fuller, Oldmixon, and all the seventeenth century with them, take it for granted that he is nothing else.[7] The same may be said of Nicholas Rowe (1709), Corbyn Morris (1742), Lewis Theobald (1750), Johnson himself officially, Mrs Montagu (1769), Giuseppe Baretti (1777), Tom Davies (1784), and Richard Stack (1788).[8] But, as often in

---

[5] *Oxford Lectures,* pp. 262-263. Here Professor Bradley seems to me certainly to be following Lamb's line in the ingenious half-truths of his essay on the 'Artificial Comedy of the Last Century.' See above, p. 45. But also he may be developing the German idealists' notion of 'transcendental farce.' Cf. above, end of chapter iv.

[6] *Essay of Dramatic Poesy* (Everyman's Library), p. 43: 'old, fat, merry, cowardly, drunken, amorous, vain, and lying'; Preface to his *Troilus and Cressida,* Ingleby's *Shakespeare Allusion-Book* (ed. Munro), ii, 246; 'a lyar, a coward, a Glutton, and Buffon, because all these qualities may agree in the same man.'

[7] Ingleby, *op. cit:*—(Fuller) i, 486, 'make-sport in all plays for a coward'; ii, 43, 'coward,' 'Buffoone'; (Oldmixon), ii, 431; (George Daniel), i, 507. Cf. Captain Alexander Smith, *Compleat History of the Lives and Robberies,* etc., 1719, i, p. 1 f., who takes it that Shakespeare intended him for 'a grand coward'; and what Mr Chandler, *Literature of Roguery* (1907), p. 175, thinks to be evidence that he thought Falstaff none, has to do only with the Fastolf of history and legend.

[8] Rowe in his Preface; Morris, *Essay of Wit,* etc., pp. 25-7; Theobald, note 1 to *A King and No King;* Baretti, the Italian critic and poet, resident for a time in London, *Discours sur Shakespeare et M. Voltaire* (1777) p. 71; Mrs Montagu, *Essay on Shakespeare* (1769), pp. 106, 107; Davies, *Dramatic Miscellanies* (1785), i. 272-3, 301; ii, 40; Stack, *Transactions of*

the history of criticism—still oftener than in human affairs, though I remember Prohibition—the voice of common sense has been drowned by the clamour of prejudice, or lulled by the murmurs of sentiment.

2.

Since Dryden's day the world has moved on a bit; yet a critical opinion on the drama propounded amid all the vagaries of the heyday of Romanticism, by one neither a dramatist nor a student of the drama, is on the face of it quite as questionable as the contrary opinion which till then had stood unimpeached. No doubt Morgann is right in insisting upon a difference. Falstaff is not, as we shall see, an ordinary stage coward; he is not even a Parolles or a Bobadill; and by no means is he a mere buffoon. But Morgann, as we have seen, goes much further. Not only is he strangely confused and contradictory in that, finding the circumstances creditable to Falstaff thrown into the background, and the 'follies and the buffoonery' thrown into the foreground, he calls us, who attach greater importance to the latter, the dupes of our wisdom and systematic reasoning; but thus and otherwise he betrays a total misapprehension of dramatic method, whether of his own or of an earlier time. It is all too plain that he cannot read score. To him, as to many another philosopher and littérateur, Shakespeare is not score to be played, but a book to be read, not to say an inscription to be deciphered; and a really great dramatist is one who dupes us, deliberately misplaces the emphasis, transcendentally baffles men's wits. Yet with all dramatists down to Dumas and Ibsen—and

Royal Irish Academy (1788). The last two, as I have learned only since the publication of the article, directly attack Morgann, and (Stack in particular) use arguments which I have employed. See below, *passim*. Mézières (1886), also, remaining, unlike Stapfer, uninfected either by English romanticism or German philosophy, has treated Falstaff somewhat as I have done, as if he were like Panurge.

even with them—the contrary is the case. What is in the
foreground is important; what is in the background is less
important, and, in Shakespeare and the Elizabethans, often
epically, rather than dramatically and psychologically, in
keeping. And what stands first in the play, as the cowardly flight from Gadshill, is most important of all and
dominates the whole. Besides these simple principles of
dramatic emphasis and perspective, which in our discussion will, I hope, constantly be illustrated, Morgann and
his followers ignore the various hints of the poet as
embodied in the established conventions of the time—the
confessions in soliloquy, the comments and predictions of
important undiscredited characters like the Prince and
Poins, and various devices and bits of 'business,' like Falstaff's roaring as he runs and his falling flat in battle. All
these are as much means of expression as the Elizabethan
vocabulary of the text, and yet they are treated as if they
had no definite meaning—as if, as someone has said, the
book had dropped from the skies,—and both the playwright and his period vanish from his play. So far has
this gone that, as we have seen, inquiry presses coolly past
him to the character's lineage, his financial and social experiences, and his past as a whole. It was but recently that
an Elizabethan scholar contended that we had a right to
do this, and that characters in plays, particularly in Shakespeare's, were not unreal like statues and paintings. They
can think, talk, and walk—they are bits of real life, not art!
But if paintings are canvas, and statues are marble, what
are dramatic characters but words and ink and paper? They
have no past or future either save as their author discloses it.

On the principle that what is most prominent is most
important there is surely no need to dwell: of art it is the
beginning and the end. Of the correlative principle that
the first impression is designedly the dominant one there
is in the case of Shylock a remarkable illustration to which

I have drawn attention above,[9] and even in the plays of Ibsen or the dramatic scenes in the novels of Dostoevsky we have only apparent exceptions to the rule. If Helmer in the *Doll's House* is not the heroic character, and Nora not the frivolous one, they may at first appear to be, that first impression is corrected, not by 'secret' impressions and insignificant details such as Morgann discovers, but by subsequent revelations which loom large and for which every preparation has been made. They do not counteract and contradict; they consummate and fulfill; and the same character advances and retires, muffles and discloses himself again, before our eyes. Ibsen and Dostoevsky lead us to adjust our conception and revise our judgment as we follow the play or peruse the book. They make us the dupes, not of our wisdom but of our stupidity, and then only for the moment. Such plays, however, are not Shakespeare's; his are far more popular, and involve processes which disclose primarily not character but events; and at the end, except for casual conversions, his characters are pretty much what they were at the beginning. Falstaff is as much of a coward sprawling on Shrewsbury Field as running down Gadshill. With a comic character, indeed, upon the stage, Ibsen's method would present great difficulties. With such Ibsen himself does not employ it.

What, then, do these facts mean? as Mr Bradley asks after having detailed the 'secret impressions.' 'Does

[9] See p. 264. This principle was fully recognized by Stack before me (see above, p. 407, note, and note 16 below), in his reply. He observes that Morgann does not follow the dramatist's order or respect the principle of emphasis; and he declares that *'first* impressions (not secret ones) are of the highest moment,' because they appeal to feeling rather than to the understanding; and if a writer should neglect this principle, he would at least avoid all early impressions of an opposite nature (pp. 6-7). Professor Feuillerat in a review (*Litteris,* April, 1926) rightly objects to Professor Schücking's rule that the first impression is always final. As I have said above (chapter 1) Shakespeare follows no rule or formula; but it is only in minor matters, and those of fact rather than of character, such as whether Ophelia committed suicide or not, that the later (and truer) impression is made to differ much from the first.

Shakespeare put them all in with no purpose at all, or in defiance of his own intention?' He never defies his own intention, I suppose, save in the hands of us critics. The incongruities, as I hope presently to show, are either necessarily or traditionally involved in the type of the *miles gloriosus* which (unconsciously) he is here undertaking to exhibit; or they are incidental to the current convention of the professsional comic person on the stage; or else they are such unimportant contradictions and irrelevancies as Shakespeare, writing for the stage and not for the study, slips into continually, examples of which in one play have, with admirable discernment, been collected by Mr Bradley himself.[10] Still others are not contradictions or inconsistencies at all, but humorous details, though they have been given a serious exegesis.

3.

Meantime we take it that, standing first, playing so big a part in the story, 'this unfortunate affair' of Gadshill is meant to prejudice us. In itself it is an example of the old device of a practical joke, delighted in by Molière and Goldoni, Goldsmith and Sheridan, as well as by the Elizabethans, not disdained by Fielding, Smollett, and Dickens, and in farce not extinct to-day. According to Elizabethan usage a foolish character—a braggart, or a coward, or a conceited ass like Malvolio, or even a merry misogynist like Benedick—is, by conspiracy, fooled to the top of his bent, and in the end made aware of it and jeered at. Of this there are many instances in the comedies of Shakespeare, as in those of Marston, Chapman, Dekker, and the rest of the craft. Always the expectations of the practical

---

[10] *Shakespearean Tragedy,* pp. 256-258; Pellissier, *Superstition Shakespearienne,* for many more. The contradictions involved in Shakespeare's time-references, again, are without number; since the days of Wilson they have been turned into a miracle of art.—For the misunderstanding of humorous touches see especially below, note 34, and section 9, end of the paragraph.

jokers—as here in Falstaff's cowardly conduct and 'incomprehensible lies'—are fulfilled, and the victim's ridiculous sayings and doings cast in his teeth. Sometimes like Falstaff he takes to his wits to cover his retreat; but at the outset he steps into the trap laid for him, unaware. There is no instance of a character making a fool of himself on purpose—playing the coward on purpose [11] and then playing the ludicrous braggart, afterward. To an audience such an ambiguous situation would, without hint or guidance from the dramatist, have been incomprehensible. The rôle of fool or butt no one loves or chooses. In Part II, when the Prince and Poins overhear Falstaff slandering them, they force him, with jeers, to admit that this time he did *not* know them as well as the Lord that made them; and so it is made clear to the audience that they have now accomplished their purpose of seeing him 'bestow himself in his true colours.' In neither incident could he have played a part any more than Parolles when he slanders and, as he thinks, betrays his master and all the leaders of his army; in either case we have a convention, a bit of

---

[11] Unlike many, Morgann and Mr Bradley do not think that Falstaff runs away on purpose, though they do think that his lying afterwards is in jest. Others think that he takes the hint and turns earnest to jest in the midst of his buckram story:

Prince Prithee let him alone; we shall have more anon.
Fal. Dost thou hear me, Hal?
Prince Ay, and mark thee too, Jack.
Fal. Do so, for it is worth listening to.

The first speech is certainly an aside—by the second that is clearly indicated. If in the last speech Falstaff shows that he is detected, still he does not save his reputation for cleverness, about which the critics are concerned, for he has been tripped up repeatedly already; and the cardinal stupidity lies in the tale as a whole. But such a speech, if really Falstaff sees, is not enough to set the audience right. After Poins's prediction of cowardly conduct and the lies of 'thirty at least' come, in due course, both cowardice and lies, and the Prince and Poins crowing, calling him coward and liar, and Falstaff wriggling out as best he may. Only by the most explicit aside could the audience be given the tip—and then only to their bewilderment. Laughter arises, as I show above in chapter vi, and below in section 18, only when the issue is plain and clear; and if Falstaff here exaggerates for fun his later embarrassment and evasions are not apparently in keeping. He should turn the tables, and unmistakably. See below, sections 13, 14, 18.

stage language, we might say, almost as precise and ascertainable in meaning as any old word or phrase in the text, but then current in the same acceptation on the Continent and in after times as well. The overhearing and confronting of backbiter or plain-speaker is a device employed in *Le monde où l'on s'ennuie*[12] as in the *Fourberies de Scapin*.

There are indeed some instances of the victim, not a fool as he had been thought, detecting the trap; but he gets even, like the Merry Wives of Windsor, not by stepping into it with a secret smile, but by leading the joker into it or setting one of his own. In that case the victim makes his detection of the trap quite clear to the audience in aside or soliloquy, or in confidences to his friends. Whenever in Elizabethan drama a character is feigning we are informed of it. That Prince Hal himself is playing the roysterer on purpose he himself tells us twice over; but that Falstaff is playing coward, liar, thief, or butt on purpose is intimated neither by him nor by anyone else. And, above all, the truth, clearly and emphatically, will out at the end, not only to enlighten the audience but to secure a comic effect. It is too good to keep, as all jokes are: expression is essential. The trickster tricked, the duper duped, the cheater cheated, the trepanner trepanned, whether it be as the libertine thwarted, the Delilah eluded, or the rook turned the pigeon's prey,—all are situations to be found in Terence,[13] Chapman, Dekker, Fletcher, Lope de Vega, in comedy (whether Latin, English, French, or Spanish) even more abundantly than in life itself; but there is no case, so far as I have seen, where the whole truth

---

[12] III, i and ii. Darkness here takes the place of disguise, as mistaken identity does in the *Fourberies* where Zerbinette has her say about Géronte to his face. Both are impenetrable save to the audience, or to such persons, and at such times, as are clearly indicated.

[13] See, for instance, the *Heautimoroumenos,* where Chremes puts Syrus up to cheat Menedemus; whereas Syrus has it already in mind to cheat, after the selfsame fashion, Chremes himself. The situation is perfectly clear, and thereby the comic effect of it is made secure.

is not imparted both to the audience and (eventually) to the victim on the stage. What a comedy, indeed, it would be, with the duper repeatedly successful and applauded, and the duper of the duper never openly to have his inning at all!

That thus we read Shakespeare, not by his own light only, but also by that of his contemporaries, appears from the parallel situation in the second and third acts of the First Part of Heywood's *Fair Maid of the West*.[14] Attacked in the fields by Bess in the disguise of a man, the boasting and swaggering Roughman shows the white feather, but afterward boasts to her of his deeds, is led on by her simulated interest and sympathy, entangled and tripped up in his lies, and, finally, when all the facts are laid bare, put to confusion. Like Falstaff he incurs ridicule, if not for counting noses or telling buckram from Kendal green when it is so dark that he cannot see his own hand, at least for justling with the enemy for the wall—in mid-field. Like Falstaff he tells how and when he 'took' the blows and 'put them by.' 'I was never so put to it' (I never dealt better). 'I think I paid him home' (Seven of the eleven I paid). 'Scap'd he with life?' (Pray God, you have not murder'd some of them). 'Ay, that's my fear: if he recover this,' etc. (Nay, that's past praying for). That Roughman is a coward no one can doubt, 'for he himself has said it'; [15] and manifestly the whole point in the 'reproof of his lies,' as of Falstaff's, is the ignominy of cowardice. As in life, the two vices are here inseparable; no dramatist—no one but a pedant or a metaphysician—would think of separating them, or of having a liar confuted who is lying merely for fun.[16]

---

[14] Published in 1631; probably written before 1603.

[15] *Fair Maid,* Part I, III, p. 296 (Works, 1874).

[16] Morgann (like his followers) says 'that it is clearly the lies only, not the cowardice of Falstaff, which are here detected.' Stack (*op. cit.,* p. 12): 'This is a kind of abstraction which I must own myself incapable of making; neither do I well conceive how the writer has done so; for these lies could in fact have had no existence, unless we imagine some foundation upon which they were raised; so that, as well in the order of our ideas as degree

4.

Falstaff's cowardice appears still more clearly when the Gadshill incident is viewed in detail. There is the testimony of the Prince, Poins, and Falstaff himself. Four times the Prince flatly calls him coward to his face.[17] The only time he attempts to deny it—on Gadshill—the Prince replies, 'Well, we leave that to the proof'; and it comes speedily. Clearer nothing could be: the question is raised, and Falstaff's roaring and running away the next moment are the all-sufficient answer. Don Juan, in the Italian scenario, bids Harlequin not betray the fact of his having killed the Commendatore. Harlequin swears secrecy. 'But if they should torture you?' 'Nothing can shake me.' 'C'est ce que nous allons voir'—'well, we leave that to the proof'—and, Don Juan presently putting on the manner of a bailiff as if to apply the thumbscrews, Harlequin makes haste to tell all.[18]

Poins's estimate of Falstaff's character just before this has been subjected to the most undramatic and hair-splitting comment imaginable:—'Well, for two of them, I know them to be as true-bred cowards as ever turned back; and for the third, if he fight longer than he sees reason, I'll forswear arms' (I, ii, 205). 'As for the third,' echoes Morgann, solemnly; 'as if the name of this veteran would have excited too strongly the ideas of courage and resistance.'[19] 'What stronger evidence can we require,' he cries,

of importance, the cowardice of Falstaff is not incidental, but the primary and essential impression.' If in the history of thought *veritas prævalet*, it is not so in criticism. By Johnson and Stack, Morgann was confuted even in his own day, to no avail. In criticism, what is wanted is not truth but ingenuity, or rather food for the prevailing taste.

[17] Part I, II, ii, 69; iv, 268, 542; Part II, II, iv. 353.

[18] Moland, *Molière et la comédie italienne* (1867), p. 196.

[19] P. 125—Morgann is not perfectly clear (though, unlike some very important commentators, he seems really to scent the understatement), but he attributes it to Poins's caution, on the one hand, and to malice on the other. 'What Poins *dares* do . . . he does!' Willing to wound, I suppose,

'than that Poins, the ill-disposed . . . than that this very Poins should not venture to put down Falstaff in the list of cowards?' Humour or the understanding of humour, particularly of that ancient Anglo-Saxon heritage the humour of understatement, which is the Englishman's possession to this hour, seems, as from most of us when saddled and ridden by a theory, to have been frequently withheld from this gifted man,—by a strange irony, the accepted chief expositor, now for a hundred and fifty years, of the foremost humorous character in literature.

Certainly the latter half of Poins's sentence contains no praise, however faint—the whole tone and context of the passage shows this; moreover, it is followed by the remark, still more explicit, about 'the incomprehensible lies that this same fat rogue will tell us,—how thirty at least he fought with, and what wards, what blows, what extremities he endured,' etc.—'a prediction,' faithfully but mournfully adds Morgann, 'unfortunately fulfilled, even beyond the letter of it,—a completion more incident, perhaps, to the predictions of malice than of affection.' What could Shakespeare have done with an audience of Morganns? Here or anywhere Poins, or Shakespeare himself in a comedy, is not the man to distinguish between conduct and character, principles and constitution, a skulker and a courageously consistent Epicurean; and the speech in question is a simple truth gilded with a pleasantry. Falstaff himself admits that he was 'a coward on instinct,' not on principle; and at Shrewsbury says to himself, 'I fear the shot here,'—'I am afraid of this Percy,' and makes his words good by stabbing the corpse. Against such an interpretation Morgann and his followers murmur, bidding us remember his age and his peculiar philosophy, the corrupting example of his associates, the odds against him, and the

and yet afraid to strike, he hints a fault—being the only bold fellow (apart from the Prince) in the whole company! Falstaff himself, a better judge, apparently thinks he dares do quite enough when he speaks, very plainly, of stabbing (see below).

suddenness of the assault; but on the Elizabethan comic stage, or any popular stage, where of course there are no relentings towards cowardice (there being none even towards things beyond our doing or undoing, as poverty, cuckoldom, physical ugliness, or meanness of birth), nobody confesses to fear but a coward, a child, or a woman. All Shakespeare's cowards, like his villains, bear their names written in their foreheads, and his true men, like Don Quixote in the eyes of Sancho, neither know nor understand what fear or dismay is. But the main objection to such considerations, as indeed to the general scheme and tenor of the prevailing Shakespeare criticism, is, as Stack well says, 'its excessive refinement.' 'Dramatic characters [particularly in comedy, I would add] are not drawn for speculative ingenious men in their closets but for mankind at large.' Such extenuations, the motives of malice, attributed to 'that Poins' and Lancaster, and the 'secret impressions' of valour,—all are inferences, 'fine-spun deductions,' to use Stack's phrase; and the like things in comedy do not count because they have not 'a strong and immediate influence.' Drama, said only the other day Mr Granville Barker, and his words are still truer of comedy), 'aims— for it must—at spontaneous appreciation.' Vous avez raison, madame,' says Dorante in the *Critique de l' École des femmes,* 'de les trouver étranges, tous ces raffinements mystérieux.' And to Shakespeare's stage they were as strange.

Nowhere is it more evident how little Morgann regarded dramatic method and stage-craft than at this early moment in the episode:

> *Peto.* How many be there of them?
> *Gadshill.* Some eight or ten.
> *Fal.* 'Zounds, will they not rob us?
> *Prince.* What, a coward, Sir John Paunch?
> *Fal.* Indeed, I am not John of Gaunt, etc.—(II, ii.)

This is found to be hardly more of a confession on his

part than the Prince's remark to Poins on his own as they plan their trick in the second scene of Act I: 'Yea, but I doubt they will be too hard for us.' The latter remark is casual or else made in mockery, but in either case it is meant only to call forth Poins's comment (quoted above) on their companions' timorous natures; whereas this speech of Falstaff's is uttered after the limelight has been turned full upon him—the audience has been apprized of his cowardice, the business is afoot, and the booty at hand. Thus everything has been nicely calculated to give his abrupt exclamation full comic value and 'bring down the house,' as would be seen by anybody who on principle had not already blurred dramatic perspective and jumbled 'values.' And Falstaff's retort is, as Stack rightly observes, a witty evasion; an effort to turn the laugh called forth by his timorousness;—not, as Morgann would have it, a hint at his discreetly courageous character, thrown out for the behoof of the audience.

5.

That Falstaff is not dissembling is still more evident from the management of the ensuing incident, in the same scene, and of the scene at the tavern. In the brief and fleeting moment of glory immediately after the robbery of the travellers he calls Poins and the Prince cowards, and swaggers. Now the coward charging the brave with cowardice,[20] like the coward boasting of his courage,[21] is a perennial situation, on the stage or off it. Parolles, Panurge, the

---

[20] Basilisco, *Soliman and Perseda* (1588), II, ii, 67-80; III, ii, 30; Parolles, *All's Well*, IV, iii, 321; *Jodelet, maître-valet*, I, iii and v; *Jodelet duelliste;* Panurge, Rabelais, IV, chap. 24. John Earle, *Microcosmography* (1628), *The Coward:* 'A coward is the man that is commonly most fierce against the coward.'

[21] In the drama all cowards boast. Cf., besides those cited above, the popular types, Capitano, Harlequin, Scaramouche; Maurice Sand, *Masques et Bouffons*, ii, 258. The combination is rooted in human nature, but it is demanded by the requirements of comic art. See chapter vi above and note 22 below.

two Jodelets of Scarron, and the cowards of the 'character'-writers are examples; and even in our time an audience knows as well what it means when such a charge comes from the lips of one already discredited as when a drunken man declares that he is not drunk and that others are. To clinch the business, immediately upon his words follows the ironical dramatic reversal and traditional comic situation of the robbery of the robber [22]—'le voleur volé'—and the fat rogue roaring and running off. What dunce in the audience would now fail to follow the drift? Morgann may think it not roaring if he pleases, for particulars in a play cannot be verified as in a history; but it is difficult to conceive how Poins could now say to the Prince on Gadshill, 'How the fat rogue roared' unless he had just been doing it; or the Prince afterwards in Eastcheap could cast it up to Falstaff in the presence of all who heard him, without fear of denial—'roar'd for mercy, and still run and roar'd,' and not like a lion, either, but 'as ever I heard bull-calf.' But to Morgann of course the play is not the whole story!

And when Falstaff with his craven crew, first bursts in, sweating to death, upon Prince Hal and Poins at the Boar's Head, he still cries out on cowards, again and again, as he drinks. Then, once he has caught his breath, come the 'incomprehensible lies' of the men in buckram and Kendal green, the acting out of the combat—'wards,' 'blows,' and 'extremities'—and the swindling exhibition of battered buckler, bloodied garments, and hacked sword. And just like the coward denying his cowardice and the drunken man denying his drunkenness, he now cries, 'I tell thee what, Hal, if I tell thee a lie, spit in my face, call me horse!' 'Wilt thou believe me, Hal?' he says on a like occasion, again much misdoubting in his bluster; 'three or four bonds apiece and a seal ring of my grandfather's.' We have seen him fighting, we know his 'old ward' and how he 'bore

---

[22] Eckhardt, *Die lustige Person*, pp. 151-52. See, above, the chapter on Shylock, p. 316; and compare Bergson.

his point,' and at these we laugh as at the 'eight-penny matter' (for so the Prince will have it) of the bonds and ring. Even if we should suspect him of saying it all for fun, on the spur of the moment, we now learn from blushing Bardolph of 'his monstrous devices'—that like the cowardly Dericke of the *Famous Victories of Henry V* [23] he had persuaded them all to tickle their noses with speargrass, and to hack their swords with their daggers. As the precious coward Parolles, who thinks also of cutting his garments and breaking his Spanish sword, plans to do, he had given himself some hurts, though 'slight' ones, and now swears he had 'got them in exploit.' [24] Here are all the conventional and traditional tricks of cowardice,[25] and on the exposure of cowardice the comic effect of the scene depends as much as on the reproof of the lies.

> Ah! je le veux charger ce maistre fanfaron:
> On ne peut l'estre tant, et n'estre pas poltron.[26]

> Tout homme de courage est homme de parole.
> —*Le Menteur,* III, ii.

> Lo que me tiene dudoso
> Es que sea mentiroso
> Un hombre que es tan valiente.
> —*La Verdad sospechosa,* II, xiii.

Such is the proverbial wisdom of the time, adopted in the drama; and when a character who is brave and yet a liar is presented, Alarcón and Corneille must needs thus make a point of it, and indicate that here is an innovation and a

---

[23] 1585-88. As is well known, Shakespeare was acquainted with the play, and drew from it the traits of Falstaff's cowardice, thievishness, and loose living, the touches of repentance and sanctimoniousness, and his friendship with Prince Hal.

[24] See *All's Well,* IV, i, for all these details; cf. Pistol, *Henry V,* V, i, 93-94;

> And patches will I get unto these cudgell'd scars,
> And swear I got them in the Gallia wars.

[25] Aside from the other instances cited, there is that in Theophrastus, *Characters,* xxvii (xxv), where the coward 'smears himself with another's blood to show,' etc.

[26] From an older play, the title of which I cannot now recall.

new departure. In this case that is not done, and in the cowardice lies the whole point of twitting him with his boasting lies and excuses;—if in fun Falstaff had run away or lied what fun would there be in confuting him?—but twice in the scene the Prince calls him coward into the bargain, and casts it up to him that he had 'hacked his sword and then said it was in fight.'[27] 'What a slave art thou!' Hal says truly.

Nor by his shifts and evasions, 'I knew ye' and 'on instinct,' does he come off safe and sound. Throughout the rest of the scene, and even in Part II, he and his companions in cowardice are twitted with them.[28] It is the Prince that does the twitting, and the Prince should know. 'No more of that, Hal,' cries the fat knight, 'an thou lovest me'; and that is not the tone of triumph. In the midst of this same scene his cowardice breaks out spontaneously anew. 'Zounds,' snarls Poins, 'an ye call me coward, I'll stab thee.' And the knight of Eastcheap sidles off, comically enough giving the words just on his lips the lie: 'I call thee coward! I'll see thee damned ere I call thee coward; but I would give a thousand pound I could run as fast as thou canst. . . . Call you that backing of your friends? A plague upon such backing! give me them that will face me!' Just so he falters, and his bluster rings loud but hollow, when in Part II the servant of the Chief-Justice begs leave to tell him that he lies in his throat. '*I* give thee leave to tell me so! If thou gettest any leave of me, hang me!' Calls he this the facing of his foes? He shouts as he retreats, he barks as he runs, he jokes and quibbles to cover up his cowardice and confusion.

6.

Through the rest of the play his cowardice is, as Morgann drolly confesses, still 'thrust forward and pressed

---

[27] II, iv, 288; 'Coward'; also lines 268, 542.
[28] II, iv, 311-35.

upon our notice.' A coward Shakespeare will have him if
Morgann won't. Even now, even after Gadshill, the
dramatist, if so he had intended to do, might have let
Falstaff retrieve himself, by actions at least, and not merely
by wit or ingenuity, and induce the world to believe, what
without deeds the world to believe would be little inclined
—that his retreat was genuinely strategic, that he ran away
only to fight another day, that his cowardice had been a
pretence or a venial and momentary aberration. Instead,
it is what Morgann will not have it be—if not 'constitutional,' at least habitual. When he hears the news of the
uprising, he ingenuously asks the Prince whether he is not
horribly afeard, and in reply is told that the Prince lacks
some of his instinct. When told by the Prince that he had
been procured a charge of foot, he cries, 'Well, God be
thanked for these rebels, they offend none but the virtuous.
I laud them, I praise them.' Like a Stoic, in his own character he finds his consolation. And when he is ordered off
to the North he wishes this tavern were his drum; and on
the eve of the fray whimpers, 'I would 'twere bed-time, Hal,
and all well,' [29] and then says his catechism of dishonour.
Standing by as Prince Hal and Hotspur come together,
he proves to be as good at encouraging others to fight as
the white-livered Moron and Panurge.[30] Then he falls
flat and feigns death as clowns and cowards did in the hour
of danger, not in England only but in contemporary Germany, Spain, and Italy;[31] and above all sets the seal on

[29] 'This articulated wish is not the fearful outcry of a coward, but the
frank and honest breathing of a generous fellow, who does not expect to
be seriously reproached with the Character' (Morgann p. 83). It is a
confession that even in our day, on the stage or off it, a character of
Falstaff's record and reputation would not risk with impunity. How much
less in more rough-and-ready times!

[30] *Princesse d'Élide,* I, iii, intermède, where, perched in a tree, Moron
urges on the archers to kill the bear; and Rabelais, II, chap. 29, where
Panurge cheers on his master.

[31] *Locrine* (1586), II, v, Strumbo; Beolco (Ruzzante), First Dialogue;
see Créizenach, iv, 340, for both; Cicognini, *Convitato di Pietra* (published
before 1650), sc. 7, where Passarino falls flat to save himself, though not

his cowardice by the dastardly blow and by hatching the scheme to take the honour of killing Hotspur to himself. 'I'll swear I killed him,' he says, 'nothing confutes me but eyes and nobody sees me'; and could anything more effectually contradict the opinion that he 'stood on the ground of natural courage only and common sense, and renounced that grinning idol of military zealots, honour,' than his undertaking, like the pitiful poltroons, Pistol, Parolles, and Bessus,[32] to filch 'bright honour,' which the man fallen at his feet had boldly plucked? Men of principle, scorning glory, do not snatch at other men's. Such wreaking of one's self on a dead body, moreover, is, like his 'playing possum,' one of the established *lazzi* of the coward on the stage. Moron beats the bear once it is dead; the Franc Archier de Baignollet (c. 1480) beats the scarecrow once he recognizes it as such; and in Shakespeare's time clowns played pranks on corpses both in England and Germany.[33] Here in the battle, then, is a little heap of *lazzi*, or bits of 'business,' all stamped as those of a coward, not only intrinsically, but by immemorial custom; and it is difficult to see how

by feigning death; *Jodelet, Maître-valet* I, v; Calderón, *Príncipe constante,* I, xiv, Brito, the gracioso; and for this 'business' in contemporary Germany cf. Creizenach, *Englische Comödianten,* p. cv. In *Have with you to Saffron Walden* (1596), moreover, Nash, referring to an epigram of Campion's on Barnabe Barnes, and much exaggerating the tenor of the text, remarks: 'He shewes how hee bragd when he was in France he slue ten men, when (fearfull cowbaby [coward]) he never heard peice shot off but he fell flat on his face.' And in the character of the 'coward' Nicholas Breton (*The Goode and the Badde,* 1616) says that he 'falls flat on his face when he hears the cannon.'—The reader must bear with me as one labouring now and then under the necessity of demonstrating what is obvious.

[32] Beaumont and Fletcher's *A King and No King.* He declares to all the audience that he will swear that the knife in his hand is all that is left of the sword which he had vowed to make his enemy eat. For Pistol and Parolles see above, note 24. Cf. the conduct of those cowards and braggarts in Renaissance epic, Martano in the *Orlando Furioso* (xvii, 108-16) and Braggadochio, in the *Faerie Queene* (V, iii). Both claim honours that others have won.

[33] *Princess d'Élide,* intermède; *Recueil,* Picot et Nyrop, line 355. Their motives, of course, are different, for Falstaff's is his fear that Hotspur may come to life and his craving for the honour and profit of killing him. Piston, another coward, robs a corpse in *Soliman and Perseda* (II, i).

Shakespeare could have effaced that impression had he tried.

7.

In the Second Part the 'satyr, lecher, and parasite' in Falstaff are uppermost, and the captain rests on his laurels. But how these were won we know, and cannot take seriously his reputation for valour with certain ladies of Eastcheap, with Davy, Justice Shallow, or even 'the enemy' at Shrewsbury and at Gaultree Forest. The effect of Dame Quickly's and Doll Tearsheet's praise of his prowesss in stabbing and foining, and the trepidations of Snare (true Elizabethan constable) at the mere thought of it, would with us be inconsiderable, even if, with most of the English critics, including Professor Bradley himself, we failed to detect the gross and palpable *double entente*.[34] And what a witness is Shallow, whose 'every third word is a lie,' whose every word is ludicrous! Well might Falstaff break Skogan's head ('some boisterous fencer,' thinks Morgann, but really Court Fool) on that day in the calendar when Shallow himself fought Sampson Stockfish, fruiterer[35]—'the very same day

[34] Part II, II, i, 15; II, iv, 252. For the former cf. Schmidt's *Lexicon* under *stab,* and *Julius Cæsar,* I, ii, 277. As for the second reference, *foin* must be used with the meaning evident in Beaumont and Fletcher's *Loyal Subject,* I, iv; so, Part II, II, i, 21-22, *thrust;* cf. the frequent instances of *double entente* in the words *pike, lance, target,* etc. Their equivalents are to be found contemporaneously in foreign languages, French, Italian, and Spanish. By strange coincidence La femme in the farce of *Colin, fils de Theuot* (Viollet-le-duc, ii, 396) complains to Theuot that the coward and braggart Colin, his son, 'empoigna ma chambrière'; for such quibbles are international. And that so certain in *stab, foin,* and *thrust,* which immediately precede and follow Quickly's remark that ''a cares not what mischief he does if his weapon be out' (l. 16), casts grave suspicion even on its simplicity and honesty of purpose, though not in Mr Bradley's eyes (*ibid.* p. 266). The Reverend Richard Stack, D.D., in 1788, in Ireland, saw the joke, though Morgann did not, even as remote from life as from the stage; and the prowess of Falstaff is but that of Colin.—Cf. also *Every Man in his Humour,* IV, iv.

[35] For the coward fighting a coward, see below, p. 433. Stockfish was 'haddocke or hake beaten with clubbes or stockes,' and a fruiterer was at least as tame as a tailor. Fruit and salads have in England always been thought an unmanly diet, weak and watery; and both diet and trade played then a bigger part in a man's life than now.

did I fight with one Sampson Stockfish, a fruiterer, behind
Gray's Inn.' That was a day that ended 'without the perdi-
tion of souls.' Jesu, Jesu, the mad days that they had
spent! Never in the history of the duello was there to be
such another till Master Slender, tall man of his hands,
'fought with a warrener.' [86] And a ballad, as Falstaff himself says, not sober history, is the place for chronicling his
capture of Colville and his drubbing of Pistol. 'The rogue
ran from me like quicksilver,' he reports, hugely to his own
satisfaction (and that of Morgann), though just before
that he had said that Pistol would not swagger with a
Barbary hen if her feathers turned back in any show of
resistance; and Colville surrendered 'more of his courtesy,'
says the caustic Lancaster, 'than your deserving.' The difference in his conduct in the two rencounters offers no difficulties. In Eastcheap he takes fire from the ladies' eyes—

> l'amour est un grand maître,
> Ce qu'on ne fut jamais, il nous enseigne à l'être;

and he is not only heated but elated and exhilarated by his
achievement, receives complacently Doll's praises and
caresses as the fit guerdon of his valour, and prolongs the
precious moment, unique and unparalleled in his experience,
by continually recurring to it:—'A rascal, to brave me!—
a rascally slave! I will toss the rogue in a blanket—A
rascal bragging slave! The rogue fled from me like quicksilver.' He fled, to be sure, but to Falstaff's delight. But
at Gaultree Forest he need not run and 'sweat for' his
captive, conquers merely by his aspect and the sheer terror
of his name, and—there is no one to believe it. So he
must needs jest and carry it off with his humour, whilst he
swaggers. Yet both pretences and also appearances of
valour, like his downright boasting and his philosophy of
discretion, only serve to heighten the comic—the cowardly
—effect.

[86] *M. W. W.*, I, iv, 29.

In either incident it is the same Falstaff; and our knight's reputation for valour had been as lightly won as that of Beaumont's Bessus, though he has not Bessus' reason to lament the winning of it.[37] Obviously Lancaster and the audience know more about that and his character, too, than Colville; and if Shakespeare had had any notion of redeeming him in our eyes, he would not have had his 'pure and immaculate valour' snubbed by his chief. The testimony of the Chief-Justice is a more serious matter; reminded by his servant that Falstaff 'had since [since the robbery] done good service at Shrewsbury,' he later tells him that 'his day's service at Shrewsbury had gilded over his night's exploit at Gadshill.' The Chief-Justice is not prejudiced in his favour; and apart from the dramatic necessity of letting the clown escape the clutches of the law, the only explanation can be that Shakespeare knows that his audience will not go astray—at Gadshill, at Eastcheap afterwards, and at Shrewsbury, Falstaff's character had already been sufficiently exhibited and demonstrated, and his reputation, in a sense, established,—and now he secures a comic effect by thus reminding us of Falstaff's martial exploits, and by letting him thus profit by this great dignitary's acceptance of his own report of killing Hotspur, through the connivance of Prince Hal;

> For my part, if a lie may do thee grace
> I'll gild it with the happiest terms I have.

It is probably not intentional on the part of the dramatist, but the Chief-Justice uses the same word *gild*.

The famous soliloquy which follows his snubbing by Prince John, on sack as the cause of all wit and valour, is the epilogue to the old reveller's military career and the epitome of his character. His is 'Dutch courage,' 'pot

---

[37] *A King and No King*, III, ii. Like Falstaff's it is not of his earning, and it embarrasses him with challenges. Falstaff indeed complains of his name being terrible to the enemy, but there he is frankly joking.

valour,' he (by the convention of the soliloquy [38]) is free to acknowledge. It is an old saw and a familiar fact that wine makes cowards brave,[39]—Wi' usquebae we'll face the devil—Siccis omnia nam dura deus proposuit—and Falstaff speaks out (though behind his hand) when he says that men are but fools and cowards without it.

8.

After this running comment on the two Parts of *Henry IV* we might, if it were necessary, further strengthen the case against Falstaff's courage by considering how the character continues and develops the dramatic and legendary tradition concerning Sir John Fastolf, or Falstaff, and Sir John Oldcastle, Lord Cobham. As is well known, our knight bore the name Oldcastle in the original draft of Part I, like the thievish loose-liver in the *Famous Victories*. These traits, as well as the rags and tatters of piety which both have about them, are taken from the Lollard as traduced in monkish chronicle and popular song. And when, at the complaint of the contemporary Lord Cobham, Shakespeare was moved to make amends to the martyr in the epilogue to Part II, and change the name to Falstaff in the text, he dropped one coward of popular and dramatic tradition only to take up another. In the *First Part of Henry VI*, Act III, scene ii, Sir John Fastolf, who in fact lost a battle in France, runs ignominiously away to 'save himself.' In real life both Sir Johns were brave and worthy fellows; [40] they are thus overwhelmed with obloquy because in the popular imagination one charge, as this of heresy [41]

[38] See above and below, pp. 468.

[39] Somerville, *The Wife*. It is a notion found in popular lore, as in the story of the mouse which, after drinking spilt brandy, cries, 'Now bring on that cat!' On the stage, Lady Macbeth confesses that she had drunk wine to stiffen her nerves (though Dr Furness will not hear of this); and the heroine in *La Tosca* actually drinks it.

[40] For Falstaff previous to Shakespeare see Gairdner, the *Dictionary of National Biography* (Oldcastle and Fastolf), and Baeske.

[41] As has been remarked by others, the Lollard Oldcastle as buffoon is a parallel to the 'Christian' as a stock comic figure in the late Greek mimus.

or that of cowardice, brings every other in its trail; but all that concerns us here is that in Shakespeare they are cowards because they were that before. Always our poet stands by public opinion, and his English kings or Roman heroes are to him what they were to his age. In the day that the name Cressida had come to be the equivalent of 'courtesan' or 'light-o'-love,' and Pandarus, of 'bawd,' how could Shakespeare on the popular stage make either anything else?[42] Even to the dramatist of our day, as Mr Archer observes, 'a hero must be (more or less) a hero, a villain (more or less) a villain, if accepted tradition so decrees it. . . . Fawkes must not be made an earnest Presbyterian, Nell Gwynn a model of chastity, or William the Silent a chatterbox.'

Sit Medea ferox invictaque, flebilis Ino.

I have suggested that many of the 'secret impressions of courage' are contradictions inherent in the type of the braggart captain. For to this type Falstaff unquestionably belongs. He has the increasing belly and decreasing leg, the diminutive page for a foil, the weapon (his pistol) that is no weapon but a fraud,[43] as well as most of the inner

---

[42] Cf. Professor Lawrence, *Columbia Shakespeare Studies* (1916), p. 207.

[43] Aristophanes' Kleonymus is of enormous size; Pyrgopolinices has long spindly legs; and most of the braggart soldiers have these, or a big paunch, or, like the Maccus of the atellans and sometimes Polichinelle, both the one and the other. Like the two latter characters and the English Punch, strange to say, Falstaff, in Morgann's time and perhaps earlier, was represented with a hump behind as well as before; for (p. 26) he recalls with horror the 'round tortoise-back,' produced by 'I know not what stuffing or contrivance.' Sancho Panza begins as a *miles,* for he has a big belly, short figure, and long legs, though afterward we hear no more of them. For the weapon see below. Their courage being called in question, as is the case with the above characters and with Falstaff and Lyly's Sir Tophas, it is in the spirit of ancient and Renaissance comic art, which delighted in physical contrasts, that their size should of itself be almost sufficient to substantiate the charge. 'When did you see a black beard with a white liver,' says Heywood, 'or a little fellow without a tall stomach?'

Capitano Spavento has a *paggio;* Ralph Roister Doister, Dobinet Doughtie; Sir Tophas, Epiton; Don Armado, Moth (Reich). Generally, like Falstaff's, the page is pert and impudent. So he is in Bentivoglio's *Il Geloso* (1543), as indeed are boys in Plautus.

qualities of this ancient stage-figure—cowardice and unbridled bragging, gluttony and lechery, sycophancy and
pride. Also he is a recruiting officer and (though it be in
the *Merry Wives of Windsor*) a suitor gulled.[44] All these
traits are manifest, except his sycophancy, which, however,
appears in his dependence on the Prince and his wheedling
ways with him; and except his pride, which appears in his
insistence on his title on every occasion, and in his reputation
for a proud jack among the drawers. Lyly's Sir Tophas,
Jonson's Bobadill and Tucca, Beaumont's Bessus, Chapman's Braggadino and Quintiliano,[45] the still earlier Ralph
Roister Doister, Ambidexter, and Thersites, as well as
Shakespeare's Pistol, Don Armado, and Parolles, have
most or many of these traits; and these descend to them, if
not from the classics directly, from the Italian popular *miles*,
Capitano Spavento.[46] The English and the Italian specimens differ from those of Plautus in that they are impecuni-
ous, the unwelcome parasites of tailor, barber, or landlady,
not the patrons of parasites. Falstaff is both the one and
the other.[47] Unlike most braggart captains, however, he is
not silly and affected—those qualities were reserved for
Pistol—boasts only when he has, not reason, but need to do
so, is not beaten and knocked about the stage but keeps a
sort of dignity, and is a humorist and wit. It is these circumstances no doubt that have made critics, even of late,
declare that the impression of his character is quite different, and is therefore not that of a coward. But all the
other traits save paunch and spindle-shanks are also the
traits of famous clowns—Panurge, Sosie, Folengo's Cingar,

[44] Both features are to be found in Pyrgopolinices.

[45] See Creizenach (1909), iv, 350. For some details of the type I am
indebted also to H. Graf, *Miles Gloriosus* (Rostock dissertation, 1892).

[46] Other names: Spezzafer, Fracasso, Matamoros, Spezza-Monti, Giangurgolo, Vappo, Rogantino, etc. (Sand).

[47] He has his landlady and his tailor; has his gull Shallow, as Quintiliano
has his Innocentio and Giovanelli, and Bobadill has his Matthew; and yet
he keeps Bardolph and perhaps Peto and Nym. How, one wonders; but
also how other people in Shakespeare and the earlier drama make or
provide a living.

Scarron's Jodelet—and even now a clown not a coward is a rarity on the stage. In that day of unanalytical but prodigally copious characterization, whereby on the stage (or as in the case of Machiavelli, Luther, and Oldcastle himself, in popular tradition) a villain engrosses all criminal traits, a comic character may be granted the vicious ones.[48] Falstaff (as clown) already a cheat, a liar, a boaster, a glutton, a lecher, and a thief, could hardly help being a coward as well. Otherwise he would have disappointed the audience: in itself cowardice is a more comical vice than the others.

Much has been said about Falstaff being done from the life—even with George Peele or Henry Chettle for a model—but except in tone or in tricks of manner it is now evident that this could not be. The whole man or a tithe of him never trod the earth. Much, too, has been said of the Capitano and the Matamore arising out of the intestine turmoil in Italy and the Spanish invasion, of the *miles gloriosus* arising out of the Roman wars in Asia and Africa, and of the *Alazon* out of the Alexandrian conquests. Something similar has been said of the *fallax servus* of Roman comedy, but Sellar's remark fits not only in this case but the others. 'Though a wonderful conception of the humorous imagination, it is a character hardly compatible with any social conditions.' [49] As I have said in a previous chapter, nothing is so rare as realism—nothing in itself so hateful to the public or by name so dear. The braggart captains,

---

[48] See above, pp. 427-28. Jodelet has been called: 'insolent, lubrique, hâbleur, et pardessus tout poltron.' Of the vices of Panurge Rabelais (II, chap. 16) gives a famous catalogue, including lewdness, cozening, drinking, roystering, and thieving, but forgetting the rest of them—boasting, cruelty, and cowardice. Cingar and Pulci's Margutte have a still more formidable array of merry sins. And the same lavish style appears in other characters of the old Italian popular comedy than the Capitano, as the Bucco of the atellans (who was 'suffisant, flatteur, fanfaron, voleur, lâche'), and Pulcinella, who besides these qualities inherits those of the Maccus, 'vif, spirituel, un peu féroce' (Sand, i, 126). Compare in the sixteenth century the popular mythopoeic characterization of Machiavelli among the northern nations, especially in the drama, and of Luther among the southern.

[49] *Poets of the Republic* (Oxford, 1889), p. 170.

the valets who beat and bamboozle their masters, the nurses
and chambermaids who scold them or thwart them in every
wish, the women who put their husbands in bodily fear, and
the timid and pureminded maidens who upon provocation
make love, and in men's clothing seek the beloved through
field and forest in lands remote, all please only by their
rarity or unreality, being incompatible with conditions under
which women and servants knew no liberty, and a soldier
stood or fell by his personal prowess alone. He sees deeper
who finds that the marvellous exploits of Alexander provoked a spirit of irony and satire in the Athenian public
and playwrights.[50] Hence—directly out of the humorous
imagination—these creations so extravagant and improbable.

9.

The braggart captain, indeed, is incompatible with himself. Cowards do not go to war, or, if driven to it, do not
become captains. Or if even that be not beyond the compass of chance and their own contriving, the clever ones do
not boast so extravagantly as to rob themselves of credence
and engage themselves in undertakings which it is farthest
from their wish to approach. The huge and delectable
contrasts of the old comedy involve contradictions as huge,
and the spectators blinked fact—if indeed they were not
blind to it—in the throes of their laughter. After Gadshill
a fellow so clever would neither have let his lies grow on
his hands nor—except on the defensive—have undertaken
to lie at all. He would have lain low, and kept out of the
limelight. But how tame for an Elizabethan, to whom
what is 'gross, open, palpable' was a delight! Bulthaupt
seriously wonders why Falstaff went to war, and concludes
that he went exalted through his humour above all fear;[51]

[50] O. Ribbeck, *Alazon*, pp. 32-34.
[51] *Dramaturgie* (1894), ii, 74. He has reached a state of philosophic
calm. 'Er scheint seiner selbst so sicher dass er seine Ruhe oder die Frei-
heit einer Seele auch in der kritischsten Lage nicht zu verlieren fürchtet.'
Bradley speaks of his having 'risen superior to all serious motives.'

and Morgann, as we have seen, like many a critic since, has thought it fine and brave of him, and has dwelt fondly on the Prince's preference of him to others for a charge of foot, on a dozen [52] bare-headed sweating captains knocking at taverns and asking everyone for Sir John Falstaff, or on Falstaff's leading his men where they are peppered.[53] He might as well wonder why a monster of a miser like Harpagon keeps a coach and horses, a cook and a troop of servants, and conclude that he must be freehanded after all. It is on the stage—it is in a comedy—and he keeps servants, as Sarcey recognizes, to stint them, and horses to get up nights and steal away their oats. And Falstaff goes to the wars to say his catechism, brandish a bottle for a pistol, fall dead, joke, cheat, and lie. In that day of prodigious contrasts and unchartered mirth a coward who does not rob on the highway or follow the wars—is no coward. To impute it to Falstaff's courage that he is in demand on the eve of war and goes to war without murmuring would mean that we must do the like to Parolles, who yearns for the wars in Italy and persuades his master to take him there; and to those 'true-bred cowards' Ancient Pistol, Lieutenant Bardolph, and Corporal Nym, who, in the later play, follow the heroic young king into France. Falstaff goes to war to furnish matter for comedy, the Prince gives him a charge to get him to the war, and the dozen captains come sweating to fetch the luxurious laggard to his charge.[54] This in itself is an anticlimactic joke, blunted by the critics. It is in Part II. Peto bursts in with the news of war for the Prince;

[52] A ballad-like exaggeration such as Shakespeare indulges himself in when it costs the Company nothing. Like Capulet's 'twenty cunning cooks' they 'stay at door'—do not tread the stage.

[53] Morgann (like Mr Bradley) comments on the fact that it is 'led' not 'sent.' If he led them there,' as Stack says, 'he there left them'; and Falstaff has just entered *solus*. *They* are peppered. 'Though I could scape shot-free at London, I fear the shot here.'

[54] It matters not that the 'charge' was given in Part I and that he was fetched in Part II. The situation is quite the same—on the eve of departure to the war.

but the hot-foot inquiry—after Gadshill, after Shrewsbury
—is for—Sir John Falstaff! Not a word about the Prince,
whom he is addressing, the hero of Shrewsbury, of Agin-
court to-be! But, as we have seen, that is not the only joke
that has been spoiled for us.

10.

Two situations in which Falstaff is placed are connected
with the *miles gloriosus* traditionally. The coward taking
a captive, as Falstaff takes Colville, is an incongruous but
mirth-provoking situation which Shakespeare found in the
Famous Victories, and repeats in *Henry V* when Pistol,
who, according to the Boy, has not a tenth of even Nym's
or Bardolph's exiguous valour, captures Monsieur le Fer;
and it appears before that in the fine old French farce of
Colin, filz de Theuot le maire (where the hero, boasting of
a prisoner, is afraid to fetch him in because of his iron-
bound staff, though in the end he turns out to be a German
pilgrim, not a Turk) as well as in the combat of Braggadochio with Trompart in the *Faerie Queene.* Colin, as
Falstaff does and Pistol ought to do, might well 'thank
thee for thee.' In all these instances, moreover, there
must have been much comic 'business,' furnished by the
actors to remind us that the captor is like unto the captive.[55] It is unthinkable that Pistol with his Frenchman

[55] Morgann denies that Falstaff roared as he ran away because there
is no stage-direction, though the roaring is remarked upon by both Poins
and the Prince. He might have supplied it. See Creizenach, *Englische
Comödianten,* p. xcviii, *Geschichte,* iv, 343-344, for evidence, if that were
necessary, that stage-directions as we have them are very incomplete. So
they are in printed plays to-day, but they vastly diminish in quantity as we
go back through three centuries. At this point we should recall Viola pitted
against Aguecheek as we have seen them on the stage, or the more explicit
text of *L'Avantureux* (1521). 'Ils reculent toujours pour prendre du
champs et crient: À mort! à mort!' Cf. *Henry V,* II, i, Nym and Pistol.
Colville, of course, is no coward, but is comically mistaken. 'Il fait de son
épée cadeau.'

should have been no funnier at the Globe than he is in the text.[56]

The other situation is that of the soldier who keeps his appetite, though scared. Another contradiction, though to the ancients and the men of the Renaissance it betokened not coolness and presence of mind but a base and besotted nature, dead to name and fame.[57] Falstaff sleeps and snores while the watch seek for him; and has his bottle on the field just as Sosie, after he has run and hidden in the tent, drinks wine and eats ham.[58] And the putting of a bottle in his case for a pistol is a stranger contradiction still.[59] According to our notions a coward would go armed to the teeth;[60] but earlier art, as we have frequently noticed, is prone to ignore analysis and present character in an outward and typical way.[61] Shaw's Bluntschli, in our

[56] The more general situation of the coward fighting the coward, or a woman, is common with the type: Falstaff fights Pistol and has a row with Quickly and her constables; Roister Doister is beaten by women; Thersites (1537) and Ambidexter fight with these and with snails and butterflies; and Giangurgolo, the Calabrian, gets into a rage with poor inoffensive people and fights with eunuchs (Sand, i, 202). Cf. Graf, p. 35.

[57] In 'contempt of glory,' says Hazlitt (ed. 1864, p. 190), determined, as always, to make him superior to circumstances. Cf. his suggestion that Falstaff may have put the tavern-reckoning in his pocket 'as a trick.' And when he falls asleep, I suppose, he is feigning once more. On the contrary, his falling asleep may be no more than a device of the dramatist's to get his pocket picked without his knowing it. Galindo, moreover, the cowardly, boastful, and impudent *gracioso* in Lope's *Comendadores de Córdoba,* must have no less than a cask to wash down the wing of a fowl; even so Falstaff requires two gallons to a half-penny-worth of bread.

[58] *Amphitryon,* I, ii. For Falstaff the wine may be there to bolster him up, or only to cool his thirst on a hot day. Cf. Part II, I, ii, 235.

[59] Mr W. J. Lawrence (*Gent. Mag.,* 1906, p. 164) thinks it must be a leather bottle, in the shape of a pistol, of which he has seen eight specimens. But that would spoil the point: the audience must be made to see for themselves that a pistol it is not.

[60] Sometimes, indeed, the Matamore was so represented. Cf. Sand, i, 197. This later realism appears in *L'Avantureux;* and in *Jodelet duelliste,* when the coward takes all unfair precautions by securing the most formidable weapons and wearing concealed a cuirass and a steel cap. Falstaff himself seems to appreciate the uses of a sword when he refuses to lend his to Hal; though this, again, may be no more than a device of the dramatist's to introduce the practical joke of the pistol.

[61] Cf. the delight in discordant sounds attributed to the Malcontents, Jaques and Marston's Malevole, and the deserted woman's wearing the

day, carries an unloaded pistol, and chocolate instead of
cartridges; yet does not therefore lose a reputation for
courage (though for commonsense) in our eyes as he does
in those of the romantic Raina. But the 'Coward' in Theophrastus hides his sword in his tent under his pillow; and
time and again in Renaissance drama the coward finds
his sword rusted in,[62] or, drawing it, can show but the half
of a blade, or, like Basilisco (in *Soliman and Perseda*) a
painted lath. Capitano had a spider's web around his
sheath; and Harlequin (like the Greek beardless satyr,[63]
Pulcinella, at times,[64] and the English Vice), wore as the
symbol of his cowardice a wooden sword, not out of keeping
with the rabbit scut[65] in his hat. M. Jusserand has
remarked upon the use of signs and symbols in medieval
drama and painting—God on the stage in the habiliments
of pope or bishop, and St Stephen painted with a stone, not
on his crown, but on his palm, St Lawrence toying with his
gridiron, or Samson being shorn in the lap of Delilah with
the ass's jawbone still in his hand![66] In the Italian paintings
of saints and martyrs the martyrdom often seems as external and as much a thing apart as in Falstaff does his cowardice; they look strangely comfortable, and Bellini's St
Peter Martyr, with a hatchet sunk in his brain and a sword
buried to the hilt in his bosom, stands before you unshaken

willow (see above, chapter vii, section 12), the melancholy woman with
her hair down and the man with his hat over his brows and his arms folded,
and the lovesick in the condition of Benedick and Beatrice described in the
next section. External though it be, this method of characterization is only
another form of the apparent self-consciousness which we have frequently
noted.

[62] T. Jordan, *Pictures of Passions* (1641), 'A Plundering Coward': 'A
heavy iron sword, which fondly grows to the kinde scabbard.' Cf. Middleton's *Witch*, V, i. The coward Aberganes cannot draw, and does 'not care
to see it—'tis only a holiday thing to wear at a man's side.' Fletcher's
cowardly Little French Lawyer is in the same plight; and compare Bentivoglio, *Il Geloso* (1545), v, p. 38, where Brandonio, the braggart soldier,
unable to draw his sword, is jeered at for it aside by his page.

[63] *Grande Encyclopaedie*, s. v. 'Arlequin.'

[64] Sand, i, 132.

[65] Sand, i, 68.

[66] See an engraving of H. Aldegraver's, 1528.

and unruffled. Even in Goldoni's *Locandiera* the chicken-hearted Marchese's sword is rusted in, and when out is no more than a stump; and in this case, as in the others, the point is not that the character is afraid of cold steel, or 'naked weapons,' but that his martial profession is a burlesque and fraud. In the *miles* it is a touch in sympathy and in keeping with the whole extravagant, external scheme.

II.

Further consideration of Falstaff's cowardice depends on the 'incomprehensible lies' of the buckram story and the problems which they involve. Not lies they are by most English critics thought to be, but mere 'waggery' to amuse himself or the Prince; [67] and by some Germans they are considered to be a case of unconscious exaggeration. [68] No one, so far as I know, [69] has suggested that Falstaff undertakes to deceive, and yet without intending a jest falls into the preposterous exaggerations and contradictions of a sailor or fisherman spinning a yarn. Still a scamp, he is no longer a wit. As for the intention to deceive, that, in the light of what we have already said about the Elizabethan practical joke should, to any student of the period, be apparent. Poins's prediction, we have seen, is fulfilled to the letter—'how thirty at least he fought with; what wards, what blows, what extremities he endured'—and is further confirmed by the purposed fraud of his 'monstrous devices.' And as for

[67] Morgann, Coleridge, Hazlitt, Lloyd, Maginn, Wetz (p. 406), Bradley (p. 264), Professor Matthews (p. 129), though it does not seem like him.

[68] Wolff, i, 426; but like most of the Germans he refuses to entertain the notion that Falstaff also meant to deceive. Bulthaupt (ii, 72-73), troubled by the inconsistency of the character, seems to take the middle course of having Falstaff half in earnest, half in jest.

[69] Gervinus (Lon., 1863, i, pp. 452, 453) and Wolff (i, 425) seem to incline to the opinion; but probably mean no more than 'witty myself and the cause that wit is in other men' (Part II, I, ii, 11). And by that Falstaff means only that he furnishes others matter for mirth by his personal appearance. Gervinus, recognizing in him the combination of wit and butt, treats it philosophically, is not troubled by the psychological incongruity.

the unconscious exaggerations and contradictions, he is like the Playboy of the Western World, who at first says that he riz the loy and let fall the edge on his father's skull; later says that he halved his skull; then that he split him to the knob of his gullet; then that with one blow he cleft him to the breeches belt.[70] Only, in Christy Mahon's case, the intervals between these exaggerations are so wide, the motivation provided in them by the admiration of his hearers and his own waxing enthusiasm so subtle and complete, that his reputation for intelligence hardly suffers. Falstaff piles up his exaggerations pellmell, despite the interrupting jeers of the Prince and Poins, and turns at once from wit to butt. 'What, fought you with them all?' cries the Prince in mock admiration.—'All! I know not what you call all; but if I fought not with fifty of them, I am a bunch of radish,' etc.—'Pray God you have not murdered some of them,' he cries again, in mock compassion and alarm.—'Nay, that's past praying for; I have pepper'd two of them. Two, I am sure, I have paid, two rogues in buckram suits.' And though the two are there before him, endeavouring to preserve their composure, upon the infatuated old rogue the truth does not break. All this, unplausible in one so clever, is, with the repetition and accumulation in the tale, highly comical; and often in drama comic effect is obtained at the expense of psychological verisimilitude. Moreover, there is here some warrant for it—on the one hand in the well-known craving of your coward for the name of courage in default of the reality, on the other hand in the exhilaration of this particular moment (after such a triumph, such an escape!) and in Falstaff's conspicuous powers of exuberant exaggeration. Thus explained, it is less unplausible than as a deliberate and unnecessary exhibition of these powers, to his own cost and discredit, and

[70] Such a comparison is not illegitimate. Synge abounds in old farcical material, dating back to the fabliaux, though, as here, treated with modern caution.

for the malicious pleasure of Poins and the Prince. And it is funnier. 'Les mots profondément comiques sont les mots naïfs, où un vice se montre à nu.'

What unplausibility is here to be found is paralleled elsewhere. The situation is the same as that in Heywood's *Fair Maid,* cited above. The only difference is that between great art and small; for in the same period a great popular artist and a mediocre one use much the same means of expression—'business,' situations, and types. That is to say, the difference is in the touch. In both cases before us there is the cowardly action, deliberately misrepresented in the report by means of bold exaggerations and contradictions,[71] satirically noticed by the hearer but without effect upon the speaker. Roughman is not witty, to be sure, nor, once started, does he let his numbers accumulate. But, like Falstaff not a fool, he too makes a fool of himself with his story. And there is another parallel in the case of Dekker's Matheo, who in similar circumstances boasts and lies about his prowess to the very man with whom he had had to do, Orlando.[72] In all alike it is an old and obvious comic situation that the audience are quick and simple enough, but the critics too deliberate and subtle, to understand—as to be comic a situation must be understood—at once. We laugh (or don't laugh) all in an instant, as the spark catches (or misses) fire.

A parallel to the general artistic method employed is to

---

[71] Morgann (p. 138) makes much of the circumstance that Falstaff's braggadocios are after the fact, not before it. But this is the case with a number of cowards. Ruzzante, in Beolco's First Dialogue, getting up from the ground, brags about what he would have done if his rival had been there alone instead of 'one of a hundred'; Swash, in Day's *Blind Beggar of Bednall Green,* echoing Falstaff, declares, 'I very manfully killed seven of the six,' though the rest carried away the money; Robin in Adam de la Halle's *Jeu de Robin et Marion;* Protaldye in *Thierry and Theodoret;* and it is so in life, of course, as well.

[72] *II Honest Whore,* IV, i, 259 ff. Cf. also Eckhardt, *Lustige Person,* pp. 352-353. The delight in lively lying, particularly with contradictions involved, is, like the delight in the play of the fancy for comic purposes, characteristic of Elizabethan times, as of those of Rabelais.

be found in the treatment of Benedick. Equally clever, he exposes his disgrace after he stumbles and falls, instead of endeavouring to conceal it. He betrays his lovesickness needlessly, without delay. Falstaff, if in real life, would not have held his tongue, to be sure, but he would not have let his lies pile up so carelessly, in the presence of his hard-hitting friends. Just so with Benedick. He falls in love despite all his railings against love and marriage; and he expects to suffer for it,—'I may chance have some odd quirks and remnants of wit broken on me.' And yet at his next appearance before others he bears upon him all the conventional marks and tokens of Elizabethan lovesickness. 'I am not as I have been,' he says himself; he shaves and rubs himself with civet; he 'is troubled with the toothache, for lovers ever are'; and he seems to have taken already to song and the lute.'[73] And he is then jeered at and laughed at, as Falstaff is. Certainly Benedick and Beatrice (for she acts similarly before the women), are the last people, as noted wits and professed enemies of love, thus to expose themselves to the gallants and lovers, just as Falstaff, a professional wit labouring under the charge of cowardice, is the last person thus to expose himself to the gibes of the sceptical Prince and the malicious Poins. Why, then, do they do it? Simply that the dramatist may secure a telling and immediate comic effect—that of the scorner scorned, the enemy of love fallen in love, the boaster and liar as a coward laid bare. Benedick and Beatrice lovesick, Falstaff boasting and lying, are treated typically, externally, somewhat as are the Capitano with his sword rusted in and Falstaff when carrying a bottle for a pistol, and that he who runs may read, that he who chatters and scuffles in the pit may laugh and not fail. Not psychological consistency but dramatic effectiveness is Shakespeare's aim, and like every

[73] III, ii. His melancholy is remarked upon by Don Pedro; and evidently he is meant, like other Elizabethans in the plight, to 'wreathe his arms like a malcontent' and pull his hat over his eyes. Biron calls Dan Cupid 'lord of the folded arms.'

other dramatist he will sell, if not his own soul, at least a character's, for a contrast.

A butt (though only for moments) and Falstaff when he is not a wit is rather to be considered naïve. In the first scene in which he appears he falters in his jollity, and vows that he will give over this life, being now little better than one of the wicked. 'Where shall we take a purse to-morrow, Jack?' asks the Prince, slily. 'Zounds!' he shouts, 'where thou wilt, lad!' On a blue Monday at the Boar's Head he is for repenting once more as he moodily contemplates his wasting figure. Bardolph complains of his fretfulness. 'Why, *there* is it. Come sing me a bawdy song; make me merry!' If in these sayings he be self-conscious, how annoying and unnatural! Those critics who to keep for Falstaff his reputation as a humorist would have him here play a part, seem to do so at the expense of their own. It is not to be wondered at in Hegel and some few German critics [74] that, with philosophy in their every thought and brain-cell, they should shake their heads at the unenlightenment of Aristophanes, and turning their backs on Shakespeare, Cervantes, and Molière, should proclaim the highest species of humour to be intentional and conscious; but it is to be wondered at in Englishmen. 'Les choses exquises quand elles sont naïves, sont doublement exquises.' What joke could be made of this equal to the unconscious comical effect of the old sensualist plunged in penitence, and spontaneously buoyed up again, as by a specific levity? 'Peace, good Doll'—and here, too, he is not jesting but saying it with a shudder—'do not speak like a death's head; do not bid me remember mine end.' The pith of the humour lies in the huge appetite for purses, or for mirth, bursting in an instant the bonds of his penitence; just as it lies in the fact of his present thirst swallowing up the memory that his lips are not yet dry. 'Give me a cup of sack! I am a rogue if

[74] Ulrici, etc., but not Gervinus; cf. Wetz, pp. 402-3; Hegel (cited by Wetz), *Asthetik,* iii, 576). I am here indebted to Wetz.

I drunk to-day.' " He is as unconscious as inconsistency has been on the comic stage ever since—as Molière's philosopher, who declaims against wrath and presently gives way to it; or the duennas of Steele and Sheridan, who deprecate love and marriage for their nieces at the moment they are desperately seeking it for themselves.

12.

Naïve, then, as well as witty, and quite as much the cause of mirth in other men when he is least aware, Falstaff is less 'incomprehensible' both in his lies and, as we shall presently see, in his conduct generally. His wit is expended, not in making himself ridiculous for the sake of a joke unshared, unuttered, and therefore no joke at all, but, by hook or crook, in avoiding that. Dryden long ago remarked as his special accomplishments his shifts and quick evasions; as did Johnson his 'easy scapes and sallies of levity.' 'His wit,' says the former, 'lies in those things he says *praeter expectatum,* unexpected by the audience; his quick evasions when you imagine him surprised, which, as they are extremely diverting of themselves, so receive a great addition from his person.' Addison, who knew the ways and haunts of humour, which many of Shakespeare's critics have too little frequented, recognizes that Falstaff has need of these dexterities in his rôle—in that of butt:

The truth of it is, a man is not qualified for a butt who has not a good deal of wit and vivacity, even in the ridiculous side of his character. A stupid butt is only fit for the conversation of ordinary people: men of wit require one that will give them play, and bestir himself in the absurd part of his behaviour. A butt with these accomplishments frequently gets the laugh of his side and turns the ridicule upon him that attacks him. Sir J. Falstaff was an hero of this species, and gives a good description of himself in his capacity of a butt, after the following manner: 'Men of all sorts (says that merry knight) take a pride to gird at me,' etc., etc.—*Spectator,* no. 47.

[75] Such instances Wetz (p. 406), under the influence of Lloyd, considers intentional jokes, despite his insistence on Falstaff's *naïveté.* Bradley and other English critics agree.

Mézières, from his foreign point of view, says the same: 'on le fait parler ou on lui joue des tours plaisants . . . Il est le plastron de Henri et de Poins.'

Morgann, Lloyd, Maginn,[76] and even Mr Bradley[77] would find this all too simple; and, wrenching both plot[78] and character in the process, have him lie in no expectation of being believed, step into traps for the fun of wriggling out of them, and bid for gibes at his own expense. Losing is as good as winning, and Falstaff is out for exercise and his health! But from Aristophanes and Plautus down through the Renaissance to the present-day Eloquent Dempsey of Mr William Boyle there is a continual succession of characters who are well content to use their wits as they may to keep from smarting for their follies. Particularly is this the case with cowards and braggarts, with Panurge,[79] Capitano Spavento, and the various Elizabethan

[76] (1860) p. 51: 'It was no matter whether he invented what tended to laughter or whether it was invented upon him.' It is true that he is not resentful or sulky, but what clown is?

[77] Oxford Lectures, pp. 264-265. In treating Falstaff's mendacity Mr Bradley fails to observe distinctions which, as it seems to me, are required by the exigencies of dramatic technique, and which would have then been observed by an audience instinctively. Falstaff's braggadocios and his vowing himself a rogue if he had drunk to-day, are, though lies, very different in spirit and purpose from the shifts and evasions by which, like Aristotle below, he turns all to merriment and half saves his face. Still another sort of lie is that which serves no practical purpose—offends no idealistic scruples—his jest about his corpulence being due to sighing and grief and his voice being cracked by singing of anthems. But Mr Bradley rhetorically asks those who think that Falstaff expected to be believed in his buckram story whether he expected to be believed in these other cases as well. To make Falstaff, if a whole-hearted liar in one case, a whole-hearted liar in all, is like making Iago a liar even in soliloquy.

'I suppose they consider that Falstaff was in earnest,' he continues; 'when, wanting to get twenty-two yards of satin on trust, he offered Bardolph as security.' That is not a lie at all—is a case in no sense parallel to the others; but certainly he was as much in earnest as when he cheated Quickly and Shallow. He afterwards makes it plain that he had expected to get the satin (Part II, I, ii, 48-50). 'Or even when he sold his soul on Good Friday to the devil for a cup of Madeira and a cold capon's leg.' And that Falstaff never says, but the jeering and jesting Poins.

[78] See below, section 13, etc.

[79] Book IV, chapter 67, where he blames for his condition the famous cat Rodilardus.

specimens of the Captain—Parolles,[80] Bobadill, Bessus, Braggadino, and Sir Tophas. After saving their bacon their dearest desire is to save their face. Even those romancing liars whose cowardice is not in grain, Peer Gynt and Christy Mahon, are far from courting failure or discredit.

13.

Some of the most famous of Falstaff's shifts are in other plays actually duplicated. In *Look About You,* printed in 1600, Fauconbridge, having in ignorance of her presence spoken slightingly of his wife, avails himself of the evasion to which, when in Part II, it is mockingly suggested, Falstaff scorns to resort for a second time, having still another up his sleeve:

> *I knew thee,* Moll; now by my sword I knew thee;
> I winked at all; I laughed at every jest—Sc. 28.

And like Falstaff he is laughed at for it as much as is his jest. In Middleton's *Family of Love* it is the woman that is caught, and she 'knew thee as well as the child knows his own father—I knew him to be my husband even by very instinct.' So in Cicognini's *Don Juan,* Passarino, still more cowardly than his equivalent Leporello or Sganarelle, when surprised in a soliloquy far from loyal to his master, cries in panic, 'Faith, I saw you coming and I was only joking.' [81] Beaumont's Bessus, again, when taken to task declares that 'Bessus the coward wronged you, and shall Bessus the valiant maintain what Bessus the coward did?' And to a man who beats him he confesses that he 'shall think him a valiant fellow for all this.' For the sayings of the three English characters this is the model:

Why thou knowest I am as valiant as Hercules; but beware instinct; the lion will not touch the true prince. Instinct is a great

[80] *All's Well,* I, i, 215, and see above.
[81] *Il Convitato di pietra,* sc. 28: 'A v'haveva vist' alla fè, e per quest'a burlava cosi.'

matter; I was now a coward on instinct. I shall think the better of myself and thee during my life; I for a valiant lion, and thou for a true prince.

Thus, before or after him, some of Falstaff's shifts, like his 'monstrous devices' and his *lazzi* on the battlefield, were the recognized property of a double-dealer and poltroon. And that in such cases 'I knew thee' is only a subterfuge or 'belle response' is apparent from many other old stories where it is employed by one caught in error, not only the Ephesian matron in Chapman's *The Widow's Tears,* but the wives in all the similar stories, fabliau or novella, listed by Child.[82]

If Falstaff steps into the trap on purpose and is, as Mr Bradley says, aware that his slanders upon the Prince will be repeated to him; and, as most English critics say, went to Gadshill only for a lark; and, as Lloyd and Maginn suspect, actually knew the Prince and Poins, ran and roared to hold the good jest up, and hacked his sword and bloodied his own and his companions' clothing on the certain calculation that he should be betrayed; why, little enough then would depend on his evasions. Actually, as with all stage cowards, here lies the centre of interest.[83] The Prince and Poins press him hard:

Prince. What trick, what device, what starting-hole canst thou now find out to hide thee from this open and apparent shame?
Poins. Come, let's hear, Jack; what trick hast thou now?—Part I, II, iv, 293.
Prince. I shall drive you then to confess the wilful abuse, and then I know how to handle you. . . .
Poins. Answer, thou dead elm, answer.—Part II, II, iv, 338.

At times his embarrassment is for the moment as manifest as their glee, and he turns from bluster to coaxing and wheedling, as in these same scenes:

[82] *Ballads* (1888), iii, p. 258.
[83] As for the Capitano, see Hermann Grimm, *Essais* (1859), p. 165; for other braggart cowards see Petit de Julleville, *Histoire du Théâtre:* La Comédie, p. 258.

Prince. Content; and the argument [*of the play extempore*] shall be thy running away.

Falstaff. Ah, no more of that, Hal, an thou lovest me!

Part I, II, iv, 310.

Falstaff. No abuse, Hal, o' mine honour; no abuse.

Prince. Not to dispraise me and call me pantler and bread-chipper and I know not what?

Falstaff. No abuse, Hal.

Poins. No abuse?

Falstaff. No abuse, Ned, i' the world; honest Ned, none. I dispraised him before the wicked, that the wicked might not fall in love with him, . . . No abuse, Hal; none, Ned, none; no, faith, boys, none.

Prince. See now, whether pure fear and entire cowardice doth not make thee wrong this virtuous gentlewoman to close with us? Is she of the wicked? Is thine hostess here of the wicked? . . .

Poins. Answer, thou dead elm, answer.[84]—Part II, II, iv, 340.

That here was the centre of interest Dryden, Johnson, and Addison, so much better judges than Morgann and his followers, clearly and explicitly recognized; and both Tom Davies and Richard Stack point out that Morgann in not recognizing this lost the effect of wit and humour in Falstaff's happy afterthoughts in Eastcheap, which half save the day.[85] They knew, as Boccaccio knew, 'quanta sia la forza delle belle e pronte risposte.' 'It is a fine thing at all times to speak well,' he says, 'but I think it a finer to do so when need arises.' [86] Dryden, Johnson, and Addison too, had recognized Falstaff's need; Morgann and the Romantics rob him of it. Even Mr Bradley notices that Falstaff is stung by any thoroughly serious imputation upon his courage, and winces at the recollection of his run-

[84] Professor Tucker Brooke (*Yale Review,* 1918, p. 353) here considers the Prince the 'victim'; and compares him with Roderigo, and Falstaff with Iago, *Othello,* IV, ii, 170. The coaxing and deprecatory repetitions of Falstaff, even after he has scored a hit, sufficiently indicate the difference between his embarrassment and Iago's cool assurance.

[85] *Dramatic Miscellanies* (1785), i, p. 272; Stack (*op. cit.*) pp. 13, 34. They both point out that Morgann spoils the effect of the nimble and agile self-extrication.

[86] *Sixth Day,* seventh novel.

ning away on Gadshill. We have seen to what lengths he goes, hacking his sword, bloodying his garments, stabbing Hotspur's body in order to prove that he killed him, and then lying; and altogether he seems not so uplifted and indifferent as the critics think. But honour pricks him on,— honour, which is 'so indispensable,' says Barry Lyndon, who like Falstaff knew whereof he spoke, 'that we should attain it anyhow.'

Such—caught in a trap and trying to explain his way out of it—was the plight of the rogue in medieval and Renaissance comedy; but it was in particular the plight of the coward. L'Avantureux and the Franc Archier de Baignollet are excellent cases in point, as we show below. Colin, filz de Theuot le maire, when taken to task by his father for losing his jerkin (or perhaps coat of mail) in action, points to the greater ease of locomotion which results:

> Ne pensez vous pas qu'en pourpoint
> On coure mieulx que tout vestu?

and there are Bessus, Jonson's Bobadill, Lodowick Barry's Captain Face (in *Ram Alley*), Scarron's Jodelet, Bergerac's Chasteaufort (in the *Pédant joué*), Regnard's Marquis (in the *Joueur*), Beolco's Ruzzante, Bentivoglio's Brandonio (in *Il Geloso, 1545*), Piccolomini's Malagigi (in the *Alessandro, 1554*), Cecchi's Rodomonte (in the *Rivali*), Wycherley's Monsieur (in the *Dancing Master*), Sheridan's Bob Acres, and many others besides,—all quibbling and shuffling braggarts and cowards and most of them soldiers too. 'Sure, I was struck with a planet thence,' vows Bobadill as he reflects upon his inaction when belaboured by Downright; 'I was fascinated, by Jupiter,' he says again, 'fascinated.' No other explanation is adequate. So Ruzzante, he said, had suffered from enchantment. 'Tis a pretty hilt,' simpers Bessus when forced to unbuckle and surrender to his enemy a sword he dare not use; 'and with all my heart I present it to you as a new-year's gift.' 'Quoi,' cries Jodelet, as if in a transport of chivalrous magnanimity; 'c'est votre neveu? Je ne me bats pas!' 'When I have made up my mind for once in my life not to fight,' quoth Chasteaufort; 'a rogue like you can't make me change it.' Brandonio, besought by his page to pursue Truffa, who has carried off his cap and mantle, exclaims, 'Let him go to the devil, I make him a present of it.' Piccolomini's Malagigi, threatened by Ruzza sword in hand, declares solemnly that they shall meet again; and attributes his subsequent flight merely to a desire not to raise a row in the town. Wycherley's Monsieur will not fight with his rival in love, for 'if I should kill you I know I should do you a kindness; therefore e'en live, to die daily with envy of my happiness.' And Acres it is unnecessary to quote.[87] So have cowards done on the stage (or in life, for that matter) to this day; and how after Falstaff's conduct on Gadshill could the audience, with never a tip or a hint, discover that this seeming coward was not really a coward, and these seeming excuses not really excuses, but all mere make-believe?

14.

In what respects, now, do Falstaff's evasions differ from those of Bessus, Bobadill, or Jodelet? In his wit and somewhat in his purpose. Theirs, comical often without humour like those of Bacchus and Xanthias in *The Frogs,* are mere excuses and subterfuges and do not save them; Falstaff's, as unplausible and far-fetched as theirs, are not so craven and timorous, are indeed gay, aggressive, triumphant, and

[87] See below, p. 476. As for the others: *Every Man in His Humour,* IV, v, vii; Hazlitt's Dodsley x, p. 349; (Ruzzante) Sand, *Masques et Bouffons* (1860), ii, 105; *King and No King,* III, ii; *Jodelet maître-valet,* IV, vi; *Joueur,* III, xii; *Il Geloso,* V; *Alessandro* V, iii; *Rivali* III, iv; *Pédant joué,* II, i, ii; IV, ii, iii. *Gentleman Dancing-Master,* V, i. Cf. also Brighella's elaborate reasons for his conduct, interrupted by tell-tale fears; Gozzi's *Mostro Turchino,* IV, vi. Some of Chasteaufort's (*Pédant joué*) when he is beaten are as ingenious and diverting as Falstaff's.

as Poins presages, they 'drive the Prince out of his revenge and turn all to a merriment.' They are laughed at; but also they turn the laugh. Of Bobadill this cannot be said when, bidden to draw, he cries out, 'Tall man, I never thought on it till now—Body of me; I had a warrant of the peace served on me, even now as I came along, by a water-bearer.' Falstaff would not have stooped to such law-abiding; he has, as Davies has said, an impudent dignity; he carries things with a high hand, and expects to bear down all before him by sheer wit and mirth alone. In his evasions he does not generally expect to be believed (there the critics are right); in his bragging lies he does expect to be believed (and there the critics are wrong)— though not when he must needs explain his flight and the motives which prompted it. As he pitches upon the notion of running away because he knew ye as well as the Lord that made ye, upon the similitude of the lion gifted with instincts and forbearing to touch the blood royal, and upon the proof which thereupon arises that he is a lion and Hal, whom he has spared, a true prince, he makes up for all that he has lost in reputation for valour by what he gains in reputation for ingenuity and gaiety. They are jests for profit, as Burckhardt [88] would no doubt have called them; but for profit and delight, and little akin to that pale species reared by philosophy and philanthropy, which craves no hearing but, like virtue, is its own reward. Though far finer, they are such jests as those of Shakespeare's clowns or fools when they beg or are threatened, those of Sancho Panza and Panurge, Eulenspiegel and Kalenberg, or those in the old fabliaux. In one of these last, indeed, the celebrated *Lai d' Aristote* of Andeli, there is an evasion, remarkably like some of Falstaff's, of which the purpose and effect are specifically indicated. We remember: 'Thou knowest that in the state of innocency Adam fell; and what should poor Jack Falstaff do in the

[88] *Civilisation of the Renaissance in Italy* (1890), p. 157.

days of villainy? Thou seest I have more flesh than
another man,' etc. Also we remember: 'I dispraised him
before the wicked that the wicked might not fall in love
with him; in which doing, I have done the part of a careful
friend and a true subject,' etc. In the same spirit Aristotle
when, having rebuked Alexander for giving way to carnal
pleasures, he is discovered as he goes bridled and saddled
and ridden by the vindictive damsel through the garden,
cries to his jeering sovereign:

> Sire, fait-il, vos dites voir!
> Mais or poés vos bien savoir:
> J'oi droit que je doutai de vos,
> Car en fin jovent ardés tos
> Et en fu de droite jouenece,
> Quant jo qui sui plains de viellece
> Ne puis contre amor rendre estal
> Qu'ele ne m'ait torné a mal,
> Si grant com vos avés véu.
> Quant que j'ai apris et léu
> M'a desfait nature en. j. eure,
> Qui tote science deveure,
> Pus qu'ele s'en veut entremetre;
> Et se jo voil dont paine metre
> A vos oster de sa prison, . . . [89]

So he too turns all to merriment. Alexander congratulates
the damsel on the revenge she had furnished them, but as
for Aristotle

> tant s'en fu bien escusés
> De ce que il fu amusés
> Qu'en riant li rois li pardonne.

Just so Falstaff seeks neither to 'amuse the Prince' nor to
excuse himself, but does both together as the better way
of reaching either end.

[89] Sire, he said, you say well. But now you see that I was right in my
apprehensions. For you are in the flush of youth, while even I, who am
stricken in years, cannot put up resistance against love, which has brought
me to this sad pass. Much as I have learned and read, nature in an hour
has undone me who have mastered all knowledge, once she undertook it;
and if I have taken pains to free you from her dominion. . . .

For the Prince, Alexander, Pantagruel, and many another in the Middle Ages and the Renaissance, are like the Master in Jonson's *Alchemist,* and 'love a teeming wit,' even to the point of excusing the roguery which finds cover under it. Nor is this spirit extinct today, in life as well as in story and anecdote. 'How's this?' said an American employer to a commercial traveller after examining his expense account; 'half a dollar, and meals in these country hotels [it was twenty years ago] cost only a quarter.' 'Yes,' he replied, 'but isn't it worth another quarter to eat them?' It is reported as a fact that he was not discharged. But in the Middle Ages and the Renaissance whole books, Italian, French and English, were compiled of such stories, because of the *belles responses,* prompted by a purpose and crowned with its attainment. The Sixth Day of the *Decameron* is devoted to stories in which by cleverness people escape pain or ridicule—'si ragiona di chi, con alcuno leggiadro motto tentato, si riscotesse, o con pronta risposta o avvedimento fuggì perdita o pericolo o scorno'—exactly Falstaff's case. But the critics turn it about—'he tells his lies,' says Professor Bradley, 'either for their own humour or on purpose to get himself into a difficulty.' To the critics Shakespeare is a cryptogram—but they vouchsafe us the key. Falstaff seeking difficulties, looking for trouble— it is contrary to the whole impression of his character. Even on his death-bed he evaded them—the big debts that may be forgiven, like the little ones that are to be paid.

15.

The principle of a looser unity, which is the main thread we have been tracing—of identity in the dramatic function and tone rather than in mental quality and processes— explains much else in Falstaff. The quickness and readiness with which he faces about, which prompts Bulthaupt to think that in his boasting he is not sincere, is due simply to the fact that here he is wit again, not buffoon. To be entertaining is required of him rather than to be plausible. And this explains his so-called presence of mind, his joking amid carnage and in the teeth of death. It is not that he is a Mercutio, game to the last, but that he jokes regardless of ultimate psychological propriety; as do Elizabethan clowns whether in battle or in the house of mourning; or as do the clever slaves in Plautus when threatened with flogging or crucifixion; or as does Sosia, trembling before Mercury; [90] or as does the *gracioso* Galindo in Lope's *El Médico de su honra,* under the eye of his enemy; or as does the *gracioso Guarín,* in Calderón's *Puente de Mantible,* though much frightened, with the giant; or the cowardly Polidoro, in *El Mayor Monstruo,* though threatened with immediate hanging. 'What could support Falstaff,' asks Morgann, 'in such a situation? What but a strong natural constitutional courage, which nothing could extinguish or dismay?' If so, most of the cowards in comedy are no cowards at all. We must allow for the 'optique du théâtre' of those times.[91] We must allow for comedy.

Looser unity, moreover, irrelevancy, or carelessness of detail—it matters not which, for probably Shakespeare seldom conceived his characters apart from the plot— explains quite as well as the tradition of the *miles* the fact that in other ways Falstaff ceases for moments to be a coward. His fighting with Pistol, from which Mr Bradley says a stock coward would have shrunk, and his capturing Colville and exchanging a blow or two with Hal and Poins on Gadshill, are like the conduct of the cowards taking cowards captive mentioned above; or of Heywood's Roughman, who like Falstaff, takes fire from the ladies' eyes—'un vaillant d'un poltron'—and beats off Forset; or of Della Porta's Captains Dante and Pantaleone [92] who defy each

---

[90] *Amphitryon* of Plautus and of Molière, sc. 1.
[91] See below, sections 21, 22, and note 114.
[92] *Fantesca,* IV, vii.

other mightily but, like the Asiatics of old, must needs be
flogged into combat; or of the *gracioso* Galindo in Lope's
Comendadores de Córdoba, who fights—and boasts of
fighting—a mulatto;[93] or of the *gracioso* Brito in
Calderón's *Principe Constante,*[94] who, after falling and
feigning death like Falstaff, starts up and secures a fresh
comic effect by chasing off the stage the two Moors who
come to rob his body; or of Ambidexter, in *Cambyses*
(1570), who beats Huf, Ruf, and Snuf before he himself
is beaten by the women; or of Thersites, who beats his
mother; or of Sganarelle, who, after his pigeon-livered
soliloquy cited below, appears, crying out upon his enemy,
in full armour—to keep off the rain! or of Bentivoglio's
Brandonio, who prevails against Truffa through the might
of his page Trinchetto when he takes to stone-throwing;
or of Panurge and Cingar, who, though cowards, having
many vices besides, exhibit them, as does Falstaff his thievishness and his bibulousness on the battlefield, as if their
cowardice were now at an end. Though 'of blows he was
naturally fearful,' in the campaign against the Dipsodes
Panurge is as bold as brass and as cool as a cucumber.[95]
And Pulcinella, we have seen, is both lâche and féroce.

16.

Elsewhere as well (and that is part of his greatness)
Shakespeare does not keep strictly to a scheme. Shylock
is conceived in prejudice, doomed to ridicule and dishonour,
yet is given now and then a touch of almost incompatible
tenderness. Polonius is sensible enough at first, yet as the

[93] I, p. 263 (Academy edition), vol. xi, 1900.
[94] I, xiv and xx.
[95] In book II, chapters 27, 29, he gives a cry of pleasure at the approaching conflict, and he creeps among the fallen and cuts their throats. Yet see
at the close of chapter 21 his fright when blows are threatened; (IV,
chap. 5) when Dingdong draws his sword; (IV, chapters 19, 23, 24) when
there is a storm at sea; (chapters 66, 67) when there is cannonading.

need of a butt arises is indeed an 'ass.'[96] And as for
the 'indecorum' of Falstaff's presence unabashed and
unreproved before the King at Shrewsbury, of which
Morgann and his followers complain (unless indeed it be
granted them as an intentional compliment to his valour,
or as evidence of his being an established courtier and
'counsellor of state'),[97] why in Elizabethan drama are fools
and clowns for ever elbowing kings or emperors without
a ghost of a pretext or excuse? To jest, as Falstaff does.
As early as 1578 George Whetstone, speaking of English
dramatists, complains that 'manye tymes (to make mirthe)
they made a Clowne companion with a Kinge; in theyr
graue Counsels they allow the aduise of fooles.' 'Peace,
chewet, peace!' cries the Prince to our 'counsellor,' once
the decorum, according to Elizabethan notions, is really
broken. About as much is to be made of Falstaff's presence
in the council as of his 'familiarity' with John of Gaunt
and with Mowbray, Duke of Norfolk. Once upon a time he
joked with the one, and in his youth he was page to the
other. In Elizabethan drama any comic character jokes
with a king and a king jokes with anybody; and Falstaff
wins little credit with us for having once tried it with John
of Gaunt in the Tiltyard. Almost the same, may be said,
we have seen,[98] of early seventeenth-century Spanish drama,
though in Spanish life, of course, etiquette and the proprieties were much more rigidly observed than in England; and the *gracioso* jests with kings and noblemen as
freely as do Touchstone and Panurge, and goes into battle

---

[96] See A. B. Walkley, *op. cit.* Urged (as usual) by the craving for unity,
critics have found the wisdom of Polonius in I, iii, jejune and insipid.
So is the Duke's, then, in *Measure for Measure,* III, i, and that of many
another moralist in Shakespeare. And even if jejune and insipid, 'hard
and unvital,' it is not silly, not asinine; and so the character is not much
more of a unit than before; Coleridge, urged by the same craving, finds
him too wise to be meant for a comic character, as he is at first.

[97] Morgann, pp. 43-44.

[98] See chapter ii, above, from which some phrases are here repeated.

or council of war as unplausibly and improperly as Panurge and Falstaff.

What, moreover, does it matter whether, as Morgann and Maginn will have it, he is a gentleman? So is Panurge,[99] and a coward, and 'a very dissolute and debauched fellow if there were any in Paris.' The pith and root of the matter is that criticism has no right thus to insist upon details and draw therefrom fine-spun deductions—upon his title of knighthood, his seal ring, his bonds, and his pension [100] (if ever he had them) as tokens of gentility—for in the treatment of such things Shakespeare and his fellows were even more careless and self-contradictory than we have already seen him to be in matters of greater importance. Sancho rides his stolen ass again before he has recovered her, and even Comus, as he welcomes 'midnight shout and revelry' and 'the secret flames of midnight torches,' now finds the star 'that bids the shepherd fold' at the top of heaven. What, then, could be expected of one who was writing not for print but for immediate comic effect? That he obtains. The to-do which Falstaff makes about his ring worth forty marks and the bonds, three or four of them, of forty pound a-piece, which he declares have been picked from his pocket, is comical not only because the ring, if lost, is only of copper,[101] 'an eight-penny matter,' but because in his pocket, when he was asleep taking his ease in his inn, was found 'nothing but papers, my lord,' the scandalous tavern-reckoning among them. If there had been bonds, Prince Hal, who had ordered the pocket-picking, would have been responsible for them. But such affluence is not likely in one whose purse, on inquiry of the Boy who bears it, contains

[99] Book II, chapter 9: 'Nature hath extracted him from some rich and noble race.'

[100] Morgann, p. 59: 'Falstaff was not only a military knight, he possessed an honourable pension into the bargain.'—The context is clear: he finds in his gout a comfort at the thought that he can make a pretext of it for a pension, Pt. II, I, ii, 270 ff.

[101] Morgann and others (see below) will not believe it.

but seven groats and two-pence; whose means, as the Chief-Justice tells him, 'is very slender and whose waste is great.' In the end the Prince puts him to his shifts once more— 'Thou knowst in the state of Innocency Adam fell,' etc.— by telling him the whole truth, which he cannot deny, that there was 'nothing in his pocket but tavern-reckonings, memorandums of bawdy-houses, and one poor penny-worth of sugar-candy to make thee long-winded' (in allusion to Gadshill). And as far as Falstaff's reputation is concerned, is it not far better to consider this (what on the surface it seems to be, what the Hostess herself declares it to be, and what is suggested by his preamble, 'Wilt thou believe me, Hal?' when he addresses the Prince) a lie, an evasion, a means of picking a quarrel with the Hostess, in order, in his penury, to escape payment of his debts, than to think that, having these bonds in his pocket, he had run up bills for his 'diet and by-drinkings, and money lent you, four and twenty pound' (not to mention the shirts she had bought to his back) and yet had not paid her before? A lie when in a pinch is less ignoble than fraud purposed from the beginning. And as for his knighthood, it must, of course, have been hereditary; he comes of gentle blood, however debauched, as his wit and fancifulness make manifest. Or if bestowed upon him, it cannot have been what Morgann thinks it, 'a military honour,' an accolade upon the bloody field—*oh, Dieu, non!* to quote again the critic-poet.

17.

So far nothing has been said of the *Merry Wives of Windsor* because of the prevalent opinion that this Falstaff is another man. Here he is a butt and dupe unmistakably. But Mr Bradley himself says that there are speeches in the play recognizable as Falstaff's in quantity sufficient to fill one side of a sheet of note-paper. Moreover, the figure of the braggart captain, which came into Shakespeare's hands from Plautus or from the Comedy of Masks, would have been incomplete if he had not appeared as the suitor gulled.[102]   Yet all that I care to insist upon is that in this play, as in *Henry IV*, the supreme comical figure is again both butt and wit.   Again for purposes of mirth he fails to see through the tricks played upon him; but, though he is clever enough, surely nobody will have him feigning and dissembling or trying to 'amuse' himself or the women of Windsor by chivalrously falling in with their vindictive schemes.

18.

All this reasoning is, I hope, founded on what is simple and sensuous, and therefore truly of the stage.   The fatal objection to the theory that Falstaff is feigning and literally 'looking for trouble' is that he keeps his joke to himself.   There are no such jokes on the stage—a jest's prosperity lies in the ear of him that hears it.   At least it must have got into a soliloquy—in Shakespeare's time it must needs have been thrust upon the notice of the Prince and Poins and have covered them with confusion. In Shakespeare the battle is to the strong, success never looks like failure, or honour like dishonour, and for him and his audience it is not a humorous thing to keep one's humour hid.   Perhaps there was never a more bewildering transformation in the history of criticism than this of our fat knight into a merry Andrea del Sarto,

> I, *jesting* from myself and to myself,
> Know what I do—am not moved by men's blame
> Or their praise either.

And, as it seems to me, only some such interpretation as that presented above is compatible with the Falstaff story as comedy.   Comic effect generally consists in a swift transition from unreality to reality or from reality to unreality; and concerning which is which there must be no uncertainty

[102] This is the lot of both Pyrgopolinices and the Capitano.

or mistake. If the reality prove unreality after all, not the solid ground we the audience thought it to be, we are puzzled, not amused. If the joke be not on Falstaff as we were led to think—if his courage so specious be real and his pretences so apparent be themselves a pretence—then we are baffled, and the wave of laughter tantalizingly eludes our lips. The joke is then not even on the Prince, so far as we notice, but on us ourselves. Reading, of course, solitary and anxious perusal and meditation of the text, does not count. It is obvious that *Henry IV, Parts I and II,* is a stage play, not closet drama, meant for playing, not reading, in a measure beyond most of Shakespeare's historical plays. Even Morgann admits that the audience ordinarily took Falstaff for a comic coward, and except as otherwise instructed they do still; and the impressions of his courage Morgann himself calls 'secret,' not patent. In so far, then, as these impressions may in the course of Part One be supposed to be borne in upon the more judicious of the audience, what can be the effect of them through the rest of the play or in Part Two, which follows? Uncertainty and bewilderment in the individual, division and disunion in the audience—and that is the death of laughter. You laugh when you and others see something to laugh at, you laugh when you do not laugh alone.

19.

A coward, then, if ever there was one, has Falstaff a philosophy? Military free-thinking has been attributed to him to lift the stigma from his name. Not believing in honour, he has been thought not to be bound by it. And by the Germans [103] and Mr Bradley, as we have remarked, the scope of his philosophy has been widened, and he has been turned into a practical Pyrrhonist and moral nihilist,

---

[103] In various degrees by Ulrici, Gervinus, Rötscher, Vischer, Graf, and Bulthaupt. The only one who explicitly dissents is Wetz. Wolff (i, 422 f.), though he finds in Falstaff no depths of philosophy, does not look upon the 'catechism' as a confession of cowardice.

to whom virtue is 'a fig,' truth absurd, and the rules and obligations of society stumbling-blocks and nuisances. In various ways, by the English and the Germans alike, he has been thought to deny and destroy all moral values and ideals of life, not only for his own but for our behoof and comfort. So in a certain sense he is inspired by principle— of an anarchistic sort—not void of it.

Only at one ideal—honour—does Falstaff seem to me to cavil, and that he is only shirking and dodging. How does he, as Mr Bradley thinks, make truth absurd by lying; or law, by evading the attacks of its highest representative; or patriotism, by abusing the King's press and by filling his pockets with bribes?[104] or matrimony (logic would not forbear to add) by consorting with Mistresses Ursula, Quickly, and Tearsheet, thus lifting us into an atmosphere of freedom indeed? It makes your head swim to see a simple picaresque narrative like that of Panurge or Sir Toby Belch brought to such an issue or conclusion as that.

As it seems to me, his catechism on the battlefield and his deliverances on honour are to be taken as coming not from his heart of hearts but out of his wits and to cover his shame. Like disreputable characters in medieval and Renaissance drama and fiction without number, he unconsciously gives himself away. His 'philosophy' is but a shift and evasion, and in his catechism he eludes the claim of honour when put by his conscience just as he does when put by the Prince and Poins. When he declares discretion to be the better part of valour, there is no more philosophy in him than in Panurge and the Franc Archier de Baignollet[105] when they avow that they fear nothing but danger; or than in himself when he swears that instinct is a great matter, and purse-taking no sin but his vocation; or than in the Roman citizens when, echoing these very words

[104] *Oxford Lectures*, pp. 262-63.
[105] *Pantagruel*, IV, xxiii; *Franc Archier*, l. 98.

to show how Shakespeare meant them, Menenius ironically reassures Marcius:—

> Nay, these are almost thoroughly persuaded;
> For though abundantly they lack discretion,
> Yet are they passing cowardly.—*Cor.* I, i, 205-7.

And when he cries 'Give me life' and 'I like not the grinning honour that Sir Walter hath,' there is no more Pyrrhonism or Epicureanism in him than there is idealism when, in defending his choice of the unlikeliest men for his company, he cries, 'Give me the spirit, Master Shallow,' meaning 'give me the crowns and shillings, Mouldy and Bullcalf.' Here, as there, he only dodges and shuffles. As in his fits of remorse we have seen, he is not 'dead to morality' or free from its claims; neither does he frankly oppose them, or succeed in 'covering them with immortal ridicule'; but in sophistry he takes refuge from them and the ridicule rebounds on his own head.

Half a dozen egregious cowards in Shakespeare's time, at any rate, talk in Falstaff's vein when in danger, and yet are not, and cannot be, thought philosophers for their pains. Ambidexter, in danger, took to his legs.

> And fell a-laughing to myselfe, when I was once gone:
> It is wisdom, quoth I, by the masse, to save one!
> —*Cambyses,* l. 302.

The coward and braggart Basilisco, with whom Shakespeare was acquainted, goes through a catechism before action, too, on the omnipotence of death and the futility of love and honour in the face of it.[106] What is at the back of his head a child could see.

> I will ruminate: Death, which the poets
> Faine to be pale and meagre,
> Hath depriued *Erastus* trunke from breathing vitalitie,
> A braue Cauelere, but my aprooued foeman.

[106] *Soliman and Perseda,* V, iii, 63-95. Shakespeare's acquaintance with the play is proved by *King John,* I, i, 244. This resemblance has long been recognized.

Let me see: where is that *Alcides,* surnamed Hercules,
The onely Club man of his time? dead.
Where is the eldest sonne of Pryam,
That abraham-coloured Troian? dead.
Where is the leader of the Mirmidons,
That well knit *Accilles?* dead.
Where is that furious *Aiax,* the sonne of *Telamon,*
Or that fraudfull squire of *Ithaca,* iclipt *Vlisses?* dead.
Where is tipsie *Alexander,* that great cup conquerour,
Or *Pompey,* that braue warriour? dead.
I am myselfe strong, but I confesse death to be stronger;
I am valiant, but mortall;
I am adorned with natures gifts.
A giddie goddesse that now giueth and anon taketh:
I am wise, but quiddits will not answer death:
To conclude in a word: to be captious, vertuous, ingenious,
Are to be nothing when it pleaseth death to be enuious.

. . . .

Faith, he can doe little that cannot speake,
And he can doe lesse that cannot runne away.
Then sith mans life is as a glasse, and a phillip may cracke it,
Mine is no more, and a bullet may pearce it:
Therefore I will play least in sight.—

There is a resemblance to the fat knight's ruminations,
even in the rhetorical method and rhythm.

20.

The other parallels are independent of Shakespeare, but
are fashioned by the same ironical and satiric spirit. In
Molière's *Cocu imaginaire* Sganarelle subtilizes on death
and a husband's honour much as Falstaff does on death and
a soldier's honour. Discretion is his pet virtue too.

Je ne suis point battant, de peur d'être battu,
Et l'humeur débonnaire est ma grande vertu;

and if in this faith he should waver, once play the bold
fellow, and get for his virtue a villainous thrust in the
paunch—

Que par la ville ira le bruit de mon trépas,
Dites-moi, mon honneur, en serez-vous plus gras?

'Give me life' (once more) not grinning honour—

> Qu'il vaut mieux être encor cocu que trépassé;

and therefore he scornfully questions whether loss of
honour can damage the limbs as Falstaff does whether the
winning of honour can mend them:

> Quel mal cela fait-il? la jambe en devient-elle
> Plus tortue, après tout, et la taille moins belle?

And before the scene is over he confesses his cowardice
explicitly: in scene xxi, as we have noticed above, it becomes
apparent in deed.

Another arrant coward, also self-confessed, Jodelet in
Scarron's *Jodelet duelliste* (1646),[107] inveighs against
honour as a silly thing, causing much inconvenience; and
considers the damage done because of it to certain important organs, through the least puncture in which the spirit
may escape—through a pinprick in heart, liver, kidney,
lungs, or an artery—gods! the very thought takes his
breath! And he 'likes not' death because it is undiscerning
(*camuse*) and too 'forward' with a fellow,

> Et sans considérer qui la veut ou refuse,
> L'indiscrète qu'elle est, grippe, vousît ou non,
> Pauvre, riche, poltron, vaillant, mauvais et bon.—V, i.

So in the earlier play, *Jodelet maître-valet*, when he considers:

> Que le corps enfin doit pourrir,
> Le corps humain, où la prudence
> Et l'honneur font leur résidence,
> Je m'afflige jusqu'au mourir.
> Quoi! cinq doigts mis sur une face!—IV, ii.

For, as in the later play, he has had his ears boxed, and the
better part is discretion.

[107] Cited in Despois, Molière, t. ii, 198-200, where also is cited the
parallel of Falstaff's catechism. Cf. also M. de Pourceaugnac (III, ii), who
disclaims the fear of death as he flees from the law in the garb of a
woman, yet thinks it 'facheux à un gentilhomme d'être pendu.'

Thus continually in the popular farces of the fifteenth and sixteenth centuries cowardice coquets with prudence, discretion, or philanthropy; but in thrusting back the claims of honour only betrays, as in Falstaff, terror at what comes in its trail. It gives itself away by an irony which recoils like a boomerang. Falstaff's discretion, Moron's 'bon sens,' Parolles' 'for advantage,' and even humaner sentiments, are the subterfuges of cowards on the popular stage in Venice and Nürnberg as in London and Paris. In the old farce *L'Avantureux,* Guillot has fled from Marolles but retired at his ease as far as—to Pontoise!—for a soldier who is quick to strike

> se doibt bien tenir loin.
> Jamais je n'eus intention
> De faire homicidation. [108]

Likewise the Franc Archier de Baignollet (1524), protests that he keeps the fifth commandment, kills fowls, not his fellows, and retreats (for to him as to Sancho retreating is not fleeing) only a trifle, from Angers to—Lyons. And he cries, not Saint Denis! but Saint George! with the English, and Saint Yve! with the Bretons, for, like Falstaff, he would fain live (l. 210). But he fears the foe not at all, though he trembles (l. 34).

This style in dealing with cowards is, as in some measure we have already seen, wide-spread, and is found not only in France but in Italy, in Germany and in Spain, Beolco's Ruzzante, in Venetian dialect, being one of the best:

[He arrives with more haste than dignity in Venice] Saint Mark's! Saint Mark's! Safe at last! I have come fast, sixty miles a day. In three days from Cremona! It is not so far as they say! . . . I am dressed like a thief, but safe. If I had been killed in the war, and were no more than a ghost, I shouldn't be here. No, by Jupiter, ghosts don't eat. I am myself, I am alive . . . I have never sought to do the enemy any ill. Why should I? He never did any to me. [Menato wonders that he bears

[108] *Ibid.,* ll. 130-140. The same sentiment is a pretext of Ruzzante's (cited below) to explain why he brings no booty home from war.

no wounds.] Valour does not consist in getting wounded and mutilated. . . . If you had been where I have been you would talk differently. You must be neither one-armed nor one-legged—to escape
from these battles, where against so many you can do nothing. . . .
I tell you it takes a lot of courage to come back alive.—Sand,
Masques et bouffons, ii, 99.

Like Falstaff he hugs life and yet clutches at reputation
too, and finds honour not in danger, in wounds or in death,
but in flight and survival. And like Falstaff, all the above,
save Ruzzante, thus expose themselves in soliloquy.

Lope's and Calderón's *graciosos* are generally cowards,
and several of them have the same philosophy as Falstaff
to support them, though they openly impart it to others.
Coquín, in Calderón's *El Médico de su honra,* like Falstaff
a coward and a thief, advises his master to break parole,
and declares that if he won't he himself will abandon him.
Must Coquín die, simply for appearance' sake? He might
go so far as to give up for his master a few days, but not
his life, for good and all; he might discard a few plain
cards and play with the face cards only; but life is a very
different game, these cards once gone then all is gone:

<pre>
Don Gutierre Dejarme tú?
Coquín   Qué he de hacer?
D. G.   Y de tí, qué han de decir?
Coq.   Y heme de dejar morir,
              Por sólo bien parecer?
              Si el morir, señor, tuviera
              Descarte ó enmienda alguna,
              Cosa, que de dos la una,
              Un hombre hacerla pudiera,
              Yo probára la primera
              Por servirte; mas no ves
              Que rifa la vida es?
              Entro en ella, vengo y tomo
              Cartas, y piérdola: como
              Me desquitaré después?
              Perdida se quedará,
              Si la pierdo, por tu engaño,
              Desde aquí á ciento y un año.—II, vi.
</pre>

Here is Falstaff, in the matter of esteeming life above reputation, considering too deeply the incontestable fact that once life is taken away it cannot be recovered, and hungering for honour if it were not for the cost.

In *A secreto agravio secreta venganza* the *gracioso* Manrique has more of the ironical, give-away method—'a squanderer when he steals, valiant when he flies' (I, vi); and when his master on the point of going over into Africa declares that there is not a knight in Lisbon who does not aspire to be first to win eternal glory through death, he replies that he is of no such mind himself! 'Aren't you going to Africa?' 'I may, but not to kill—not to break the law by which I live, in which I believe, Thou shalt not kill—Christian nor Moor, as I take it; and not for me is it to expound or limit the word of God'—

> No á matar, quebrando en vano
> La ley en que vivo y creo;
> Pues allí explicar no veo
> Que sea moro ni cristiano.
> *No matar,* dice. Y los dos
> Esto me veréis guardar;
> Que yo no he de interpretar
> Los mandamientos de Dios.—II, iii.

A play with the title *El Médico de su honra* was written also by Lope de Vega; and in it the coward *gracioso* Galindo has a somewhat similar joking or frankly give-away method in the face of danger, blustering till the bluff is called. 'The man who fights with my master, I will show him who I am.' 'Who are you, then?' 'He who calls himself Galindo. And I know what to do, *vive Dios!* if I am attacked.' 'What'll ye do?' 'Run away,' [109]—and no sooner said than done. But like Falstaff he says what in real life, of course, he would have done without saying.

Possibly the closest parallel to Falstaff's gammon about honour appears in a fifteenth-century *Fastnachtsspiel,* in

[109] End of Act I.

which the faint-hearted knights excuse themselves from
following the Emperor into battle. Shall I die, cries the
Second Knight, for honour that I shall never know?—

> Scholt ich mich da geben zu sterben,
> Das ich da mit solt er erwerben,
> Was möcht mir die er gefrumen
> Wenn ich nit mocht her wider kumen?
> Wann ich hab selbs daheim er und gut
> Und ain schöns weib, das gibt mir mut.[110]

The others express somewhat similar sentiments, and the
Fourth Knight stipulates that he shall be permitted to ride
to the charge behind the Emperor, because to ride before
does not beseem him, and—he will look after him,

> ich will eben zusehen
> Von wem euch Schaden sei geschehen.

On both Emperor and Ausschreier all this makes but one
impression—and at the end they say as much—that of
cowardice unalloyed. Somewhat the same are the sentiments of Panurge, and in him the ironical method is more
obvious than in any:

Let's whip it away. I never find myself to have a bit of Courage
at Sea: In Cellars and elsewhere I have more than enough. Let's fly,
and save our Bacon. I do not say this for any Fear that I have; for
I dread nothing but Danger, that I don't; I always say it, that
shouldn't. . . . We'll lose no Honour by flying. Demosthenes saith,
That the man that runs away may fight another day.—IV, chap. 55
(cf. chap. 23).

21.

Both Falstaff's philosophy and his philosophic method,
we conclude, were widely disseminated, even before his
time, but only among cowards like himself. These 'principles' are held by those who have no principle; this military free-thinking is military apostasy and treason. Like
Falstaff these others make of their principles a veil of dis-

[110] Keller (1853), no. 75.

simulation, and drolly peep from behind it. Here lingers medieval satire as we find it in capital form in the *Wife of Bath's Prologue,* or in Heywood's *Four P. P.,* where the Potycary avers that he beats the record of both Palmer and Pardoner in the matter of sending souls to heaven [111]; or in the old farce of the widow who hears, as the bells toll for her husband's death, the tintinnabulated heavenly admonition, as in the verse we hear it still,—

Pren ton valet, pren ton valet; [112]

and people clever enough to take that for nothing but the unconscious confession of one to marriage much inclined, might so take Falstaff's and these other fellows' discretion and prudence, and aversion to grinning honour and undiscerning death, and not for what to our eager sympathy they seem to be.

And that in all its transparency this satiric and ironical understatement is not foreign to Shakespeare's method with Falstaff in general appears not only in many of his evasions, as we have seen, but in his famous talk with Bardolph, alluded to above:

—virtuous enough, swore little, diced not above seven times a week, went to a bawdy-house not above once in a quarter—of an hour, paid money that I borrowed—three or four times.

It is employed in soliloquy also by Benedick when to his dismay he finds himself in love. He betrays himself, or rallies himself, and beats about the bush with his principles, quite in Falstaff's manner:

Why it must be requited—I must not seem proud—doth not the appetite alter? No, the world must be peopled. When I said I would die a bachelor I did not think I should live till I were married (II, iii, 231).

And the Second Murderer in *Richard III* pooh-poohs conscience and complains of it as Falstaff does of honour:

[111] ll. 153-6; 407-17.   [112] *Robinet Badin.*

It was wont to hold me but while one tells twenty.

1 Murd. What if it come to thee again?

2 Murd. I'll not meddle with it; it is a dangerous thing; it makes
a man a coward. A man cannot steal, but it accuseth him;
a man cannot swear, but it checks him; a man cannot lie
with his neighbour's wife, but it detects him. . . . It
beggars any man that keeps it. It is turn'd out of towns
and cities for a dangerous thing; and every man that means
to live well endeavours to trust to himself and live without
it.—I, iv, 120-148. [113]

His reasons like Falstaff's are ignoble reasons which recoil
upon his head. And all these philosophical soliloquies and
apologiæ pro vita sua in the Renaissance resemble Falstaff's, although Sir Walter Raleigh thinks the soliloquy
on honour might have been spoken by Hamlet. It might
have been—if words alone counted, and tone, and accent,
and context were nothing at all—if the speaker did not
wink, or stick his tongue in his cheek, or so openly give
his words the lie by his conduct.

22.

We have hesitated in the interpretation—how far these
self-revelations are to be taken as conscious or unconscious,
it is hard to say. Autolycus certainly is deliberately jesting
when he declares, 'If I had a mind to be honest, I see
Fortune would not suffer me'; but certainly Shylock is
not jesting in his comical afterthoughts (whatever may
be said of Falstaff in his) when he cries

I would my daughter were dead at my foot—and the jewels in
her ear. Would she were hearsed at my foot—and the ducats in
her coffin. . . .

and in this same device of comical afterthoughts as
employed by Molière or by Sheridan, or by so recent a
dramatist as Robertson, the humour, like that involved

[113] Mr Harris points out the similarity of the two catechisms but interprets
both differently.

in Falstaff's 'incomprehensible lies' and his remorse, seems meant to be unconscious, not intentional. [114]

One reason why in Falstaff we fail to penetrate this mask of unrealistic and malicious portrayal, and we take his words to heart, is that they are in soliloquy. A man does not banter himself, does not address himself with his tongue in his cheek—'c'est qu'il est par trop contre nature qu'un homme se moque si clairement de soi-même'; [115] but on the stage both in those times and before them a man did, [116] and all soliloquy was then phrased more as if the character were addressing another or the audience than as if he were thinking aloud. Really, Falstaff's philosophy is but a bundle of evasions, to escape (this time) from himself, not Poins and the Prince. Or it may be described as the ironical method of Anatole France shifted to the first person, a method employed by Fielding, Sterne, Molière (as we have seen), Cyrano de Bergerac, Le Sage, and Voltaire, and by Thackeray (as with Barry Lyndon) in both first and third. Sarcasm, the only method for realism, as we have seen in Italy, France, and England in the Renais-

[114] See the chapter on Shylock above, section 18, for the discussion and for illustrative passages from Molière and the rest.

[115] Stendhal, *Racine et Shakespeare*. He is speaking of a similar method in Voltaire; and Stendhal must know. It is clear that the acting in comedy in those days was to suit. Lamb, in his essays *On Some of the Old Actors* and on *Stage Illusion*, laments the passing away of the artificial conventionalized manner, whereby the comic actor 'kept in secret correspondence with the company before the curtain, and the coward let out by a thousand droll looks and gestures that his confidence in his own resources had never once deserted him.' Possibly this consideration might seem to lend support to Morgann's opinion; but in both the penning of the lines and the playing of them it is not so much a matter of character as of technique. In so far as character (or actor) steps out of the rôle and winks at the audience, he is not a character at all—is an actor only. As we now think, he should act as if there were no audience there. But it was a prodigious wink that I saw given them at St Malo the other day, by a mother-in-law when about to confess, falsely, to improper conduct—such as would have suited Falstaff as he descanted on the duty of discretion, or Benedick, on that of replenishing the earth.

[116] Even in Plautus. Cf. the soliloquies in the *Menæchmi*, I, i (Peniculus); *Stichus*, II, i (Gelasimus); and *Bacchides*, IV, iv (Chrysalus), where the rogue or parasite jokes in soliloquy at his own expense.

sance, has become steadily less obtrusive, until Henry James
dreamed of the ultimate novelist as 'entirely purged' of it.
It is from without, strange to say, and by way of irony as
well as of sympathy, that the point of view of questionable
characters was gradually approached.   This appears as one
follows the development from Fielding to Thackeray.
Jonathan Wild is quite like Falstaff in his soliloquies on
honour, greatness, and glory, on the mutations of all life
and the ticklish chances of his own, on robbery and murder
as the policy of statesmen and monarchs, or on himself when
thwarted in these as 'a great though an unhappy man.'
But in *Barry Lyndon* the irony is so free from exaggeration—so closely fitting—that often it is hardly distinguish-
able from the fairly unconscious hypocrisy natural to
blackleg and rogue or even that self-esteem which is natural
to us all.   Comic effect is sacrificed but the effect of reality
is heightened.   In the Renaissance soliloquy, however,
allowances are to be made, as when Falstaff holds forth
on sack as the cause of valour, which is another under-
hand confession of cowardice, and when Benedick declares
that the world must be peopled, which is a confession too.
It is an irony which touches the speaker, not the thing
spoken of, and dissolves away, not all the seriousness of
life, but the speaker's pretenses; it is the exposure, not
(as has been thought) the expression, of his 'inmost
self.' [117]   When Falstaff seems to be talking principle, he
is, as we now say, only 'putting it mildly': in his own time
he gave himself away; in ours he takes the learned in.

   And we fail to penetrate the mask because, in or out
of soliloquy, this particular method of characterization
(even when modified as we have seen it above) is a thing
outworn, outgrown.   *Jonathan Wild,* they say, and *Barry
Lyndon* itself are now little read, and certainly the older
style is not in favour.   Characters are no longer driven to
banter or expose themselves, or the better audiences resent

[117] Wetz, pp. 402-3, quoting Rötscher.

it if they are. Psychology—born of sympathy—will have
none of it, as a method too external, ill-fitting, double-
tongued. If the person be taken to be consciously jesting—
the widow about wedding in the moment of mourning, Falstaff about the vanity of honour, or Robertson's Eccles
about the wholesomeness of work—he seems then and there
to be out of character; yet it is hard to see how he can have
been unconscious, either, and it is manifest that the author
is more intent on the jest, or, in the case of Quickly above,
on the *double entente,* than on the main philosophic drift;
—and yet (once again) this self-consciousness and mirth
surely do not imply, as in the writing of to-day imply they
must, 'freedom' or detachment, any measure of indifference
or superiority to the pleasure of incontinently taking to
one's valet, keeping one's arms and legs whole, or sponging
in bibulous sloth. If in Renaissance drama joking to oneself
about oneself be a sure sign of superiority to fear, then
Bergerac's Chasteaufort, craven and boastful, beaten and
ingenious in excuses for not striking back, is as unaf-
frighted—as Falstaff. He must flee, he says—'sans dire
adieu au Roi? Ah, a, a!' He laughs—not even Falstaff
is so cool! The pith of the matter, then, is that the lines
of the character are, for us, confused; the author seems
to peer through and wink at the audience; and our modern
sympathy and craving for reality are vexed and thwarted,
somewhat as they are by the self-consciousness of the villains
or by the butt-and-wit-in-one. Indeed, unless the character
be taken to be unconscious, we seem here to have a case of
butt-and-wit-in-one at one and the same moment. For these
reasons this method of ironical self-betrayal, which goes
back at least to the Middle Ages, and occurs not only in
Elizabethan comic drama but in the greatest comic drama
since—in Congreve and Sheridan, not to mention Molière—
has, like butt-and-wit-in-one or self-conscious villainy, been
dropped by the modern spirit as a strange, ill-fitting
garment, and, since Robertson and Gilbert, has been rele-

gated to frank satire and farce. When, accordingly, we come upon it in works of the greatest genius,—why, then, as usual, we adjust it to the modern spirit instead of adjusting ourselves to the Elizabethan.

In what is perhaps the finest comedy of the Italian Renaissance, the *Mandragola* of Machiavelli, Fra Timoteo the rascally monk has in our day been misunderstood after the same fashion and for the same reason as Falstaff. Disguised for his scabrous part in this intrigue, he soliloquizes in self-defence: Evil communications corrupt good manners, and as often as not one goes astray from sheer good-nature. Here was I, he says, so devoutly engaged in my cell, when in came that devil of a Ligurio (the Lover) with his proposals:—

E' dicono il vero quelli che dicono, che le cattive compagnie conducono gli uomini alle forche; e molte volte uno capita male, così per essere troppo facile e troppo buono, come per essere troppo tristo. Dio sa ch'io non pensava a ingiuriare persona: stavami nella mia tella, diceva il mio ufficio, intratteneva i miei devoti. Capitòmmi innanzi questo diavolo di Ligurio, che mi fece intignere il dito in un errore, donde io vi ho messo il braccio e tutta la persona, e non so ancora dove io m'abbia a capitare.—IV, vi.

Signor Sanesi points out that by one critic this has been taken to mean that the Friar was at bottom a good fellow; Signor Sanesi rightly declares that it proves him utterly void of moral sense; [118] but neither he nor the other critic seems to see the shuffling and irony. It would be, and should be, all hypocritical gammon to an audience. Have they not already, in Act III, scene iii, seen how he was engaged with the lady? And have they not in Act III, scene ix, heard him pondering in soliloquy on the way he had been taken in and how he in turn would take in others?

23.

How petty and personal Falstaff's philosophy is on the

[118] *Commedia* (1912), 212.

face of it! It is a philosophy for profit and a purpose, which is the negation of philosophy. Bulthaupt, Gervinus, Ulrici, Rötscher, and others after them, speak of him sapping the foundations of morality; and Bulthaupt compares him, 'picking the notion of honour to pieces,' with Trast in Sudermann's *Ehre!* There indeed, or in *Arms and the Man,* or in *Major Barbara,* honour reels and totters; but here it comes 'unsought for,' 'pricks' our captain on, and drives him to hide from before its face. By word and by deed he shows that he is not more indifferent to a soldier's honour than is Sganarelle to a husband's, and like him he snatches it greedily when he can. It is the 'grin' that he 'likes not,' and since the beginning of things no philosophy has been needed for that.

For Falstaff is as simple and un-cynical as the dramatist and his times. By him the chivalric ideal is never questioned: Hotspur is comical only for his testiness, for the extravagance of his imagination and language, not for his derring-do. To some critics Falstaff seems a parody or burlesque of knighthood, and they are reminded of the contemporary Quixote and his Squire. But the only parallel or contrast [119] between knight and clown suggested is on the battlefield; and there, as in Calderón's comedies, the ridicule is directed at the clown alone. In the story of Cervantes himself it is so; the chivalric ideal stands unchallenged, though the romantic and sentimental extravagances are scattered like the rear of darkness thin. Even by these Shakespeare is not much troubled; and true to the spirit of the Renaissance all his heroes cherish their fame and worship glory, as they do in the dramas and romances of France, Spain, and Italy. The Renaissance passion for fame, honour, and glory, in

[119] The parallels discovered by Ulrici, such as the robbery as a withering travesty of the Hotspur rebellion, or the whole Falstaff episode as intended to parody the hollow pathos of the political history and to assist in scattering the vain deceptive halo with which it has been surrounded, are further symptoms of the craving for a more intimate unity from which all impressionistic and philosophical critics suffer.

which the traditions of feudalism and the ancient world met
and conspired, assumed in literature, and in life perhaps as
well, almost unbelievable proportions; [120] and though Shakespeare was nothing of a cavalier, and little of a humanist,
Mr Harris says of him not untruly that his heroes have no
other motive for brave deeds than love of honour, no other
fear than that of shame with which to overcome the dread
of death.   In Shakespeare or in lofty and pious Milton even
(Hazlitt goes so far as to say that his works are a perpetual
hymn to fame), there are no such sentiments as Fichte's—
'Durst nach Nachruhm ist eine verächtliche Eitelkeit'—or
Tennyson's—'Fame, merely the pleasure of hearing oneself
talked of up and down the street,' or those in the same
vein of Robert Louis Stevenson.   The poet of the war,
Georges Pioch, in *Les Victimes,* is said to be obsessed by a
hatred of 'la gloire'; and Monsieur Barrès, one of the greatest of recent writers, has of late remarked on the fact that
in the young Frenchman in arms 'there was not the least
preoccupation with glory.'   But to Shakespeare, as to
Molière and Cervantes himself, Moron's confession that he
had rather live two days in the world than a thousand years
in history, or Bessus' avowal that if he might stand still in
cannon-proof and have fame fall upon him, he would refuse
it, would, even in less compromising circumstances, have
seemed but clownish and craven, though to us it would seem
neither, in our mystical adoration of life and indifference
to fame.   'Give me life!'—we sadly mistake the ascetic,
stoical, chivalric principles, coming down from the earliest
times through the Renaissance even to our own, if we fancy
that in England or in Italy [121] then there were many who

[120] See an article on the conception of honour in Lope and Calderón, by
A. Castro, *Revista Española,* 1916. Cf. Burckhart, *Renaissance,* Pt. ii, bk.
3; Symonds, *Revival of Learning* (Holt), pp. 38-9, 76, 80; Owen, *Skeptics
of the Italian Renaissance* (1908), p. 165. For Shakespeare, see Harris,
pp. 98-9; F. C. Sharp, pp. 15, 80.
[121] Bruno would have come nearest to it.   Men like Aretino, as in his
letter to Strozzzi, in 1537, say it cynically.   When moved, all Elizabethans,
at least in tragedies, think of death; and so do the Italians of the Renaissance.

could keep a good conscience and say it. Romeo, Hamlet, Brutus, Othello and Desdemona, Antony and his queen, are, like the ancients, far from saying it, though only happiness, not honour, is at stake. The noblest characters, even the children, in Shakespeare and the Renaissance drama in general, die willingly, often eagerly, and with Senecan contempt of life. And off the stage, the men of the Renaissance, like the ancient Greeks, loved life because they had found it sweet, but—especially the Elizabethans—they had not learned to think much better of it than the world had thought before. They loved it as well as we, but not, like us, from principle and as a tenet of their faith. That spirit came with scepticism, as the other world retreated from view. La Fontaine would have us leave life as if it had been a banquet, thanking our host; Voltaire learned from Horace—

À mépriser la mort en savourant la vie;

and that is the spirit of Browning and Ruskin, Swinburne and Meredith, 'glad for what was.' In Shakespeare they are glad (if at all) only of their glory.

24.

Little disposed as is Shakespeare (in the person of his heroes) to swerve from the conventional standard of honour himself, he enters with little more sympathy into the spirit of them that swerve. For his clowns the standard is set as for his villains. Sometimes, indeed, though only as rebels, the villains set up a standard of their own, as when Iago asserts the supremacy of his will, and calls virtue a fig and reputation an idle and most false imposition. But Falstaff is neither rebel nor critic. As clown he could be supposed to have neither philosophy nor anti-philosophy, being a comic contrast and appendage to the heroes and the heroic point of view. His cavillings at honour are made utterly nugatory and frivolous, and his jokes are but tell-tale parries

and feints.   Like all stage cowards from Colin to Acres he
fulfills the requirements of Mr Bradley's definition, 'feeling a painful fear in the presence of danger and yielding to
that fear in spite of his better feelings and convictions.'
There indeed lies the old-time 'humour' of our knight on
the battlefield—quaking and joking as honour pricks him
on.   In his fits of remorse or in his incomprehensible lies
he is not only merry but also 'an object of mirth.'   He is
funny, not only because he feigns and really is 'free,' but
because at uncomfortable moments he pulls so hard on the
bit.   On his deathbed, I suppose, he was not feigning, and
no enfranchised 'Ephesian' would there have cried out of
sack,[122] of women—or the Whore of Babylon, as Quickly's
loyalty and piety would have it.

In that last glimpse, for all the humour and pathos of
it, there is not the indulgence of to-day.   But according to
Mackenzie, the Man of Feeling, his cowardice is 'less a
weakness than a principle.'   He lives as he thinks, as how
few of us do!   He renounces the 'grinning idol' says Sir
Walter Raleigh, and 'runs away or counterfeits death with
more courage than others show in deeds of knightly dar-
ing.'   Such transcendental paradox, on the one hand, such
tenderness with temperament and 'principle' or point of
view, on the other, were unknown to the Globe, to the man
of Stratford and his time.   As I have shown in connection
with Shylock and the villains, if so Falstaff should think or
do, the worse for him!   But the fact is, as we have seen,
that Shakespeare lets Falstaff at heart think like everyone
else, and calls a spade a spade.   For him and his fellows a
coward in a comedy is such regardless of distinctions
between character and conduct, constitution and principle,
and might as well at once have done with them and stick
the rabbit scut in his hat.   Even in his serious work he

---

[122] Giuseppe Barone (*Un Antenato di Falstaff*) mistakes the expression,
and has him cry out *for* sack and women.   Just so he would have been
presented to-day: living or dying, our funny men are not troubled with
compunctions.

presents no such paradox, no contrast such as Fielding's between outward propriety and probity, on the one hand, and goodness of heart and generosity of feeling, on the other. He knoweth the secrets of the heart, but in the story he makes little of them—of intentions or impulses, be they good ones or bad ones—as apart from or opposed to deeds. In the comedies of Morgann's own day, as in the medieval farces, all extenuating distinctions were without a difference. 'Look 'ee, Sir Lucius,' cries Bob Acres, like another Colin or Jodelet; ' 'tisn't that I mind the word coward—coward may be said in joke. But if you had called me a poltroon, Odds daggers and balls!' And when in mellower (or flabbier) times Mr Shaw in *Candida* attempted to establish a difference, and to represent, not one cowardly in principle and courageous by constitution, but one courageous in principle and cowardly by constitution—a compound less dubious and mistakable—what a deal of exposition and manipulation was required! The fact is, an audience at a comedy is like the coarse harsh people outside the theatre: they have no mercy on anything that looks like a subterfuge. We all know how they took the high-flying idealism of President Wilson's 'too proud to fight'; the laugh rang round the world. A humorist— a comic dramatist—would have quite expected it. The world took Mr Wilson's words as it later took the Germans' last official military reports in the war: 'We have put the Divette region between ourselves and the enemy,' instead of saying, 'We have retreated beyond the Divette'; 'The town of X—now lies before our lines,' as if it were the town itself that had moved. The words 'strategic retreat' were freely used on either side and as freely laughed at on the other. Can we expect less of an audience which listens to Falstaff's repeated subterfuges and evasions and quibbling and shuffling philosophy—or of the artistic foresight of one of the greatest of all humorists?

25.

All this becomes clearer when we examine the approximations on the stage to such a mixed character as Morgann and his followers conceive. In Shakespeare's time I know of none in England save Fletcher's Little French Lawyer, who, a coward, forced to fight, turns, by reason of his good luck in the combat, into a swash-buckler, and then, when a trick is played on him, turns coward again. This farcical stage figure teaches us nothing. But later (yet before 1638) in Tirso's El cobarde más valiente, Martin Peláez, nephew of the Cid (and his servant Batija with him), cowardly at first, has a taste of blood, and then and there undergoes a total change. And there are other Spanish plays, later still, in which not experience but love is the transforming power—El amor hace valientes (1658) and El noble siempre es valiente (1660). Here it is not really a mixed character at all; the youth wakes up and is a hero; and is not suffered to remain in that debatable land where endless explanation and apology are necessary. Once the coward takes the leap he knows no fear, and is a paladin.

Cases more in point are Don Quixote in Shakespeare's own day, and Farquhar's Sir Harry Wildair, in the Constant Couple (1699), a hundred years after. As for the former, in his history too we find an instance of Morgann's 'venial and momentary aberration,' in extenuation of which may be pleaded 'age,' indeed, though not 'corpulence.' In the twenty-seventh chapter of Part II Don Quixote takes flight when, on Sancho's braying, they are attacked by two hundred armed villagers. But aside from the mere fact of the flight, he and Falstaff have obviously nothing in common. Don Quixote's career has been so heroic that it was high time that he betrayed some slight touch of human weakness in his makeup. Here is Morgann's true 'single exception,' which therefore is comic; whereas with Falstaff the comic exception is not his cowardice but his prowess, not Gadshill or Shrewsbury but the taking of Colville captive. Moreover, his enemies here number hundreds; and even in running away he is faithful to his ideal, 'for I would have thee know, Sancho, that the valour which is not based on a foundation of prudence is called rashness, and the exploits of the rash man are to be attributed rather to good fortune than to courage; and so I own that I retired, but not that I fled; and therein I have followed the example of many valiant men who have reserved themselves for better times; the histories are full of instances of this,' etc. He protests too much, but he is more troubled than he need be; with such a record as his, fleeing from enemies so many, Falstaff might have roared as he ran and still kept reputation safe.

As for Sir Harry Wildair, in him we find at last Morgann's enlightened Epicurean philosopher. He won't be troubled with business, revenge, or any other annoyance; nor will he fight 'without reason,' for a woman least of all. Far enough himself from the spirit of reform, he probably reflects the change, just then coming about, when Steele and others began the crusade against the code of honour and the duello. At all events the character is clear, not ambiguous and paradoxical as on Morgann's showing Falstaff's, if he were really at bottom courageous, must be. Though humorous, cynical, and impudent, Wildair is courageous enough. His enemies, Vizard the villain and Standard the hero, acknowledge it; [128] and (as is emphatically not the case with Falstaff) the facts, for all his equivocal conduct, bear them out. Wildair has a philosophy; he has, as we have seen, prudence and 'discretion,' but he is not thereby exposed and laid open to ridicule. He holds no bantering soliloquies; the nearest he comes to it is when he is hesitating whether to marry or to fight, and then he heroically chooses, not discretion and the better part, but

[128] I, i; IV, i.

'Damn it!' he cries, 'cowards dare fight; I'll marry!' Nor does he boast or brag. In short he has no vestige of the *miles gloriosus* clinging to him, though that figure was still on the stage—or rather for that reason. Neither is he stained with the other vices which on the Elizabethan and Renaissance stage keep cowardice company—drunkenness [124] and gluttony, cheating and stealing. And above all there is no Gadshill, no Shrewsbury, with the roaring, falling flat, and running away, no stabbing of corpses, bloodying of garments, or bandying of the word coward back and forth. When he first appears, singing, Standard remarks that he had behaved very bravely in Flanders. 'Why not!' rejoins Vizard; 'dost think bravery and gaiety inconsistent?' Now the audience know—here is their cue. Even in Tirso's play, cited above, the coward about to turn hero does not appear cowardly on the stage but is only so reported. In that day deeds of prowess in the sequel could hardly efface in the minds of the audience such shame and ignominy, directly presented, at the beginning. And in both Peláez and Wildair the impressions of valour are not secret. In almost every way Farquhar, who, like Shakespeare (but far less perfectly) knew the stage language of his time—all the traditions and associations of ideas—took pains, as Shakespeare with Falstaff did not, that Wildair, in his careless gaiety, should not be misunderstood, not taken for another sort. Here, nearer his own time, is the sort of man that Morgann and his followers seem to be thinking of, a gay Epicurean, who, for reasons, does not fight; but in almost all other respects he is not what Falstaff is and does not as he does.

26.

As for Falstaff, he is not only subtilized but also sentimentalized! Mr Bradley does not mind saying that he for

---

[124] In V, i, he drinks too much burgundy, or rather, just enough. It was suggested to him and there is a motive for it.

one is glad that Falstaff ran away on Gadshill; Monsieur Stapfer declares that morally he was no worse than you or I; Hazlitt, lost in sympathy with him on the blighting of his hopes at the succession, resentfully asserts that he was a better man than the Prince; and another critic, mentioned by Sir Walter Raleigh, 'takes comfort in the reflection that the thousand pounds belonging to Justice Shallow is safe in Falstaff's pocket, and will help to provide for his old age.' That is, the character is lifted bodily out of the dramatist's reach. Falstaff is a rogue, and as such people cannot like him: twice Morgann protests that in order to be comical at all he must be 'void of evil motive. Lying for profit and jesting for profit, the cheating and swindling of your un-sophisticated admirers, gluttony, lechery, extortion, highway robbery, and cowardice—pray, what is funny about all these? Hence the profit has been turned to a jest, the mis-demeanours to make-believe. Not otherwise, Hercules in the *Alcestis* was thought by Browning to get roaring drunk, not for his own private satisfaction but for that of the mourners [125]—and there is another in a play who, in the good cause of human happiness, does not mind making a fool of himself! So it must be, when we take a character to our bosom out of an old play like a pet out of the jungle —we must extract his sting. This has by the critics been duly done, to Falstaff as to Shylock. Our 'white-bearded Satan' has had his claws pared.

For they that have not learned to think historically can-not stomach the picaresque. It matters not to them that nearly all the professional comic characters of Elizabethan drama, as of all drama before it, have a vein of roguery in them—Sir Toby as well as Autolycus, the Clown as well as the Vice; or that in those days high and low were rejoic-ing in the roguery romances, English, French, or Spanish. Such people must have delighted in Falstaff as unreservedly as does the Prince in the play. That they did not take him

[125] See Jebb's comment, article 'Euripides,' *Encyclopædia Britannica*.

for an innocuous mimic and merrymaker numerous allusions in the seventeenth century, as we have already seen, attest. And Hal loved him as Morgante loved Margutte, as Baldus loved Cingar, and Pantagruel—'all his life long'— loved Panurge, not for his humour only but for his lies and deviltry. They had their notions of 'a character' as we have ours. With endless variety of repetition Rabelais revels in notions of mendacity, drunkenness, gluttony, and lasciviousness, and in tricks of cheating and cruelty, as things funny almost in themselves. With what gusto he tells of the outrages perpetrated by Panurge on the watch, the difficult Parisian lady, and Dingdong and his flock, and of Friar John's slaying and curiously and expertly mutilating his thousands with the staff of the cross in the abbey close! And yet, frowning down the facts, the critics declare that Falstaff had no malice in him,[126] and though he laments the repayment, had had no intention of keeping the stolen money, repays Quickly full measure and running over with his company, and after all does no mentionable injury to Shallow, who has land and beeves. 'Where does he cheat the weak,' cries Maginn, 'or prey upon the poor?' There is Quickly, poor, and weak at least before his blandishments, 'made to serve his uses both in purse and in person'; and there are Bullcalf, who has a desire to stay with his friends, and Mouldy, whose dame is old and cannot help herself, both swindled in the name of the King, as Wart, Feeble, and Shadow, the unlikeliest men, are wrongfully pressed into service. All this was once funny and is now base and pitiful,[127] but why should we either shut our eyes

[126] Raleigh, p. 189; Wolff, i, p. 423; but consider Part II, III, ii, 353-57; IV, iii, 137-42. If he has no malevolence in him it is only as a thief, swindler, bilker, and barrator may have none, thinking not of others but himself.

[127] The scenes (Part I, III, iii; Part II, II, i,) in which Falstaff, upbraided by Quickly, retorts in impudently clever vein, resemble the scene in *Le Médecin malgré lui,* in which Sganarelle does the same to his long-suffering wife. And the scene in which the doctor imposes on the country bumpkins with fraudulent remedies resembles that in which Falstaff and Bardolph fleece the conscripts,—both scenes not meant for pathos!

to it or bewail it? Surely we cannot with Morgann make allowances for his age and corpulency (how that would have staggered an Elizabethan!) and corrupting associations; or with Maginn trace the pathos of his degradation, hope after hope breaking down; or with Swinburne discover the well of tenderness within him, his heart being 'fracted and corroborate,' not through material disappointment, but for wounded love.[128] With this last the present Chief Secretary for Ireland [129] is properly disgusted, though in being less sentimental he is hardly more Elizabethan in spirit as he calls him 'in a very real sense a terrible character, so old and so profane.[130] About as properly 'terrible' as was the nurse Sairey Gamp of late to an eminent literary critic writing, for the *Times,* though truly it would have been a fearful thing to fall into the hands of the living Sairey. Yet Mr Birrell remembers Falstaff (where others have been but too glad to forget him) with Doll at the Boar's Head; and he reads an unexpurgated text. And if he does not look with the eyes of an Elizabethan, he looks honestly (though shamefacedly), with his own, and sees the old rogue and satyr in his heathen nakedness, not in the breeches that, like

[128] If Shakespeare means that he really is heart-broken—(which Mr Birrell denies) it is not the first or the last time that the dramatist permits himself a bit of sentiment upon the death of the unworthy. But this is unlikely, and Swinburne somewhat sentimentalizes. Mrs Quickly says, 'The King has killed his heart'; yet we need not take that too seriously. The phrase is fairly common in Elizabethan literature. It often means disappointment to one in his hopes or expectations, not necessarily in affection.

Why that contempt will kill the speaker's heart
And quite divorce his memory from his part.—*L. L. L.,* v. ii, 149.

He that hath far to go tells it by miles;
If he should tell the steps, it kills his heart.—*Edward III.*

[129] In 1914, Mr Birrell.

[130] *Renaissance Shakespeare, Henry IV,* Part II, pp. xvi, xviii. Cf. p. xv: 'Falstaff's words "Kiss me, Doll," followed by his cry, "I am old, I am old," together with other touches in the same scene, might well stand for the last words of disgust and horror.' They were meant, certainly to be funny. Funniest of all, no doubt, was the worst, at the end of the scene, where Bardolph, from within, cries, 'Bid Mistress Tearsheet come to my master,' and 'motherly' Mistress Quickly bids her run.

Volterra in the Sistine, the critics have hastened to make him.

Morals and sentiments alike, in the lapse of time, obliterate humour. Laughter is essentially a *geste social,* as Meredith and Professor Bergson have truly told us; and the immediate and necessary inference, which no doubt they themselves would have drawn, is that it languishes when the tickled *mores* change. The discussion of wit and humour and the examples of both in Castiglione's *Courtier* are illuminating.[131] Much that was funny to the Elizabethans, or to the court of Urbino, or of the Grand Monarch, has since become pathetic, as in Shylock and Harpagon, Alceste and George Dandin; and 'disgusting' or even 'terrible,' as in Falstaff or Tartuffe. Of this we have just seen repeated instances, and of the process of critical emasculation which ensues. Even the form and fashion of the older humour have given offense. Most of the English critics apparently have not seen Falstaff on the stage, but those who have cannot recall him without a shudder. The roaring, the falling flat, and above all the padding—'a very little stuffing under the waistcoat,' one of them pleads, 'would answer all the requirements of the part.'[132] And the padded bulk of his humour, as of his person—'out of all measure, out of all compass'—about his name being terrible to the enemy and known to all Europe, and Turk Gregory never doing such deeds, is so reduced by anachronizing Procrustean critics as to contain 'nothing but a light ridicule.'[133] His ancestral ring seems to have been really of gold, not copper,—Morgann 'believes it was really of gold' just as he 'thinks he did not roar,' though 'probably a little too much alloyed with baser metal.'[134] And his 'old ward,'

[131] See the chapter on Shylock, above, p. 310.

[132] *Fraser's,* xlvi, p. 409; Morgann, p. 26, etc.

[133] Morgann, pp. 41, 83; Bradley, *Oxford Lectures,* p. 267—'must not be entirely ignored.'

[134] Morgann, p. 54. These contrasts, between fact and pretense, are essential, as we have seen, to comic stage effect; and the critics blur and obscure them.

like his 'manhood,' Prince Hal might have remembered if he would.[135]   What of the multitudinous knaves in buckram and Kendal green, or of the knight himself at Hal's age not an eagle's talon in the waist or an alderman's thumb-ring, or of the nine score and odd posts he foundered as he devoured the road to battle in Gaultree Forest? Even his laugh, which must have been big as his body, riotous as his fancy, lingering and reverberating as the repetitions of his tongue, has been taken away.[136] 'The wit is from the head, not the heart. It is anything but fun.' If we are to depend on the bare text or stage-directions there is no laughter in Sir Toby either, or almost any other jovial soul in Shakespeare.[137] In robbing these fat knights of their fun critical treason has well-nigh done its worst, though before that it robbed audiences (at the cost of truth though to the profit of morals) of the fun got from Shylock, Harpagon, Dandin, and Tartuffe. On the stage and in the study much of the comedy in Shakespeare and Molière has been drained out of them from the Romantic Revival unto this day, and yet we smile at the Middle Ages Christianizing the classics.

27.

And yet people like Falstaff, however they may interpret or explain him, as I hope my reader still can. Men do, if not women; Englishmen do, if not foreigners. It is partly, no doubt, because of the tradition that he is the supreme comic figure, and they have endeavoured and laboured to like him. But it is more because, however much in the centuries they have changed in morals, humour, and taste, Englishmen have not outlived their human nature—

[135] *Ibid.*, p. 148.

[136] Maginn, p. 56: 'he never laughs.'

[137] It is remarkable that in text or stage directions in Shakespeare (see Bartlett, 'ha, ha, ha') there is almost no indication of laughter, though in Italian comedy of the sixteenth century there is plenty of it, without the aspirate, phonetically reproduced. See above, note 54.

Shakespeare's art. Their pleasure in the picaresque they have not wholly lost: virtue cannot so inoculate our old stock but we shall relish of it. Moreover, there is something in Falstaff's appeal that is immediate and perpetual; it lies not so much in his conduct as in his speech. He talks prose but is supremely poetic, and his is in many ways the most marvellous prose ever penned. It pulses with his vast vitality and irrepressible spirit, it glows with the warmth of his friendliness and good humour, it sparkles with his fancy and wit. No prose or verse either is so heavily charged with the magnetism of a personality, or has caught so perfectly the accent and intonation of an individual human voice. It *is* a voice,—rich, full, and various. In dialogue or stage-direction there is nothing to indicate his laughter, but the words and phrases as they ripple and undulate in repetition amply suggest it or involve it. He rolls a jest as a sweet morsel upon his tongue,—food for powder, food for powder; they'll fill a pit as well as better. Tush, man, mortal men, mortal men! With that he laughs, and all the audience with him.

Englishmen cannot escape that strong infection, if Frenchmen and Germans, Spaniards and Italians may. Mézières, and perhaps most foreigners that read English no more readily than Spanish, prefer Sancho; and for a Spaniard possibly Sancho's speech may have an equal charm. The Squire, certainly, is tenderer, more naïve, more moral, than the Eastcheap knight. But to Englishmen he seems much less vivid and real, less alive in every phrase and syllable, less prodigiously entertaining. Falstaff is depicted with—and endowed with—a greater gusto. He never bores you as Sancho with his proverbs sometimes does. He is voluble but never long-winded; he is the very spirit of comradeship, the genius of converse, always ready with something to say, which provokes an answer— which provokes a better answer in turn. He both speaks and also (as some clever ones do not) listens, both sways and is swayed, and knows the mutual precipitate exhilaration—as in song and dance—of good company. Conversation is to him a thing of infinite moment: in words, not in deeds, are, not all his delights, to be sure, but all his triumphs. Time is nothing to him—he is always for making a night of it, like the moral Dr Johnson, who therefore, no doubt, forgave him. And so it is that he is the life of the party, the king of companions, the prince of good fellows, though not good. There, in the idiom, lies embedded the contradiction which justifies the contradiction in Falstaff himself. We, too, after all, like Prince Hal and Mrs Quickly, take to a man because of his charm, if it be big enough, not because of his virtue; and as for Falstaff, we are bewitched with the rogue's company, even to the point of forgetting everything else, and like Mrs Quickly even momentarily attributing to him that one thing which (none should know so well as she) he lacketh:—'Well, fare thee well! I have known thee these twenty-nine years, come peascod-time; but an honester and truer-hearted man—well, fare thee well!' What a testimony and tribute, entirely fallacious! Or, as Hal, thinking him dead, puts it more soberly and truly, 'I could have better spared a better man.' Under the spell of his presence and speech Mrs Quickly forgets what he owes her, for his diet and by-drinkings, the shirts bought for him and the money lent him; and, did we not stop to think, we should do the same.

But it is not merely by Falstaff's speech that we are kept under his spell; it is by all Shakespeare's comic art in the play. Here is another case of *isolation,* of comic emphasis such as we have seen in Shylock, until at the end of the Second Part he meets with the rebuff from the King. Shakespeare does not insist on Falstaff's sins and vices; he subordinates them, as we have seen, to his comic effects,—does not let them become serious, 'terrible.' In what Maginn says there is half a truth—'where does he cheat the weak or prey upon the poor?' His treatment of the travellers, and of Quickly, Bullcalf, Mouldy, Wart, Feeble, and Shallow, we are not suffered (or at least not expected) to take to heart or sternly remember against him. His boasting and lying is not a needless, silly, and chronic affair as it is with many braggart soldiers; it is the revival of enthusiasm after ignominious lapses, the glow of reaction after an escape. And his cowardice,—Morgann is right in insisting that it is not continual and contemptible like that of Parolles and Bobadill. That there is a difference between his and their evasions we have already noticed. In short, his roguery is not professional but human and incidental. No other coward is so attractive because none has such a variety of deportment, can in the presence of others put on such an air of dignity or pathos, or in the face of danger seem so philosophical and cool. He may run, roar, whimper, or fall flat upon the field, but so scared is he only for moments. When he hears the sheriff is at the door, he says to Prince Hal, 'If you will deny the sheriff, so; if not, let him enter'; and he debates the matter of his gracing a cart and the gallows to bring tears to the eyes of others, though there are none in his own. And again, when on the eve of the engagement, he cries, 'Hal, if thou see me down in the battle and bestride me, so; 'tis a point of friendship.' He has the manner; he can assume a virtue, though he has it not the next moment—'I would 'twere bedtime, Hal, and all well.' Yet the moment after (though for that moment only) he rallies, in soliloquy, the slender forces of manhood within him:—'Well, 'tis no matter; honour pricks me on.' It is a feint—a transport—a flash in the pan! 'Yea, but how if honour prick me off when I come on? How then?'

And his promptings of conscience and remorse touch us not too nearly. They are real but not too real. A quick shift of the burden to the villainous company he keeps, or a call for a bawdy song, ends them when in health; Quickly's

deathbed comfort that there was no need of such thoughts
yet, ends them forever. They had troubled him, though,—
thoughts of honour, duty, religion; thoughts of his sins—
his swearing, dicing, stealing, and lechery; thoughts of
death—of God and Hell. 'Peace, good Doll!' he had
said in his latter heyday; 'do not speak like a death's-head,
do not bid me remember mine end.' He winces a little
when he is reminded of them, they prick him a little on the
battle-field, they for a moment at the last peer in at him
upon his pillow. He is not perfectly 'free,' not, as Professor Bradley thinks, wholly happy or at his ease, or he would
not be so funny or so human. He is, as we have seen, not
exalted above name and fame and duty; and the droll and
delightful thing about him is the quick way he has of dodging or overriding all such obstacles and stumbling-blocks to
happiness in his path. He makes shift to rise superior to
his debts and duties—to all immaterial things (which, as
such, are immaterial to him)—but not to circumstances.
He puts on a bold face as he receives the public rebuff at
the hands of the king; and he jests on gamely, perhaps
brazenly, as he gives Shallow the thin satisfaction of a
formal acknowledgment, *coram* Pistol and Bardolph, of
his debt of a thousand pounds, assures his creditor that the
king will send for his indispensable friend 'soon at night,'
and bids him 'fear no colours,' punning on the word. But
he does not laugh at being cast off, we have noticed, till the
welkin rings, as Mr Beerbohm would have him do, and as
he would do, if Rötscher's, Bulthaupt's, and Professor
Bradley's conception of him quite fitted. This, at last, is
to him no laughing matter; and if he have a philosophy it
is not adversity's sweet milk, which fortifies. He is planted
on this earth, and cannot dispense with her favours; he is
not the one (if really he had it) to live on honour, on 'air,'
like a chameleon up a tree. And prison, in his old age,
without creature comforts, or company, is quite too much

for him. Not that he is heart-broken—'killed his heart,'
we have seen, need not mean that—and though he had
delighted in Prince Hal's company he on his death-bed does
not remember him. Love he does not so much as crave
love: Hal owes him his love, he once told him; and it
pained and surprised the old fellow that Prince John,
though with no particular reason to do so, did not warm
up to him:—'Good faith, this same young sober-blooded
boy doth not love me.' He is not self-sufficient like a philosopher or a cat. Though not devoted himself, he likes the
quality, insists on 'good fellowship,' and even on thieves
being true one to another; he banks on it but all too fondly
in the Prince. For he is by nature a guest, as Mr Beerbohm
would say, not a host; to receive he has ever found more
blessed than to give; and her guests he prays his hostess to
cherish. But now the sun no longer shines; in the Fleet
there is no cherishing; and while from duty he can dodge
and sidle, he cannot from discomfort and cold fact.[138] His
comedy is at its period; reality, kept in the background,
steps up and with disenchanting touch puts a stop to the
merry make-believe; and Shakespeare is a tragic dramatist
as well.

We may rightly complain of the King's priggish speech
and harsh conduct; we may rightly complain perhaps that
our comedy ends thus soberly; but both character and situation are true. The jig is up; the game of evasion could
not last ever;—though afterwards, on his death-bed, he
still contrived to evade the scruples which troubled him,
and went away an it had been any christom child. But the
facts, unlike the scruples and principles, that stood in the
path of his happiness, he could not brush away, and he
knew not how to laugh and face them. If Falstaff has,

[138] Compare Dowden and Professor Bradley, to whom I am here
indebted. Some of the notions in these last paragraphs, moreover, have
been taken from my introduction to *Henry V,* by the kind permission of
Messrs Holt and Company.

though much mirth, no philosophy, the poet has both; and Falstaff holds us under his spell not only in his own right but also in that of his maker.[139]

[139] Only after the proofs were returned to the printer have I come upon two extensive criticisms of my *Falstaff* as it first appeared, one by Miss Wales, *University of Wisconsin Studies* (1923), and one by Mr E. C. Knowlton, *English and Germanic Philology*, April, 1926. I regret that I am unable to take notice of one or two of their strictures; although, as the reader versed in the current criticism will himself have observed, I have, out of respect for his interests, endeavoured in the book to refrain from mere controversy and to put behind me the temptation to retort. Both critics, but particularly the latter, seem to me concerned to *sentir le rôle plutôt que le comprendre;* and Mr Knowlton only brings Morgann up to date. Shakespeare's intention and the various language of the Renaissance stage which he faithfully employs to convey it, as well as the chivalric spirit of Shakespeare and his time, are ignored; and the reader is invited to consider Falstaff as a picture of the cynical, disillusioned soldier of to-day. Does such a one brag and bluster, I wonder. 'Discretion' is by Shakespeare treated comically, satirically; by Mr Knowlton, sympathetically and with respect. Nowadays, apparently, it *is* the better part. And Falstaff is still called a 'veteran'—by mere repetition of Morgann's word Mr Knowlton would carry his point—and the fat knight is granted a veteran's license. He is free not only to play the robber but (without loss of reputation) to turn tail when robbed. 'There is no implication that Falstaff was bound by duty to stay,'—not by duty, certainly! 'Discretion would point to flight,'—of the four from before the face of two! And the writer declares that 'Commines might justly have numbered him among the few people in his life who knew the right to flee.' If so, these are more numerous now, and the Age of Chivalry is truly gone. Several times Mr Knowlton calls in question my sense of humour. If really Jove ever laughs, it must be when two Shakespeare critics bring that charge against each other, or when either denies it. Only to Jove and the reader can the great question be referred—and as evidence on the one side I would submit not only Mr Knowlton's remarks above but others, as that about Falstaff being as a recruiting officer 'really fair and efficient,' and (this for the reader overseas above all) the serious and troubled consideration of the deeper significance of the soliloquy on sack and of Shakespeare's 'ultimate views concerning liquor' (p. 209). *Il ne fallait que ça,* in Shakespeare criticism!

I should like to add to note 59 that while, unlike most other braggart soldiers, Falstaff betrays the fact that his weapon is a fraud of his own accord, and he thereby wins further credit for good-humour, he wins none for courage. We are inclined to take him here for a Bluntschli, but are not intended to do that. As I have shown above, he exposes himself as other cowards do, in soliloquy; and in company, when the jig is up and the only refuge open to him is a jest. Since Gadshill, moreover, the secret is out betwixt him and Prince Hal. Just in the previous scene he has whimpered, 'I would 'twere bed-time, Hal, and all well.' The point is, not that he is cool and careless in the teeth of peril, but deaf to the higher call. There is a time for all things. 'What,' cries the Prince when he sees the bottle, 'is it a time to jest and dally now?'

INDEX OF AUTHORS, CRITICS, AND ACTORS, PLAYS AND CHARACTERS

(Topics of discussion may be found by the *Table of Contents*. Unless dealt with frequently or at length, plays are indexed under the author, and characters under the plays. More important references are in italics.)